# Critical Perspectives on Activity

The last two decades have seen an international explosion of interest in theories of mind, culture, and activity. This unique collection is the first to explicitly reach back to the tradition's original critical impulse within which the writings of Karl Marx played such a central role. Each author pushes this impulse further to address leading contemporary questions. The contributors include a diverse array of international scholars working from the fields of education, psychology, philosophy, sociology, anthropology, communications, industrial relations, and business studies. The book is broken into three main sections – education, work, and everyday life. Each chapter builds from an analysis of practice and learning as social cultural participation and historical change in relation to the concepts of activity, contradiction, and struggle. This book offers insight into an important complex of overlapping practices and institutions to shed light on broader debates over such matters as the "knowledge economy" and "lifelong learning."

Peter H. Sawchuk is Professor of Sociology & Equity Studies in Education as well as Industrial Relations at University of Toronto. He is the Chair of the International Advisory Committee for the Conference on Researching Work and Learning. He is also a founding member of the University of Toronto's Centre for the Study of Education and Work.

Newton Duarte is a full professor in Philosophy of Education at the Universidade Estadual Paulista (UNESP) in Brazil, where he is the Director of the PhD Program in School Education. He holds large-scale grants from the Brazilian National Governmental Institution for Scientific and Technologic Development and has won post-professorial honors at UNESP.

Mohamed Elhammoumi is Associate Professor in the Department of Psychology, College of Social Sciences at the Imam Muhammad Ibn Saud Islamic University in Saudi Arabia. He has published numerous papers on child development, cultural psychology, and the role of culture and family structures on the development of mental abilities, proportional reasoning, and cognitive development including "Socio-Historicocultural Psychology: Lev Semenovich Vygotsky: A Bibliographical Note."

# Critical Perspectives on Activity

*Explorations Across Education, Work, and Everyday Life*

Edited by

**PETER H. SAWCHUK**
*University of Toronto, Canada*

**NEWTON DUARTE**
*Universidade Estadual Paulista, Brazil*

**MOHAMED ELHAMMOUMI**
*Imam Muhammad Ibn Saud Islamic University, Saudi Arabia*

**CAMBRIDGE**
UNIVERSITY PRESS

CAMBRIDGE UNIVERSITY PRESS
Cambridge, New York, Melbourne, Madrid, Cape Town, Singapore, São Paulo

Cambridge University Press
40 West 20th Street, New York, NY 10011-4211, USA

www.cambridge.org
Information on this title: www.cambridge.org/9780521849999

First published 2006

Printed in the United States of America

*A catalog record for this publication is available from the British Library.*

*Library of Congress Cataloging in Publication Data*
Critical perspectives on activity : explorations across education, work & everyday life / edited
by Peter H. Sawchuk, Newton Duarte, and Mohamed Elhammoumi.
    p.   cm.
Includes bibliographical references and index.
ISBN-13: 978-0-521-84999-9 (hardback)
ISBN-10: 0-521-84999-3 (hardback)
1. Social psychology.   2. Culture–Psychological aspects.    I. Sawchuk, Peter H. (Peter Harold),
1968–   II. Duarte, Newton.   III. Elhammoumi, Mohamed, 1956–   IV. Title.
HM1011.C75   2005
302–dc22          2005017463

ISBN-13   978-0-521-84999-9 hardback
ISBN-10   0-521-84999-3 hardback

*In memoriam,*
*Mario Golder & Joachim Lompscher*

# Contents

# Contributors

**Paul S. Adler,** School of Business, University of Southern California, United States.

**Alessandra Arce,** Department of History of Education & Childhood Education, Universidade de São Paulo, Brazil.

**Joe Berry,** Chicago Labor Education Program, University of Illinois-Urbana-Champaign, United States.

**Newton Duarte,** Department of Philosophy of Education, Universidade Estadual Paulista, Brazil.

**Mohamed Elhammoumi,** Department of Psychology, Imam Muhammad Ibn Saud Islamic University, Saudi Arabia.

**Yrjö Engeström,** Department of Adult Education, University of Helsinki, Finland.

**Jean Lave,** Department of Education and Geography, University of Calfornia-Berkeley, United States.

**D. W. Livingstone,** Department of Sociology, University of Toronto, Canada.

**Joachim Lompscher,** Department of Educational Psychology, University of Potsdam, Germany.

**Ray McDermott,** Department of Anthropology, University of California-San Diego, United States.

**Maria Célia Marcondes de Moraes,** Department of Philosophy of Education, Universidade Federal de Santa Catarina, Brazil.

**Peter H. Sawchuk,** Department of Sociology and Equity Studies in Education, University of Toronto, Canada.

**Helena Worthen,** Department of Industrial Relations, University of Illinois-Urbana-Champaign, United States.

# Foreword

The historical development of the cultural–historical research tradition can be understood conceptually in a simple dialectic of "oral-written-oral." From the 1920s through roughly the 1970s, persons actively engaged in doing research in the cultural–historical tradition were likely to be living in Moscow, to have studied in Moscow, or to have regular access to persons who were living or had studied there. In short, the dominant form for coming to understand and work with the cultural–historical tradition was to be engaged in dialogue with others who were working in this tradition. Starting in the 1970s, many translated and secondary texts became available in several different languages and later included online and course materials. At present, interpretation of written texts is the dominant form by which persons learn about the cultural–historical tradition, without necessarily having access to the participants of the oral tradition from the previous historical period. During this "written" period, awareness, interest, and acceptance of the cultural–historical tradition has grown internationally, without a corresponding dialogical interaction among its "readers." There is now a considerable diversity in which aspects of the historical tradition are known, emphasized, and investigated (which explains in part the variety of its descriptive labels, such as socio-cultural, cultural–historical activity theory, socio-historical, and so forth).

The appearance of a new oral period is desirable, but dialectical logic does not require such a transformation. It depends necessarily on the actions of researchers who work in this tradition, as well as the conditions that have developed until now. An important step in this direction was the constitution of the International Society for Cultural and Activity Research (ISCAR) in 2002, reflecting the culmination of a process that started in the early 1980s and early 1990s, when researchers from the oral tradition started to organise conferences and scientific organisations. The integration of these organisations into ISCAR represents, in part, a commitment by active researchers to avoid the sectarian responses (observed all too often within both scholarly and political traditions), in which persons with similar, minority views form semi-closed communities, differentiated and isolated from each other by subtle distinctions. ISCAR's commitment to open dialogue is reflected in the fact that "cultural and activity research" in ISCAR's name does not refer to anybody's current or previous research practice! In this way, ISCAR can be understood as an open invitation for researchers to further the development of the theoretical tradition by engaging in a living, dialogical practice, including an exploration and assessment of theoretical sources that have historically motivated its development. I hope that further historical developments will result in 2002 being recognized as the beginning of the dialectical transformation of the cultural–historical tradition from a written period to an oral period that has an interiorised understanding of the theoretical commitments that motivate the research tradition.

The significance of the present volume can be understood against the background of this brief sketch of the historical dynamics in the development of the cultural–historical research tradition. Productive discussions presuppose a certain amount of common knowledge and common assumptions about what issues and problems need to be investigated and discussed. Two related historical conditions noted before were the diversity of knowledge about the cultural–historical tradition and the disjointedness among partially overlapping networks of researchers who have been interested in the cultural–historical tradition. The volume makes many important contributions to realising a new oral period by addressing the relevance of Marx's ideas for the further development of the cultural–historical tradition. Despite the generally acknowledged significance of Marx's ideas in the historical development of the cultural–historical tradition, it is still rare to find texts in the cultural–historical tradition that explicitly address Marx's ideas in relation to research about concrete, historical practices (such as education, work, and play). This volume helps to address this seemingly paradoxical situation, with its inspiringly wide range of topics and themes that are being considered or oriented by a dialectical perspective, as well as several different disciplinary perspectives.

In relation to overcoming disjointedness, it is good to see that the authors in this volume come from North America, South America, and Europe and that most, but not all, have participated in research communities that have formed ISCAR. It is also encouraging to see new participants in this "multi-disciplinary set of conversations" (editors' introductory chapter in this volume), which is important in creating an oral tradition, and I hope this dialogue will continue with other participants, including colleagues from Asia, Australia, and Africa who are already prepared for such discussions.

Finally, in the spirit of contributing to a living dialogue, I hope that readers will explore these chapters critically (i.e., not to passively accept the texts as authoritative sources to be strictly followed). For example, it would have been useful if this volume confronted more directly how the term "Marxist" is to be understood, including some explicit discussion about the historical political systems that have referred to Marx's thought as a main source of justification and guidance.

The focus of this volume on Marx may explain, in part, why Hegel is not also included for examination, despite the great significance of Hegel's work for Marx, for Vygotsky (who had a working knowledge of Hegel that was drawn into his own works), and more recently for Davydov, who drew from Hegel in his analysis of theoretical thinking. Hegel is not easy to understand, and many commonly accepted misunderstandings make it all too easy to dismiss his work with casual mention of such phrases as "idealist" or "mystical shell." A recognition of Hegel's significance in the cultural–historical tradition allows us to understand this tradition as a continuation of this dialectical tradition, both substantively and methodologically.

Personally, I think the cultural–historical tradition is part of a dialectical tradition synthesised by Hegel and further developed by many others, including Marx's monumental contribution of a concrete historical analysis of the dialectical logic of political economy. One advantage of characterizing cultural–historical research as being in the dialectical tradition is that one can be committed to the concerns of Hegel and Marx to understand the consequences of humanly created institutions for supporting or hindering full human development, while seeking analyses that aim to understand the conceptual logic in relation to which these institutions develop in their concrete histories, including critical evaluation and development of Marx's analyses.

The unity of cultural–historical research as a living research tradition must be created through a dialogue among the diversity of its participants – a dialogue both about existing texts and ideas – but also through formulation of ideas and issues that are not yet sufficiently interiorised that they can be exteriorised again in texts. This volume formulates ideas and issues that need to be explored and interiorised (through critical discussion) as part of the tradition's further development. In years to come, I hope these issues will also become part of the living dialogue in the rise of a new oral cultural–historical tradition.

Seth Chaiklin
Department of Educational Psychology
The Danish University of Education
October 2004

# Acknowledgements

In volumes like this one, one often presumes a pre-existing, tightly knit community of scholars with a significant foundation of shared understanding and communication. Our volume, however, began with only a modicum of these things. Some authors we'd worked with for years; others not. However, in the process of our discussions with individual authors, the bases for what we've called a "critical perspective on activity" have clearly been fortified. For these discussions, and for their creative and engaged chapters, we need to thank the contributors. We would also like to acknowledge the fine work of the editorial staff at Cambridge University Press and especially Phil Laughlin, whose interest, insight, and foresight allowed this work to come to fruition.

Peter H. Sawchuk
Newton Duarte
Mohamed Elhammoumi
September 2004

# Introduction

*Exploring Activity Across Education, Work, and Everyday Life*

Peter H. Sawchuk, Newton Duarte,
and Mohamed Elhammoumi

### INTRODUCTION

Clearly, there has been an international explosion of interest in theories of mind, culture, and activity over the last two decades. This interest is well founded. The traditions involved in this explosion speak to some of the most pressing and obvious challenges facing the social sciences. These include the increasingly inter-disciplinary nature of problem solving; the complexity of social systems; the role of technologies, tools, culture, divisions of labor, and other mediating factors; the role of cognition, social interaction, and learning; and, perhaps most importantly of all, how and why such systems – from classrooms, to schools, to organizations and beyond – undergo change. There are very few analytic traditions that offer so much to students, scholars, and perhaps even policy-makers. In this collection, theories of mind, culture, and activity are also rooted in a long and rich tradition of social criticism as well. These traditions have been recovered, developed, and expanded.

Today, there are flourishing journals, scholarly associations, conferences, and powerful research programs widely available. Reports, monographs, articles, books, and collections such as this one are circulating across international and linguistic boundaries more than ever before. However, despite this, and, in particular, despite the existence of several high-quality collections devoted to representing this explosion, there remain several important gaps that must be addressed. This collection seeks to respond to these gaps by posing, illuminating, and answering important questions that define these gaps in two principal ways.

First, each of the chapters in this collection represents an original and cutting-edge analysis in its own right. Many provide the grist for important new lines of research to be taken up and expanded. All authors orient to the concept of social cultural participation in relation to the concept of "activity." Activity in this tradition is not used in the everyday, common-sense way, however. Rather, it is a specialized and, in fact, highly contested concept. To begin with, it is defined as the minimal unit of analysis for the understanding of cognitive development, human participation, and change. It inherently contextualizes practice in cultural and historical terms. It is, in our view, the most comprehensive analytic framework for analyzing human practice and learning currently available. At its heart it affirms that all human practice is mediated by symbolic, cultural, and communal, as well as material, resources or tools; it is through these forms of mediation that human practice is understood as both dynamic and historical. This conceptual approach allows important, integrated forms of analysis. In this collection, for example, some authors explore activity vis-à-vis education and economy, and its relation to the reproduction of inequities and contradiction. Others examine activity in relation to the nature of work and learning processes, job design, and the institution of schooling as a workplace. And still others develop new understandings of activity in the context of everyday life. Importantly, one of the original contributions this collection makes to the corpus is that these varied topics have been carefully selected to generate additional "meta-level" observations. In other words, our chapters do not simply represent reports on discrete, unrelated phenomena. Rather, they offer a profile of, and insight into, an important "complex" of overlapping practices and institutions in contemporary society: Activity at school, at work, and in everyday life are connected forming a mutually dependent set of activity systems. We return to the interconnectedness of these foci at the close of this chapter, but suffice it to say here that, in this way, the collection seeks to penetrate and inform a broader societal debate over the nature of "knowledge economies" and, by now one of the most frequently discussed policy issues of all, "lifelong learning."

The second gap to which this collection seeks to respond relates to the fact that, although application and development of the concept of "activity" have seen remarkable growth, and although many of the leading writers in the broad area of Cambridge's "Learning in Doing" series have (albeit sporadically) noted the importance of recovering and evaluating the larger influence of the writings of Karl Marx on current and future research directions, as yet there exists no collection devoted to critical dialogues of this kind specifically. We seek to reflect seriously upon the importance and theoretical influences of what we refer to in the title of the book as a "critical perspective." It builds more or less explicitly on the writings of Marx. Marx's work was, of course, central to the genesis of theories of activity beginning with the work of Vygotsky, Leont'ev, Luria, and others in what has become known as the Cultural Historical School. Across our collection, contributors engage in critical exploration of Marx's writings and concepts. Some authors examine the issues of Marx as a "founding influence." Others explore specific concepts, including "estranged labor," "alienation," "relations of production," "class consciousness," "class struggle," "ideology," "labor process," and theories of "value" – all original preoccupations of Marx and Marxist analysts since him.

The research observations and theoretical debates collected and initiated in this collection offer specific directions for research on mind, culture, and activity with empirically grounded arguments. But it is also our hope that the collection will ultimately benefit the development of the tradition as a whole whether people choose to pursue the directions mapped out or not. An important element of making a contribution to broader debates, as we've said, is inter-disciplinarity, and this collection is remarkably diverse. Inter-disciplinary dialogue is vital to anyone facing real, concrete challenges. To us, it seems clear enough that one doesn't solve complex problems in the real world by strict reference to any single academic discipline. Interestingly enough, in the first decades of the twentieth century, a significant feature of Marxism's broader appeal in the academy, political spheres and political parties, labour unions, and assorted working-class movements, was its multi-disciplinarity. At that time, in academia, scholars contributing to this research tradition working from the fields of economics, anthropology, history, and jurisprudence, as well as philosophy and sociology, were evident. In his work *Essays on the Materialistic Conception of History* (1908), Antonio Labriola commented,

[t]he various analytic disciplines which illustrate historical facts have ended by bringing forth the need for a general social science, which will unify the different historical processes. The materialist theory is the culminating point of this unification. (p. 149)

This "inter-disciplinary impulse" is an important point of similarity between Marxist scholarship historically and the Cultural Historical School today that we wish to develop further. We'll return to the importance of this multi-disciplinarity in relation to a critical, dialectical analysis in a moment, but in the case of this volume, we note that its genesis lay in dialogue between an educational scholar, a psychologist, and a sociologist. In turn, we each recognized the need to extend this impulse further as we included leading international scholars working from the fields of philosophy, anthropology, communications, industrial relations, and business studies as well.

## A CRITICAL PERSPECTIVE?

Within the field of mind, culture, and activity as a whole, there are important, recent predecessors to this book (e.g., Chaiklin, Hedegaard, and Jensen 1999; Chaiklin 2001; Robbins and Stetsenko 2002). Each is an important volume that has informed thinking for us and many others. For our purposes, an exemplar in this regard is Engeström, Miettinen, and Punamaki's *Perspectives on Activity Theory* (1999). That volume had as one of its explicit goals to collect diverse sets of scholarship that were often "hybrid" in nature. Contributors frequently combined a range of theoretical traditions in dialogical relation with Cultural Historical Activity Theory (CHAT). Topics addressed there were wide-ranging and included sections devoted to play, learning, and instruction, as well as technology and work. As a whole, that collection offered a concentrated primer in historical roots and current trends. Our volume can be thought of as a complement to that collection. As our title indicates, however, our unique contribution lies in its interest to express a type of "critical" perspective on activity and to recover, express, and press forward many of the original Marxist elements of the Cultural Historical tradition.

So, it is appropriate that we turn to the question of what exactly is meant by this notion of a critical perspective. In return, and by way of an answer, we pose what we see as an important question. Although much is said in the Cultural Historical tradition about context and history, why is it that the concept of capitalism, the contradictions inherent in the commodity form, conflictual social relations, and class struggle remain latent or, worse, ignored by so many scholars? Indeed, many of the most powerful and insightful contemporary writers in this tradition seem to prefer to speak of general principles that run across historical periods such as mediation, co-construction, and so forth. For us, although provocative, these are particularly abstract abstractions in the sense that, by omission, they deny a coherent statement about the particular kind of social, political, and economic – let alone historical – world in which we are, in fact, engaged.

Of course, we wish to be careful to avoid the impression of dogmatism. Indeed, it will become obvious that our collection does not programmatically eschew the contributions of non-Marxist traditions. Nevertheless, throughout we are persistent in claiming the importance of recovering Marxist and related critical elements, and more than that, pressing these elements into service for further development of future, international, and multi-disciplinary conversations. In this sense, we hope that our collection becomes an important resource for those wishing to engage with such perspectives whether, in the end, they apply them directly themselves or not. We begin, however, with a *prima facia* observation that Marx forms the central philosophical and social analytic root of the Cultural Historical tradition. We emphasize the need to go further than the otherwise correct observation that "a careful and critical study of Marx's work" is necessary (Engeström, Miettinen, and Punamäki, 1999, p. 5). Indeed, for us, what is most remarkable about Marx's work is not simply its role in the genesis of this tradition, but that it maintains an extraordinary power for understanding its future.

At the same time, frequently noted in activity-based scholarship is the overlap of CHAT with questions emerging from sometimes vastly different traditions. The debate over the meaning of activity is central to our book. So, whereas many authors have been both quick and insightful in noting and exploring the overlaps of CHAT with other intellectual traditions, we nevertheless suggest that there needs to be some clarification. Our claim is that the ultimate value of such overlaps, if it is to be something more than merely intellectually fascinating, is to be found in integration within the rubric of a critical approach to activity rather than the other way around. At the very least, the re-assertion of original elements of activity in relation to a "critical" and/or Marxist perspective should be actively debated. Thus, in defining what we mean by the term "critical" in relation to the original germ cell of "activity" we propose a re-vitalization of Marxist analysis.

Given the preceding explanation, we can now more meaningfully state that by "critical" we mean approaches that ultimately have an interest in describing, analyzing, and contributing to a process of historical change and human betterment along the lines of Marx's *Eleventh Thesis* on Feuerbach, that is, an emphasis on change with a clear-eyed understanding of the social, political, economic, and historical bases of material reality. Building on this basic idea, though, we recognize some differences amongst authors in the collection; we note their shared beginnings in this impulse as well as the recognition that there are dialectical contradictions at play in the various phenomena of interest. These contradictions are, of course, far from apolitical and far from irrelevant to the larger questions we face as a society. Thus, critical perspectives on activity understand that "revolutionary practice" is not limited in the least to overt political activity: It is activity that is historical, incorporating elements of fundamental individual and, necessarily, social change. Perhaps most apposite to our claim is the observation that the fundamental nature of this change, in the Marxist sense, is understood as the resolution of contradictions. As a form of politics, then, all activity is at its heart contested or conflictual; it is, in a phrase, deeply shaped by collective as well as individual struggle. Struggle, in our definition of "critical" is crucial. In this collection, we see the notion of struggle expressed in a variety of ways: as politicized, theoretical struggle to retain a means of understanding individuals, societies, and change processes; as struggle to argue for the relevance of Marx's concern with the labor process (in school, higher education, as well as other workplaces); as a struggle to break down ideological boundaries between work and education, learning and everyday life, different forms of social consciousness, and forms of value creation; and most centrally, as struggle against inequities rooted in the diversity of class experiences and class-based organizations and social systems.

The question of defining a "critical perspective," then, is rooted in dialectical thought. Dialectical thought, in the Marxist tradition, is defined by the union of "materialist" thought associated with the scientific revolution and the Enlightenment and Hegel's dialectics, itself rooted in even older philosophical traditions. It seeks to break the boundaries between thought and ideology on the one hand, and concrete, material reality on the other by demonstrating their co-constitution: the dialectic of base and superstructure. As an analytic method, Marxist dialectics seems remarkably well suited to the contemporary, globalized context more often treating change as a given fact whereas dealing with apparent stability as something to be explained.

Although we cannot provide an extensive introduction to Marxist dialectics here, nonetheless, as a starting point for understanding our use of the term "critical" we must, at the very least, speak to some of its important general principles. To do this, we start by recognizing the significant challenges that ideological barriers create in any attempt to analyze and understand culture, institutional forms, and human development as a process of historical change. This is, after all, perhaps the first achievement of the concept of activity as it inherently challenges and, in turn, helps us transcend powerful ideological individualizing boundaries reflected in dominant understandings of human development and learning. Marxist dialectics, as a central element of this original thinking, is seen as a critical approach that allows us to question the ideological distortions embedded in dominant, taken-for-granted definitions. Does this mean we dismiss, for example, the notion of "institutions" as a mere ideological distortion? Hardly. Such categories or boundaries can be used critically when they are historicized and contextualized through the specific techniques of dialectical abstraction (e.g., Ollman 1993): a process ably demonstrated in the chapters of this volume. It is, after all, only through such forms of analysis that we can begin to assemble a sense of the overall societal or rather, societal–historical, picture, what is called in the language of this method, "totality." Moving in the opposite direction of the well-known post-modernist refusal to acknowledge notions of totality, this collection adopts the assumption that a critical approach to human activity is impossible without a critical theory on capitalism as a "totality of many determinations and relations" (Marx, in Tucker, 1978, p. 237). Capitalist relations are not confined to economical fields of social practice. We all live and act as part of a totality named capitalism necessarily making us all part of the dialectical struggle between humanization (or emancipation) and alienation.

An expression of this impulse in third-generation CHAT scholarship, for example, is when we extend our exploration of local systems of activity (e.g., a classroom, a department in an organization, etc.) to the notion of *systems* of activity systems, each with dynamics of change and historical trajectories. Dialectics, as the likes of Marx, Ilyenkov, Ollman, and others have so consistently demonstrated, brings "ideas" under the yoke of analysis rather than the other way around. It is, in fact, a dialectical observation to say that ideas should be treated as artifacts: tools that mediate activity but which can also be re-made by people to allow us to change ourselves and our world.

Before concluding this section, it makes sense to briefly reference one final distinction of Marxist dialectics: the basic difference between philosophies of "external" and "internal" relations. To begin, first we acknowledge that an awareness of both internal and external relations is necessary. In the same way that Marx originally sought to conjoin idealist philosophy with concrete, material analysis, likewise a critical approach as we understand it seeks to combine analyses of both internal and external relations, a form of anti-essentialism developed long before the ground was claimed by what is now known as post-modern social theory. Specifically, a strict philosophy of external relations focuses analysis on the interaction between two seemingly self-contained spheres, institutions, or fields of practice that may, in turn, interact to produce a third separate effect whereas the original two spheres remain largely unchanged. A philosophy of internal relations, on the other hand, allows an analytic focus on the nature of a particular part of a system as an element in relation to the whole, necessarily reflecting in it the central defining relations of the total socio-historic system, or totality. A philosophy of internal relations explores the nature of any single part deeply. It abstracts elements inherent in one analytic object through time, through the dialectical techniques of generalization, extension, contradiction, and the recognition of alternate standpoints (see Chapters 1 and 2 of Ilyenkov 1982; Part II of Ollman 1993).

To ground this explanation, a brief example suitable to the topic of the volume may be in order. For this we can look toward schooling. A philosophy of internal relation allows us to understand how schooling – in itself through individual testing, competition, differential reward systems, and so on – produces learning as a "credential" that is, at the same time, recognizable as a form of commodity. Students obtain credentials that have as one of their organizing features an exchange-value. In this way, claims about the nature of credentialism can be made on the basis of internal relations within the educational process, which also express a key relation defining the broader socio-economic system of capitalism. A key contradiction then becomes apparent. The credential-granting process is subject to the contradictions between use-value and exchange-value inherent in the commodity form. Use-value in the context of this example is what most students, parents, teachers, and administrators might understand as "education as valuable in itself." This relation thus represents the classic "unity of opposites." As most educators would agree – and as two of the chapters in this volume directly demonstrate – credential production as an "exchange-value" has increasingly come to govern its internally related opposite, educational "use-value" to produce a specific form of development on the basis of internal relations. The contradiction within this unity tells us a great deal about the struggle that goes on within the walls of every school under capitalism. At the same time, we cannot ignore external relations. In our example, schools as institutions have an important relation to the separate institutions of paid work and, more directly, labor markets. Tracing interactions between these separate spheres is an important element of understanding how the contradiction above plays itself out in the concrete.

As we've suggested, it will always be inadequate to try to provide a thumbnail sketch of the development of Marxism as a system of thought, let alone as a practical/political movement in this context and space. All the same, one might still ask: What is Marxism? The answers, of course, have been the subject of volume upon volume of clarifications, refutations, and constructive development over the past 130 years. Perhaps the most often recognized and concise statement concerning the foundational elements of Marxism, as provided by Marx himself, is the Preface to *A Contribution to the Critique of Political Economy* (1859). The authors in this collection have not sought to re-hash what is already widely available; suffice it to say here that through the history of the corpus, we define Marxism broadly. It is a critique of political economy from the standpoint of the proletariat. It is also a specific form of dialectical analysis and a materialist conception of history and change. It is expressed, perhaps most simply, in the relations between "being" and "consciousness," relations that the founders of activity research took very seriously indeed: that "being", the sum total of material practice/production, is the root of historical change in relation to the super-structure of civil society, including "consciousness." This relation according to Marx, lies in opposition to the Hegelian radicalism that privileged consciousness. To conclude, we might add that, in this broad definition, if there is a critique of other non-Marxist sciences, it is that, although not necessarily inaccurate, they are historically bounded by capitalism as a social, cultural, and economic period of history.

It is the purpose of this volume to collect applications of this type of critical perspective on activity across a number of social spheres. As Marx did, through his now-famous immersion in the governmental Blue Books of the British Museum and the social, political, and economic questions of the day, our collection seeks to understand, with the help of empirical resources, the real contradictions of the day leading to change. Marxist dialectics is not a generic theory of change. It is a theory of change that is rooted in actualities of particular historical epochs. In our current historical context, it is a theory of change within and beyond capitalism specifically.

## MAJOR THEMES ACROSS THE COLLECTION

Following this introduction, Mohamed Elhammoumi's Chapter 2, "Is There a Marxist Psychology?," provides a fascinating account of the mind in action, an essay on the thinking through of key questions of Marxist psychology as well as Marxism as a whole – its past, present, and possible future. It is highly personal, shedding many of the clothes of confident appraisals, preferring good questions to partial answers, and thus serves well as our initial presentation. Elhammoumi begins noting the parallel between the methods of Vygotsky in arriving at his theory of higher mental functioning and Marx's own method in the study of the development of human history. Returning to the historical roots of radical psychologists in discussions of the Austro-Marxist School, German critical theory, Freudo-Marxism, Pavlov's

Materialism, Soviet Psychology, Frankfurt School, Berlin Critical Psychology, Western Marxist Psychology, and other forms of Materialist Psychology, Elhammoumi responds to a provocative question: Was Vygotsky the Feuerbach of psychology or was it Marx? Along the way, he emphasizes how Vygotsky's thinking obviously responded positively to the role of various social relations (social relations of production, social interaction, cooperation, collaboration, etc.) in individual development. Exploring the explicit Marxist questions Vygotsky entertained and the variegated tradition of Marxism more broadly, the author arrives at a focus that he argues may be crucial to the future of both. This focus is spatio-temporality, an issue that the author claims sets the limitations of Marx's own theoretical development. What are the inconsistencies in treatments of abstract and concrete labor, in treatments of "leisure time," in the dialectic of use-value and exchange-value, and so on? Theories of activity, in particular, are said to require an assessment of the forces of spatio-temporality if they are to become truly formative conceptions. Springing from such issues, among other important insights, is a radical re-engagement with notions of individuality, that is, the social production of the individual, understood by Elhammoumi as the "individual form."

Joachim Lompscher's Chapter 3, entitled "The Cultural–Historical Activity Theory: Some Aspects of Development," is the second chapter of our sub-section on "Theoretical Foundations." It presents an original, critical profile of the developmental history of CHAT with the hope of stimulating a further elabouration and debate. He begins with a grounded description of Vygotsky and collaborators, taking careful steps to show key theoretical origins and foci of work, including its divergent patterns of development amongst Vygotsky and Leont'ev specifically. Throughout, the author shows the key theoretical elements as they underwent development. He directly addresses the question of whether or not the works of Vygotsky and Leont'ev represent two different stages in CHAT development, an issue that contributes to an understanding of the overall relation of critical theories of activity to current scholarship. As Lompscher discusses, it is now known that Leont'ev did in fact write a private letter to Vygotsky, which openly argued for a return to earlier preoccupations that included the notion of collective human activity. Nevertheless, Lompscher concludes their work remains deeply intertwined with later work building on the earlier elements. Following this, Lompscher delineates schools and sub-schools of Russian and non-Russian CHAT research approaches, providing a detailed account of several works, some not widely available in the English translation, across a range of key concepts, covering the research of the three generations of Leont'ev scholarship and the work of Asmolov, Davydov, and others. By the end of the chapter, the author offers constructive directions forward for analyses in the CHAT tradition, highlighting the lack of careful consideration of the socio-technical and economic role of the forces of production, namely computer technology and the Internet, as an underdeveloped area of research.

A key element of our opening discussions of CHAT theory is the concluding chapter of this section. Maria Célia Marcondes de Moraes' Chapter 4, "Epistemological Scepticism, Complacent Irony: Investigations Concerning the Neo-Pragmatism of Richard Rorty," offers a useful antidote to the free-flowing search amongst many CHAT researchers to find other traditions that offer more suitable paths of development than those already offered. The author takes on one that is, perhaps, most central to current discussions: neo-pragmatism. Moraes methodically affirms the importance of a dialectical, historical materialist reality in understanding activity that is, she argues, incompatible with the path that neo-pragmatism, as embodied in the work of Rorty, suggests. Moraes provides a searing assessment of Rorty's claims about knowledge and truth in the context of "hypercontextualism." Hypercontextualism in this context is said to reduce every knowledge and every ethical value strictly to conventions shared by people in a specific cultural set. In this sense, the knowledge is neither true nor false; it is only good or not good depending on its instrumental function; the truth is just something taken as true by people in a particular social practice. Importantly, this cultural relativism is considered by many to be the same as the Vygotskian conception of human beings as cultural and historical beings. But the real question is, can a Marxist theory such as Vygotsky's be connected with the pragmatic philosophical tradition? Moraes' critical analysis of Richard Rorty's philosophy is a contribution toward the negative. Moraes' contribution is a strong and persistent argument against the post-modernist appropriation of Vygotskian theory, addressing epistemological questions as well as the educational, ethical, and political consequences of Rorty's neo-pragmatism. It should give pause to those assessing theories of activity generally and especially those enthusiastically taking up the pragmatist tradition, including the writings of Dewey, Mead, and others.

Following our more general assessments of theories of activity, we move to our second sub-section on "Education." First in this section is Alessandra Arce's Chapter 5, "The Importance of Play to Pre-School Education: Naturalization Versus a Marxist Analysis." Here, we see a critical comparative perspective on play, pre-schooling, and child development in which she takes up the perspectives developed by Elkonin and Leont'ev from the CHAT tradition against the perspectives of Froebel. Her critique of Froebel demonstrates the problems associated with ahistorical and universalistic modes of analysis with a focus on naturalism or rather "primordialism." The significance of the comparison comes, first, in its careful analysis but also, perhaps in particular, when we note the "genetic role" that early theories of education and pedagogy had, and thus still have, within dominant conceptions of education. In other words, the history of education, specifically in the West, carries with it a lasting influence of such philosophies. Arce begins by agreeing that Froebel's emphasis on play was important to understanding the modern educational enterprise. Like Moraes' paper, which is a contribution to a criticism of the linkage between CHAT and Pragmatism/Neo-pragmatism, Arce's paper shows the problematic nature of the association between CHAT and the so-named "Active Education" or "Active School" in Europe and "Progressive Education" approach of North America. Arce's comparative analyses of the idealistic conception of Froebel on play in childhood and the historical–materialistic approach of Leont'ev and Elkonin is particularly enlightening in terms of the critical perspective on activity adopted in this volume generally. This chapter can be taken as an example of how much the dialectical conception of totality is important to the analysis of specific kinds of human activity.

In Chapter 6, "Estranged ~~Labor~~ Learning," Jean Lave and Ray McDermott begin with key statements on the subject of capitalism vis-à-vis Marx's well-known essay, "Estranged Labor" (from *The Economic and Philosophic Manuscripts of 1844*). The authors carefully situate the basic axioms of one of capitalism's hidden secrets and then do what dialectics demand, they apply it to see if indeed the hidden secrets of capitalism's commodity form, its alienation, and so on can be understood as an inherent part of the concrete educational process. Of course, it can. This chapter's analysis of social practice and activity goes back to several first principles of Marxist analysis through careful, line-by-line analysis of Marx's own writing and transposes them directly to an inventive overall critique of contemporary schooling under capitalism. As they remark, "In critiquing the theories of political economy available in 1844, young Marx unwittingly wrote a quite devastating critique of the theories of learning available in 2004." And through this type of reading, the authors emphasize the political economic turn in analyses of learning and activity to which this collection hopes to contribute. Herein are covered concepts central to Marxist educational theory, but given fresh life. As editors of this collection, we note with satisfaction that the authors invite the reader into the process of production itself – an act of de-fetishization – rather than to simply view the final scholarly product (a commodity). It is a practice to be emulated. Indeed, the spirit of critical dialogue that inspires the collection as a whole is represented here in the subtle and not-so-subtle divergences between ideas. This critical dialogue is an intentional characteristic of this collection, and we invite the readers to elaborate their own positions inside the debates.

Helena Worthen and Joe Berry's Chapter 7, "'Our Working Conditions Are Our Students' Learning Conditions': A CHAT Analysis of College Teachers," begins with the quoted statement: "Our working conditions are our students' learning conditions." What is the significance of this, as well as the details of the struggle to which it refers, in the broader context of the collection? Can a critical perspective on activity open new questions that are not yet widely posed for this international phenomenon at the intersection of education and work? Worthen and Berry think so. They offer a dialectical analysis of schooling *as* work and work *as* schooling, emphasizing the political economic dimensions of the teaching/learning conditions amongst contingent faculty in American higher education. The authors ask: What is meant by the "good teacher"? This is a matter of dialectical contradiction within a system of activities that are through and through formed by the confluence of educational as well as economic elements of a "higher education industry." What standpoints are relevant to understand or map what's going on? To begin with, the standpoints of the worker–teacher (in particular, the contingently employed worker–teacher) and that of educational management, but, in addition, there is the parallel system that accounts for the practices of tenure-track teachers as well.

In Chapter 8, "Contradictory Class Relations in Work and Learning: Some Resources for Hope," D. W. Livingstone begins with an analysis of contradictory (and, ultimately, polarizing) class relations and its effects on work and learning. It is the first of three chapters that form the sub-section entitled "Work." Covered in Livingstone's contribution are discussions of unemployment, underemployment, and theories of work–education relations. Above all, there is evident need, according to the author, for critical theories of learning to pay more concerted attention to contradictory class relations. An important discussion that springboards analysis is the expansion of the narrow conceptual boundaries of both work and learning. CHAT is used to interrogate various alternative conceptions of learning (tacit, informal, non-formal, and formalized learning), whereas work, it is argued, must be viewed in both paid and unpaid forms if class relations are to be brought fully into view. In some ways similar to the chapter that follows, the socialization of labor is central. In Livingstone's case, he is concerned with the forces of knowledge production, that is, the central contradiction between the "socialized forces and privatized relations of knowledge production." The sites of development of the socialized forces of knowledge production are, according to Livingstone, both the sites most often ignored by educational scholars and the sites that form the starting point of revolutionary change.

Following, in Chapter 9, "From Labor Process to Activity Theory," Paul Adler takes as a starting point Marxist Labor Process Theory (LPT) as understood in the tradition inspired by Harry Braverman. He outlines how a return to Marx's original discussions of the fundamental contradiction between the socialization of the labor process on the one hand and the persistence of the constraints of capitalist profitability on the other provides a constructive way of invigorating labor process analysis. How can contemporary LPT address the problem of de-skilling, that is, what is the nature of the "de/en-skilling" debate? A critical perspective on activity as well as a close – "paleo-Marxist" – re-reading of Marx's work itself, according to the author, allows us to see and partially resolve the problems within LPT. To ground discussion, Adler draws on a case study on the rationalization of work in the software development sector in the United States. The analysis of the socialization of labor processes provides a fascinating argument that reaches back to Marx's critical commentary on what he called "craft idiocy." As these craft boundaries break down, a greater number of participants find the complexity of their work increased. Could it be that en-skilling occurs at a societal level as the socialization of, in Adler's case, software design processes becomes more standardized, allowing greater international exchange? His analysis leads directly to issues of the development of a lived experience of the "collective worker" as well. Implications of social versus technical division of labor abound. At the same time, the author juxtaposes the contradictory internal unity of this socialization effect with the valorization effect through which the familiar disabling forces of capitalism on cooperation, free exchange of ideas, and the production of higher quality use-values are seriously threatened by inter-capitalist competition, heightened managerial control, and, in general terms, commodification/profit requirements.

In Chapter 10, "Values, Rubbish, and Workplace Learning," Yrjö Engeström takes a critical approach to the issue of value. As the author indicates, "Values at Work" is frequently the subject of scholarly and popular concern. Citing the common-sense perspectives, widely reproduced in psychology, education, and other disciplines that suggest the notion of "values" as a largely mentalistic and discursive phenomenon, the author argues for the importance of seeing values as structurally embedded as contradictory objects/motives of activity: "The articulation, questioning, and expansive transformation of values can eventually only succeed at the level of collective activity systems. Problem solving and reflection-in-action at individual or dyadic levels will not suffice." He takes as the central problem the many transformative cycles of objects, in provocative fashion, drawing and significantly expanding upon the fascinating work of Michael Thompson's 1979 book *Rubbish Theory*. How are values, in this context, shaped? Here, the value of objects of activity is in constant flux but with discernable and distinct patterns: A car of considerable exchange-value is purchased, its value plummets, possibly through multiple instances of re-sale, to the point of worthlessness or rubbish, but, in some cases, re-emerges again as a "durable," a collector's find that then may increase in value over time. From these rudiments, an elaborate set of alternative pathways of objects and values are traced, illuminating the roles of production and consumption in addition to exchange. Drawing on concrete examples in health care service work, it is in these phases that Engeström finds "invisible resistance and emergence." Here, we trace the career, as it were, of "difficult," "demanding," and "complex" patients and ultimately the so-called lost causes or "rubbish cases," their lives translated into a rubric of "commoditization," price, and (exchange) value that define the central contradiction of health systems around the world. Building into the model instances of self-care, re-using of equipment, re-diagnoses, and self-medication (as well as poverty and self-abuse), Engeström embraces the central tenet of a critical approach in asking: How do these patient cases become rubbish? And how might they become durables? Three trajectories, perhaps, hold the key for moving forward: playful conversion, caring revitalization, and engrossed appropriation. The implications for health care work and other contexts are many.

The final sub-section of the collection is "Everyday Life." It begins with Newton Duarte's Chapter 11, "Education as Mediation Between the Individual's Everyday Life and the Historical Construction of Society and Culture." Here Duarte presents observations on the studies he has carried out over the last decade and a half. The focus of this chapter is on the relations between three theoretical approaches. The first one is historical and philosophical anthropology in the Marxist tradition. This chapter deals with two key dialectical relations: the relationships between humanisation and alienation on the one hand and the relation between objectification and appropriation on the other. The second theoretical approach, represented in Leont'ev's collective works, concerns theories of activity that incorporate Marx's anthropology and develop the analysis of the relations between the structure of activity and the structure of consciousness. Two important topics of Leont'ev's theory of activity are specifically noted: the role in the formation of the individual of the appropriation of the socio-historical experience objectified in the material and non-material culture, and the alienation produced by capitalist society. Duarte demonstrates how alienation is analyzed by Leont'ev, taking into consideration not only the barriers that drastically limit the possibility of appropriation of culture by the individual, but also the rupture between meaning and sense of most of the actions taken by human beings. Finally, the third theoretical approach is the Theory of "Species-Essential Objectivations" proposed by Agnes Heller (1984) in her book *Everyday Life*, written between 1967–68. The conceptual tools the author draws from Heller allow an exploration of a number of key topics. These topics include the differences and relations between "species-essential objectivations in itself" (everyday life) and "species-essential objectivations for itself" (what does not pertain to everyday life), the main characteristics of the everyday activities and the forms of thought and knowledge of everyday life, and, finally, the concept of person and the distinction between "particularity" and "individuality." The chapter concludes with a defense of the relevance of these three theoretical approaches for contemporary studies across philosophy, psychology, education, and sociology.

Finally, in Chapter 12, "Activity and Power: Everyday Life and Development of Working-Class Groups," Peter Sawchuk undertakes an assessment of contemporary Cultural Historical theories of activity for their ability to explain and analyze specific patterns of change in political consciousness. He links his discussion with broader social trends related to the so-called new knowledge society and economy. An important matter for Sawchuk's argument is the notion of "class struggle," which must be analyzed in relation to changes in consciousness vis-à-vis structural shifts in the workings of specific activity systems. Key contributions to the CHAT rubric can be made, according to the author, by other conceptual sources, such as Michel de Certeau's notion of the tactical and the strategic, Henri Lefebvre's understandings of resistance and *le detournement*, and especially Pierre Bourdieu's concept of "class habitus." Sawchuk presents a three-type model of changes in political consciousness in the form of complex everyday learning activity systems undergoing forms of contracted and expansive development. Forces of fragmentation and, what Sawchuk calls, interstitiality (everyday resistance) shape and ultimately provide an account for changes in class consciousness. The class habitus is said to be the key mediating cultural artifact. Tracing changes in its content as well as structural position within activity, it is proposed as a master artifact in many ways primary to language.

## ACTIVITY ACROSS EDUCATION, WORK, AND EVERYDAY LIFE: VISIONS OF LIFELONG LEARNING

According to the Organization for Economic Cooperation and Development (OECD), "lifelong for all" is now a major policy perspective amongst Education Ministers around the world. Built on the concept of lifelong learning originally developed over three decades ago by the OECD, UNESCO, and the Council of Europe, comparative international statistics on performance now increasingly orient policy affecting the majority of countries in the world. The World Bank and the International Monetary Fund, likewise, now orient to, amongst other matters, this issue as well. Importantly for this volume, "learning" in this rubric encompasses practices of early-childhood, through compulsory, and post-compulsory, education and training throughout everyday life: "from cradle to grave," as the OECD puts it. Four features mark the edges of the policy implications of such views according to the OECD (2004, p. 2): learning objectives, structure of provision, content, and resource provision/management. One of the main goals of this collection is to contribute implicitly to a critical conception of the fact that, in the contemporary capitalist society, people are expending more and more time in their lives in learning activities or learning processes. Critical analyses of what this social and historical fact really means is necessary to move the policy beyond the mere rhetoric of "lifelong learning society," "knowledge society," or "educative society" adopted by the leading international institutions.

Although policy discussion is not the focus of this collection, in the broader sense of the work, it should not be ignored. In the case of our volume, it is not hard to see that this collection poses useful, powerful, and perhaps even vexing questions for such discussions. The contents do, after all, provide a potent mix of empirical specificity and theoretical depth in its assessment of learning/practice that encompasses the life course. What vision of lifelong learning does this collection, exactly, afford?

Reading across our first sub-section on theory, we can begin to piece together interesting points of tension that national and international policy-makers rarely have the time, resources, or expertise to entertain. First, we note that it is important to remember that theory does matter. Frames of reference and relevance that we apply to analyses shape what one attends to, denies, and ignores. How we understand the very concept of "learning" (a concept chronically presumed rather than defined in policy documents) has radical implications for how something like a "knowledge economy" or "lifelong learning society" might be organized. Taken as a whole, the writing of Lompscher, Elhammoumi, and Moraes present important clues about key fallacies, theoretical dead-ends, and mistaken directions to be avoided in understandings of learning itself. The lesson to be taken from this opening section is that, although not discounting a range of important differences, a Cultural Historical view of learning as mediated human activity provides a broad, systematic, and inter-disciplinary basis for defining, tracing, and in turn understanding the phenomenon. Our understanding of the idea of a "critical approach" is oriented by an assessment of major contradictions that define societal history; this view is largely conflictual, it is rooted in actual material practices, and it refuses to paper over real inequities, including their systemic and historical roots. At the very least, it is clear that policy discussions that refuse to acknowledge the highly uneven and hotly debated theoretical roots of the concepts of learning and knowledge production can scarcely recommend new forms of practice with confidence.

The discussion within our "Education" section provides policy-makers with further pause for thought. Is it simply an abstract observation to note that our society's future rests on early visions of what childhood means, what it means to learn and, in particular, play? We think not. The daughter is the mother of the woman; that is, a life-course perspective must acknowledge that there can be no adequate understanding of learning in society without a critical assessment of the experience of childhood. Arce's chapter is clear that how pedagogy frames these experiences and shapes them incurs important choices, some of which connect with actual Cultural Historical practice and modes of knowledge acquisition better than others. We might juxtapose this argument, once again, with Worthen and Berry's observation (quoting college teachers): "Our working conditions are our students' learning conditions." The dynamic analyzed by Worthen and Berry can easily inspire reflection on teaching as a whole; the hidden economic constraints on pedagogy, whether it is early-childhood or post-compulsory, cannot be left to one side as we discuss lifelong learning. Similarly, Lave and McDermott's political economic framing of the credentializing and theorizing practices of the educational realm bring into question the true function of schooling in our society. Can lifelong learning policy continue to ignore these central contradictions?

The discussion in our section on "Work" shows the real constraints on skill and learning development in the work process (seen as both paid and unpaid). Policy discussions are rife with presumptions of what "knowledge work" is, typically viewing it as largely consensual and unproblematic. Livingstone and Adler each show that there are important contradictory forces at play that would easily undermine any simplistic policy initiative. The socialization of labor processes and the forces of knowledge production are both constrained and partially constituted by a powerful opposing force that few policy analysts openly acknowledge. It may be absurd to proclaim any lifelong learning policy involving, for example, greater support for workplace training without first understanding the system, as outlined by these contributors, in which these practices are enmeshed. Engeström's grounded analysis of alternative forms and pathways of "valuing," equally, suggests that understanding the complex workings of work must be taken into account in proclamations of its future.

Finally, in our fourth section "Everyday Life," we begin to open up critical dialogue about the link in the trajectory of lifelong learning policy that is perhaps the most inadequately addressed of all. To date, lifelong learning policy rests on tallies of how many attended school and took training courses, apprenticeship programs, and so on. With notable exceptions, across the globe, the learning that goes on outside organized courses remains difficult to assess and challenging to fit into conventional policy frameworks. More often than not, policy initiatives rest on simplistic survey constructs and correlations. In contrast, Duarte offers a powerful philosophical starting point for beginning to understand the nature of everyday life and through it learning in its broadest forms. Objectively, different relations between human beings and their modes of objectification/appropriation provide a means of sorting out what most theory fumbles around as it attempts assessments of the vast flow of human experience that is "lifelong learning." Sawchuk, likewise, attempts to bring a sense of shape to what might appear to be a complex and arbitrary set of different trajectories of development in the context of everyday learning. Why and how is it that there are such differences in experiences, outcomes, and development in the realm of everyday life? Learner motivation and generalized correlations between prior school experience and socio-economic situation, are the state of the art of lifelong learning analysis, and as such leave much to be desired. Both Duarte and Sawchuk show conceptual means of sorting out questions of who, how, and why in the development of everyday learning so essential for a comprehensive lifelong learning strategy.

**CONCLUDING REMARKS**

Our approach to activity has a great deal to offer those wishing to embrace the complexity of learning through the life-course in changing times. Interdisciplinary dialogue is as essential as a recovery of a critical perspective. The concept of "activity," however, remains broad. The usage throughout the collection recognizes this and presents analyses of activity as a process of change. Learning is at the center of our analysis because it evokes an image, along the lines of Marx's original compliments of Hegel's work, "[h]e grasps the self-creation of man [*sic*] as a process . . . that he therefore grasps the nature of labour" (from Bottomore 1963, p. 202). Labor produces and shapes human individuals. Just as the concept of labor allowed Marx to overcome Cartesian dualism, the concept of activity does the same for the social sciences with regard to learning. The concept of activity unites the subject and object, and overcomes the dualism of lower versus higher mental functions, inner world of meanings, and outer world of determinations. Through labor or productive activity, human individuals objectify themselves and their potentialities. Learning is, in this sense, the labor people individually and collectively do on themselves. Labor might be used interchangeably with activity, and labor/activity becomes, for us, the cardinal representation of social relations, social organization, and culture. According to Leont'ev (1974), these forms of relations are nothing other than the total logic of human life processes inclusive of the division of labor.

In many ways, we might say that our collection tries to reconcile the theories of activity with Marx's concept of labor. Authors review several key areas of research with a view of assessing and evaluating the premises, categories, and concepts, as well as epistemological, methodological, and philosophical foundations. We should conclude, however, that whereas the research program of the Cultural Historical School formulated by Vygotsky, Luria, and Leont'ev has been very fruitful and promising, its overall ambition to provide a properly elaborated theory of human higher mental functions remains, to date, unfulfilled.

Finally, we note that the theoretical and political importance of this dialogue on "work, education, and everyday life" lies in the attempt to trace the contours of life under capitalism starting from the key loci that seem to uniquely define the period. Each section lays out key questions on the meaning and potentials for a vision of lifelong learning society or knowledge economy. At the same time, answers given in the text can only be partial. Science is a collective endeavor, each of us standing on the shoulders of others, forming the platform for still others who follow. Moreover, for in-depth analyses, there is always a sacrifice of breadth. In the case of our collection, authors address either local, national, or a narrow range of international contexts and specific conceptual matters, populations, and institutions. What should be clear, however, is that studies of mind, culture, and activity such as these offer a powerful means of moving forward on central questions of our time. At the broadest level, it can be said that policies of lifelong learning and most articulated visions of a knowledge economy are, at this stage, perfunctory: a richly fragranced stew with little meat. Beyond the intellectual nourishment this text may offer, studies herein, and those like them, promise to add sustenance to the overall societal debate.

# CRITICAL PERSPECTIVES ON THEORY

2

# Is There a Marxist Psychology?

## Mohamed Elhammoumi

We do not want a brand-new and trivial name from history. We want a name covered by the dust of centuries. We regard this as our historical right, as an indication of our historical role, our claim to realize psychology as a science. We must view ourselves in connection with and in relation to the past . . . That is why we accept the name of our science with all its age-old delusions as a vivid reminder of our victory over these errors, as the fighting scars of wounds, as a vivid testimony of the truth which develops in the incredibly complicated struggle with falsehood.

(Vygotsky, 1927/1997a: 336–337)

La psychologie ne détient donc nullement le "secret" des faits humains, simplement parce que ce "secret" n'est pas d'ordre psychologique [Psychology by no means holds the "secret" of human affairs, simply because this "secret" is not of a psychological order].

(Politzer, 1928: 170)

Pourquoi la théorie? Comme le plus court chemin vers la realité.

(Verret, 1999: 10)

### INTRODUCTION

Vygotsky, whose premature death occurred at the age of thirty-seven in 1934, was a serious loss to Marxist psychology. He will be remembered for three things. Firstly, he played a major part in reviving the Marxist approach to psychology, which had been suppressed by the positivism–scientism versions of Marxism. Secondly, in his major works, Vygotsky made a positive and original application of Marx's method, which in Marx's works often suffered from vulgar dialectical materialism. Thirdly, Vygotsky is the Feuerbach of psychology, but not yet the Marx of psychology.

Vygotsky had read many texts by Marx and on Marxism. His ideas were grounded in a philosophy that was both dialectical and materialist.

Doubtless, he did possess the necessary skills – philosophical, political, literary, economic, historical and cultural – to bring to a successful conclusion to the extremely complex and difficult task he had set himself. This task was to create psychology's own *Das Kapital*, which is based on dialectical and historical materialism. Materialism maintains that there is an objective concrete reality that exists outside of human perception, and social totality is perceived as a concrete historical totality. To paraphrase John Locke, there is nothing in human thought that is not first in society. Or, to extend the implications, each of us is constituted by social relations and is inseparable from ongoing social processes of change. My attempt has been to make intelligible a range of social relations, or relational forms in which individual activity derives its content, sense, or meaning from its placement within the extended and interconnected social relations (Sève, 1966, 1975; Shames, 1984, 1987, 1990; Elhammoumi, 2001a, 2002, 2004). Dialectical materialism maintains that all constituents of concrete reality as well as human mental life are in a constant state of change that occurs according to certain laws of development and change. Historical materialism is the application of dialectical materialism to human society, including human higher mental functions. In this perspective, a Marxist approach to psychology is an ensemble of principles that apply to the study of human higher mental functions, including consciousness, personality, and all spheres of human activity. In Vygotsky's conceptions, Marx's theoretical framework (Marx, 1963, 1971a, 1971b, 1973) offered an intellectual tool for analyzing the psychological fabric of human higher mental functions. Vygotsky's psychology is rooted in the principles of Marx's philosophy. He was committed to Marx's writings, but did Marxist psychology under the influence of Vygotsky rise to the level of Marx's thought or stay at Feuerbach's pre-Marxist categories?

## VYGOTSKY: THE FEUERBACH OF MARXIST PSYCHOLOGY

For the last eight decades since 1920, Marxist psychology has not achieved its goals. Most of its leading psychologists, such as Lev Vygotsky, Georges Politzer, Henri Wallon, Alexis Leontiev, Alexander Luria, Serge Rubenstein, René Zazzo, Klaus Holzkamp, Lucien Sève, Ethel Tobach, Carl Ratner, and Carl Shames, among others, operated within the categories of the pre-Marxist research program. In other word, Marxist psychology, in its present form, operates at the level of Feuerbach, not yet Marx. Three stages were identified in the evolution of a Marxist psychology. The first stage can be characterized to some extent like that of the young left Hegelians (Wilhem Reich, Henri Wallon, Georges Politzer, Alexander Luria, Alexis Leontiev, René Zazzo, Klaus Holzkamp, and Lucien Sève, among others); the second stage can be characterized like that of Feuerbach's pre-Marxist categories (Lev Vygotsky, Carl Ratner, and Carl Shames), and the third stage is Marx's radical categories. In my view, Marxist psychology has not yet been able to move from the Feuerbachian categories to Marxist categories. In this critical review, I focus on Marxist psychologists and their theoretical inspirations. Since the 1920s, Marxist psychologists have presented their concepts and ideas "in a much more artful form, and confused by the use of a 'new' terminology, so that these thoughts may be taken by naïve people for 'recent philosophy'" (Lenin, 1908: 20), in other words, for Marxist psychology. Naïve radical psychologists have taken Austro-Marxist School, German critical theory, Freudo-Marxism, Pavlov's Materialism, Soviet Psychology, Frankfurt School, Berlin Critical Psychology, Western Marxist Psychology, and other forms of Materialist Psychology for a truly Marxist psychology. In this respect, Vygotsky pointed out:

When the eclectic and unprincipled, superficial and semi-scientific theory of Jameson is called Marxist psychology, when also the majority of the influential Gestalt psychologists regard themselves as Marxists in their scientific work, then this name loses precision with respect to "Marxism." I remember how extremely amazed I was when I realized this during an informal conversation. I had the following conversation with one of the most educated psychologists: What kind of psychology do you have in Russia? That you are Marxists does not yet tell what kind of psychologists you are. Knowing of Freud's popularity in Russia, I at first thought of the Adlerians. After all, these are also Marxists. But you have a totally different psychology. We are also social-democrats and Marxists, but at the same time we are Darwinists and followers of Copernicus as well. (Vygotsky, 1927/1997a, Vol. 3: 341)

As Marxism controlled the social organization in the Soviet Union to a great extent, the early goal of the Marxist psychologists was to establish a psychological model following Marxist philosophy. They part from the assumption that changing the social relations of production that govern the patterns of society can change human nature. Vygotsky (1997b) argues:

From the standpoint of historical materialism, the fundamental causes of all social changes and all political upheavals must be sought not in peoples' minds ... and not in their views of eternal truths and justice, but in changes in the means of production and distribution. They must be sought not in philosophy, but in the economics of each epoch. Thus, in mankind the production process assumes the broadest possible social character, which at the present time encompasses the entire world. Accordingly, there arise the most complex forms of organization of human behavior with which the child encounters before he directly confronts nature. (p. 211)

This theoretical framework led Vygotsky to emphasize the role of various social relations (social relations of production, social interaction, cooperation, collaboration, etc.) in individual development. He developed the concept of the zone of proximal development in which the axis individual–society is dialectically constituted. The chicken–egg dilemma of priority of the individual or the society has been solved according to the following formula: In *potentiality*, the human individual is prior; in *actuality*, society as an expression of social relations is prior. This brings us to the Marxist argument that human individuals are full of undeveloped potential that can only be realized after the structural reorganization of the social relations of production of the entire social organization of the society. In other words, human potential can be fully developed only in a society in which the social relations of production are regulated by the formula, each according to his/her needs.

An investigation of the full range of Soviet and Western Marxist psychologists' thinking will be examined in detail within the context of Marxism.

## SOVIET AND WESTERN MARXIST PSYCHOLOGISTS: ARE THEY MARXIST OR YOUNG LEFT HEGELIANS?

In the mid-1920s, Lev Vygotsky formed the Troika, a group of "young" Marxist psychologists who gathered at Moscow University in the turbulent years of the rise of Stalinism from 1925 to 1934. The central figures were Lev Vygotsky, Alexander Luria, and Alexis Leontiev. Many others were attracted to their ideas.

The Troika was an intellectual group of psychologists whose common theme was the ongoing application of Marx's dialectical method and philosophical conclusions to the study of human higher mental life. Their views of psychology were radical and critical of the competing schools within Soviet and Western psychology.

Vygotsky's initial formation was as a member of the radical "young Marxist" school of social criticism, which emerged in Russia after the revolution of 1905 and which contributed to the ferment of ideas leading to the revolution of October 1917. Initially influenced by Marx, his earliest writings were devoted to the critique of art, literary critics, and philosophy from a radical humanist perspective. However, he soon came to appreciate Marx's ideas that human consciousness, rule-governed behavior, and activity have their roots in material conditions and socially organized practical activity. Henri Wallon and Georges Politzer were reaching similar conclusions as a result of their experiences with psychology in France (Wallon's *dialectical psychology* [1925], and Politzer's *concrete psychology* [1929/1969]). Vygotsky collaborated on a number of works attacking his contemporaries who drew their theoretical inspirations from Pavlov's physiology, Freud's psychoanalysis, Darwin's natural selection, behaviorism, hermeneutics, Hegel's idealism, and positivism–scientism for their idealism. From this emerged the "cultural–historical theory of human higher mental functions," the theory which, Vygotsky says, served as the guiding thread for his psychological studies throughout the remainder of his life.

Vygotsky and his colleagues made an important contribution toward a Marxist psychology, but their efforts were at the level of Feuerbach, not yet Marx (Carl Shames, 1984 1988, 1990; Elhammoumi, 2000, 2001a, 2001b, 2002, 2004). Vygotsky and his colleagues (Leontiev, Luria, and others) were similar to the young left Hegelians who tried to put an end to Hegel's idealistic philosophy. The same ambition attracted Vygotsky and his colleagues to put an end to the idealistic schools that dominated psychology and brought it to a deep crisis. In his critical review of Hegelian philosophy Vygotsky pointed out that:

When Hegel strives to subordinate the unique activity of man to the category of logic – arguing that this activity is the "conclusion", that the subject (man) plays the role of a "component" of the logical "figure" "conclusion" – this is not only stretching the point, it is a game. There is a profound point there, a purely materialistic one. We must reverse it: man's practical activity must bring the repetition of various logical figures a billion times in order for these figures to become axioms ... And further: "Man's practice, repeated a billion times, anchors the figures of logic in his consciousness." (1987, Vol. 1: 88)

And he added that:

What is man? [Human being] for Hegel, he is a logical subject. For Pavlov, it is soma, an organism. For us, man [human being] is social person = an aggregate of social relations, embodied in an individual (psychological functions built according to social structure). (1989: 66)

Vygotsky suggested, correctly in my view, that what drew Marx to Hegel was apparently Hegel's ability to anchor the realm of human freedom in the vicissitudes of human history. In this respect, Vygotsky is the Feuerbach of Marxist psychology. According to Vygotsky,

L. Feuerbach's wonderful phrase might be taken as the motto to the study of development in abnormal children: "That, which is impossible for one, is possible for two." Let us add: That which is impossible on the level of individual development becomes possible on the level of social development. (1993, Vol. 2: 218)

It was Feuerbach who prepared the road to Marx and the conceptualization of Marxist philosophy. In his article *Critique of the Hegelian Dialectic,* Marx viewed Feuerbach as "the only one who has a *serious, critical* attitude to the Hegelian dialectic" and credited him for having "laid the foundation of genuine materialism and real science" (Marx, 1844: 197). If Vygotsky is the Feuerbach of Marxist psychology. Who will be the Marx of Marxist psychology? In my view, Marxist psychology is in need of its own Marx, a Marx who will rework and rebuild on the Feuerbach (Vygotsky) of Marxist psychology. In conclusion, Soviet psychology and Western materialist psychology have produced the Feuerbach of psychology (in this case, Vygotsky), but not yet the Marx of psychology.

### THE STRUGGLE FOR A MARXIST PSYCHOLOGY

The struggle for a Marxist psychology in dialectical thought is far from being a new one. It was the object of long and searching discussions and debates – between the years 1920, 1930, and 1940 – involving the principal theoreticians of the various tendencies of Marxist thought, notably Lev Vygotsky (1923, 1925, 1927, 2003), Henri Wallon (1925, 1936, 1937, 1946, 1951), Pavel Blonsky (1928), Georges Politzer (1928, 1929), Wilhem Reich (1929, 1934), Konstantin Kornilov (1930), Sergi Rubenstein (1934, 1945), Otto Fenichel (1934), Junius Brown (1936, 1938), Alistair Browne (1937), Reuben Osborne (1937), Angel Flores (1938), Burrill Freedman (1939, 1940), and Pierre Naville (1946), a discussion carried on in numerous articles, monographs, and books of very high intellectual investigations. To understand the origins of these scientific investigations, we must first of all place them in the context of Marxist thought of the 1920s and 1930s. Psychologists working within Marx's theoretical framework were not aware of fragmentations and versions of Marxism. The 1920s and 1930s were characterized by a break with the dialectical Marxist tradition and the progressive triumph of historicism and scientism. The methods of natural science became the effective tools to investigate human phenomena in general and human higher mental functions in particular. Thus, psychologists working within Marx's theoretical framework had come back to the idea of a radical division between sciences and social engineering, division between academic thought and socialist thought or, in Marx's view, division between judgments of fact and judgments of value. The conception of scientism rapidly became dominant among the main theoreticians of the so-called orthodox Marxism who transformed the dialectical concept of social organization into a concept of natural science. Most Marxist psychologists at that time were less informed about the conflicts within Marxism. The determinist movement triumphed. We must remember that Marx was not a determinist and the *Third Thesis on Feuerbach* is a good example. In a letter to J. Bloch, Engels (1890/1978, p. 204) asserted that, if somebody says that "the economic element is the *only* determining one, he transforms that proposition into a meaningless, abstract, senseless phrase."

Marxist psychology is, of course, a complex subject. Psychologists working within Marx's thought held a variety of views of psychology, often brilliantly formulated but not always consistent.

### SOME IDEAS ABOUT THE PROJECT OF MARXIST PSYCHOLOGY

In general, I think most work in *Marxist psychology* has stayed too close to both the form and content of bourgeois psychology and psychoanalysis. In addition Western psychologists with an interest in Marxist approaches to psychology have tended either to turn to psychoanalysis, such as Freudo-Marxism, Frankfurt School of Critical Theory, and other positivism versions of Marxism, or to concentrate upon demonstrating the limitations of Western Bourgeois psychology. The leading thinkers of the Frankfurt School (Adorno, Horkheimer, Marcuse, Fromm) as well as Wilhem Reich attempted to reinterpret Freud's concepts in order to develop a new mode of thought for understanding topics such as authoritarian personality, alienation, false consciousness, unconsciousness, prejudice, ideology, communication, sexual repression, sexual alienation, dialectic of civilization, and antagonism. The use of psychoanalytically based concepts has not led to the development of a genuine Marxist psychology (Reich, 1929, 1934). In this battlefield, a Marxist approach to psychology was suppressed. Marxist psychologists (Leontiev, Luria, Holzkamp, Zazzo, and others) did some very important work and have made some real contributions, particularly in the field of human mental development, but in general I think they tried to produce a Marxist version of psychology that has the same form as pre-Marxist psychology, fitting neatly into the same academic categories: cognition, motivation, perception, intelligence, attention, development, etc. This is understandable in the context of the academic politics at that time, but in the long run, I think Marxist psychology will look very different. As you can see, Marxist psychologists (this is now past tense) have stayed within a too narrow set of ideas – and here I would include Leontiev, Holzkamp, and, in fact, just about everyone. In the next section, human activity, both abstract and concrete, will be examined as the fabric and the basis of human life.

### ABSTRACT AND CONCRETE ACTIVITY

Marxist psychologists tended to understand "abstract and concrete activity" in a positivist sort of way, as though we can take the individual and draw a chart of when he is engaging in abstract activity and when he is engaging in concrete activity. I think this contradiction is at the core of all ontology and the elements can't be separated, and the resolution of the contradiction will result in an entirely new individuality. Western Marxist psychologists (Sève, Holzkamp, and others) had also come under great pressure from the "psychoanalysts" who claimed they didn't have enough understanding of the field of psychology and from others who claimed they didn't have enough understanding of biology – this resulted in a debate that consumed their energies and yielded no concrete advance of Marxist psychology (Sève, 1966, 1977, 1984). So in general they haven't had any allies for a more radical interpretation. As a result, they have been hesitant to re-enter a field where they were easily accused of being non-professional – in psychology on one hand and in Marxism on the other hand.

What I said about a more radical starting point for Marxist psychology is vital. I do believe that Vygotsky, Leontiev, and Sève were genuinely attempting to produce a Marxist psychology, and they made some important contributions, but this is just a beginning – still at the level of Feuerbach, not yet Marx. The question then is, what now? I have several preliminary concerns rooted in a fundamental question: How will a Marxist psychology develop?

1 – Will Marxist psychology spring from itself, or through some transformation of existing psychological content? This raises the general question

of the development of Marxist science. Does it develop as an elaboration of its own categories, or through some kind of assimilation and transformation (Lucien Sève speaks of "critical assimilation") of existing science (Sève, 1978)? Here, I think Marxism needs a Marxist theory of the development of Marxist theory.

2 – One way or another, I think it is important to study the evolution of bourgeois psychology as it confronts and tries to resolve its own contradictions and limitations. Here, as in other sciences, as in society itself, there are internal dynamics in which insoluble contradictions are created and the need for revolutionary transformation comes from within, as well as seemingly from the outside. In other words, Marxism doesn't come to psychology only as an "outside agitator" but from its own internal needs as well.

An important factor I think is the very gradual emergence of temporality as a theoretical dimension. I have very little evidence of this, but I know it has to happen. I think it is important to trace the development from the original mechanical, naturalistic conceptions, to the spatial-based systemic and interpersonal conceptions – systems theory, field theory, and various interpersonal theories – to the emergence of temporality as a dimension. I think it is ultimately here that Marxism can find its link at the most fundamental level, and this is Vygotsky's and Sève's deepest contributions – seeing that Marxism is ultimately about temporal logic, or the temporal relations of life (Shames, 1987; Elhammoumi, 2002, 2004).

3 – Finally with regard to academic psychology – whereas it is true that psychology, as with the other sciences, will sooner or later have a need for Marxism, this will be resisted for a very long time. In other words, Marxism is "the humus of every particular thought and the horizon of all culture" (Sartre, 1960: 17). Mainstream psychology will prefer fragmentation, dualisms, reductionism, and meaninglessness to a full confrontation with Marxism. Why? There are no "neutral" moments in Marxism, no neutral terrain. The attempts to create such a neutral terrain have done so by denaturing and altering Marxism. Every moment, every category, every aspect is revolutionary, pointing to the need for social transformation. So, frankly, I think the call for academic psychology to recognize the contribution of Marxism will not be heeded.

My effort was an attempt to apply Marx's concept of value-form, abstract and concrete labor, alienation, etc. I believed, and still believe that this is the core of Marxist psychology: alienation and the dialectic of abstract and concrete, individuality as a form. It is from these attempts that I have concluded that Marxist psychologists never transcended the positivist position of Leontiev.

The contradiction between abstract and concrete is an ontological fact that pervades and in a sense forms our existence itself. So "the individual" doesn't engage in these activities, but, as a form, is created by the contradiction at the core of all activities. Vygotsky's and Sève's concept of "individuality-forms" is unclear on this. What is the form of forms? How can we avoid positivist interpretations here? The form of all forms is alienation, or this contradiction itself. I have discussed this with colleagues many times, but I am still not clear as to their final thinking on it. I do not hesitate to push such a radical assertion (the individual-form). Today, I have tried to go beyond this, in a sense – in that I am trying to understand everything in terms of temporal relations. I think we need a specifically Marxist theory of time, and the difference between abstract and concrete will ultimately be expressed in terms of relation-to-time (Shames & Elhammoumi, personal correspondences). Here, I think Vygotsky, Leontiev, and Sève have laid the groundwork – seeing Marxism as ultimately a theory of temporal relations – that is, all the relations can ultimately be expressed temporally, but I don't think these authors have developed this sufficiently. In the next section, I will discuss the challenge of Marxist activity theory.

### ACTIVITY THEORY

Activity theory actually could and should be based on a Marxist concept of spatio-temporality. In this sense, it really would and should be a formative concept. But, firstly, as I said, we don't really have a Marxist concept of time, and activity has been reduced to a positivist concept. It seems to me that time, with regard to human affairs, has either remained external, as in positivist thought, or internal, as in hermeneutics, Heidegger, etc. For Marx, it must combine the two – and this is the meaning of Marx combining social and natural history, and in fact the basis of his overcoming all duality of classical thought. This is what I'm trying to think about – and this is where I think a truly Marxist psychology must originate – but I'm afraid my life has not allowed much time for theoretical pursuits in recent years. I want to say a few more things about abstract activity. When I wrote this chapter, I looked up as much as I could find on Marx's concept of abstract labor and, amazingly, despite the centrality of this concept, there was very little deep research on this question. Everyone simply takes it for granted, and there have been few attempts to look at it more directly and really examine this concept. The concept raises profound logical and philosophical questions. What is it; whose labor is it? I tried to think this through more than had been done. When you look at it, you can see the time dimension as fundamental. For Marx, *abstract labor* is defined as the *time creating value*, whereas *concrete labor* is the *time creating use-value*. But are these different periods of time performed by the same person? Or is it an ontological relation that is more fundamental than the individual, a relation of the "essence" to temporality, within which individuality is formed? How to conceptualize this? Labor as such is an abstraction conception, concretely; it comes into real being only in divided form. This divided form gives birth and produces social relations and antagonisms. In my opinion, the more we look at it, the more we find this concept to be incomprehensible using ordinary concepts of *time and individuality.* Here I think we are up against the *conceptual limits of Marx's work itself,* where we truly have to go beyond the pre-Marxist concept of *time* and the *individual* as a pre-existing individual, functioning in external, "natural" time. Of course, we now know that this conception is a product of the modern era. We then added internal, hermeneutic time, brought to its height in Heidegger. So the Kantian duality between the natural and the social is expressed in the duality between time as inner human experience and as purely outer reality. With the mechanistic separation of base and superstructure, and the Feuerbachian individual, Marxists have never challenged this. We need an *Aufhebung,* in which time is both natural and social, just as the "subject" of human activity must become the essence – that is, as Vygotsky and Sève said, the subject does not have a human form. This essence is both social and natural. Hegel, toward the end of the Logic, said that forms of alienated being could be expressed in terms of temporal shapes. In this sense, *property relations are ultimately temporal relations* – ownership over someone else's labor and its products is ownership of that time. Unfortunately none of this was developed, and the whole human core of Marxist thought remained in a Hegelian stage. Another example is the way Marxists have thought about "free time." Traditionally, we have thought that Marxism tells us that the individual needs more "free time" in order to develop as an all-around personality and this is given as the goal of socialism. The *Grundrisse* certainly seems to be telling us this. In my opinion, this is a very linear simplistic way of thinking that doesn't get at the fundamental point of Marxism: ontological transformation – the transformation to a new type of being. Interestingly, when you look at the *German Ideology,* in many places, Marx is not saying "free time," as in the simplistic usage of time after work for pursuit of leisure, etc., but "freed time." Maybe I am making too much of the difference, but the second seems to imply a qualitative change in relation to time, not a simple quantitative addition of more leisure time. It seems to me to imply a liberated relation to time. In any case, I think we have to respectfully recognize that *Marx was here at his conceptual limit.* It simply wasn't possible for him to theorize or even imagine the ontological transformation that his theory calls for at the individual level, and his own language reflects a certain ambiguity on this. He speaks of "the individual," even though the whole point of the Grundrisse is the "*social production of the individual*" (unfortunately this is incorrectly translated in most English versions, into "*social production by the individual*"). When we recognize the individual as a *produced form,* then we have to find the way to theorize the transformation to the *next form* – which of course is not just another form, because it is the *negation* of the type of *form* that *has characterized all history in class society.* The abolition of class, property, and money is also the abolition of individuality, as we have known it, toward a more *fluid individuality.* This change is already happening in many ways. So these are the things I'm thinking about these days.

For me, the idea of Marxist psychology is inseparable from the idea of bringing to life and literally to earth a Marxist vision of human nature as well as human future and the scientific understanding of how we might get from here to there. I literally believe this can't be done without a great elaboration and development of Marxist human scientific visionary thought.

Although it is true that the Soviet psychologists derived most of their influence from Western psychologists, isn't it true that there was influence in both directions? Berlin in the twenties and early thirties was alive with new thinking – systems approach, ecological approach, Marxist psychoanalysis, field theory, etc, all of it influenced in some way by Marxism and much of it making its way to the Soviet Union. This relation was cut off under Stalin, when Pavlovism became the official psychology.

I believe anyone who takes *the individual* as a starting point is guilty of Feuerbachianism, and this includes every Marxist psychologist, despite all their efforts to base their theories on social historical dynamics. The key, I think, is to discard "the individual" for the *individual-form*. The barrier between individual and social determinations is thus overcome. Even Holzkamp, despite all his efforts, seems to have failed to truly overcome the barrier between relations and individual. This is true of Wallon, Politzer, Leontiev, Zazzo, and others.

I think Marxism is a developmental, transformative process and that the form of Marxist knowledge is different from its pre-Marxist form. In other words, Marxism at this time of its history is not a completed body of knowledge but a transformative process in relation to bourgeois thought in which new forms and transforming content are in a dialectical relation. I think that Marxists in all areas of science have suffered losses due to this expectation that there would be a Marxist physics, Marxist biology, Marxist psychology, Marxist sociology, Marxist anthropology, and so on, that somehow corresponded to its equivalent positivist version. But whatever all this means, I think a fundamental fact is that Marxism is a study of the *historical movement of forms* – and particularly the historical origin of the commodity-form and the individual-form. All of psychology must be subsumed under the understanding of this motion. Put another way: alienation and de-alienation. This is what I am trying to get at in the idea of the contradiction between abstract and concrete activity as the fundamental ontological issue and its negation as the basic fact in a new ontology. Unfortunately, this is a grand conception, and I haven't made much progress myself in elaborating it.

## CONCLUSION

As I said, I am particularly interested in the possible emergence of *temporal conceptions to replace spatial ones*. I really believe Vygotsky, Leontiev, Sève, and others have opened doors to a true advancement and development of Marxist psychological thought. They have shown how Marxism can "return to itself" after a self-alienation in humanism and anti-humanist conceptions. After reading Heidegger, particularly *Being and Time*, and understanding his vast influence on twentieth-century thought – both existentialist and anti-humanist – I have a deeper appreciation for Vygotsky, Leontiev, Sève, and others. I truly believe they are the first to find the key to breaking the grip of Heideggerianism and allowing Marxism to fill the spaces that Heidegger occupied for much of the twentieth century. However, when you see Heidegger's formulation on the human essence and how this was absorbed into both existentialism and anti-humanism, you can see in what way these authors moved this forward. Interestingly, I haven't seen anything from the Vygotskians putting this all together. I suppose it is more important to support the myth that anti-humanism, "post-structuralism," and "post-modernism" are Western Marxist creations. Here, of course, is an example of people running in horror from Stalinism and embracing Heidegger instead. But this is just one example of the embrace of bourgeois thought.

In conclusion, psychology is in need of Marxism because Marxism is a brilliant tool for *interpreting* human higher mental functions and *changing* ruled-governed behavior and consciousness. Marxist psychology of the last century was predominantly Feuerbachian, which led to a definite close elaboration of a unified and integrative theoretical framework of human higher mental functions.

Is there a Marxist psychology? Marxist psychology, as I said, existed only in its infantile Feuerbachian form. In this chapter, we viewed Vygotsky as the only one who had serious, critical insight into the competing schools within Soviet psychology and credited him for having laid the foundation for genuine Marxist psychology.

# 3

# The Cultural–Historical Activity Theory

*Some Aspects of Development*

## Joachim Lompscher

The cultural–historical activity theory (CHAT) is a relatively young theory, but nevertheless it has its history already. Created in the twenties and thirties of the last century in Russia by some psychologists and further developed by their numerous collaborators and students, it became internationally known over several decades – a process that is still going on today. Especially, beginning in the eighties, more and more philosophers, sociologists, psychologists, pedagogues, and others in a growing number of countries became interested in this theory and began to study, to use, and to develop it even further. So, today, we may speak of an inter-disciplinary and international activity-theoretical movement as it presents itself in publications, congresses and conferences, workshops, and unpublished discussions, etc. A look at the development of this theory may serve for a deeper understanding of its fundamentals and potentials. It is the aim of this chapter to make a contribution to the theory by studying its historical development. Of course, in one chapter, it is impossible to show this history in detail. Perhaps, the chapter may stimulate colleagues to describe other aspects of this development and thus promote the theoretical discussion.

First, I give a short description of what is meant by CHAT today. After that, I look back to the beginnings and to the process initiated by the founders of CHAT. Finally, I try to discriminate three stages of this development and argue for the necessity of further development as its fourth stage.

### CONTENT AND POSITION OF ACTIVITY THEORY

Activity theory was developed within cultural–historical theory and became its constituent as its methodological basis having principal significance for all human sciences, not only for psychology, in the framework of which it was elaborated based on philosophical positions of classical German idealism further developed by Marx in a materialist sense.

To understand human life and development and to create conditions for their improvement, it is necessary to understand them as activity interpreted as the basic form of human existence, as human-world-interaction. Elsewhere, I wrote:

People as societal beings exist as they themselves create and re-create the conditions of their own life. They do not only accomodate themselves to the surrounding world, but they also actively change it to a certain degree (and an ever-growing one in the course of history). Activity is the fundamental, specifically human form of relationships between human beings and the world, the content of which is *the goal-oriented modification and transformation of the world on the basis of culture as it is appropriated and further developed by people* (Yudin, 1978: 268). Human interaction with the world is necessarily mediated by objects, methods, norms, values, and other aspects of culture that are produced by human beings. Thus, this interaction is mediated by the historically developing culture, by the experience and knowledge of previous generations, by the manifold relationships between people. It is through these active transformations that people come to reveal and reflect on the conditions and regularities in nature and social life. The knowledge gained in the process of these transformations is the critical precondition for human beings to be able to continously form new goals of activity and put them into practice. In this historical process, humans gradually become aware and conscious of themselves, of their position in the world, of their potentialities and conditions as subjects of activity. (Lompscher, 2002: 80)

This interpretation concerns both the human society as a whole, individuals, and their groups. Of course, as a starting point for analyses, it is, as yet, still very abstract. The following seven aspects may serve as a first step of concretisation. First, activity is a unity of subject–object (person–world) and subject–subject (person–person) relations. There is no activity without an object that serves as the main source of motives and goals and no activity without a subject interacting with other subjects. As a rule, activity is joint activity transforming its object in this or that respect. Second, activity exists in two basic forms mutually conditioning and penetrating each other: material and mental activity. Third, activity is characterized by fundamental features, such as transformation, cognition, communication, value orientation, and development. Fourth, activity has a macrostructure consisting of subjects interacting with objects (and each other), executing certain actions and operations under concrete conditions, using certain means in order to put into practice their goals and satisfy their needs and motives, resulting in objective and subjective changes (transformations). Fifth, activity may be subdivided into several general activity classes based on the diversity of objects, means, conditions, etc. Sixth, activity exists in the form of several kinds of activity, the most important ones being physical reproduction, play, learning, communication, political activity, and work. And finally, seven, these aspects name directions of further analysis (see Lompscher, 2002).

Affirming activity theory and trying to apply it in this or that field today means, first of all,

- to understand and approach a human situation as activity, that is, as process and system: to analyze, model, and change its components (at first, may be, as an attempt) under the aspects of a theoretical or practical goal – the (mostly collective) subject, the object, and its transformation (being at the beginning, may be, not very clear) into a new result or product, the potential means and rules, the division of labor or functions, and the community in the frame of which all this is going on, aiming at finding out the interrelations between these components and opportunities for a solution;
- to analyze the activity under study and transformation in its dependencies and interrelations with other activities or activity systems and to be aware of its socio-cultural and historical embeddedness;
- to look at activity systems under study and transformation as development, that means to include their history into the study and determine their zones of proximal development;
- to reveal the basic contradictions and seek ways for overcoming and solving them (and thus producing new ones); and
- to look at transformation both as a method of analysis and as a value in its own right and act correspondingly, that means not to restrict ourselves to description and interpretation (which is necessary as well), but to stimulate and advance transformations permitting the revelation of inner connections within the corresponding activity systems and their potentials for development and to put them into practice serving the interests of people.

Activity theory has developed from the first ideas and statements to a – more or less – elaborated real theory. From the very beginning, central problems of psychology (and much beyond its boundaries) – such as essence and structure of human consciousness, polyfunctionality and systemic character of psyche, unity and interrelation of individual and social, of thinking and speech, development and education, scientific and everyday concepts – were raised and ways for their solution were shown, problems that for the "ordinary" science became essential (partially) only decades later.

In the next section, I try to describe the beginnings of this development in a brief overview.

## VYGOTSKY, LEONTYEV, AND LURIA: THE FOUNDERS

When Vygotsky sought a way out of the crisis of psychology in the middle and second half of the twenties, one of the cornerstones in his theoretical and practical work was the orientation toward activity. As Davydov (1996: 497) indicated, at that time, Vygotsky could not have an elaborated theory of activity, but he had a historico-sociological concept of activity as it was elaborated by Hegel, Marx, and others. For example, Vygotsky's view on psychic development as going on in interaction and cooperation with others, in social situations of development, as transition from inter-psychic to intra-psychic processes, and his idea about zones of proximal development and their transition into zones of actual performance by cooperation, support, help, and/or modeling would be impossible without this type of historico-sociological concept of human activity. It became the starting point of the elaboration of activity theory by Leontyev and others for which Vygotsky created important theoretical prerequisites. As seen by Davydov (1996: 500–501), Vygotsky's contributions consisted in the orientation toward the joint work mediated by means as the key for the analysis of psyche (mediation of psychic processes by signs and meanings instead of an immediate connection between stimulus and reaction). It also consisted of the discovery of different genetic roots of action and speech and their uniting as the basic prerequisite for human consciousness. Furthermore, it involved the discovery of word meaning as unit of analysis, which made the relation of consciousness and activity accessible. And finally, it stressed the fact that behind the psyche is the human life, which meant the real human activity (for which the correct name was at that time still absent).

These theoretical ideas became the foundation of Vygotsky's practical work with handicapped children, of his engagement in socio-political activity and, especially, of his empirical research, where he concentrated on the problem of consciousness, and its substance, structure, and development as published posthumously in 1934 in his famous book *Thinking and Speech* (translated into English in several versions, the first one in 1962 in a very abbreviated form). In this process of scientific research and work he, so to say, forgot or neglected his theoretical starting point: human activity. He tried to find access to consciousness via speech, word meaning, its generalization, and so on. But in the same period (the early thirties) he began to study the problem of human emotionality (his unfinished book of 1933 was first completely published in 1984), which could bring him again to activity "from another side" via motivation. But early death from tuberculosis (in the thirty-eighth year of life), which had for many years forced him to hurry his work, finally stopped its movement.

Without any doubt, Vygotsky was an outstanding thinker (often named a genius), but he was not alone. Leontyev and Luria joined him very soon after he began to work in Moscow, and they formed together the famous *troika*, which then became a *vosmyorka*: five young people (Zaporozhets, Bozhovich, Slavina, Morozova, and Levina) became their collaborators and, with time, well-known scientists in their own right, making substantial contributions to the elaboration of CHAT. The troika and then the vosmyorka worked very closely: Everyone participated in the elaboration of new ideas. So, for example, in the late twenties, Luria made important empirical and theoretical contributions to the new cultural–historical developmental theory (see Lompscher, 1994). It is well known that he became one of the founders of neuropsychology and that his research had important significance for the further cultural–historical analysis of such problems as memory, speech, and consciousness, and the psychological functioning of normal and handicapped children, etc.

Further important contributions to cultural–historical theory were made by Leontyev, especially with his investigation of the development of memory published in 1931. When he had the impression that Vygotsky left their joint materialist position that the human psyche can be revealed only through the analysis of activity, he placed it at the center of his own scientific work. He formed a new research group in Kharkov and began to elaborate the problem of activity systematically – a work he continued over decades, the main result of which was his famous book *Activity, Consciousness and Personality* (1978).

In 1932, on the eve of his departure for Kharkov he wrote a dramatic letter to Vygotsky (which was found only recently; see Leontyev and Leontyev, 2003) in which he described the critical situation of the troika caused by a massive unqualified "critique" of so-called (undialectic, mechanistic) "Marxists" (Vygodskaja and Lifanova, 1996, showed some examples) and its own theoretical difficulties. Leontyev requested that Vygotsky return to joint work and struggle based on the positions elaborated together to that point. Leontyev began new cycles of investigations aimed at the analysis of human activity and its role for psychic development and functioning. Vygotsky continued his work (see previous discussion). No response to Leontyev's letter was ever found. But in the spring of 1934, some months before his death, Vygotsky included Leontyev together with other colleagues in his proposals for a new research institution. Leontyev returned to Moscow and began the work Vygotsky had planned.

## THE ACTIVITY THEORY: THREE STAGES OF DEVELOPMENT

It may seem (and several authors see it this way) that Vygotsky and Leontyev mean two different stages in CHAT's development. However, I don't think so. Leontyev and his disciples very soon understood that they elaborated the fundamental theoretical principles laid out by Vygotsky. They continued the work that they understood as continuing in the Vygotskian tradition. Leontyev himself stressed this several times (e.g., Leontyev, 1994; see also A. A. Leontyev, 2001a: 134–138). The speculation about a "breakage" between Vygotsky and Leontyev (upon the discovery of the letter), about Leontyev's "betrayal" of Vygotsky, and the like appear to be without foundation. Moreover, a postcard written by Vygotsky in 1933 or so with greetings to Leontyev (found in the archive) disproved such speculations as well. Vygotsky stayed in Kharkov several times in this period and observed the work of Leontyev and his colleagues. Obviously, the communication between the two scientists and their groups was never interrupted, despite disagreements concerning the principal way to continue their work.

Leontyev, of course, went his way for several decades together with Vygotsky's and his own collaborators and students before passing away in 1979. CHAT unfolded and was concretized and applied to different problems and domains (from developmental and educational psychology to engineering psychology, ergonomics, psychophysiology, and other branches). The period of Stalinism brought difficulties and limitations for this work (Vygotsky's name disappeared for twenty years, Leontyev lost his job for some time, publications were forbidden, etc.), but nevertheless the work went on.

During World War II, Leontyev and several of his colleagues worked in military hospitals (Leontyev and Zaporozhets, 1946). After the war, especially in the fifties, a new generation came into science. Young people appropriated the cultural–historical theory and began to work in this framework under the guidance of those who immediately worked together with Vygotsky (Leontyev, Luria, Zaporozhets, Bozhovich, Morozova, and others), with Leontyev (Galperin, P. I. Zinchenko, and others), or with Luria (Cvetkova, Khomskaya, Akhutina, and others). Here, a new stage of development began. Concerning Leontyev and the other scientists of his generation, we may say that they made substantial contributions to the first and to the second stage of development (see, e.g., Voyskunsky, Zhdan, and Tichomirov, 1999; A. A. Leontyev, 2001a).

The second stage of development is characterized by a broad application and further development of the cultural–historical theory in different directions, by the formation of different "schools" within the general "school" (having a general theoretical basis, but several differences in opinions and approaches as well), by expanding toward different domains (beyond psychology), and by a growing interest in this theory abroad, leading to translations of Vygotsky's, Luria's, Leontyev's, and others' works, and also to the development of cultural–historical research in other countries, international conferences, journals, and organisations. In one chapter, it is impossible to trace the features of this development fully, so I focus on what was done in this respect by several "second-generation" Russian representatives of CHAT whose work is less well known in the West.

One aspect of further development consists of elaboration of theories concerning different kinds of activity: play (Elkonin, Zaporozhets, Kravcova), learning (Galperin, Talyzina, Davydov, Repkin, Lazarev, Gromyko), work (Munipov, V. I. Zinchenko), socio-political activity (Feldshtejn), and communication (Andreeva, Lisina, Lomov, A. A. Leontyev). Much was done concerning the analysis of actions (their development and formation) as main components of activity in their relation with motives, goals, etc., for example, motor actions (Zaporozhets), perceptive actions (Gordeeva,

V. I. Zinchenko, S. A. Smirnov), memory actions (I. P. Zinchenko, A. A. Smirnov), thinking actions (Rubinshtejn, Tikhomirov), and learning actions (Davydov, Rubcov, Zuckerman).

As an example, I give a brief overview of the work of Aleksey A. Leontyev (the "second-generation Leontyev," that is, the son of A. N. Leontyev). I begin with his book *The Active Mind* [Deyatelnyj um] (2001a), which is a serious contribution to the analysis of the substance and history of CHAT. It presents material concerning the reconstruction of the development of the activity theory from the beginnings in Blonsky's, Bassov's, Uznadze's, Rubinshtejn's, and others' work as well as the psychophysiological prerequisites (Sechenov, Ukhtomsky, Pavlov, Anokhin, Bernshtejn) via the connections between the work of Vygotsky, A. N. Leontyev, and the Kharkov group. In a certain sense, this book gives a broad picture of the cultural–historical activity theory as it developed in the USSR/Russia to the current period. This is true not only for the concept of activity, but also for such central problems as reflection and image, the relation between sign and meaning, and between sign, activity, and personality.

One of the main topics in A. A. Leontyev's research work is the analysis of communication. His starting point is the principally societal character of human communication. This topic is about more than mere exchange of information, as is often interpreted. Following Marx (who used the concept *Verkehr*), communication is understood as social exchange of experiences, ideas, interrelations, activities, and their results – not only, but mostly based on the means of language. This exchange goes on, not among isolated individuals, but among members of society who are born into and shape different societal relations. Social exchange is determined by activity and may stand in different positions in the structure of activity – as a necessary component of every activity, as communicative action within a non-communicative activity (play, work, etc.), or as a special activity. The genetically initial form of communication is the exchange as a necessary component of object-related, motivated, goal-established joint activity, the subject of which is an active community. Socially oriented forms of communication in the sense of specific influences on smaller or larger parts of society are directed toward a certain kind of transformation of social relations within the society, of its social or social–psychological structure, and of the societal consciousness or social activity of its members. This is a process of inner organisation or self-regulation of society – one part acts on another part aiming at optimization of the whole society or individual sectors. Differentiated analyses are given for language in general as well as for specific forms, for example, a university lecture, radio, TV, art, and foreign language acquisition (Leontyev, 1999: 2001b). A. A. Leontyev worked on different educational problems as well and was one of the initiators of a large school reform program titled *School 2100* with detailed materials for teachers and school managers (Leontyev, 2003).

As a psycholinguist, A. A. Leontyev worked much on the problems of sign and meaning in the history of general theory, linguistics, semiotics, and activity theory. In this connection, he differentiated, for example, four forms of meaning:

1. Linguistic meanings based on a system of specific *quasi-objects* (signs). Thus, the significance is discriminated from the concrete situation and may be stored, on the one hand, and make it the object of actions, on the other.
2. Object meanings based on the sensoric (direct or indirect) image. They have an immediate relationship with the object and the situation.
3. Role meanings based on the sensoric image of dynamic components of the activity itself, such as social norms and roles.
4. Operational meanings also based on the sensoric image of dynamic components of the activity, but related to normative schemata of action procedures.

Meanings are the ideal existence of the reality becoming individualized and subjectivized in individual consciousness, which, at the same time, maintains a historical–societal character and thus objectivity. Individual meanings contain a cognitive invariant in the sense of their relation to the societal activity and its projection in signs, on the one hand, and a communicative invariant in the sense of operations with signs and rules of their use in more complex communication structures on the other. Individual meanings differ from amodal societal meanings in that they have sensoric and emotional components and vary concerning their potential explicativity. In relation to the activity process, four functions of meaning are discriminated: motivational, goal-setting, formation of a comparative standard, and operational function (Leontyev, 1997, 2001a, 2001b).

Beginning with Vygotsky and Leontyev, in the framework of CHAT, a difference is established between meaning and sense: a differentiation closely connected with the interrelations between activity, consciousness, and personality. Usually, individuals perceive objects and words in their objective (societal) meaning, but at the same time, via the *glasses* of their individual experiences, interests, and motives, the meaning "for me" as an individual personality. Several authors have dealt with this topic. A differentiated theoretical analysis of the history and substance of the sense problem was presented by Dmitrij A. Leontyev (that is, the "third-generation" Leontyev). He discriminates three facets of sense:

1. The ontological level (relation between subject and world): The *life sense* objectively characterizes the position and role of objects, phenomena, and events of the reality, as well as the actions of the subject himself in his life.

2. The phenomenological level (image of the world in the subject's consciousness): The *personality sense* is the form of the subject's knowledge concerning his life senses.
3. The regulational level (unconscious inner regulation mechanisms of the life activity): The *sense structures of the personality* form a whole system and guarantee the activity regulation with correspondence to the logic of life necessity.

Sense is, in his interpretation, the relation between subject and object, which is determined by the objective position of the object in the subject's life, emphasizes this object in the subjective image of the world, and embodies itself in the personality structures that regulate the subject's behavior in concern of the corresponding object (Leontyev, 1999: 305). Six different sense structures of personality are characterized: personality sense and sense sets as the lowest level; motives, sense constructs, and sense dispositions as the second level; and personality values as the highest level, which influences the sense formations that follow. All these phenomena are analyzed in detail that can not be reproduced here. D. A. Leontyev asks the question: Why do people do what they do? And the answers are based on different logics, which don't deny, but rather inter-penetrate one another:

... because I will ← logic of satisfying needs
... because he began ← logic of reacting on a stimulus
... because all the time I do it this way ← logic of stereotype or disposition
... because all the people do it this way ← logic of social normativity
... because it's important for me ← logic of sense or life necessity
... and why not? ← logic of free choice

The sense problem is not the only aspect of the personality under study in the context of CHAT. Personality and its development can be understood only in the context of culture. This was one of the principal starting points of the cultural–historical theorizing. But for a long time, this was a relatively abstract statement. Luria's comparative investigations in Middle Asia in the early thirties were to be published (though not very widely) in 1974; whereas his investigations concerning psychic development in different milieus of the Soviet society at the end of the twenties were mostly unknown. As Tulviste (1999) indicated, the founders of the cultural–historical theory at first wanted to find evidence *that* higher psychic functions grow up by appropriation of human culture and change together with the changes of culture, whereas the question concerning *how* this is going on, *which* aspects or components of culture participate in that process, could not yet be answered. Activity theory made the explication of these processes possible: In a culture, different kinds of activity are carried out and different tasks given. This made the use of semiotic and other means necessary. Activities call for and make possible the acquisition of culture (selective parts of it) and thus lead to the formation and development of corresponding psychic functions and features. Cultures differ in the kind and multitude of activities and means of exchange and therefore also in the development of concrete thinking styles, social forms of behavior, etc. Leontyev's theory shows the principal connection between culture, on the one hand, and activity and personality, on the other, but was not yet concretised in terms of different cultures. In this respect, though the discussion is beyond the scope of this chapter, substantial contributions were made in the West (Cole, Scribner, and others).

Speaking about contributions of second-stage activity-theorists, it is necessary to mention Aleksandr Asmolov (2001, 2002). He is especially engaged in methodological aspects of cultural–historical theory and problems of personality. In 1979, he published a study about the relation between activity and set (ustanovka), a topic that was heavily discussed as an absolute contradiction between representatives of activity theory and Uznadze's theory of set. Asmolov showed that sets are a necessary component of every goal-oriented activity as its stabilizer and at the same time being a conservative moment in the process of adaptation to new conditions and situations. He discriminated amongst different kinds of sets and described their function in the process of activity. They interact with *hypersituative activity* overcoming situative necessity and adaptive tendencies, as well as sets established in the activity previously. In this process, activity qualitatively changes, the potentials grow, expanding over the conditions at hand and stimulating the subject to take a risk, maybe even against his or her own interests.

In connection with this problem, he analyzed the relation between conscious and unconscious components in the psychic regulation of activity using the results obtained in different domains of science. He discriminated four classes of unconscious phenomena. First, hyperindividual, hyperconscious phenomena – the field of societal meanings, such as concepts, symbols, roles, rituals, and social patterns of behavior, that is, the manner of behaving, knowing, and action schemata typical for a cultural community appropriated by its members in joined activity and not necessarily conscious for a subject. Individual and group represent here an unsolvable unity, for example, in the form of mainstream, Zeitgeist, and the like. The second class of phenomena involved unconscious motives and attitudes of personality – stimuli and not realized action dispositions emerging in the process of activity and directed toward their object. They cannot be reproduced as clear meanings or formalized, and express themselves in the form of seemingly incidental and unmotivated deviations from "normal" behavior in a situation. To change such unconscious motives and attitudes, mere verbal influence is not enough – a change of the activity itself, including social relations and emotions, is necessary. Third, he identified operational sets and stereotypes – unconscious regulators of action execution coming from experiences in analogous situations and anticipating corresponding events and procedures. They release the consciousness by making possible that information can be processed at different levels at the same time. Such unconscious components may become conscious, if their position in the activity structure changes, for example, if the process of activity or particular aspects or phases of it are made the object of control by the subject. Voluntariness and consciousness of psychic processes and states presuppose each other. And fourth, he identified unconscious reserves of sense organs – information processing below the threshold of consciousness leading to objectively measured reactions and adaptation to conditions and their changes not consciously noticed, but reaching the aim of an activity. If such processes or their stimuli are made the object and goal of activity, they may become conscious and be used as additional potentials for the activity regulation. Recently, for instance, it could be shown that acoustic and optic stimuli below or at the threshold – a principally important problem of control and regulation in many modern technological systems – could be noticed and differentiated when organized as solving sensoric tasks, as goal-oriented activity of a subject. The operational structure of that activity and the use of cultural means for its execution was formed in special experiments.

It is impossible here to interpret the whole oeuvre of Asmolov. Nevertheless, a certain impression may be given by his own characterization of his approach to the problems of personality:

1. The human being is an *element* of different systems in which he or she appropriates and expresses different features characteristic for the corresponding systems.
2. A human can be studied and understood only by analyzing the history and evolution of the different physical, biological, and social systems bringing him about.
3. A necessary moment for understanding humans is the analysis of goal determination of different systems, including the investigation into the emergence, development, and functioning of goal-oriented systems (the so-called objective-teleological approach).
4. System approach calls for the necessity of the emergence of the personality phenomenon, that is, why personality becomes necessary within the process of development of nature and society.
5. System approach necessarily is seeking those "fundamentals" of systems, by means of which the interaction between humans and nature, society, and themselves is going on.

Joint goal-oriented activity is interpreted as the foundation for human participation in the world of culture and for self-development of personality. It isn't the hierarchy of activities as such that is the personality's "center." Rather, as wrote Leontyev, it is *what* is brought about by different activities, *for what*, and *how* a human being uses social norms, values, and ideals that gives a sense of the personality in one's life. In the process of development, the relation between personality and activity is the basis of change:

The joint activity in a concrete social system also further determines personality development, but personality individualizes in a growing extent and selects those activities or forms of life by him-/herself which determine his/her development. A transition is going on from a regime of using and appropriating culture toward a regime of constructing different social worlds. (Asmolov, 2001: 188)

In this connection, he discriminates three aspects of interiorization (internalization):

• individualization, that is, the transition from inter-psychic to intra-psychic processes (sensu Vygotsky);
• intimization, that is, the transition from "we" toward "me" – the development of self-consciousness;
• construction of the inner level of consciousness, that is, the transition from external to internal ideal actions (sensu Galperin).

The personality problem is treated by many representatives of activity theory (I speak here only about Russian authors). Vasily Davydov is one of them. He is, first of all, well-known as a researcher in the field of learning activity (see Davydov, 1988, 1996; Hedegaard & Lompscher, 1999). But he had much to say in several fields of theory and practice, including the field of personality theory. For him, personality is connected with creativity (Davydov, 1996). Personality is characterized by such features as capability to comprehend new societal needs; to act – even in complicated situations – in a way corresponding with one's own convictions, independence, and responsibility. Therefore, looking at the development in childhood, the role of fantasy becomes especially important as the basis of creativity. Fantasy is characterized, first of all, by the capability to see a whole earlier than its parts, to establish the connection between abstract knowledge and a concrete fact, between the general and the particular. On this basis and under the conditions of interaction with other people, the child can produce new images and ideas based on abstraction, transfer, symbolization, and modeling and come to new actions and artifacts.

Davydov was intensively engaged in the problems of further development of activity theory. His critique, ideas, and proposals are expressed in several publications, including posthumous ones. In 1991, he formulated eight unsolved problems of activity theory, which remain relevant now (see Davydov, 1991, 1993, 1999). These involve the need to understand transformation, collective and individual activity, structure and components of activity, different kinds of activity, communication, connections to other theories, organizing inter-disciplinarity, and stages in the study of activity. Many researchers have tried and continue to try to solve these problems, Davydov's collaborators among them, and there is clearly much to be done yet in these respects.

My overview is very incomplete. Many researchers had to be named. Space does not allow this. As Davydov said in one of his last lectures, Vygotsky's approach in Russia today is represented by different "schools" with different objects, but the same theoretical basis. These are Luria's, Leontyev's, Zaporozhets's, Galperin's, Bozhovich's, and Lisina's schools, (Davydov, 1998) and others could be added yet (especially, Davydov's own school of developmental education). In a summary, we could say that the second developmental stage of CHAT could be characterized by the unfolding, extension, application, and concretization of what was elaborated during the first stage.

During the second half of the twentieth century, especially during its last decades, societal life essentially changed in all respects and spheres – political, economic, technological, cultural, scientific, and social. This was a challenge for CHAT (discussed among Russian colleagues, as well). New problems emerged, new solutions and answers had and have to be found. Though the second stage of CHAT's development, in some ways, hasn't ended, a third stage began. The challenge was taken up, first of all, by Yrjö Engeström, who elaborated a broader concept of activity based on Vygotsky's and Leontyev's views and successfully applied it for analyses of new phenomena. Beginning in the eighties, he published a great many theoretical and empirical investigations, most of them in English (e.g., Engeström, 1987, 1999b, 2001, this volume), so that there is no necessity to describe them in detail here. He founded the Center for Activity Theory and Developmental Work Research in Helsinki, which became not only a place for a range of very fruitful scientific works, but also a place for numerous visitors to learn and discuss activity theory today as well as to collaborate in approaching new theoretical and empirical problems.

Engeström took seriously two fundamental ideas of CHAT's founders: first, the mediated character of human life and activity by material and ideal means, especially signs, as parts of human culture and the artifacts of human activity, and second, the collective character of human activity realized by actions of the participating individuals. During the second stage of development, the collective character of activity gradually moved to the background (though it did not disappear in research and practice completely) and was mostly replaced by individual activity (in the context of analyses of individual psychic processes and features). The unity of activity and culture was lost, and these two aspects were analyzed more or less in isolation from each other – the aspect of activity in the East and the aspect of culture in the West (see Stetsenko & Arievitch, 1996; Stetsenko, 1999; A. A. Leontyev, 2001a). Engeström re-established the unity of these aspects. This brought forth a fresh look at the activity structure with six main interrelated components (his well-known *triangle*) and a new approach to the analysis of collective activity seen as a system and an object of transformation. He placed at the center of his analyses modern work and adult learning. This approach during the last years was applied and elaborated by numerous collaborators and further colleagues in very different branches of societal activity (technology, science, industry, agriculture, health care, and many others).

Engeström (2001) formulated five principles of activity theory at its third stage of development; a key excerpt of his work is worth quoting at length:

The first principle is that a collective, artifact-mediated and object-oriented activity system, seen in its network relations to other activity systems, is taken as the prime unit of analysis. Goal-directed individual and group actions, as well as automatic operations, are relatively independent but subordinate units of analysis, eventually understandable when interpreted against the background of entire activity systems. Activity systems realize and reproduce themselves by generating actions and operations. The second principle is the multi-voicedness of activity systems. An activity system is always a community of multiple points of views, traditions and interests. The division of labor in an activity creates different positions for the participants, the participants carry their own diverse histories, and the activity system itself carries multiple layers and strands of history engraved in its artifacts, rules and conventions. The multi-voicedness is multiplied in networks of interacting activity systems. It is a source of trouble and a source of innovation, demanding actions of translation and negotiation. The third principle is historicity. Activity systems take shape and get transformed over lengthy periods of time. Their problems and potentials can only be understood against their own history. History itself needs to be studied as local history of the activity and its objects, and as history of the theoretical ideas and tools that have shaped the activity. [. . .] The fourth principle is the central role of contradictions as sources of change and development. Contradictions are not the same as problems or conflicts. Contradictions are historically accumulating structural tensions within and between activity systems. The primary contradiction of activities in capitalism is that between the use value and exchange value of commodities. This primary contradiction pervades all elements of our activity systems. Activities are open systems. When an activity system adopts a new element from the outside (for example, a new technology or a new object), it often leads to an aggravated secondary contradiction where some old elements (for example, the rules or the division of labor) collides with the new one. Such contradictions generate disturbances and conflicts, but also innovative attempts to change the activity. The fifth principle proclaims the possibility of expansive transformations in activity systems. Activity systems move through relatively long cycles of qualitative transformations. As the contradictions of an activity system are aggravated, some individual participants begin to question and deviate from its established norms. In some cases, this escalates into collaborative envisioning and a deliberate collective change effort. An expansive transformation is accomplished when the object and motive of the activity are reconceptualized to embrace a radically wider horizon of possibilities than in the previous mode of the activity. (pp. 136–137)

These principles are both theoretical presuppositions of and generalizations from the many empirical analyses and transformations in the societal practice described by Engeström and his collaborators. They proved to be very fruitful for investigations into new phenomena, the problems of societal life, and their active transformations. At the same time, they stimulate the exchange with other theoretical positions concerning central problems and developmental trends of the world today.

## IS THERE A NEED FOR A FOURTH STAGE OF CHAT?

It seems that one aspect of modern society is insufficiently valued by mostly all representatives of both the second and the third developmental stage of activity theory. This is the computer. As a rule, it is seen as a tool and artifact and as others have noted, a very strong one. But is this enough?

Though several investigations concerning computer technology and its use in contexts of work, learning, and so on have been carried out from the point of view of activity theory (Bertelsen and Bödker, 2000; Kaptelinin, 1996, 2003; Sawchuk, 2003; and others), modern activity theory as a whole (as an interdisciplinary theoretical and practical movement with a multitude of actors, goals, and methods) has not yet grasped the principal far-reaching role of the computer and the Internet for society and for all kinds of human activity. Taken in this way, activity theory has not had much to say and, perhaps, has not yet even put forth the necessary questions. In interviews I conducted with several outstanding representatives of activity theory, questions concerning this topic were answered much less concretely than other questions: As a rule, the computer was interpreted only as a new tool making specific kinds of human activity easier and quicker. Likewise, the Internet was seen as a large, useful memory (though with much unnecessary information). Occasionally, warnings were even given not to overestimate computers and the Internet (see Lompscher, 2004).

However, over the last few decades, the computer has become the *new leading productive power* (Haug, 2003: 38), penetrating and transforming all aspects and domains of production, including management, distribution, consumption, scientific research, and so on, and producing a new stage or form of capitalist mode of production – the transnational *high-tech capitalism* (the title of Haug's book) with the Internet as its medium. National and international economic processes have changed and continue to change dramatically with serious and far-reaching political consequences across the globe. As a result, human activity is changing in all spheres, including the borders between men's and women's work, between outside and self-regulation, and between work and learning, as well as between work and leisure time.

Much is written about the role of the computer and the Internet as the third scientific–technological revolution. Here is not the place to go into detail on these processes; however, we can ask some important questions. How does activity theory interpret these and other corresponding processes? What about such labels as information society, knowledge society, and the like; topics inherent across this collection. Which challenges, dangers, and opportunities across the different spheres of societal life are, or should be, examined? Can computer literacy be compared in terms of its cultural–historical significance with reading literacy and the like? There are several voices within activity theory trying to answer such questions (e.g., Fichtner, 1999; Giest, 2001; Rückriem, 2003; Sawchuk, 2003), but it seems to me that CHAT as a whole has to develop further, in both theoretical and method-ological respects, to be able to adequately create concepts and methods for studying and to put to use and transform these processes. Perhaps, in this way, a fourth stage of development will be reached.

From the point of view of Rückriem (2003), computer technology is more than a tool. Principally differing from other new technologies playing the role of tools in human activity, computer technology is in fact without any alternative, unavoidable, irreversible, general, and even universal. It changes not only one specific concrete activity but revolutionizes the societal activity structure as a whole and the complete relations of activity and consciousness (i.e., the economic, social, and psychic status of any tool available). It really integrates every existing communication technology without any exception. And it even seems to mark an already ongoing process of new drafts of our societal existence as a whole emerging. This urges us to reflect on digital information and telecommunication technologies as catalysts of a new social system emerging. At least this is the unanimous appraisal from McLuhan up to modern media theorists.

Activity theory has to overcome the one-sided orientation toward computer technology as a tool instead of a medium, Rückriem argues. Communication by media is the modus operandi of social systems. Media are basic conditions and prerequisites of any communication. And media are both material substratum and meaning, actuality and potentiality at the same time. They store not only specific technologies but the specific form of so-cietal activity. To take media into the concept apparatus of activity theory, it has to be analyzed whether activity theory is compatible with media the-ory and system theory. If we understand activity theory by means of system theory, we will overcome the previously argued bias. And what is more, I am sure, that systemic thinking can be shown to be an inherent quality of Leontyev's theory itself.[1]

From its first steps seeking a fundamentally new approach to problems of human beings and their development up to the state of CHAT today, a long and complicated developmental process has been undertaken. Begin-ning within psychology (but on a deep philosophical basis and with a dif-ferentiated knowledge of the sciences of the time), activity theory has been adopted by scientists of other branches who began to use it for solving their theoretical and practical problems. Through this connection, another new

---

[1] The whole argumentation given by Rückriem may be read at www.ich-sciences.de.

challenge has emerged: to establish new interrelations with other theories. Modern development in sociology, culturology, and sciences of work and organization, of science, of communication, and others led to knowledge and methods having much in common with activity theory (for instance, orientation toward human activity and its components, projection, and transformation). It is a task of today to find out conditions and ways (maybe, limits as well) of synthesis or synergy with other theories or conceptions concerning human existence and development to tackle theoretical and practical problems emerging today and tomorrow.

# 4

## Epistemological Scepticism, Complacent Irony

*Investigations Concerning the Neo-Pragmatism of Richard Rorty*[1]

### Maria Célia Marcondes de Moraes

**INTRODUCTION**

In recent years, researchers (Duarte, 2002a, 2003a; Moraes, 2001, 2003; Evangelista and Shiroma, 2003) have been trying to provide the objective means to understand the political and epistemological agenda that, in its cultural crusade to disqualify the school institution, have been proposing the formation and training of teachers with poor intellectual capacity, detached from the experience of thinking. Such a project is articulated with another, the one that limits the horizon of knowledge to sensitive experience. Research in education and in social sciences is therefore discredited, because it is regarded as a simple collection of empirical data, the development of tools to control those data in order to describe their probable future behaviour, an intervention strategy, or even, in its "post" versions, as a series of fragmented narratives, mere descriptions of the multiple aspects of everyday school life (Moraes and Muller, 2003). As Duarte (2003a: 1) put it, we are facing an agenda "that devalues school knowledge and an epistemology that devalues theoretical/scientific/academic knowledge."

Researchers also denounce the epistemological scepticism (Bhaskar, 1989, 1991, 1986; Eagleton, 1991, 1999, 2003; Callinicos, 1989, 1991; Duarte, 2002a, 2003a; Moraes, 2001, 2003; Duayer, 2001, 2003) of the postmodern, poststructuralist, and neo-pragmatic currents with their different features and subtleties. Although they envisage signs of weakening in some of these trends, these researchers recognise the persistence of the epistemological scepticism, which along with a rising anti-realism and relativism, impoverishes the understanding of science and reduces the scope, strength, and depth of the gnosiological field. Under these circumstances, the capacity

[1] This work is part of the results of a research project entitled "Emergent Paradigms: New Conceptual Designs in Educational Policies" (supported by CNPq/Brazil). I would like to thank Mário Duayer and Olinda Evangelista for their criticism and suggestions concerning the opinions expressed here.

of apprehending the functional relations of the empirical phenomena is impaired (Duayer, 2003). The epistemological scepticism presents knowledge as the field of practical vocabulary against that of theory and asserts that it is time to break the limits between objective knowledge and the way we use things. Objective knowledge becomes out of favor these days, and reality is dissolved to a mirror of pragmatic desires. As Eagleton (2003: 67) affirms: "Reality itself had now embraced the non-realistic, as capitalist society became increasingly dependent in its everyday operations on myth and fantasy, fictional wealth, exoticism and hyperbole, rhetoric, virtual reality and sheer appearance."

In this context, it is thought-provoking to recall Richard Rorty's neo-pragmatic proposals as a kind of "absent presence" to this frame of questions. He is known as the most notable and influential representative of contemporary neo-pragmatism and perhaps is one of the most debated and controversial authors of the Western academic world. The book that established his international reputation, *Philosophy and the Mirror of Nature*, was published in 1979 and had a great impact, especially in the North American academic sphere, dominated by analytical philosophy up to that moment. In its conscious isolation, such philosophy ignored the effervescent philosophical ideas that existed in Europe by then and presented itself – and indeed still does where it prevails – as an extension or condition for the progress of natural sciences, logic, and mathematics, a fundamental rupture with what it considers to be a pre-scientific or pre-analytical philosophy. Although criticism coming from North American post-analytical philosophers, such as Quine, Sellars, and Davidson, was already widely spread, the analytical hegemony was indisputable in the universities of the United States when Rorty's book was released.

The eclectic and controversial pragmatism reinvented by Rorty puts into question the constructive efforts of the analytical way of conceiving philosophy and welcomes or revives the influence of a wide variety of thought. On the one hand, Rorty's work reveals features of the traditional North American pragmatism, represented by Pierce, James, and mainly Dewey. On the other hand, it is influenced by the post-analytical philosophy of language, especially by the previously mentioned authors, Quine, Sellars, and Davidson. But that is not all. The dialogue he established with other American thinkers, such as Putman and Kuhn, or European figures, such as Derrida, Heidegger, Nietzsche, and Wittgenstein, amongst many others, is patent in his work.

Rorty's texts are difficult to read, not because of their general ideas, which are highly recurrent, but due to the impressive number of interlocutions and the references he uses, mainly those related to logic and the philosophy of language. Nevertheless, maybe as a consequence of its polemic nature, his work has moved beyond the confines of academic life and reached the general public. The ironic comments, his iconoclastic style, his conscious abandonment of the arid terminology of analytical philosophy, and even the caricature he portrays of Western philosophy make the reading of his texts quite pleasurable. Moreover, when Rorty presents his neo-pragmatic conception, he addresses key questions of the contemporary debate, either theoretical or practical: those related to knowledge and logic, social and political life; theses about the philosophies of language, education, law, and religion; discussions about gender and so on; and several other topics that are common in the media nowadays. Furthermore, his ambitious proposal to synthesise writers and philosophers, either in a technical or literary way, has given him certain legitimacy and the attention of innumerable intellectuals of other areas besides philosophy.

For all these reasons, proposing the discussion of Rorty's arguments in a single short article is certainly too ambitious. Therefore, we just focus on some aspects of his thought. Having in mind the profound articulation of the issues that Rorty dealt with, we first focus on his criticism of Western philosophy, mainly of the traditional conceptions of knowledge and truth. Then we consider the pragmatic social theory formulated by him, its subsequent liberal utopia, and the expected role of education (or edification) in this context.

## THE "PLATO-KANT SEQUENCE": A NEO-PRAGMATIC META-NARRATIVE OF PHILOSOPHY

The Rortyan *pragmatic* turn tries to obliterate the distinction between analytic and synthetic, theory and observation, science and literary criticism, or science and fiction. Its main argument moves in a definite direction: the criticism of the gnosiological predominance in Western philosophy and the conceptions of knowledge and truth he considered implicit in it. In these circumstances, the basis of the argument is a radical criticism of knowledge as representation, truth as a cognoscitive concept resulting from the correspondence of thought to the intrinsic nature of things, and language as a transparent and literal medium, an alleged vehicle for "clear and distinct ideas." Thus, neo-pragmatism censors[2] the Cartesian conviction – *bête noir* in this story – that the only kind of true knowledge is the one that provides accurate mental representations of an objective and real world, independent of the mind of the cognoscente subject.

We could say *grosso modo*, that Rorty's procedure expresses itself along two main axes. On the one hand, it reviews the Western philosophical tradition, the "Plato-Kant sequence" as he calls it, from a pragmatic meta-narrative. His aim is to demystify its characteristic dualisms, such as knowledge/opinion, scheme/content, reality/appearance, and also the idea that a rational

---

[2] Bernstein (1998) used this ironic expression.

investigation would reveal a hidden truth, an intrinsic nature behind or beyond apparent reality. Rorty also rejects the corollary of that proposal, that is, the idea that knowledge or access to the truth of things would presuppose a rational and critical distance from them. On the other hand, he evokes and reconstructs what he considers the edifying history of the liberal North American institutions and their continuous cultural and political vitality (Norris, 1993: 151).

Rorty's story dates the beginning of the crystallisation of Western philosophy in a distant past. He actually finds in Plato – one of the great villains in the Rortyan meta-narrative – the gnosiological deviations that would affect the later procedures of Western philosophical thinking. This process, continues the story, would reach its final form in the modern era, when philosophy started to be influenced by the "Cartesian anxiety"[3] and had to find an Archimedes' point, some pivotal point from which the conditions for knowledge and truth could be guaranteed at the risk of falling into a complete epistemological nihilism. These were the times of the modernity of Descartes, Locke, and Kant, when the problems of knowledge and the epistemological doubt were elected as the main subjects to be investigated by philosophy. It was the time when Kant defined the conditions of possibility of knowledge and established the differences among science, metaphysics, and religion. Rorty regards that moment as the starting point for the supremacy of the metaphor of the mind as a "mirror of nature" or "mind as lamp" of the correspondence theory of truth and of "philosophy as a discipline whose main aim is to examine, polish and focus this mirror, accurately and in detail" (Duayer and Moraes, 1997b: 29). According to Rorty's criticism, such aspiration made philosophy search for the ultimate foundations of knowledge and for the vocabulary that would "explain and justify its own activity as an *intellectual activity*, and therefore discover the meaning of life itself" (Rorty, 1994a: 20). He adds that such an attempt made philosophy "inflate" truth with unique and immutable criteria. The story Rorty tells us is an attempt to explain, in his terms, of course, "how philosophy-as-epistemology attained self-certainty in the modern period."

Rorty asks for a revision of that story. He promises to reach the aims that, according to him, were set by Wittgenstein, Heidegger, and Dewey, the three "most important philosophers of our century," those who placed philosophy on a distinct level compared with its previous forms, now fallen into disuse. Such aims would be: to break free from the Kantian conception of knowledge, to put aside epistemology and metaphysics, and to present a therapeutic and edifying philosophy instead of a constructive and systematic one (Rorty, 1994a: 21;22), a philosophy that would be just one more kind of writing, just some other actor in the contemporary conversation of humanity.

[3] Bernstein (1998) used this ironic expression.

According to Rorty, Wittgenstein, Heidegger, and Dewey opened entirely new possibilities in the territory of human activities. In their charts, there would be no room for the vocabulary inherited from the seventeenth century, especially that which ratifies knowledge as the representation of reality and truth as correspondence. In fact, in Rorty's view, there is "no such an activity called 'knowledge' that has a nature to be discovered" (Rorty, 1987) and it is "the vocabulary of practice rather than of theory (. . .) in which one can say something useful about truth" (Rorty, 1982: 162). This means being "in contact with reality in all areas of culture – in ethics as much as physics, in both literary criticism and biology – so that 'in contact with' does not mean 'representing in an accurate and rational way', but simply 'caused by and causing'" (Rorty, 1990: 22). In another essay, Rorty states the need to blur the boundaries between knowing and using things, as we no longer have to represent reality but only investigate how to use it in a more appropriate way.

Therefore, Rorty puts aside the need to investigate truth, objectivity, or what could be considered a correct interpretation or apprehension of reality. Strictly speaking, he redefines these terms from a different perspective. He states: "The notion of 'accurate representation' is simply an (. . .) empty compliment which we pay to those beliefs which are successful in helping us to do what we want to do" (Rorty, 1979: 10). Thus, the question of knowledge as representation is replaced by the acceptance of useful beliefs, which are explained in terms of reflexes in a stimulus–response psychology, instead of normative aspects of epistemology. As Norris points out, the causal theory is enough to keep cultural conversation flowing and, in the Rortyan construct, it seems to be given *carte blanche* to do anything: "reinterpret meanings, replace old beliefs, revise scientific theories, reconfigure those various 'metaphors we live by,' and constantly re-weave the fabric of belief according to present needs and purposes" (Norris, 2000: 76).

We could then try to investigate what a rational being would be from a Rortyan perspective. Neo-pragmatic rationality, as we can infer from the comments mentioned earlier, does not reject the web of beliefs of a specific group of people and, in this respect, it accepts that any group has its own rationality, in other words, beliefs that are useful and reliable for them. Being rational means getting used to reaching a consensus by means of persuasion and not by force and, from that viewpoint, rationality is also outlined in the learning of persuasion techniques, types of justification and forms of communication, conversation, and social practice. Conversation substitutes confrontation, solidarity replaces objectivity. For Rorty, being rational means being in agreement with what "our" culture considers to be rational.[4] In other words, as we shall see later, rationality, truth, and language

---

4 Rorty frequently uses the word "we": "we, pragmatists," "we, liberals," "we, North Americans," and so on.

have their origin in arbitrariness and contingency, and they are considered "tools," useful resources that are available so that we can deal with "our" everyday life. As such, they are essentially related to purposes and interests that are also variable and contingent and are defined by the role they play in the context of the debate. Therefore, rationality, truth, and language are always ethnocentric, notions of a given culture (Duayer and Moraes, 1997a: 119). To Rorty, "all there is to say about truth or rationality are the descriptions provided by familiar procedures of justification that a given society – *ours* – uses" (Rorty, 1987: 42). Truth, knowledge, and rationality, Rorty asserts, are just laudatory terms used for beliefs socially justified.

He coherently claims that: "what justifies a conception of justice is (...) its congruence not only with our comprehension of ourselves and our aspirations, but also with our understanding, which constitutes the most reasonable doctrine for us, given our history and the cultural traditions rooted in our public life" (Rorty, 1994b: 183). The question of whether justifiability to the community with which we identify ourselves contains the truth or not is simply irrelevant (Duayer and Moraes, 1997a: 123), as from the Rortyan perspective there is no interesting connection between the concept of truth and the concept of justification (Rorty, 1987: 33). Such connection is broken when beliefs turn out to be mere justifications that satisfy the expectations of a social group at a given moment. Outside the community – or the audience – one can only return to transcendentalism. Under these circumstances, as Norris states, theorising becomes a strictly inconsequential activity: "At most it provides just an added measure of rhetorical or persuasive back-up for beliefs and convictions that can make no sense unless they are already shared by a large enough section of our own 'interpretative community'" (Norris, 1996: xi).

Therefore, Rorty regards justification as a social phenomenon and not as a transaction between a "cognoscent subject" and "reality." It is not "a matter of a (...) relation between ideas (words) and objects, but of conversation, of social practice (...) We understand knowledge when we understand the social justification of belief, and thus have no need to view it as accuracy of representation" (Rorty, 1979: 170). It is not necessary to mention that any conception of science as objective knowledge of reality is dismissed. Neo-pragmatism regards science as "one genre of literature" (Rorty, 1982: xliii); in fact, it proposes literature and arts as enquiries at the same level of scientific research. Science would be just one of the many areas of culture – and not even the most privileged or interesting one. Literature becomes the most important discipline in our culture, displacing religion, science, and even philosophy (Rorty, 1982: 155). As a consequence, Rorty admits that if there is any difference between physics and literary criticism, this difference is not epistemological but sociological.

For Haack, such characteristics show the essence of Rortyan propositions. Different criteria, from historically diverse times and cultures, are considered incommensurable; that is, for Rorty there are no criteria to establish which beliefs are correct or not. As Haack states, "Justification is not only a social question, but also something completely conventional: there is no sense in assuming that our custom to criticise or defend beliefs might be based upon any other thing external to such customs." Thus, the Rortyan conversation results in two theses: "contextualism in what concerns explanation and conventionalism in what concerns ratification" (Haack, 1997: 253; 260).

Among other aspects, the new vocabulary introduced by Rorty reveals a supposedly anti-realist character. However, he warns us that his anti-realism is not tantamount to denying the existence of reality. In a text in which he engages in a polemic with the "realist" Searle, using his characteristic style and in apparent contradiction with the quotations previously mentioned, Rorty declares:

No one has ever stated that there are no truths or objective validities. What we say is that you gain nothing for the pursuit of such truth by talking about the mind-dependence or mind-independence of reality. There is nothing to talk about except for the procedures we use to reach agreement among researchers. (Rorty, 2000:100)

What is at stake, according to Rorty, is the ambiguity of the notion of independence, that is, its causal or non-causal meaning. Assuring the non-existence of a reality that is independent of the mind does not mean, for instance, denying the existence of mountains before having the idea of mountain in our minds or the word "mountain" in our language, nor stating that mountains are an effect of either our thoughts or our language. What pragmatic authors investigate, Rorty says, is if "it is pointless to ask whether there really are mountains or whether it is merely convenient for us to talk about mountains." And he continues: "it is pointless to ask whether reality is independent of our way of talking about it" (Rorty, 2000: 100). One of the obvious truths about mountains is the evidence that they already existed before we started talking about them. If someone does not notice this fact, Rorty says, it is simply because "he does not know how to play the language-games that employ the word 'mountain.' But the utility of those language games has nothing to do with the question of whether reality as it is in itself, apart from the way it is handy for human beings to describe it, has mountains in it" (Rorty, 2000: 100). In this respect, Norris points out, Rortyan neo-pragmatism allows one to be as "realist" as one likes about objects, physical stimuli, etc. However, it denies "that one's beliefs are fixed – or one's range of creative 'redescriptions' in any way limited – by the requirement that they should somehow 'correspond to reality'" (Norris, 2000: 80).

Thus, for Rortyan neo-pragmatism, the world continues to exist, contain the same objects, and cause the same effects, no matter what description of it we provide or what theories we can eventually construct in order to explain it. We will continue to live our lives issuing descriptions and developing theories, even though, by definition, any possibility of asserting a correspondence with "facts" is excluded. Therefore, the pivotal point of the argument is that admitting we live immersed in reality is not tantamount to stating that this or that content of our mind or our language represents or corresponds to this or that element of reality (Rorty, 1991a). Theories will always be products of a language-game or of a socialised scientific practice. Although Rorty does not go as far as to deny the existence of reality, he refutes the possibility of having access to it outside the sphere of culture, language, or human interests. That is to say, despite the affirmation of the existence of reality, the system of significations prevents access to it (Duayer and Moraes, 1997b).

Any possibility of a referent that transcends the "marks and noises" of a culture is therefore eliminated. In other words and in conformity with this guideline of neo-pragmatism when dealing with the world, knowledge is limited to the choice between alternative hypotheses and is not capable of discovering anything that "makes" one of them true. As we have mentioned, enquiries about the objectivity of value, the rationality of science, and the causes of the viability of our language-games are rejected. Adopting such an approach means substituting all these "theoretical questions" by "practical questions" concerning the desirability and/or necessity of "maintaining or not our current values, theories and practices" (Duayer and Moraes, 1997b). The only restrictions to research, according to Rorty, are related to conversation and not to the nature of the object, the mind, or the language. For this reason, Norris points out, "persuasion (or rhetoric) is indeed the bottom line of enquiry, and (...) truth-talk or kindred high-toned appeals to fact, evidence, theory or principle are just so many ploys for enlisting assent among members of the relevant peer-group community" (Norris, 1997: 3).

The same conclusions could be drawn from an analysis of language. Rorty, once again influenced by Heidegger, Dewey, and Wittgenstein, highlights the impossibility of using non-linguistic items in order to discriminate between true and false linguistic items. From an anti-representationalist point of view, this is impracticable for a very simple reason: There is no human way of collecting a non-linguistic item – all human things are intrinsically linguistic (Duayer and Moraes, 1997a). For Rorty, the idea that something – the world or we ourselves – could exist "detached from language, detached from a description" is just a pseudo-problem created by the essentialist philosophic tradition. A pragmatist must insist "that it is only possible to compare languages and metaphors to each other and not to something called "facts," which are beyond language" (Rorty, 1989a: 20). As Haack points out, the assertion that nothing can be described without the use of language is radicalised in the declaration that there is nothing outside language that could make possible a description without it (Haack, 1997: 253).

But what is Rorty's conception of language? As we have previously mentioned, he conceptualises language as a tool or toolkit that enables us to deal with the world. In such interpretation, vocabularies are instruments and not representations. Once again, what matters is not correspondence to reality, but the fact that language allows us to move around the world, that is, it allows us to deal with the world and with culture, to search for happiness, to satisfy our needs and wishes. Therefore, language is affirmed by its usefulness and efficacy (Duayer and Moraes, 1997b: 38). Rorty regards language as the means through which "human beings use marks and noises to get what they want" (Rorty, 1991b: 127). In this respect, it is possible to talk about knowledge only when it becomes a useful description for our current purposes (Rorty, 1987: 45).

If by any chance one would ask "useful for what?" there would be no possible answer but "useful in creating a better future," Rorty says. If other questions followed and someone enquired "better according to which criterion?" pragmatists would add nothing but the notion that "better" would be what "contains more than what we consider good and less than what we consider bad." If others asked "what exactly is considered good?" the answer would be "variety, and liberty" or "growth" (Rorty, 1987: 14–15). And how can we achieve growth, variety, and liberty? Well, a pragmatist would say, through the exchange of ideas, conversation, and free and open encounters!

The epistemological scepticism in Rorty's thought is obvious. This scepticism, in its effort to set knowledge free of any trace of transcendence and in the attempt to naturalise and deflate it, ends up trivialising the problem of truth, making it intrinsically disposable. In fact, this proposal goes beyond the scope of epistemology. Nowadays the debate about scepticism is not confined to the limits of a controversy concerning knowledge and the criteria for its validation. On the contrary, it is a broad ideological discussion in which the different protagonists of the contemporary intellectual scene take part and confront each other, including Rortyan neo-pragmatism. In this context, the proposal of truth as consensus deliberately coincides with the *modus operandi* of "practices and institutions of liberal democracies," at least "the North-Atlantic ones" (Duayer and Moraes, 1997a: 102).

Before concluding the first part of this chapter, it is important to mention that Rorty's criticism of Western philosophy, epistemology, and the notions of truth and representation is not separate from his social theory, or his liberal utopia, which from my standpoint expresses and nourishes the spirit of our time. Rorty seems to offer a radical scepticism, presenting himself as a libertarian critic of any oppression (truth, authority, universals, etc.). However, Rorty may also be considered as an advocate of a rhetoric that preventatively disables any criticism or social practices that confront the "consensual values" of liberal democracies and, by doing so, is a means toward the accomplishment of his own presumptions. "Therefore, understanding the pragmatic proposals is also relevant in the realm of social and political struggle, mainly because what is at stake in this area is whether or not the so-called ideas of modernity (truth, justice, liberty, and emancipation) are still pertinent" (Duayer and Moraes, 1997a: 102).

## REJUVENATED LIBERALISM AND ITS IRONISTS

The Rortyan social theory and conception of education are intimately articulated and both have a strong link with the propositions about knowledge, truth, and language mentioned earlier. Rorty's ideas about the "liberal utopia" and its heroine, "the liberal ironist," presented in *Contingency, Irony and Solidarity* (1989a), constitute the starting point for the second part of this exposition. We will then try to define the role of education within this utopia.

In agreement with his propositions that all lexicons are a human creation, a tool rather than a medium, and "meaning is simply the ability to substitute sensible signs (...) for other signs (...) and so indefinitely" (Rorty, 1989c: 211), Rorty proceeds to invent a lexicon that is appropriate for the description of his liberal utopia. In such a process, he redescribes both terms – "utopia" and "liberal" – depriving them of their original meaning.[5] It is worth pointing out that, according to Rorty, redescribing does not mean enunciating a "true description" or finding a "vocabulary which accurately represents something, as a transparent medium" (Rorty, 1989a: 75) but attempting to avoid or solve problems, conflicts, or anomalies by reweaving our current speeches with a new vocabulary. In these circumstances, redescription does not aim at offering arguments against current vocabulary we are familiar with, but at substituting with another more attractive one, rich in metaphors, able to describe a wide variety of topics.

It is common knowledge that the word "utopia" – from the Greek oὐ τόποξ – contains a tremendous ideological power. Whether in the classic sense proposed by More or Campanella, or in the sense identified as an interpretation of Marxism[6] as a negation and inversion of a dominant *topos*,

---

5 Rorty also redescribes the term "irony." Exploring this aspect is beyond the scope of this chapter, but if we consider Socratic irony, which never disregarded philosophy, we will realise how restrictive the Rortyan conception is. What is more, Socrates would not be an "ironist" according to the Rortyan definition.

6 Certainly not in the sense of the proposals made by Marx and Engels. These two authors used the term utopia in a pejorative way, as a synonym of good intentions without the effective capability to transform reality. For them, the socialism proposed by Saint Simon, Fourier, and Owen, who believed they could transform the material and economic conditions of society through reforms that would bring happiness and justice to humanity, was utopic. As opposed to what they called utopic socialism, Marx and Engels proposed a scientific socialism based on an analysis and a real and radical criticism of capitalist society (Riu and Morato, 1996). As Eagleton indicates, "if Marxism has traditionally set its face against utopia, it is not because it rejects the idea of a radically transfigured society, but because it rejects the assumption that such a society could be, so to speak, simply parachuted into the present from some metaphysical outer space" (Eagleton, 1999: 34).

the oppressing capitalist order, the term utopia – which is related to *eutopia,* happy place – indicates an ideal model of social organisation, a just society in which the existential miseries of both individuals and communities would be solved. In a utopian society there would be no misery or exploitation of any kind and people would no longer have to submit themselves to the division between their personal inclinations and social obligations, between the private and public sphere. The utopian society would therefore be a harmonious society that would realise the principles of justice, the achievement of the dream of human emancipation. Although utopia is *ou-topos,* that is, does not possess any spatial locus, this does not imply that it is *ou-chronos,* non-temporal, as it is generally imagined as something that may be realised or a horizon that guides our actions (Riu and Morato, 1996). In this respect, a utopian future is anchored to radical criticism of the present; otherwise, it would not be a utopia but a fetish.

Rosenow reminds us that, abandoning the traditional meaning of utopia, Rorty does not offer any criticism of the dominant social situation. Likewise, there is no indication of innovative social systems and institutional organisations or of a non-existent utopian society in the classical sense of the expression (Rosenow, 1998: 256). Strictly speaking, that would not be necessary. There is nothing new to propose at this level, as Rorty considers "the rich North-Atlantic liberal democracies" as the best of what humanity has produced so far – because they favour the "bourgeois freedoms," the open encounters, and permit the free conversation and the introduction of new ideas. Such democracies, he asserts, already contain "the institutions for its own improvement" (Rorty, 1989a: 63).

But Rorty sketches a utopia whose main concern is not society. On the contrary, it is focused on the ideal person "deserving to live in the already existing social order (. . .) a woman (. . .) 'the liberal ironist', and she is contrasted with her masculine counterpart, who appears as the metaphysician or the intellectual theorist" (Rosenow, 1998: 256).[7] The liberal ironists are the citizens of his utopia. The way to reach the utopia is through the *universalisation* of the liberal society (Rorty, 1982: 82). That is perhaps a way to be followed by the progressive expansion of the borders of liberal democracies, maybe a globalisation of Western liberalism, in which the expansion

---

[7] Obviously, in this case, Rorty does not stick to the limits of gender and includes among the ironists Nietzsche, Proust, Heidegger, Foucault, and Nabokov. Among the liberals are Marx, Dewey, Mill, Habermas, Berlin, and Raws. Although from a Rortyan perspective, both groups of thinkers share the repudiation of metaphysical foundationalisms, the ironists are primarily interested in self-perfection, in the desire to achieve auto-creation, in an autonomous life. On the other hand, liberals are inspired by the "wish to have a more just and free human society" (Rorty, 1989a: p. XIV). His definition of liberal, borrowed from Judith Shklar Rorty, includes such thinkers because they agree that "cruelty is the worst thing we do" (Rorty, 1989a, p. XV). The conflict between ironists, "authors of autonomy," and "liberals," "authors of justice," makes their vocabularies incommensurable.

of a certain vocabulary, the liberal one, will allow the possibility of sharing it with a growing community with intentions that are similar to "ours," the liberals (Critchley, 1998: 53).

Furthermore, Rorty also redescribes the term "liberal," and when doing so, only takes into account the ethico-political dimension of the term, disregarding, *tout court*, its inevitable economic side – liberty defined in terms of a free market. This difference allows him to adopt a comfortable discourse, advocating tolerance, the rejection of cruelty, and the development of solidarity. These words, which obliterate the imperialism, racism, and colonialism that constitute the expansion forces of those "liberal North-Atlantic societies" are easily spoken. However, one cannot forget the severe effects of the worldwide complex economic game that accentuate the separation between winners and losers, between those who really matter and those who are disposable. Rorty is benevolent and rejects the idea of criticism of liberal thinking, even when, more recently, he mentions the abysm between the rich and the poor or the degrading conditions and starvation salaries, or when he talks about the aftermath of September 11.

Critchley mentions the risks of that political complacency which, after all, could be interpreted as "(re)descriptive excuses for the iniquity, intolerance, exploitation and lack of liberty that in effect exist in the present liberal democracies" (Critchley, 1998: 55). As a matter of fact, from what we know about *corporate democracy* or about the farcical nature of the bourgeois parliamentary democracy and the so-called "crisis of representativity," only an extreme condescension could provide a positive political and institutional balance of liberal democracy. At the "imperial times" of the third millennium, the farcical nature of Western democracy is clearly exposed.

In any case, as Topper points out, Rorty's view of a liberal society constituted "by our loyalty to other human beings" may well be one of the most ambitious attempts to rejuvenate the old ideals of liberalism, namely, tolerance, pluralism, liberties, etc. (Topper, 1995: 958). However, when designing his utopia, Rorty reaffirms with disconcerting frankness an aspect that is part of the capitalist mercantile societies: the separation and incommensurability between the public and private spheres. In agreement with his criticism of Western thought, Rorty argues that neither philosophy nor "any other theoretical discipline" is able to find a way that allows us to maintain self-creativity and justice, private perfection, and human solidarity within a broad philosophical mentality or a unique point of view. As Rosenow (1998) affirms, there is no metaphysical or theoretical solution to the contradiction between public and private matters. Such contradiction is a problem that the individual must solve after personal deliberation (Rorty, 1989a: 194). In other words, one cannot unify but only "accommodate in a practical way" those two spheres that are equally valid yet inexorably incommensurable, the private demand of self-creation and the public project of human solidarity (Rorty, 1987: 50; 1989a: XV, 68).

The private sphere is exemplified by the ironic attitude. The "liberal ironist" aims at encouraging tolerance and minimising suffering and sees cruelty as the worst evil. She confronts the contingency of her main wishes and beliefs, that is to say, her dependence on the cultural context and the process of socialisation. She is the one who includes in her "unfounded wishes" her own hope that "suffering will be diminished, that the humiliation of human beings by other human beings may cease" (Rorty, 1989a: XV). As an ironist, she acknowledges the contingency of her beliefs and desires and does not look for philosophical grounds for her actions. She has permanent doubts about her "final vocabulary." Knowing that this vocabulary cannot be corroborated or invalidated by "facts," she is aware that every "final vocabulary" is necessarily contingent. The ironist believes that nothing has a unified or absolute essence or nature and that there is no objective criterion to distinguish between right and wrong for there is nothing '"beneath' socialisation or prior to history which is definatory of the human" (Rorty, 1989a: XIII). She knows that anything "can be made to look good or bad" through its description and, therefore, "she has radical and continuing doubts about the final vocabulary she currently uses" and should not be taken very seriously (Rorty, 1989a: 73–74). She constantly recreates and redescribes herself, emphasising the spirit of playfulness, expanding and innovating her idiosyncratic vocabulary. Therefore, Rosenow (1998) reminds us, she tries to learn as many diverse final vocabularies as possible. Insofar as she regards philosophy as a kind of writing, simply a final vocabulary among many others, or just an illusion (Rorty, 1982: 92), she opts for literary criticism, an activity that is related not only to literary works and philosophy, but also to all textual products of human culture (Rorty, 1989a: 81).

Rosenow indicates that Rorty's worry focuses on "the self-image which a democratic society must have" and "the rhetoric which it should use to express its hopes" (Rorty, 1989a: 67). According to Rorty, what liberal culture needs is a redescription of liberalism as the hope that culture as a whole can be poeticised. This is how liberalism should be described: a "poeticised" culture based on the "compromise" between the private wishes of individuals to achieve autonomy and their liberal wish to avoid humiliation, cruelty, and pain. Rosenow thinks that in Rorty's utopia:

this compromise is achieved by the liberal ironist, who knows how to privatise her attempts 'at authenticity and purity' while relegating her liberal hope to the public sphere (. . .) In other words, Rorty commends a 'split between private and public concerns' (. . .) a 'compartmentalization of the self' (. . .) into two distinct realms. Accordingly ironists 'reconcile themselves to a private-public split within their final vocabularies' and to the fact that there is no connection between their doubts about private final vocabularies and their liberal hopes for solidarity. (Rosenow, 1998: 257)

Contrary to what many thinkers in the Western philosophical tradition wished, Rorty states the impossibility to unite, reconcile, or go beyond the public and private domains (Rorty, 1989a). Therefore, by restricting the irony and the ironists to the private sphere – in a kind of psychological bi-cameralism (Critchley, 1998: 56) – Rorty rejects the strategy of a public irony that could expose the violence that liberalism, *malgré tout*, tries to hide.

Several philosophers understood that the solution to the problem of the relation between public – sphere of rights – and private – sphere of individual interests – could be the key to human happiness. On the other hand, Rorty asserts that this duality or division should not be overcome or abolished but, on the contrary, cultivated and encouraged. As a consequence, instead of solving the problem of dualism, he perpetuates it. In other words, he transforms the question of the individual versus society from problem into solution.

For Rosenow, what distinguishes Rorty is not only the separation between private and public, but his inability to articulate or conjoin them. In his own words:

His contingent conception of personhood enables him to present his ironical position lightheartedly, but his democratic and liberal attitude gets him into trouble since he is unable to substantiate the need of solidarity on the basis of such a conception of personhood. He therefore is forced to dichotomize the private and the public. The separation between these two domains is not the point of departure of his utopia, but an inevitable outcome of his postmodern position. Rorty's commitment to Dewey is mystificatory, since Dewey regarded the abolition of dualism as the most important task of democracy and education. Rorty is, in spite of his declarations, unable to follow Dewey in this respect: as a liberal he is committed to democracy, but as a postmodernist he can justify its principles only in terms of an idiosyncratic and arbitrary preference. He therefore has no choice but to renounce Dewey's vision of a person in whose consciousness the private domains are fused together. Rorty instead creates its reversal, the divided person. (Rosenow, 1998: 263–264)

The profit with this substitution, the author continues, is extremely meagre: Rorty not only fails to construct a liberal utopia with aesthetical premises, but he is also unable to derive a liberal ideology from them. This may be the reason why Berstein presents the character O'Brien in Orwell's *1984* not only as a "double that haunts Rorty's redescription of liberalism" but also as a true "disciple" of Rorty, the one who has "diabolically mastered the lesson of the contingency of all vocabularies" (Bernstein, 1990 as quoted in Rosenow, 1998: 264).

I agree with Rosenow (1998) when he affirms that, strictly speaking, Rorty's utopia is not attractive. It not only lacks any critical or revolutionary orientation, but also its objective seems to be to assert the preservation of the establishment. That may precisely be his intention.

## EDUCATION IN THE RORTYAN LIBERAL UTOPIA

In *Contingency, Irony and Solidarity*, Rorty does not refer to education directly. However, in this book, there is a sentence that allows us to clearly identify what his ideas on this issue are. In his words: "I cannot imagine a culture which socialized its youth in such a way as to make them continually dubious about their own process of socialization" (Rorty, 1989a: 87). This fragment is congruent with his conception of education,[8] presented in a text published in 1990 and specifically aimed at philosophers of education. Although in this text he expresses his doubts "about the relevance of a philosophy of education" or about whether a philosopher could have anything relevant to say concerning the dilemmas of contemporary education (Rorty, 1990: 41), he formulates some propositions about the subject.

In his opinion, the objective of education is not the transfer of knowledge about epistemological questions or the discussion about the truth of "facts" – it could not be, considering what was exposed in the first part of this text. As mentioned earlier, Rortyan neo-pragmatism proposes substituting "theoretical questions" with "practical questions" about the desirability and/or necessity to maintain or not our current values, theories, and practices or, more precisely, by a permanent process of adjustment to the different cultural interests and necessities. It is coherent that he states that: "From the educational, as opposed to the epistemological or the technological point of view, the way things are said is more important than the possession of truths" (Rorty, 1994a: 353). Furthermore, as he regards the term education "a bit too flat, and *Bildung* a bit too foreign," he prefers another one, "edification," which he thinks is more appropriate to stand for "this project of finding new, better, more interesting, more fruitful ways of speaking" (Rorty, 1979: 360). But what is the Rortyan concept of education?

To understand Rorty's ideas of education, it is necessary to remember his non-essentialist view of human nature and his celebrated assertion: "human beings are centerless networks of beliefs and desires and (...) their vocabularies and opinions are determined by historical circumstances (Rorty, 1991a: 191). If this is so, says Reich, "education plays an enormous role in forming those beliefs and desires, and directing that shaping and molding. For without a notion of 'the core essence of man' *humans learn, or are taught, everything*" (Reich, 1996: 2).

Rorty assigns two different tasks to the educational process corresponding to its division into two components: a period of socialisation and another of individuation. As in the public and private spheres, in this educational theory, we also find the "bicameral I." The first task of the educational process corresponds to initial education, a phase of socialisation in which education tries to implant in the student the sense of citizenship and adapt the child to the society in which he/she lives. Such a task is consistent with his idea that it is unthinkable that a culture socialises its youth so as to make them doubt their own process of socialisation. Education, he believes, "has

---

[8] Although Rorty has dealt with educational questions in other texts (1982, 1989b, 1994a), here we refer mainly to the article published in the magazine *Educational Theory* (1990) about the educational meaning of his philosophy.

to start from acculturation" (Rorty, 1979: 365). To re-create themselves, the children must first be socialised into the dominant discourse and conventional descriptions of their community. As Reich points out, not everyone achieves self-individualisation or self-creation: "Some are merely socialized, becoming people who unselfconsciously accept the given vocabulary of the day and describe themselves in words that reflect the conventions of the community" (Reich, 1996: 4).

The role of the teacher at this stage is described with incisive words: he/she "should aim primarily at communicating enough of what is *held to be true* by the society to which the children belong" (Rorty, 1990: 42). In this context, it is not the educator's role to decide what "is or is not true." It is essential that the history about society students know coincides with that of their parents; otherwise, the latter may consider schools as "subversive institutions." Thus, at the initial stage, the teacher must conceal his possible doubts about such history and, if he believes that society is built upon a lie, then "he had better find another profession" (Rorty, 1990: 42). The initial phase in the educational process, therefore, is the socialisation of students in their environment, the neo-pragmatic learning of the "marks and noises" of their culture, the conscious reproduction of the consensual values of the society in which they live. In Rorty's words:

Education up to the age of eighteen or nineteen is mostly a matter of socialization – of getting the students to take over moral and political common sense of the society as it is (. . .) Primary and secondary education will always be a matter of familiarizing the young with what their elders take to be true, whether it is true or not (. . .) The point of non-vocational higher education is (. . .) to help students realize they can reshape themselves (. . .) the proper business of the university is to offer a provocation to self-creation. (Rorty, 1989b: 200)

The objective of higher education then, is a provocation to self-creation, the "individualisation" of the "I" that was initially acculturated (Rosenow, 1998: 261). In other words, the task of higher education is to provide stimulus for individuals so that they can "recreate" or "reinvent" themselves (Rorty, 1990: 41, 43). In this phase, there is scope for academic freedom and permission, so that doubt and social criticism become the central point of the educational process (Rorty, 1990: 42). In another article, Rorty states that this stage means a revolt against the process of socialisation (Rorty, 1989b: 200). It is therefore expected that higher education propitiates the process through which adult students find the path of self-education – or edification – so that they become ironists, privileged characters in the Rortyan liberal utopia. At this stage, students have present-day teachers and authors from the past and, for this reason, this is also a stage of aesthetic and literary education that enriches and helps students to invent "new forms of human freedom" and make use of "liberties never taken before." Under the circumstances, the edificating discourse must be "abnormal," aiming at taking us "out of our old selves by the power of strangeness, to aid us in becoming new beings" (Rorty, 1994a: 354).

Strictly speaking, Rorty does not offer any explanation for the division he proposes for the educational process. It is not clear why socialisation and individuation must be separate and distinct processes. Rorty derives from Dewey the principles of education at the two levels, initial and higher, but he does not take them literally. Instead, he "updates" Dewey, translating him pragmatically into his own vocabulary. Rosenow (1998) asserts that Rortyan Dewey presents "inspired narratives and fuzzy utopias" (Rorty, 1989b: 201) that lead us in a process of socialisation through which the child at the initial stage of the educational process acquires an image of himself as an inheritor of the North American democratic tradition, incorporating "the narrative of liberty and hope" proclaimed by that tradition (Rorty, 1989b: 202). The problem with this proposition is, among others, that it encourages a non-critical understanding of those values.[9] However, such criticism is expected of the subsequent moment, the process of individuation that takes place by means of the erotic and aestheticizing encounters of students and teachers, in which they learn to create themselves in an increasing irony, to develop their imagination, to renew their vocabularies, to re-describe their references of thought (Rosenow, 1998: 261). We should investigate, as Beck does, the following question: How can a society break the "crust of convention" to which Dewey made reference, if all youths up to the age of 18 and all their teachers only reinforce these conventions? (Beck, 1994: 8). As a matter of fact, "individuation understood as the provocation of the imagination may be fruitfully included at any level of education" (Reich, 1996: 8).

Finally, Rorty openly admits that, in the realm of virtues of liberalism, there is still an abysm between the current political practices and the utopia of the ideal of "free and open encounters," in which ironist education would play an important role. However, as Topper mentions, he does not examine what inhibits the development of a freer, open, inclusive, and democratic discourse; he elides those questions concerning the specific measures that are necessary to achieve such an objective (Topper, 1995: 963). Instead, he offers vague suggestions such as that "discoveries about who is being made to suffer can be left to the working of a free press, free universities, and enlightened public opinion." He adds that the only way to avoid the perpetuation of "cruelty within social institutions is by maximizing the quality of education, freedom of the press, educational opportunity, opportunities to exert political influence, and the like" (Rorty, 1989a: 67).

---

9 As Reich says: "If Rorty intends to maintain the 'entirely distinct' divisions of education in his liberal utopia, he cannot expect everyone to have an equal shot of self-creation, and he cannot expect anyone but a select elite to become liberal ironists. Rorty's liberal utopia begins to look like a small island of ironists surrounded by a vast ocean of commonsensicalists." (Reich 1996: 7).

What then does the Rortyan idea of education stand for? It represents a curious idealism, apparent good intentions and, mainly, a strong adequation to his liberal utopia and to the development of his ironists, as described in *Contingency, Irony and Solidarity*: the "bicameral I," the two diverse and incommensurable vocabularies, the private and the public realms. I agree with Rosenow's statement (1998) that Rorty's point of view about education must be considered not only in the organisational or curricular sphere, but also from the perspective of the complex consequences of the relation that he establishes between public and private. Only then will we be able to grasp the scope of his ideological horizon.

## CONCLUDING REMARKS

The rhetorical game permeates Rorty's works. There are recurrent ideas and succeeding persuasive arguments and criticism, frequently expressed in beautiful linguistic articulations, which make the reader feel uncomfortable to some extent. Is there anyone who opposes democracy or solidarity or who does not feel the "horror of cruelty"? Is there anyone who consciously affirms a reality inflated by a philosophy with a capital P? However, a closer analysis reveals to a large extent that we are presented with just a fallacy: We can either opt for the illuminist rationality – more specifically for the caricature of it done by Rorty – or eliminate the very possibility of knowledge; we can either opt for the Cartesian subject or for the subject diluted in language-games; for metaphysics or for the contingency of the best argument; for truth as correspondence or for the question regarding the uses of truth within a certain language or audience; for foundationalism or hyper-contextualism. In other words, we can either opt for pragmatism or for no other way of thinking.

It is common sense that the "marks and noises" of a culture determine different perspectives and personal convictions, different political or cultural intentions, different linguistic or conceptual pictures. They also shape and colour any description or narrative of reality that we offer. However, this multiplicity of views does not ratify the hyper-contextualism proposed by Rorty, nor does it confuse us with the ingenuity of the fallacious options.

We cannot deny the fact that, beyond such marks and noises, beyond the neo-pragmatic objectivity defined by consensus, beyond "being caused," beyond the metaphor of amplitude, we have the tense and complex relations of what we call ontology – the complex effectivity of the social being, what is real in the essentiality of concrete relations that institute and constitute economic, politic, and cultural relations in the contradictory process that is a historical product of human acts. That is why the complexity of the social being is intelligible. It is a real effectivity open to knowledge, clear understanding, and human intervention.

These questions are of great interest to education. Perhaps not so much to a bipartite education like that offered by Rorty, but mainly to education as

a privileged social practice that, as such, supposes subjects: not mere transmitters or receptors of justified beliefs that guide them in their actions, but
educators and educatees, in the most profound sense of these terms. These
subjects are aware of the important role of acculturation that education has
and also of the resistance that is typical of it. Holding this view of education, they accept resorting to analysis, either in order to criticise the current
social practices or to show us how we can alter, preserve, extend or dare
them. Such subjects admit the necessity to understand the interaction of
social and linguistic practices, privileges, differences, and distortions that
they harbour. In conclusion, they do not ignore the fact that the transmission of knowledge and the truth of events are instruments of fight – both in
classrooms and social movements.

Norman Geras, a critic of Rorty, reminds us that if we cannot talk about
truth, we cannot talk about injustice either. In other words, if truth is entirely
relativised, limited to private discourses, or to language games or unjustified
beliefs, then there is no injustice. This is so because those who protest or
are victims lose, in this context, their best and most efficient weapon: telling
what really happened (Geras, 1995: 110). All they can tell "is their history,"
one among others within the convictions and institutions of a certain culture
(Moraes, 1996: 55). It is worth remembering Walter Benjamin's belief that it
is the knowledge of the past, the memory of the dead from a time of slavery
and oppression, that leads men and women to fight for transformation and
change and not future dreams of freed descendants at all costs.

Rorty believes that the horizon of male and female rights transcends the
sheer identification of our actions with the community of persons who think
like we do (Rorty, 1987: 97). Moreover, despite neo-pragmatic objections,
moral and ethical responsibilities are linked not only to individual discern-
ment but also to the universality of reason. There is a universality that is
typical of the public use of reason, a transcendence regarding the contingency of practical life that prevents the ethical deliberation from being
considered merely as a calculation that operates within the immanency of
the immediate possibilities (Leopoldo and Silva, 1996: 354). In this realm,
there is only room for scepticism and the cynical lack of compromise that
lower everything to the same level with the facile argument of a pseudo-
realism. A more serious proposition, because it is so attractive, is the one
that dismisses reason as the sign of human solidarity, morality, and freedom
or circumscribes truth in the realm of publicly shared beliefs, of the contingency of the best argument, and of the utopic hope of a "less distressing"
society.

Even when, in *Achieving our Country* (1998a), Rorty calls upon the North
American "cultural Left" to be less cultural and address economic inequality,
to think again of the abyss that separates the rich and the poor, his discourse
does not fail to confirm a new de-politisation and cooptation in politics and,
therefore, in education. He postulates the direct link between education

and the celebration of the virtues of the exalted liberal utopia (and the North American values) in everyday life. He also contributes to removing from the political discussions and the educational process the relevance of the theoretical analysis, the discussion about the excluding side of consensus, the effective ways of dominance and exclusion, and the ways through which the past is articulated with the logic of historical and cultural forms of the present.

Rorty does not seem to realise that social life is not guided by discussion and by the conscious consensual decisions of the members of society. As Kuntz states, "The Democratic procedure is not prior to the galvanising effects of the 'social physics' of anonymous markets, but post-posed. Therefore, all the decisions of democratic institutions do not represent an autonomous use of the symbolic collection of resources, but are previously made by the automatism of the economic system that, as such, is not open to debate" (Kunz, 1999). "We Latin-Americans," who suffer the brutal galvanising effects of the social physics of contemporary liberalism, believe those are crucial questions.

# EDUCATION

# 5

## The Importance of Play in Pre-School Education

*Naturalisation Versus a Marxist Analysis*

Alessandra Arce

The main aim of this chapter is to analyse the similarities and differences between Froebel on the one hand and Elkonin and Leontyev on the other, taking into account the contributions that these authors have made to child development psychology and pre-school education. To this end, we will make a comparison between Froebel's ideas and those of Activity Theory with respect to the role of play in child development at pre-school age. The text is organised into three parts. The first one aims at presenting a brief description of Froebel's conception of child development and the role of play. The objective of the second part is to analyse Elkonin/Leontyev's conception of the same subjects. In the third section, we present some conclusions that have been drawn from this comparative analysis.

### PLAY ACCORDING TO FROEBEL — SELF-ACTIVITY AND THE VITAL UNITY WITH RESPECT TO CHILD DEVELOPMENT

To present the principles of child development that are the foundation of Froebel's conceptions of play, we take into account three works by this author: *The Education of Man, The Mottoes and Commentaries of Friedrich Froebel's Mother Play*, and *Pedagogics of the Kindergarten*.

In his book *The Education of Man*, Froebel (1887) explains how human development, especially that of children, occurs. He affirms that God is the beginning of all things and that the life of human beings must seek to harmonise itself with Him and with all other aspects of divine creation. The divine nature of everything that exists on earth reveals God's essence. Human beings must seek this divine essence within themselves to cultivate it and externalise it in their own creations. According to Froebel, Jesus is an example of the divine struggle, in which we must also engage searching for our own perfection and for the union with God and with Nature. This divine and eternal law to which Froebel referred guides the development of all beings on earth. This is the reason we find a constant comparison between the development of children and that of seeds in Froebel's works. For the German educator, children are like a seed to be cultivated and, consequently, the educator seeks the harmonisation of humankind with Nature from the very earliest age. From his viewpoint, the principle that establishes that all humans are equal is found in the relationship between childhood and Nature. Only by understanding the links between childhood, Nature, and God can individuals know themselves and accept their rightful place in our society. As a consequence of this process, we would have a better society. Froebel (1987) uses a triangle to represent the connections between God, Nature, and Humanity. Each of the three elements in the triangle is inseparable from the others. This triad forms what Froebel called the *Vital Unity*, on which education should be founded to promote the full development of the individual. Within this principle of Vital Unity, the processes of internalisation and externalisation are fundamental, as they lead to clarification of conscience and self-knowledge, that is, to education. Moulding and development occur thanks to what human beings receive from the external world, but become effective only when they know how to "touch their internal world." The process of internalisation consists of receiving knowledge from the outside world into the internal part of human beings, always following the same sequence: from the most simple to the complex, from the concrete to the abstract, from the known to the unknown. Activity and reflection are instruments of mediation in this non-directive process, as they guarantee that the seeds of knowledge will sprout and be discovered by the child in the most natural way. The opposite process is called externalisation, in which children express what is within them. Children need to work in concrete activities, such as art and play, which are excellent sources of externalisation. Once they externalise their internal self, they begin to become self-aware and understand themselves better. This is how education takes place. According to Froebel, education should be founded on the Vital Unity (Humanity, God, and Nature), and the processes of externalisation and internalisation should direct any methodology used with children. Such processes require actions to mediate them; they need life and activity and not words and concepts. Froebel regarded them as the concretisation of something natural within the children. Therefore, educators must always be attentive to these two processes, as all external activity is the fruit of the child's internal activity.

For Froebel, to act thinking and to think acting was the best way to avoid any kind of teaching that would impair or harm the development of the pupil's talents by being overly abstract. This method would allow the pupils to comprehend the triad, the guiding principle of their whole lives, thus opening the doors to attain perfection whereas still being human. To learn in doing, as proposed by Froebel, respects above all the natural methodology of children. According to him, the maxim that education should follow is "(...) to observe, only to observe, as the child itself will teach you" (cf. Cole 1907: 26). Only then will teachers be able to know their students, understand their internal dynamics, and discover their human essence, their talents. In his book, *Pedagogics of the Kindergarten*, Froebel (1917) reinforces this principle and affirms that all efforts of education and educators must be focussed on favouring the free and spontaneous development of the individual. Every human being, having been created by God, also possesses immense creativity.

Working with the Vital Unity principle in education enables the child to be aware of God's presence and of His works, especially those found in Nature. This kind of education also would allow children to recognise themselves within the Vital Unity, harmonising with it. Working in a fragmented form, a school cannot perceive this unity, and its work is impeded; the exterior and the interior are juxtaposed, making learning impossible. The educator should respect Nature, the action of God, and the spontaneous manifestations of the pupils. Education must follow their free development without being prescriptive, deterministic, or inventive, as this destroys the pure Nature origin of the pupil. Based on experience, this pedagogy centres around the orientation and awakening of the child's spontaneous activity, disseminating qualities and annihilating defects through the full development of the harmony between Humanity, God, and Nature.

In *The Education of Man* (1887), the German educator makes the first steps toward the utilisation of a developmental psychology as the basis for education. He divides human development into three stages that he presents in more detail than Pestalozzi: "man in earliest childhood, the boyhood of man and man as a scholar or pupil." Froebel attributes to each phase a type of education with specific characteristics. This is made clear in one of the passages, entitled "Man in Early Childhood." In this text, Froebel explains that if the adult observes play, for instance, or the speech of a child, he will be able to comprehend the level of development at which the child is. This means that the observation of a child's spontaneous activity, such as play or speech, is of great importance when undertaking educational activity.

To acquire self-knowledge with freedom, Froebel elects play as his major instrument, together with toys. Play is the mediator in this self-knowledge process through the exercise of externalisation and internalisation of the divine essence in each child, and thus causes the recognition and acceptance of the Vital Unity. Froebel was the first author to regard play as the activity through which children express their vision of the world. According to him, play is also the main activity in early-childhood development, which he considers the most important period of human life, a period that constitutes the source of all individual characteristics and personality traits. Therefore, play is a serious and important activity to those who really wish to know the child:

Play is the purest, most spiritual activity of man at this stage, and, at the same time, typical of human life as a whole – of the inner hidden natural life in man and all things. It gives, therefore, joy, freedom, contentment, inner and outer rest, peace with the world. It holds the sources of all that is good. A child that plays thoroughly, with self-active determination, perseveringly until physical fatigue forbids, will surely be a thorough, determined man, capable of self-sacrifice for the promotion of the welfare of himself and others. Is not the most beautiful expression of child-life at this time a playing child? – A child wholly absorbed in this play? – A child that has fallen asleep while so absorbed? As already indicated, play at this time is not trivial, it is highly serious and of deep significance. Cultivate and foster it, O mother; protect and guard it, O father! To the calm, keen vision of one who truly knows human nature, the spontaneous play of the child discloses the future inner life of the man. The plays of childhood are the germinal leaves of all later life; for the whole man is developed and shown in these, in his tenderest dispositions, in his innermost tendencies. The whole later life of man, even to the moment when he shall leave it again, has its source in the period of childhood – be this later life pure or impure, gentle or violent, quiet or impulsive, industrious or indolent, rich or poor in deeds, passed in dull stupor or in keen creativeness, in stupid wonder or intelligent insight, producing or destroying, the bringer of harmony or discord, of war or peace. His future relations to father and mother, to the members of the family, to society and mankind, to nature and God – in accordance with the natural and individual disposition and tendencies of the child – depend chiefly upon his mode of life at this period; for the child's life in and with himself, his family, nature, and God, is as yet a unit. Thus, at this age, the child can scarcely tell which is to him dearer – the flowers, or his joy about them, or the joy he gives to the mother when he brings or shows them to her, or the vague presentiment of the dear Giver of them. Who can analyze these joys in which this period is so rich? If the child is injured at this period, if the *germinal leaves of the future tree of his life are marred at this time, he will only with the greatest difficulty and the utmost effort grow into strong manhood; he will only with the greatest difficulty escape in his further development the stunting effects of the injury or the one-sidedness it entails.* (Froebel 1887: 55–56)

In his book *Pedagogics of the Kindergarten* (1917), Froebel reinforces the idea discussed earlier, expressing that play is the key for us to know and communicate with the small child. The author continues to highlight that play develops the human characteristics of the child, helping boys and girls to find and to exercise from the early years the roles that they will play in society.

Many human traits develop themselves in the child by its play with the doll, because thereby its own nature will become at some time objective, and hence recognizable to the child and to the thoughtful, observing parent and nurses. Hence there makes itself visible later, by and through this, the spiritual difference, the difference of vocation and life between the boy and the girl. The boy will be longer delighted with the play with the sphere and cube as separate and opposite things, while the little girl is, on the contrary, early delighted with the doll, which inwardly unites in itself the opposite of the sphere and cube. The inner significance of these facts is that the boy early presages and feels his destiny – to command and to penetrate outer Nature; and the girl anticipates and feels her destiny- to Foster Nature and life. (Froebel 1917: 93)

Froebel admits that games vary depending on the age of the child. The teacher should not underrate this aspect but, on the contrary, pay attention to it and work so as to facilitate the development of the child. In the chapter about childhood in *The Education of Man*, Froebel (1887) highlights the differences between games in early childhood and in boyhood. In early childhood, games are more centred on activity, movement, and the initial externalisation process of the child. In the period that Froebel calls boyhood, the game is more group-based. This produces the moral development of children and prepares them to live together in harmony.

(...) For, while during the previous period of childhood the aim of play consisted simply in activity as such, its aim lies now in a definite, conscious purpose; it seeks representation as such, or the thing to be represented in the activity. This character is developed more and more in the free boyish games as the boys advance in age. This is observable even with all games of physical movement, with games of running, boxing, wrestling, with ball-games, racing, games of hunting, of war, etc. It is the sense of sure and reliable power, the sense of its increase, both as an individual and as a member of the group, that fills the boy with all-pervading, jubilant joy during these games. It is by no means, however, only the physical power that is fed and strengthened in these games; intellectual and moral power, too, is definitely and steadily gained and brought under control. Indeed, a comparison of the relative gains of the mental and of the physical phases would scarcely yield the palm to the body. Justice, moderation, self-control, truthfulness, loyalty, brotherly love, and, again, strict impartiality – who, when he approaches a group of boys engaged in such games, could fail to catch the fragrance of these delicious blossomings of the heart and mind, and of a firm will; not to mention the beautiful, though perhaps less fragrant, blossoms of courage, perseverance, resolution, prudence, together with the severe elimination of indolent indulgence? Who ever would inhale a fresh, quickening breath of life should visit the playgrounds of such boys. Flowers of still more delicate fragrance bloom, and the spirited, free boy spares them as the spirited horse spares the child that lies in the path of his dashing career. These delicate blossoms, resembling the violet and anemone, are forbearance, consideration, sympathy, and encouragement for the weaker, younger, and more delicate; fairness to those who are as yet unfamiliar with the games. (Froebel 1887: 112–113)

In *Pedagogics of the Kindergarten*, Froebel (1917) also presents us with some toys he created to stimulate child play without harming natural development. He called his toys or educational materials *gifts* because they were a kind of *present* for the children. They were tools to help them discover their own gifts, that is, to discover the gifts that God had given each of them. With these toys, Froebel defined important concepts with respect to play. He observed, for instance, that play only works if the rules are well understood. The continuation of the game requires the introduction of new materials and ideas. For this reason, there are many occasions when adults should play with children to help them and to keep their interest alive. All Froebel's games using the gifts always began with the people forming a circle, dancing, moving, and singing so as to attain perfect unity. In this kind of play, Froebel also saw the great power that symbols had for children. Therefore, he elected games and toys as mediators not only of the child's process of apprehension of the world but also of his process of self-knowledge through externalisation. As a consequence, the creator of the kindergarten understood that toys and play could not be chosen at random. They must be studied so as to offer the children more adequate activities for their level of development.

It was in his kindergartens that the author sought to develop his work with the gifts fully. There he managed to unite all of his educational principles. According to Liebschner (1992), it was difficult for Froebel to find an adequate name for this kind of institution. He did not want to use the word "school," as he believed this would imply putting things into the minds of the children and teaching something, which was not the true purpose. The aim was to use play to guide, direct, and cultivate divine tendencies in children, their human essence, occupations, and free-time activities, such as God does with plants in Nature – the German word "kindergarten" (children's garden) manages to unite all these ideas and principles. Thus, the institution in which the above precepts could be applied in all their plenitude was created. Froebel naturalised children's development. Consequently, human development follows the same path, and education is subordinated to this process. The naturalised development process is the key to education, the principle on which it must be based.

## THE ACTIVITY THEORY AND PLAY — ELKONIN AND LEONTYEV AND CULTURAL HISTORICAL PSYCHOLOGY

In our attempt to make a comparison between Froebel and Cultural–Historical psychology, we cannot forget the fact that Froebel lived in a completely different cultural and social context. We must also recognise his pioneering spirit and his achievements, especially considering that he developed his conceptions at a time when psychology still had not become a field of science. When we compare Froebel on the one hand and Elkonin, Leontyev, and Vygotsky on the other, our focus is mainly on their ideas about human beings and society and, consequently, on their views on play and child development.

As we have mentioned previously, Froebel made important discoveries with respect to play and child development in his studies. However, his discussions centred on naturalised divine and universal childhood. Froebel believed that the fruit of divine childhood pertains to what is purest and best in the human being. Therefore, this period of human life requires time, just like a flower. This stage of human development should be preserved and kept from anything that might disturb it. For Froebel, there is a divine and eternal law, which governs child development and everything that exists in nature. Flouting this law would be the same as destroying the most perfect seed created by God: the child and its childhood.

In the first half of the twentieth century, a school of Soviet Marxist educators, producing their writings to build a socialist society in the Soviet Union, studied child development and the role of education in a way that was opposed to the Froebellian perspective. Among these researchers, we find Vygotsky, Leontyev, and Elkonin. But why would the approach of these Soviet Marxist scholars be different from Froebel's when considering child development and the role of play in the education of children below the age of six?

In his text *Toward The Problem of Stages in The Mental Development of Children*, Elkonin (2000) discusses the complex question of the division of child development in stages according to age groups or based on levels of cognitive development. In the second paragraph he affirms:

The correct solution of the problem of developmental periods will in large measure determine the strategy employed in constructing a comprehensive educational system for the coming generation in our country. The practical significance of this problem will increase as we approach the point when we must elaborate the principles for a unified public system of education encompassing the entire period of childhood. We must emphasize the fact that the construction of such a system in compliance with the laws of developmental stages of childhood is possible only within a socialist society; for it is only in such a society that has a maximum interest in the full and harmonious development of the abilities of every one of its members, and, consequently, in the fullest possible use of the potential of each development stage. (Elkonin 2000: 1)

Being a psychologist dedicated to the establishment of a socialist society, Elkonin understood that schooling should have the same aim. Only in this way would it contribute to the full development of the human being. Based on this dialectical materialist conception of man and society, Elkonin, Leontyev, and Vygotsky created a branch of psychology that studied human development and, as part of their studies, analysed the role of play in education and in child development in children under the age of six.

Unlike Froebel, these authors believed that childhood and development were closely connected to education and to the society in which the child is inserted. Elkonin (2000), whose theories were supported by Blonski, affirms that a universal, singular, and natural development of childhood does not exist. Child development may undergo changes in each historical setting. The children of today do not develop in the same way as those of the eighteenth century. Childhood is not immutable and eternal, nor does it depend mainly on the subjective element that exists in each individual, within his/her interior. Cultural, economic, social, and historical conditions are decisive factors in this development. Children living in the same historical period may present diverse processes of development as a consequence of the differences that exist in their activities. These activities are always cited within a specific social and cultural context. Elkonin, Leontyev, and Vygotsky did not believe in a human essence with its origin in the divine and spiritual. Had they based their studies of human development on this type of principle, they would be placing themselves well away from science and the Marxist presupposition that human beings make their own history and at the same time are made by history. Therefore, Leontyev states his views in a text entitled *Man and Culture*[1] :

If an intelligent being coming from another planet visited the Earth and described the physical, mental and aesthetic aptitudes, the moral qualities and the behavioral traits of men belonging to different classes and social strata or who dwell in different regions or countries, he would not easily admit to be dealing with representatives of the same species. But this inequality among men does not come from their natural biological differences. It is the product of economic inequality, of class inequality and of the consequent diversity of his relationships that flesh out all of the aptitudes and faculties of his human nature, which are formed over the discourse of his socio-historic process. (Leontyev 1978: 274)

This socio-historical theory of the formation of human beings is opposed to Froebel's conception. As we have already seen, he did not believe childhood was influenced and produced by the historical process of humanity as a whole. Froebel's romantic and idyllic view on human childhood enabled him to think of eternal, divine, natural, and universal development.

Vygotsky affirmed that child development is a dialectical process. The passage from one stage to another is marked not by simple evolution, as Froebel stated, but by a revolution that implies qualitative life changes within the child. This process cannot be aseptically separated from the insertion of the child within the society and the effect this has on his needs, motives, and intellectual development. Elkonin believed that the attempt to separate child development into different parts is a characteristic of the search for its naturalisation, given that this separation produces many of the dualisms that are present in various existing approaches in developmental psychology. Only by overcoming this form of development study can we be capable of fully understanding it.

---

[1] That compilation, entitled *The Development of Psyche*, is the translation of the French edition. Although most of the texts are the same in the English edition (Leontyev, 1981), some were just published in either one of them. This is the case of the text quoted here, which was not included in the English edition.

Underlying this dualism and parallelism is a naturalistic approach to the child's mental development (...). Such an approach, first of all, views the child as an isolated individual for whom society is merely 'an environing habitat' sui generis. Second, mental development is viewed merely as the process of adaptation to the conditions of life in society. Third, society is seen as the union of two mutually disjoint elements, a 'world of things' and a 'world of people', both of which are primordial elements of the given in this 'environing habitat'. Fourth, it is the development of two fundamentally distinct sets of adaptive mechanisms – for adaptation to the 'world of things' and to the 'world of people' – that constitutes mental development. Mental development, then, is viewed as the development of adaptive mechanisms within two mutually disjoint systems: the system of 'child-things' and the system of 'child-other people'. (Elkonin 2000: 4)

Leontyev, Elkonin, and Vygotsky's ideas about play and games in pre-school education appear within this theoretical framework. These authors agree that play is the leading activity in this period of childhood. Their starting point is a view of child development that is opposed to that of Froebel and their studies on play also provide different principles.

For Leontyev and Elkonin, whose views were also supported by Vygotsky, play is not an instinctive activity for the child. According to these authors, play is objective because it is an activity in which children make the real world of human beings their own in any way they can at this stage of development. These authors state that fantasy and imagination, which are indispensable components of play, do not have the function of providing children with a world that is different from that of adults. Instead, they open up the possibility of making the adult world their own, bridging the gap of impossibilities that children face when trying to accomplish the same tasks that are undertaken in the adult world. "The play action, it must be stressed, does not come from the imaginary situation, but the latter, on the contrary, is born from the discrepancy between the operation and the action; thus it is not imagination that determines the play action but the conditions of the play action that make imagination necessary and give rise to it" (Leontyev 1981: 374). For instance, when children play at being bus drivers, they need to use fantasy to substitute the operations carried out by a real bus driver for others that are within their reach. However, this is not a way of distancing themselves from the real world in which the bus driver exists, but an attempt to bring themselves closer and closer to it.

In preschool play a child's operations and actions are thus always real and social, and in them it assimilates human reality. Play (as Gorky said) really is 'children's path to understanding the world in which they live and which they are called on to change'. Play therefore does not at all arise from autistic fantasy, arbitrarily building the child's imaginary play world; the child's fantasy itself is necessarily engendered by the game, arising precisely on this path of the child's penetration of reality. (Leontyev 1981: 377)

Froebel believes that play is part of the child's nature, and as such it is the main activity of this age group and the only way children can express their internal world, know themselves, and harmonise themselves with the Vital Unity triad. Children need to symbolise their interior using objects, and play makes this symbolisation possible. It also helps children to discover their divine essence and allows the adult observing children at play to discover where these children are situated in the Creator's plans for human beings.

According to Leontyev and Elkonin, play is the leading activity in the pre-school period, but the reasons for this affirmation are different from Froebel's. To begin with, Leontyev describes the status of the leading activity in child development:

What is this 'leading type of activity?' Purely quantitative indices are by no means the criterion of leading activity. The leading activity is not simply the one most often encountered at a given stage of development, the activity that a child devotes much of its time to. We call leading activity that activity of a child that is characterized by the following three attributes. 1 – It is the activity in whose form other, new types of activity arise, and within which they are differentiated. For example, instruction in the narrowest sense of the term, which first develops already in preschool childhood, arises first in play, i.e. precisely in the leading activity of that stage of development. The child begins to learn by playing. 2 – Leading activity is the activity in which particular psychic processes take shape or are reorganized. The child's processes of active imagination, for example, are moulded first in play, and processes of abstract thinking in studies (...). 3 – Leading activity is the activity on which the main psychological changes in the child's personality observed at a given period of development depend in the closest way. It is precisely in play that the preschool child, for example, assimilates people's social functions and appropriate standards of behaviour ('What is a Red Armyman?', 'What does the director, the engineer, the worker do in a factory?'), and this is a very important moment of the moulding of its personality. Leading activity is therefore the activity whose development governs the chief changes in the psychic processes and psychological features of the child's personality at a given stage of its development. (Leontyev 1981: 396)

We can therefore see that play constitutes the leading activity because in pre-school aged children it provokes these *revolutions* in child development. Vygotsky (1984) believes it is incorrect to affirm that play is a prototype of the child's everyday activity. This statement does not contradict the theory developed by Leontyev and Elkonin, who stated that play, the leading activity of pre-school aged children, allows the child to act on a daily basis in a fantastical manner, moved by his imagination and not by objective reality. Leontyev clearly states that the rupture between sense and meaning that takes place while the child is at play ceases to exist when the activity stops. This means that, in everyday life, children act on the basis of their objective reality and do not allow themselves to be dominated by fantasy, which exists while they are at play.

Play, according to Vygotsky (1984: 117), is the leading activity because it creates a zone of proximal development for the child. In other words, when children play, they do things that are not typical of their age, interacting with the world around them and trying to comprehend it. Therefore, imagination appears to have an emancipating role: children use it when playing as a means to carry out operations that they do not undertake due to their age. When they play, children reproduce a real situation in which they extrapolate their real condition, using the imaginative aspect to help them make an impossible operation real. Make believe comes to the fore, according to Leontyev (1981), generating a discrepancy between the operation that must be undertaken (for instance, riding a horse) and the actions that are part of it (saddling the horse, mounting the horse, and so on). As children cannot use a real horse, they may for instance use a broomstick instead. This occurs because children have the process, not the action itself, as their objective. Another example is that of play with a doll. When a girl plays with this toy, she repeats or re-enacts things that happen in adult life, such as looking after a baby. By doing that, she imitates the way her mother takes care of her little brother or sister. This is why Vygotsky (1984: 177) states that play "is much more the reenactment of something that actually occurred than actions generated by imagination." Leontyev (1981) believes that all actions and operations that children at play undertake are real and social. Through them they seek to learn reality. Leontyev provides the example of some children enacting vaccination against smallpox. In this game, they imitated the real sequence of actions undertaken for vaccination. First, the skin was cleaned with alcohol, then the vaccine was given. The adult researcher observing the children proposed to them that they should use real alcohol, and they welcomed the idea with enthusiasm. He then said that he would get the alcohol from another room and told them to continue applying the vaccines while he was away, leaving the real alcohol for the end of the process. The children did not accept this suggestion. They preferred not to use alcohol but to keep the real sequence of events. From this example, Leontyev extracts the following conclusion:

In a game the conditions of the action can be changed: paper can be used instead of cotton wool, a sliver of wood from building material, or simply a stick, instead of a needle, imaginary liquid instead of surgical spirit, but the content and the sequence of the action must obligatorily correspond to the real thing.

(...) So we again reach a rather paradoxical result: we do not find any fantastic improbable elements in the structure of play in which there is so much fantasy. What does the consciousness of the playing child really reflect? First of all, the image of a real stick calling for real operations with it. Then the content of whatever action the child is reproducing in play, and reproducing with great pedantry, is reflected in its consciousness. Finally, there is the image of the object of the action, but there is nothing fantastic in it; the child imagines the horse, of course, quite adequately. So, in the psychological *premises* of the game *there are no fantastic elements*. There are a real action, a real operation, and real images of real objects, but the child, all the same, acts with the stick as with a horse, and this indicates that there is something imaginary in the game as a whole, which is the *imaginary situation*. In other words, the structure of play activity is such that an imaginary play situation arises. (Leontyev 1981: 373–374)

When playing, a child creates a rupture between the meaning and the sense or notion of an object. In other words, for a child, an object such as a small cylindrical piece of wood does not lose its meaning, but during play it can become a syringe for giving vaccines. It is important to point out that the child does not make this rupture either before beginning to play or after the game is finished. Only during the activity does imagination become necessary.

But what type of play is the most appealing to pre-school aged children, those ranging from three to six years of age? Role-playing games in which the child acts out a situation or imitates a person. According to Elkonin (1998: 31), in this type of game, the major influence is the realm of human activity, especially work and relationships among people. Therefore, the child is precisely trying to reconstruct these aspects of reality. This reality that surrounds the child, according to the author, may be divided into two spheres: that of the objects and that of human activity. At the beginning of their lives, children concentrate their activities on objects and on the actions that adults carry out with these objects. However, as the role-playing game begins to evolve, the focus is shifted to the relationships that adults establish among themselves, using the actions performed with those objects as guidelines. In other words, children become more interested in the relationships that exist among human beings and begin to reproduce them when they play.

Elkonin (1998: 35) states that human activity and relationships have such a great impact on role-playing games that, even though the theme may vary, the content always remains the same: "the activity of people and their social relationships with other people."

It is in the pre-school years that role-playing games develop intensely, and they reach their highest level when children leave the stage of manipulation of objects. It is important to point out that, according to Elkonin, it is necessary to allow children to face different situations and human productions, as the larger and richer their immersion into the world that surrounds them, the better children will develop their capacities. Elkonin states that:

(...) The basis of the game is precisely social and so is its nature and its origin. That is to say that play is born out of the living conditions of the child within society. The theories of play that are deduced from instinct and internal impulses in fact marginalize the question of their historical origin. At the same time, the history of the rise of role playing games is exactly the thing that can reveal its nature to us. (Elkonin 1998: 36)

Thus, Elkonin believes that role-playing games foster child development during the pre-school years. Play is one of the mechanisms that help children to learn the set of riches produced by humanity, while generating revolutions in their development. Given the importance of play at the pre-school age, Leontyev highlighted the necessity of controlling and guiding this leading activity to aid and enhance child development. Moreover, he emphasised the need to know in depth what play consists of, seeking to consciously understand the child's mental development at that age. Therefore Leontyev and Froebel held opposing points of view, as the latter thought that spontaneity was essential and led to naturalisation.

The leading role of play at the preschool age is recognized by practically everyone, but in order to master the process of the child's psychic development at this stage when play had the leading role, it is certainly insufficient just to recognize this role of play. It is necessary to understand clearly in just what the leading role of play consists; the laws of play and of its development have to be brought out. A child's mental development is consciously controlled mainly by controlling its main leading relation to reality, by controlling its leading activity. In this case play is the leading activity; it is consequently essential to know how to control a child's play, and to do that it is necessary to know how to submit to the laws of development of play itself, otherwise there will be a breakdown of play instead of control of it. (Leontyev 1981: 396)

### CONCLUSIONS

The study presented here has a preliminary character, as the brief exposition of both sets of theoretical approaches makes it possible to visualise the major distinctions between them. On the one hand we have Froebel harnessing childhood and child development to Nature and to the Divine, on the other we find Leontyev, Elkonin, and Vygotsky seeking to capture childhood within a set of aspects as a whole, aspects that make up our social organisation as the product of the history written by humanity. Therefore, Froebel points to a romantic and naturalised conception of both child development and play, whereas the Soviet school of psychology is based upon dialectical, Marxist, and historical materialism to study the same areas. Two different periods of human history have crossed paths within this text, as we have taken as our starting point a view of man and society centralised upon a mystical, subjective, naturalised, and alienated concept. It is one that regards man as an actor playing a role and a product of history, allowing him to apprehend this movement and the riches therein produced. We must also mention that Froebel influenced many educators and stood out as a pioneer within the movement that would later be called "Progressive Education" in North America and "New Education" or "Activity School" in Europe (Ferrière, 1927; Selleck, 1968). Thus, when we refer to his theoretical foundations, we must include all those educators who established similar principles underlying child development. Ferrière was very explicit in this respect: "the Education Movement in Europe had its theoretical origins in Rousseau, Pestalozzi, Herbart, Froebel and John Dewey" (Ferrière, 1927: VIII).

This implies that the attempt to conciliate the Activity Theory and the "Activity School" or "Progressive Education" is a rather problematic area. One of the aims of my brief analysis of Froebel's ideas is to question the parallelism defended by some contemporary authors in the field of the Activity Theory, such as Reijo Miettinen:

John Dewey's attempt to resolve the problem of schooling in industrialized society may be relevant here. Many features of Dewey's pragmatism are closely related to the central tenets of activity theory. Thus, it is not altogether surprising that his education vision proves to be rich source of insights for activity theoretical attempts to analyse and resolve contradictions of current school learning. (Miettinen, 1999: 331)

There are obvious differences between Froebel and Dewey, and we must therefore admit that the critical analysis of Froebel's thinking may not always reveal correspondences with Dewey's educational ideas. However, it is also evident that both authors belong to the same educational movement, which has its roots in distinct conceptions of the human being, society, and knowledge that are very different from that of Marxist authors. If we admit that the Activity Theory has its roots in Marxist dialectics (Ilyenkov, 1974, 1982), our conclusion can only be that the Activity Theory does not reflect Dewey's pragmatism, neither from the philosophical nor from the pedagogical point of view.[2]

A consistent articulation of the Activity Theory and education requires the development of Marxist studies in the field of the history of education. Such studies are necessary to enable us to go beyond the general criticism of the *traditional school* and to develop a pedagogy that gives value to the main role of schooling: the transmission of knowledge to new generations.

---

[2] For a critique of the philosophical ideas of pragmatism and neo-pragmatism, see the chapter entitled "Epistemological Scepticism, Complacent Irony: Investigations Concerning the Neo-pragmatism of Richard Rorty," by Maria Célia Marcondes de Moraes, included in this compilation. For a study of a pedagogy that applies the Marxist principles of the Activity Theory, refer to another chapter in this compilation, "Education as Mediation Between the Individual's Everyday Life and the Historical Construction of Society and Culture by Humankind," by Newton Duarte.

# 6

## Estranged ~~Labor~~ Learning

Ray McDermott and Jean Lave[1]

### INTRODUCTION

This chapter is in praise of the labor of reading profound and rich texts, in this case, the essay on "Estranged Labor" by Karl Marx. Comparing in detail what Marx wrote on estranged labor with current social practices of learning and education leads us to comprehensive and provocative ideas about learning – including the social practices of alienated learning. We then emphasize the importance of distribution in the institutionalized production of alienated learning. And we end this chapter with critical reflections on the importance of alienation for the relation between teaching and learning in the social practice of scholars.

In 1844, Karl Marx wrote "Estranged Labor," an essay with a radical philosophical and political claim: labor, prices, profit, and ownership do not exist as things independent of historical circumstance. Rather, they exist only in relations between persons and their productive work. To make matters worse, claimed Marx, the same is true of the words and categories we have available to understand, confront, and reorganize these building blocks or any other relations that define and control our lives: the very content of our minds "takes for granted what it is supposed to explain" (Marx, 1844: 106).[2] Together, the two claims have it that the world is both complex and hidden, terribly so and politically so, even to us, its builders.

Note: A previous version of this article appeared in *Outlines: Critical Social Studies*, 4(1), 2002.

[1] This chapter is a product of co-learning so intricate that questions of authorship feel inappropriate. The usual criteria – who did what, who did it first, who did how much – are the very stuff of estranged learning. For making a claim we must attend to, Karl Marx is the lead author, and the present paper is intended to be read in between two readings of Marx's essay on "Estranged Labor." Ole Dreier, Rogers Hall, Gill Hart, Rebecca Lave, Meghan McDermott, and Philip Wexler offered warm and helpful advice, and Seth Chaiklin's relentless critique forced us to phrase the limitations of our effort. In Tokyo, Naoki Ueno generously arranged the first public presentation of our struggles with the text. Our appreciation to each and all.

[2] Hereafter citations of "Estranged Labor" are limited to paragraph numbers (1–75).

To make the case, Marx delivered a phenomenon that, upon examination, could convince readers that every named thing in human life is tied to every other named thing in ways that (1) feed current arrangements in the political economy and, worse, (2) keep the logic and consequences of the arrangements obscure, hidden from their participants, and reflexively constitutive of problems participants might want to solve. Marx makes the case with a neat reversal of common-sense assumptions about the relation of labor to profit. Here are the four sentences of Paragraph 7:

The worker becomes poorer the more wealth he produces, the more his production increases in power and size.

The worker becomes an even cheaper commodity the more commodities he creates.

With the *increasing value* of the world of things proceeds in direct proportion the *devaluation* of the world of men.

Labor produces not only commodities: it produces itself and the worker as a commodity – and this in the same general proportion in which it produces commodities.

Counterintuitive? Yes. Arresting? No less. The harder someone works, the more the very same someone is rewarded. So goes Adam Smith's (1776) optimistic prognosis, and so now goes the cultural mainstream.[3] But Marx sees, and so does anyone who looks beyond immediate rewards, that many of the hardest at work get the least pay, rarely enough to make more than the necessities that bring them to work for another day: "labor produces for the rich wonderful things, but for the worker it produces privation" (paragraph 17). And then Marx sees further. Even those who are seemingly paid well are only paid off momentarily, until it is their turn, until their inalienable rights are also sold off, until alienation becomes the primary fact of their lives. People, all people in a capitalist society, labor only to have their products taken from them, alienated, literally alienated, turned over to others, and legally so. This is neither the spirit of capitalism nor the Protestant ethic as Max Weber (1904) stated them. If alienation is ubiquitous in the human situation, and most destructive under capitalism, there is reason for doubting where we stand, how, and why. There is reason for supposing that learning in schools might also be a commodified and alienated practice.

Theorizing economy as abstracted and isolated from ongoing activity was troublesome for Marx in 1844. Theorizing learning as abstracted from

---

3 The opening words of *The Wealth of Nations*: "The annual labor of every nation is the fund which originally supplies it with all the necessaries and conveniences of life which it annually consumes, and which consist always either in the immediate produce from other nations, or in what is purchased with that produce from other nations. According therefore, as this produce, or what is purchased with it, bears a greater or smaller proportion to the number of those who are to consume it, that nation will be better or worse supplied with all the necessaries and conveniences for which it has occasion" (Smith, 1776: lix).

situations of use and desire was similarly troublesome for Charles Dickens a decade later, as in the classroom of Gradgrind and M'Choakumchild:

"You are to be in all things regulated and governed," said the gentleman, "by fact. We hope to have, before long, a board of fact, composed of commissioners of fact, who will force the people to be a people of fact, and of nothing but fact. You must discard the word Fancy altogether. You have nothing to do with it. You are not to have, in any object of use or ornament, what would be a contradiction in fact. You don't walk upon flowers in fact; you cannot be allowed to walk upon flowers in carpets. You don't find that birds and butterflies come and perch upon your crockery. You cannot be permitted to paint foreign birds and butterflies upon your crockery. You never meet with quadrupeds going up and down walls; you must not have quadrupeds represented upon walls. You must use," said the gentleman, "for all these purposes, combinations and modifications (in primary colours) of mathematical figures which are susceptible of proof and demonstration. This is the new discovery. This is fact. This is taste." (Dickens, 1854: 11)

Learning seems long away from the school grind choking these children. Yet the people characterized by Dickens have built an institution just for learning, and there they insist children repeat on demand the facts of learning. They were hard on children who did not do it well. Factory life, "in all things regulated and governed," delivers a narrow range of fact for learning and a narrow range of categories for thinking about learning. Gradgrind's theory of learning no doubt "assumes what it is supposed to explain."

And what about now? The illusion of measured learning makes substantial what is not and reifies it into numbers that align children within hierarchies that replicate injustices in the distribution of access and rewards. Institutionalized education has done to the productive learner what Marx revealed was done to productive labor: schools have commodified learning to the point that every learner must worry more about what others know than about what might be learned if people worked together. The contemporary state offers schools in which every child, like every capitalist in the larger world, has to do better than everyone else. Similarly, every learner, like every laborer under capitalism, is alienated from his or her own learning by virtue of the dominant concern for what every person does and does not know relative, and only relative, to each other.

Marx opposed a double-entry account book version of the human situation – the version that records how much money comes in, against how much money goes out, with as much as possible left over for profit. Dickens agrees: the same "just the facts" bottom line version strangling labor could strangle learning as well. Imagine Marx's response to the pretest/posttest, double-entry account book version of the human mind that we use today to strangle children in schools.

On the chance that reading Marx as if he were writing on estranged learning can suggest what he would say about contemporary schooling and give us as well a new slant on the political economy of learning, we have been rereading "Estranged Labor" and keeping track of the changes that follow from our initial alteration. Our method, to use Seamus Heaney's (2000) phrasing, pays careful "duty to text," loaded with our own concerns, of course, but careful to take Marx seriously on his own terms.[4] The rewrite starts as simply as dutifully: Whenever the word labor occurs, with occasional exceptions, it is replaced by the word learning. Marx's argument and imagery stay intact, and we get to approximate his opinion on an issue of moment over a century later. "Estranged Labor" uses about 5,000 words grouped into approximately 75 paragraphs (depending on the edition), and we have found it productive to spend more than an hour on many paragraphs translating from the English of political economy to the English of learning theory. This method of "reading" has led to a deepened understanding of Marx's essay with unanticipated ideas about the relations between estranged labor and estranged learning. It has helped us critique – in parallel and simultaneously – theories of political economy and theories of learning, and it has led to questions about how ideas of learning, intelligence, creativity, genius, stupidity, and disability have developed in tandem with ideas about production, consumption, exchange, and distribution.

Because we allow our analytic path to develop in detail along with Marx's text, the reader might need an account of where we are going. Simply put, in critiquing the theories of political economy available in 1844, young Marx unwittingly wrote a quite devastating critique of the theories of learning available in 2004. This is possible because education has been institutionalized under advanced capitalism as an integral part of the political economy. In *Capital*, twenty-three years later, Marx gave a strong hint of the relation between the two spheres of production:

If we may take an example from outside the sphere of material production, a schoolmaster is a productive worker when, in addition to belaboring the heads of his pupils, he works himself into the ground to enrich the owner of the school. That the latter has laid out his capital in a teaching factory instead of a sausage factory, makes no difference to the relation. (1867: 677)

The same critique applies to the workings of both economy and education because they are two facets of the same history, two versions of institutions rooted in alienated relations of production, consumption, distribution, and exchange, one officially of goods, the other officially of ideas, and in both cases, two sides of the same coin, the filthy lucre of commodified manual and mental labor.[5]

---

4 Translating from one topic to another demands more than a subjectivism: "the self-consciousness of one facing a text in a distant language, should not be confused with subjectivism, as some have suggested, for it is just the opposite – a respect for another voice, not an obsession with one's own" (Becker, 1995: 138).

5 We are not the first to reread "Estranged Labor" in other institutional registers: For a congruence, variously conceived, between Marx on estranged labor and language, see Volosinov

In addition to what we might learn about Marx, about learning, and about Marx on learning, there is a historical continuity behind our re-reading. It is close to how Marx himself proceeded. He read voluminously – Smith, Hegel, Feuerbach, Hess, Proudhon – and would enter into his notes systematic changes in their phrasing. Even the older Marx, in *Capital* (1867) and the *Ethnological Notebooks* (1880–1882), manipulated textual detail. Lobkowicz gives a glimpse of Marx at work around the time of "Estranged Labor":

> Commenting upon Hegel's text paragraph by paragraph, and sometimes word by word, more often than not he became lost in a thicket of verbal arguments instead of trying to survey Hegel's political philosophy as a whole. Still this piecemeal procedure brought forth some remarkable results. (1967: 249–250; see also Struik, 1964; Wheen, 1999)

Sometimes Marx would keep track of his editing, sometimes not.[6] A good example of his making analytic use of his changes comes from the following commentary, in *Theories of Surplus Value* (1860, Book 2: 349–50), on a paragraph from Adam Smith (1776, Book I, Chapter IV: 61), which Marx underlines as he reads (here in italics) and adds, first, a running commentary in parentheses inside Smith's paragraph, then a comment on the paragraph, and finally a rewrite of Smith side by side with Smith's own words:

"As in a civilized country there are but few commodities of which the *exchangeable value* arises *from labour only*" (here labour is identified with wages) "*rent* and *profit* contributing largely to that of the far greater part of them, so the *annual produce of its labour*" (here, after all, the commodities are the *produce of labour*, although the whole value of this produce does not arise from labour only) "will always be sufficient to *purchase* or *command a much greater quantity of labour than what was employed in raising, preparing and bringing that produce to market.*"

Marx's comment on and rewrite of Smith's paragraph:

The produce of *labour* [is] not equal to the *value* of this produce. On the contrary (one may gather) this value is *increased* by the addition of profit and rent. The produce of labour can therefore command, purchase, more labour, i.e., pay a greater value

---

(1929) and Rossi-Landi (1968); on estranged labor and science, Sohn-Rethel (1976); on estranged labor and sexuality, MacKinnon (1982).

[6] An example of not making his edits visible: "in a 'translation' from French to German of Peuchet's essay on suicide," Marx (1945) "bends [the] text a bit, here changing Peuchet's phrase 'fundamental defect' to 'deficient organization' and thereby making the critique more social and less moralistic. At another point, without indicating that he has done so, Marx adds a phrase of his own, writing that 'short of a total reform of the organization of our current society,' any attempt to lower the suicide rate 'would be in vain'" (Anderson, 1999: 13).

in labour, than the labour contained in it. This proposition would be correct if it ran like this:

| *Smith says:* | *According to Marx himself, it should read:* |
|---|---|
| "As in a civilized country there are but few commodities of which the *exchangeable value* arises *from labour only*, rent and profit *contributing* largely to that of the far greater part of them, so the annual produce of its labour will always be sufficient to purchase or command a much greater *quantity of labour* than *what was employed in raising, preparing, and bringing that produce to market.*" | "As in a civilized country there are but few commodities of which the *exchangeable value* resolves itself into *wages* only and since, for a far greater part of them, this value largely *resolves* itself into rent and profit, so the annual produce of its labour will always be sufficient to purchase or command a much greater *quantity of labour* than what had to be *paid*" (and therefore employed) "in raising, preparing, and bringing that produce to market." |

This is roughly the genre of translation we are offering. There is a version of science ideally done this way, but not enough of it. Apprenticeship to text may be far easier than duty to children in school, but they are identical in their respect for complexity, their delight in cooperative learning, and their appreciation of surprise.

We are engaged in reading and learning about alienated labor, alienated learning, and relations between them. We try to show what it is like to re-braid the text after introducing one significant change of topic, and then to move forward by trying different ways of recasting what follows to deepen the rewriting. We have read this text together and with students many times. Still, it would be a mistake to think of the rewrite as a concluded, polished, definitive "translation" displayed for the reader's consumption. It is not our intention to be supposed experts on Marx, nor are we offering a predigested account of our knowledge on work. Instead, if we can share our work bench, readers might follow the *process* of reading and re-reading, and work with our re-writing in their own way, on their way to working further on "Estranged Labor" and other texts.

The first two parts of the paper stay closer to how we did the work and the textual changes that developed along the way. Marx should not be read quickly, and our play with his text certainly insures that the reader has to slow down. In Part I, we offer the first paragraph of Marx's essay and explain how we worked out a sense for the demands of the text and its possibilities, for what Becker (1995) calls deficient and exuberant readings of the text. In Part II, we move to an only slightly quicker account of Paragraphs 2–4 for a gloss of Marx's argument, and we apply our changes to institutional education in general and the diagnosis of learning disability and the ascription of genius in particular.

After working through the thorny thickets of paragraphs 1–4, readers might benefit from a view of the forest. "Estranged Labor" elaborates a theory of alienated labor in four successive steps encompassing the first half of Marx's essay. Part III of "Estranged ~~Labor~~/Learning" does the same, rereading the main points of that theory in terms of alienated learning. Part IV is a selective rereading of the second half of Marx's essay. At one point, Marx proposes an exercise for the reader, and we take up the challenge. He suggests that relations internal to the keywords of political economy can be derived from alienated labor and private property. For our exercise, we focus on education as a distributional phenomenon and – still engaged in a process of re-reading "Estranged Labor" as "Estranged ~~Labor~~/Learning" – explore how alienated distribution can be derived from alienated learning and private (educational) property. Our intervention challenges common ways of reading Marx and brings his work to bear on a current concern. It is serious work done twice. At the end of the paper, we draw together what we have learned about alienated learning and consider its relations with our practice of reading.

### PART I: ALIENATED CATEGORIES

In the beginning is Marx's first paragraph:

We have proceeded from the premises of political economy. We have accepted its language and its laws. We presupposed private property, the separation of labor, capital and land, and of wages, profit of capital and rent of land – likewise division of labor, competition, the concept of exchange-value, etc. On the basis of political economy itself, in its own words, we have shown that the worker sinks to the level of a commodity and becomes indeed the most wretched of commodities; that the wretchedness of the worker is in inverse proportion to the power and magnitude of his production[7]; that the necessary result of competition is the accumulation of capital in a few hands, and thus the restoration of monopoly in a more terrible form; and that finally the distinction between capitalist and land rentier, like that between the tiller of the soil and the factory worker, disappears and that the whole of society must fall apart into the two classes – the property *owners* and the propertyless *workers*.

Now we can develop our own first paragraph. Once we have turned the topic from labor to learning, we must alter the first sentence: "We have proceeded from the premises of. . . ."

Many substitutes are possible: educational psychology, most specifically; educational ideology, most politically; the educational establishment, most generally. Our choice is to use the most general reading, and if the text insists

---

[7] As written, Marx describes a direct relation: the more richly the world's possibilities are produced by workers, the more workers are deprived of them; usually, he makes the same point by describing an inverse relation: as workers produce more and more for those who pay their wages, they receive less and less of what they are producing for themselves. We comment only because this phrase has brought our reading to a halt repeatedly.

on a tighter formulation, that can be made obvious as we move through the paragraph. So we have our first line, and the second line is generic enough to require no change:

> We have proceeded from the premises of *the educational establishment.*
> We have accepted its language and its laws.

Now it gets difficult. Marx gives us:

> We presupposed private property,
> the separation of labor, capital and land,
> and of wages, profit of capital and rent of land –
> likewise division of labor, competition, the concept of exchange-value, etc.

As a substitute for private property, one of us suggested "controlled and standardized knowledge (curriculum)" and the other suggested "inherent intelligence":

> a.  We presupposed *standardized knowledge (curriculum)*...
> b.  We presupposed *inherent intelligence*...

This is a difference that seems to make a difference, the first focused, as Marx would appreciate, on an institutional phenomenon, the educational banking system (Freire 1969), and the second focused more on the individual account, or seemingly so, and available for institutional analysis only after careful thought. The differences hardly make themselves felt in the rest of the sentence:

> We presupposed *standardized knowledge (curriculum),*
> the separation of *learning, academic success, and natural capacities,*
> and of *grades, credentials, and earning potential*–...
> We presupposed *inherent intelligence,*
> – the separation of *learning, knowledge, and assessed potential,*
> and of *learning, degrees, and success*–...

If we continue to follow the two choices – curriculum vs. intelligence – through subsequent paragraphs, they do not organize readings as divergent as we anticipated. Although inherent intelligence at first invites other psychological terms to populate its semantic tree, it gives way to a picture of the institutional arrangements that make an exaggerated attention to measured intelligence, reportable, recordable, and consequential. We can use *standardized knowledge* (in the first line of translation a.), which constrains only slightly our choices for the second line. We cannot resist combining the translations of "rent of land"; instead of "natural capacities" (in the second line of a.) and "assessed potential" (in the second line of b.), we opt for *assessed capacities,* for there are two uses of the word "assessment" in modern

English: one for measuring land value, the other for measuring the value of a person's mind. The fit is difficult to ignore.

The remainder of the sentence stands on its own:

> – likewise division of labor, competition, the concept of exchange-value, etc.

In education as in political economy, the division of labor is ubiquitous in its relevance. Competition is everywhere. The concept of exchange-value, by which everything is theoretically exchangeable for everything else, for example, knowledge in exchange for career line and/or profit, speaks to the heart of what most people seek when they go to school (and certainly what people must attend to when they leave school). So now we have three sentences rewritten:

We have proceeded from the premises of *the educational establishment.* We have accepted its language and its laws. We presupposed *standardized knowledge (curriculum),* the separation of *learning, academic success, and assessed capacities,* and of *grades, credentials, and earning potential* – likewise division of labor, competition, the concept of exchange-value, etc.

We have translated "capital" into *academic success* and "profit from capital" into *credentials.* Both, of course, are won in competition: academic success is always achieved over others, and credentials are less about what they allow their owners to do than their non-owners not to do. This is consistent with Marx's haiku-like definition of capital in the *Manuscripts*:

> Capital,
> private property
> taken from other people's labor?
>     (1844: 79, poetic license ours)

Good news: with variation, changes made in the first paragraph can last through the essay. The variations are interesting to trace, but are mostly self-explanatory. In Tables 6.1 and 6.2, we separate the terms we had to change (as we began analytically to pull apart, first, labor and learning and, second, political economy and education) from a few terms we did not have to change because they apply equally to both of these thoroughly enmeshed spheres of production.

*Nota bene*: The conceptual shifts are not one-to-one. The concepts in Marx's text are mutually defined, and so it must be for the educational terms. The changes must be read from top to bottom as well as from left to right. The appearance of a one-to-one correspondence across terms would require the assumption of a one-to-one, and likely distorting, fit between political economy and education. The power of the rewrite lies ultimately in the relations among and across both sets of concepts as they have been historically established and fitted to different spheres of activity across quite

TABLE 6.1. *Conceptual Changes – Political Economy to Education*

---

Paragraph 1: Initial rewriting of Marx's concepts of political economy into educational terms (variations from later paragraphs are listed in parentheses)

   political economy and its classical theory → educational establishment and its
      theory (educational theory, learning theory)
   private property → controlled and standardized knowledge (curriculum
      and tests)
   labor → learning
   capital → academic success (achievement), all at the expense of others
   land → capacities (access)
   wages → grades
   profit of capital → credentials, appropriated from others
   rent of land → assessed capacities
   capitalist → knowledge accumulator (scientists and scholars)
   land rentier → knowledge distributors (teachers and testers)
   his (man, him, he) → their (humankind, people, she and he)

---

different time lines. Although we stress similarities across concepts that serve both theories of political economy and theories of education, what does not translate is just as revealing, as when we argue, in Part IV, that production in education might be more akin to what Marx calls distribution in political economy.

The rest of the first paragraph turns into education as it might get articulated in a class-based democracy:

On the basis of *educational theory* itself, in its own words, we have shown that the *learner* sinks to the level of a commodity and becomes indeed the most wretched of commodities; that the wretchedness of the *learner* is in inverse proportion to the power and magnitude of his production; that the necessary result of competition is the accumulation of *academic success* in a few hands, and thus the restoration of monopoly in a more terrible form; and that finally the distinction between the *knowledge accumulator (scientist and scholar)* and the *knowledge distributor (teacher and tester)*, like that between the *kinds of learner*, disappears and that the whole

TABLE 6.2. *Conceptual Continuity – Political Economy and Education*

---

Paragraph 1: Concepts applicable to both domains (variations from later paragraphs are listed in parentheses)

   division of labor
   competition (meritocracy, showing off )
   exchange-value
   production
   commodity
   monopoly (nobility, knowledge)

---

of society must fall apart into the two classes – the credentialed and the non-credentialed.[8]

## PART II: ALIENATED PROBLEMS AND ALTERNATIVES

For the next three paragraphs, Marx develops his argument: Experts on political economy can populate the world with supposed entities abstracted from the sensuous give and take of daily life and then struggle to write laws for how the entities interact, but they cannot explain how the entities have developed historically along with the partial perspectives that make them look real. For most modern thought, reality has been irremediably perspectival, but for Marx, all perspectives are also irremediably political. Objective reality not only depends on where one is standing, but where one is standing in relation to everyone else, whether measured by lineage, money, or access to power.[9] Might the same be true for a critique of theories of education? Might where one stands in relation to everyone else be measured as easily by grades earned as by lineage, money, or access? For Paragraphs 2–4, we present the economic arguments of "Estranged Labor" and the educational arguments of "Estranged Labor/Learning" side-by-side for an easy to view contrast:

Paragraph 2:

| | |
|---|---|
| (2) Political economy starts with the fact of private property, but it does not explain it to us. It expresses in general, abstract formulas the *material* process through which private property actually passes, and these formulas it then takes for *laws*. It does not *comprehend* these | (2) *The educational establishment* starts with the fact *of standardized knowledge*, but it does not explain it to us. It expresses in general, abstract formulas the *material* process through which *curriculum* actually passes, and these formulas it then takes for *laws*. It does |

---

[8] A note on the concept of production: In "Estranged Labor," the internal relations of "production" that give it its meaning are labor under capitalism, workers' relations with what they produce in the workplace, workers' relations with capital and capitalists, and relations between alienated labor and private property. We explore comparable relations among learners, their self-formation, learning, the commodified products of learning in schools, learners' relations with teachers, schools, and the educational establishment including its theorists and apologists. We compare the latter to the classical political economists, exploring with respect to educational theory Marx's critique of political economic theory. Later in the chapter we consider production/distribution relations as a matter of alienated labor and learning. We are aware that exploration of the relations between political economy and education potentially raises distinctions between production and reproduction, distinctions of which we are critical. To maintain a critical perspective, we must remember that relations between labor and learning, political economy and education, the learning implied in estranged labor and the labor in estranged learning, are multiple and entangled.

[9] Objective reality: "all that is appropriate to, noticeable within, and marked by the self-directed, or practical, actions of collectivities in situations of conflict" (Brown, 1986:15).

laws, i.e., it does not demonstrate how they arise from the very nature of private property. Political economy does not disclose the source of the division between labor and capital, and between capital and land. When, for example, it defines the relationship of wages to profit, it takes the interest of the capitalists to be the ultimate cause, i.e., it takes for granted what it is supposed to explain. Similarly, competition comes in everywhere. It is explained from external circumstances. As to how far these external and apparently accidental circumstances are but the expression of a necessary course of development, political economy teaches us nothing. We have seen how exchange itself appears to it as an accidental fact. The only wheels which political economy sets in motion are *greed* and the war amongst the greedy – competition.

not *comprehend* these laws, i.e., it does not demonstrate how they arise from the very nature of *standardized knowledge*. *Educational theory* does not disclose the source of the division between *learning and achievement*, and between *degrees and assessed capacity*. When, for example, it defines the relationship of *grades to credentials*, it takes the interest of the *knowledge accumulators* to be the ultimate cause i.e., it takes for granted what it is supposed to explain. Similarly, competition comes in everywhere. It is explained from external circumstances. As to how far the external and apparently accidental circumstances are but the expression of a necessary course of development, *educational theory* teaches us nothing. We have seen how *teaching/learning exchanges* and *knowledge distribution* appear as accidental fact. The only wheels which *educational theory* sets in motion are *ambition* and the war amongst the *ambitious* – competition.

---

Substitutions become more complex in Paragraph 3. The argument is more layered, and each substitution must be paired across levels of analysis. In Paragraphs 1–2, Marx could say we had terrible problems and little analytic vocabulary for confronting them, an argument that holds for education as well as political economy. In Paragraph 3, Marx claims that the resolutions we devise for our historic problems are not only inadequate, but systematic products of, and thereby reflexively constitutive of the very same problems. In defining a problem and articulating a possible solution, it is possible to lose sight of the conditions that created the problem and move forward with the proposed solution:

Precisely because political economy does not grasp the way the movement is connected, it was possible to oppose, for instance, the doctrine of competition to the doctrine of monopoly, the doctrine of the freedom of the crafts to the doctrine of the guild, the doctrine of the division of landed property to the doctrine of the big estate – for competition, freedom of the crafts and the division of landed property were explained and comprehended only as accidental, premeditated and violent consequences of monopoly, of the guild system, and of feudal property, not as their necessary, inevitable and natural consequences.

It is a difficult paragraph. In Table 6.3, we offer a schematic of how Marx develops the argument in three parts of four steps each:

TABLE 6.3. *The Logic of Paragraph 3*

| Problem | invites | Apparent Solution | because | Apparent Causes | masking | Real Conditions |
|---|---|---|---|---|---|---|
| Doctrine of Monopoly | ←→ | Doctrine of Competition | ← | Accident | ← // ← | Necessity |
| Doctrine of Freedom of Guilds | ←→ | Doctrine of Freedom of Crafts | ← | Premeditation | ← // ← | Inevitability |
| Doctrine of Big Estates | ←→ | Doctrine of Division of Landed Property | ← | Violence | ← // ← | Naturalness |

It is tempting to read Marx's argument from left to right, across the rows one column at a time, as if the problem and solution pairs, say Monopoly ←→ Competition, could be understood, mistakenly, as caused by Accident, whereas the real connection is one of Necessity. Because we cannot always tell the difference between Necessity, Inevitability, and Naturalness and do not always see reasons for traditional political economists choosing between Accident, Premeditation, and Violence, we have merged these categories considerably. So we have three problem and solution pairs, each accounted for, inadequately, by Accident, Premeditation, and Violence, whereas each might be better accounted for by Necessity, Inevitability, and Naturalness.

1. In an economy of monopolistic control, access to competition must look like a wonderful alternative. But monopolies are the systematic outcome of competition run amuck. Monopolies make competition visible and attractive. It is not noticed that the institutionalized competition that led to monopolies *necessarily, inevitably, and naturally* led to a reform by the invocation of still more competition.[10]

2. In an economy of repressive guilds, access to free crafts must look like a wonderful alternative. Guilds are the systematic outcome of access to a market run amuck. Guilds make free crafts visible and attractive. It is not noticed that the market freedoms that led to repressive guilds *necessarily, inevitably, and naturally* led to a reform by the invocation of still more freedom.

3. In an economy of big estates, access to a more equitable division of landed property must look like a wonderful alternative. Big estates

---

[10] So long as there is no disruptive transformation in the terms of debate, prescriptions for "new solutions" inevitably end up reproducing old problems, albeit in new trappings. We read "*necessarily, inevitably, and naturally*" (the italics belong to Marx) in hegemonic terms, not as a statement of absolute determination.

are the systematic outcome of the relations of private property run amuck. Big estates make individual land holding visible and attractive. It is not noticed that the rules of land ownership that led to big estates *necessarily, inevitably, and naturally* led to a reform by the invocation of still more private ownership.

Now we can rewrite Marx to see if it gives us an account of a reasonable, but invidious pairing between educational problems and educational solutions, all produced in ways that confuse "*accidental, premeditated, and violent consequences*" with "necessary, inevitable, and natural" ones. As Marx gives three examples, we give three examples. Marx's examples – struggles to replace monopolies with competition, guilds with free crafts, and large estates with a more equitable division of land – are quite distinct from each other. Our educational examples – struggles to replace access to knowledge by elites only with a meritocracy, replacing education by privilege with equal access to education, and transforming an enforced conformity to a cultural cannon with self-cultivation – seem less distinct. As much as we are pointing to the continuities from political economy to education, the differences are also instructive. Marx was talking about large social changes across many centuries, whereas we are focusing on much smaller changes within a specific institutional setting across the last century.

[Paragraph 3] Precisely because *educational theory* does not grasp the way the movement is connected, it was possible to oppose, for instance, the doctrine of *meritocracy* to the doctrine of *elite knowledge*, the doctrine of *level playing field* to the doctrine of *privileged access*, the doctrine *of cultivation of the self (individualism and multiculturalism)* to the doctrine of *a forced allegiance to a cultural* – for *meritocracy, level playing fields*, and *self-cultivation* were explained and comprehended only as accidental, pre-meditated and violent consequences of *nobility*, of *privileged access*, and of *a forced allegiance to a cultural cannon*, not as their necessary, inevitable and natural consequences.

1. The enforcement of a meritocracy may well look better than inheritance by a nobility, but neither challenges the principle of unequal access. The systematic outcome of competition among elites run amuck, displays of inherited knowledge make competition visible and attractive, if only because they developed together, as part of the same economic circumstances. It is not noticed that the institutionalized competitions that led to inherited entitlement *necessarily, inevitably, and naturally* led to a reform by the invocation of still more competition.

2. Equal access to education certainly sounds preferable to access to expertise by privilege, but it leaves hierarchy eventually in place. The systematic outcome of access to a market run amuck, expertise by privileged access makes meritocracy visible and attractive. It is not noticed

that the institutionalized freedoms that led to repressive expertise *necessarily, inevitably, and naturally* led to a reform by the invocation of still more expertise.

3. A focus on self-cultivation (self-realization, self-actualization, self-efficacy) simply wallows in decency in contrast with an enforced celebration of elite culture, but, no matter how hard fought for, individual rights are hollow until paired with control of the conditions for staging selves in relation to each other; in education, a focus on the motivated cognitive self seems an improvement over *race* and *gender* as explanations for school success and failure. Even if successfully claimed, it can still leave everyone relatively mired in place until the conditions for redefining knowledge, intelligence, and success are more in the service of the poor and disenfranchised than in the service of the already rich and knowledgeable. The systematic outcome of commodified selves run amuck, enforced conformity to a cultural cannon, makes a private cultivation of the self visible and attractive.[11] It is not noticed that the cult of well-groomed self-expression that led to the successful individual as the center of social relations *necessarily, inevitably, and naturally* led to a reform by the invocation of still more attention to personal desire.

The logic of Marx's argument in Paragraph 3 lends itself to a more extended reading of problem and solution pairs popular in contemporary education. For example, two products of contemporary educational theory are learning disabled children and geniuses. The first is about seventy years old. The second has a longer history (Latin: genio), but has referred to a single person consistently of great ability for only about 300 or 400 years.[12]

---

[11] On this point, see an excellent discussion by Wexler (1983, 1993).

[12] See Murray (1988) for historical biographies of the term "genius" in use and DeNora and Mehan (1993) on the relation between genius and learning disabilities. A rough reconstruction of genius, starting with Huarte (1575), distinguishes:

- a medieval and renaissance genius as the medium of moment for rare gifts from supernatural sources, often tied to madness, mystical states, and drunkeness;
- an eighteenth-century genius, still rare, as a kind of person across context and circumstance;
- a turn-of-the-nineteenth-century genius, less rare, as a social role, with every generation its representatives;
- the romantic nineteenth-century genius, as role and goal, sought after, trained for, and dependent on others to realize and celebrate.

In the late nineteenth century, the very idea of genius begins to fragment and becomes:

- an inheritance and soon thereafter a genotype,
- a stereotype in invidious racial comparisons,
- an identifier of what most people are not, and therefore a source of unproductive alienation.

If the terms have developed along with the rise of capitalism, they should fit into Marx's critique of terms from political economy.

And sure enough, Learning Disability (which is, so they say, smart, but not quick to learn reading and writing) could develop as an alternative to a school system that was rendering so many children officially stupid, a theory of multiple intelligences could hold out hope for school failures, and appeals to self-esteem could be opposed to the hard truth that, in a system in which everyone has to do better than everyone else, there is only so much self-esteem to go around (McDermott, 1993; Mehan, 1993). Paragraph 3 translates easily into disability discourse:

Learning Disabilities in Paragraph 3:

Precisely because *learning theory* does not grasp the way the movement is connected, it was possible to oppose, for instance, the doctrine of *learning disability* to the doctrine of *stupidity*, the doctrine of *multiple intelligences* to the doctrine of *one general intelligence*, the doctrine of *self-esteem (individualism and multi-culturalism)* to the doctrine of *institutional discipline* – or *learning disabilities, multiple intelligences,* and *self-esteem* were explained and comprehended only as accidental, pre-meditated and violent consequences of *theories of stupidity, general intelligence, and institutional discipline*, not as their necessary, inevitable and natural consequences.

Similarly, genius can be read as a possible solution to the problem of how to talk about persons who think in new ways in a system articulate about, gauged by, and limited to celebrating performances by a chosen few on tests with a culturally pre-established content in a predigested format. Through the middle ages, the category of genius overlapped considerably with madness, and creativity was easily confused with special breeding and high birth. A few centuries later, the same people were more likely to be thought of as ingenious, exceptional, and creative individuals. This seems like a great improvement until the search for creativity became routinized into a search, by way of IQ tests and the like, for children who know what has been predefined as knowledge by adults. The limits of the first system of categories (genius as madness) invites solutions (genius as conformity) that get reworked to fit new relations of production, consumption, exchange, distribution, and representation. If intelligence cannot be measured by how much a person knows the answers to standardized questions, but is better tested by what a person does when no one knows what to do, then high degrees of intelligence, of genius, should be virtually unrecognizable and certainly untestable by non-geniuses working at testing services. The world of tests offers no new terrain for brilliance, and if it did, who would be able to grade it?

Genius in Paragraph 3:

Precisely because *learning theory* does not grasp the way the movement is connected, it was possible to oppose historically, for instance, the doctrine of *genius* to the doctrine of *madness*, the doctrine of *exceptional individuals* to the doctrine of *privileged access*, the doctrine of *creativity* to the doctrine of *high birth and good breeding* – for *genius, exceptional individuals,* and *creativity* were explained and comprehended only as accidental, premeditated and violent consequences of *madness, privileged access, and high birth*, not as their necessary, inevitable and natural consequences.

Paragraph 4 nicely sums up the situation from the point of view of political economy and educational theory[13]:

| | |
|---|---|
| (4) Now, therefore, we have to grasp the essential connection between private property, greed, and the separation of labor, capital and landed property; between exchange and competition, value and the devaluation of men, monopoly and competition, etc. – the connection between this whole estrangement and the money system. | (4) Now, therefore, we have to grasp the essential connection between *standardized knowledge, ambition*, and the separation of *learning, achievement*, and *access*; between *teaching* and competition, between *diagnostic assessment* and the devaluation of *children*, between *knowledge and showing-off*, etc. – the connection between this whole estrangement and the *educational banking* system. |

## PART III: ALIENATED LEARNING

Alienation, Marx tells us in four steps, is created, first, in labor's products (paragraphs 7–8) and, second, in the process of laboring (paragraphs 20–23). Third, it follows from the first two that alienation characterizes human relations with nature and with the self (paragraphs 25–36). Finally and together, these relations result in the alienation of everyone from everyone else (paragraphs 36–42). These four aspects form the armature of the concept of alienation in "Estranged Labor."[14]

---

[13] The theoretical "essential connections" of paragraph 4 should not be construed as fixed in functionalist terms, for those very essential connections in practice – like those we are discussing in relation to schooling – slip, twist, get mangled and transformed, often sustained by efforts to address what they are supposed to be, but are no longer.

[14] There is an order to the way Marx analyzes estranged labor. He proceeds dialectically from abstract accounts of how labor functions in capitalism and gradually rises to a concrete historical comprehension of real persons suffering estrangement. Marx gives flesh to the concept of alienation as he moves from:

– the abstract political-economic fact of alienation in production (in the first sentence of paragraph 7:

"The worker becomes poorer the more wealth he produces, the more his production increases in power and size.")

– to an analysis of the relations that compose the concept of alienation in (roughly) the first half of the essay,
– then turning to brief observations on the relations of alienation in real life,
– interspersed with a discussion of other relations that must be elaborated to discern alienation in a wide range of social events, for example, learning (on Marx's own descriptions of method, see paragraphs 43–51; also, Marx, 1847: 112–137; 1857: 112–137; see also Hall, 1973; Beamish, 1992).

Just as estranged labor is not about the unusual predicament of a few workers, estranged learning is not limited to a few individuals who might learn in peculiar or agonized ways. Instead, Marx's essay is a disquisition on the organized, structured character and effects of political economic relations, the only game in town, by which everyone goes about making their lives and fortunes through their own labor or other people's labor. Alienation lays an indelible shape on all aspects of their lives, including learning.[15] It will have its effect on:

1. What workers produce through daily efforts,
2. the processes of doing so,
3. their collective relation to nature and to themselves, and
4. their relations with each other.

The analysis of alienated labor provides a logic for analysis of the products and practices of learning and equally of how learners can be alienated from themselves and each other.

### Aspect I

Paragraph 7 plunges directly into the first of the four conceptual relations, the alienation produced in the *product* of labor:

The worker becomes all the poorer the more wealth he produces, the more his production increases in power and size. The worker becomes an ever cheaper commodity the more commodities he creates. With the increasing value of the world of things proceeds in direct proportion the *devaluation of* the world of men. Labor produces not only commodities: it produces itself and the worker as a commodity – and this in the same general proportion in which it produces commodities.

The last sentence contains not one, but several relations internal to the initial observation that "the worker [learner] becomes all the poorer the more wealth [learning] he produces. . . ."

| | |
|---|---|
| labor produces commodities | *learning* produces commodities |
| labor produces labor | *learning* produces *learning* |
| labor produces the laborer as a commodity | *learning* produces the *learner* as a commodity |

Just as the result of alienated labor is embodied in the things produced, so the object of alienated learning becomes material in the things learned – as lessons with exchange-value. Just as a product becomes a market thing, so learning becomes a school thing; and just as labor itself becomes a product, so being a pupil or a student is a thing one becomes. Similarly, learning becomes embodied in a credential, and being credentialed is a thing to

---

[15] We do not grapple in this essay with distinctions between the terms "estrangement" and "alienation," but see the work of Torrance (1977).

become. This bundle of objects confronts the alienated learner as "something alien, as a power independent of the producer" (paragraph 8), and "the learner becomes all the poorer the more learning he produces" (paragraph 7). The learner becomes all the poorer the more he becomes subject to the whim of the educational system. Poverty is as much a condition of the mind as of the account book. Three years after "Estranged Labor," Marx reiterates just how poor a thinker can be: "The same men who establish social relations comfortably with their material productivity, produce also the principles, the ideas, the categories, comfortably with their social relations. Thus these ideas, these categories, are not more eternal than the relations which they express. They are historical and transitory products" (1847: 119).

We have left the commodity concept untouched to this point (see Table 6.2), for it lives almost as obviously in the educational sphere as elsewhere in relations of capital. But what kinds of commodities does alienated learning produce? We have several registers available: The first can be found in any school office where homework, school assignments, test performances, test scores, grades, report cards, student records, educational credentials, academic degrees, and assessed potential all get recorded. A second register can be found most easily among parents or school counselors who reify alienated categories of learners from official and other professional perspectives. There is also a budget line attached to each of these categories, and these make us understand learners as commodity producers who produce themselves as objects of the expert labor of the educational system – as, say, the gifted, the slow, the disadvantaged, the learning disabled, the emotionally disturbed, etc. A third register is perhaps the most ubiquitous and develops a most invidious distinction between commodified products of learning and things that are interesting. Just as Marx (paragraph 20) says of the laborer:

He feels at home when he is not working, and when he is working he does not feel at home.

We can say of the learner:

He feels interested when he is not learning in school, and when he is learning in school he does not feel interested.

The distinction lies at the pivot where the use-value of exploring the as-yet-unknown parts company with its exchange-value. We can now rewrite Paragraph 7, keeping in mind that "learning" here refers to the alienated character of learning under capitalism:

The *learner* becomes all the poorer the more *learning is produced for others to assess, compete with, diagnose, and remediate,* the more *the learner's* production increases in power and size. The *learner* becomes an ever cheaper commodity the more commodities he creates. With the *increasing value* of the world of *commodities* proceeds in direct proportion the *devaluation* of *learning in everyday life*. Alienated *learning* produces not only commodities: it produces itself and the *learner* as a commodity – and this in the same general proportion in which it produces commodities.

The point: the *product* of laboring to learn is more than the school lessons learned. Over time, laboring to learn produces both what counts as learning and learners who know how to do it, learners who know how to ask questions, give answers, take tests, and get the best grades. Making what counts and making those who seek to be counted, these together compose the product of learning-labor.

   This works for Paragraph 8 also:

---

| | |
|---|---|
| (8) This fact expresses merely that the object which labor produces – labor's *product – confronts it* as *something alien,* as a *power independent* of the producer. The product of labor is labor which has been embodied in an object, which has become material: it is the *objectification* of labor. Labor's realization is its objectification. In the sphere of political economy this realization of labor appears as loss of *realization* for the workers; objectification as loss of *the object* and *bondage to it*; appropriation as *estrangement,* as *alienation.* | (8) This fact expresses merely that the object which *learning* produces – the *learner's product – confronts it* as *something alien,* as a *power independent* of the *learner*. The product of *learning* is *learning* which has been embodied in *a test score or promised credential,* which has become material: it is the *objectification* of *learning. Learning's* realization is its objectification. In the sphere of *learning theory* this realization of *learning* appears as loss of *realization* for the *learners*; objectification as loss of *the object* and *bondage to it;* appropriation as *estrangement,* as *alienation.* |

---

Marx clarifies what he means by objectification (paragraph 11–16).[16] Human praxis is a matter of doing and being in relations with objects – things and people – external to the person. But the reification of labor and learning under capitalism results in estrangement and loss to learners and other workers, as learning is turned into the product of educational theory, school organization, teaching, testing, and credentialing. Learners are diminished by their own industry. What they are given to learn is not theirs but the school's product – including objectifications of the learner by more powerful others. Marx reiterates (paragraph 16) the view of traditional political economy that expresses the alienation of the worker in a mystified way – it speaks of the worker as becoming barbarous.[17]

---

[16] Marx treats objectification as inherent in human praxis and also argues that the historical character of objectification under capitalism – alienation – has a political-economic character that creates and expresses profound social dislocation in the name of surplus value. We emphasize contemporary relations of alienation, though we are aware of interpretative debates over the history and bounds of the concept with respect to objectification.

[17] The text: "The laws of political economy express the estrangement of the worker in his object thus: the more the worker produces, the less he has to consume; the more values he

So the school speaks of students as becoming barbarous. Not farfetched, consider a recent newspaper front page article:

School Lockers are Making a Comeback.

...after receiving relentless complaints from parents and students, officials in the Pasadena Unified School District have begun unsealing lockers that had been shuttered since the 1970s. "There was this perception that each locker was a den of iniquity," said Bill Bibbiani, director of research and testing for Pasadena Unified. "But there are better ways to handle problems than to treat each locker as if [it is] a hole-in-the-wall gang hide-out." (*Sunday Los Angeles Times*, Orange County Edition. September 2, 2001)

The solution offered from the school district is an expensive system of surveillance cameras and lockers that can be locked down from the principal's office. The parents complain, with data in hand, that it is their children's backs that are suffering from carrying heavy books around all day – a case of descriptive accuracy and analytic obtuseness. Political economy, official and parental views, and educational practice conceal alienated labor-learning. Marx argues that this concealment is brought about and sustained by a refusal to draw front and center the direct relation between workers and production, between learners and their learning.

*Educational theory* conceals the estrangement inherent in the nature of *alienated learning* by not considering the direct relationship between the *learner* and production (*of learning*). (paragraph 17)

This conclusion is obvious, but easy to ignore under current arrangements: To understand learning, in all its complexities, keep the investigative eye fixed – if you can imagine this – on learning.[18]

### Aspect II

The second aspect of alienated learning follows from the first. Active alienation is manifested in processes of production, that is, in the activities of production.

How could the *learner* come to face the product of his activity as a stranger, were it not that in the very act of production he was estranging himself from himself? The product is after all but the summary of the activity... In the estrangement of the object of *learning* is merely summarized the estrangement, the alienation, in the activity of *learning* itself. (paragraph 20)

creates, the more valueless, the more unworthy he becomes; the better formed his product, the more deformed becomes the worker; the more civilized his object, the more barbarous becomes the worker; the more powerful labor becomes, the more powerless becomes the worker; the more *ingenious labor* becomes, the less ingenious becomes the worker and the more he becomes nature's bondsman" (paragrph 16).

[18] Dreier (1993, 1997, 1999) points to the "desubjectification" of family therapy and similarly the curriculum in schools as foci that evade attention to learning.

What constitutes the alienation of learning processes? Alienated learning is "external to the learner," not freely undertaken. In his work, the learner does not ". . . affirm himself but denies himself, does not feel content but unhappy, does not develop freely his physical and mental energy but mortifies his body and ruins his mind" (paragraph 22). It is activity experienced as suffering. Alienated learners are only themselves when they are not learning – think of common distinctions between "real learning" and "real life" (Lave, 1988). Such learning does not satisfy a need: It is coerced, forced, and a means to satisfy needs external to it. If it belongs to learners, it is second-hand, on loan from others. It is a loss of self.

### Aspect III

Alienation reduces collective life to the individual and utilitarian: Estranged from nature and the most productive life activities, estranged labor – and no less estranged learning – changes the life of the species into a means, merely the means, of satisfying the need to maintain physical existence, and further it becomes only a means to *individual* life.

First it [labor under capitalism] estranges the life of the species and individual life, and secondly it makes individual life in its abstract form the purpose of the life of the species, likewise in its abstract and estranged form. (paragraph 27)

Marx's dense discussion of the alienation of humankind from nature and from themselves (their "own active functions" and their "life activity") develops as he contrasts the relations of people and animals to nature, in theory and in practice, and as matters of consciousness and activity. Relations of humans to nature are multiple, mutually constitutive, and contradictory. Marx's vision is dialectical: All of nature is theoretically included in human consciousness. In practice, nature is part of human life and activity. . . . Nature is his direct means of life, and the material object and instrument of his life activity. Man lives on nature, man's physical and spiritual life is linked to nature and thus nature is linked to itself.

  Without exploring all dimensions of Marx's argument, it is possible to trace his path from collective social and spiritual relations with nature to the isolated individual caught in a web of utilitarian relations. Marx takes the "life of the species" – in a wonderful phrase, "life-engendering life" – to consist of "labor, life activity, productive life." Alienated labor disrupts collective life and its relations in/with nature. By working upon the objective world (the active species life), people prove themselves part of the species being. Through labor, through production, nature appears as their work, their reality. The object of labor is the objectification of specifically human collective life. The argument thus arrives at human life as a practice of objectification.

Now consider the specifically, historically, alienated character of objectification under capital. "In tearing the object of his production away from man, estranged labor tears him from his species life, his real objectivity as a member of the species" (paragraph 33). Marx explains in this way how alienation from nature and society derives from the alienation of workers from their own products (the first aspect of alienation). Then he shows how estrangement from nature and society derives from the alienation of productive activity (the second aspect of alienation). Aspect III follows from the first two: In degrading spontaneous free activity to a means, estranged labor makes species life a mere means to physical existence. The consciousness that people have of their social being generally and collectively is transformed by estrangement into life as only a means.

Read in terms of "Estranged Labor," alienation at work reverses the relation between collective and individual life, and collective life becomes the means to pursue individual life rather than the other way around. Read in terms of "Estranged ~~Labor~~/Learning," alienation – at school (and no less at work or at home) – reverses the relation between collective and individual life, and schools become the means to pursue careers and not the way to contribute to collective well-being.

### Aspect IV

Finally, the fourth aspect of relations of alienated labor:

An immediate consequence of the fact that learners are estranged from the product of their learning, from their life activity, from their species being is the estrangement of person from person. When learners confront themselves, they confront other learners. What applies to a learner's relation to his work, to the product of his learning and to himself, also holds of a learner's relation to the other learner, and to the other learner's learning and object of learning. (paragraph 38)

Marx directed us to the relations of competition, ambition, and monopoly in the opening paragraphs of "Estranged Labor." This final aspect of alienation suggests *how* learners enter into their own alienation, coming to see others, what they know, what they might know, etc., as fearsome comparative dangers that make failure a possible, even necessary, consequence of struggles to acquire school learning (McDermott, 1993, 1997; Varenne and McDermott, 1998). The puzzle of learning as a competition is pursued further in the next section.

*Observations*: If learning is alienated in the comprehensive ways labor is alienated, Marx's text allows for three immediate conclusions: First, the problem of alienated learning, like alienated labor, is ubiquitous. Second, it is not enough to understand learning problems, like other production problems, as simply an absence of knowledge or even a well-situated absence of knowledge, but necessarily as a mystification, a false focus, a problem that hides more than it makes available to reform. And, third, if "remedies" are devised, but only for those mystified problems, such "solutions" are never enough and, often, not even a little bit helpful.

1. Alienated learning is endemic: Marx's analysis distinguishes between apparently free labor and a darker underlying reality of alienated labor, and greatly expands the scope of analysis required to characterize labor in practice. The same is true if we follow Marx's analysis of the four aspects of the relations that compose alienated labor to arrive at an equally relational conception of alienated learning. This conceptual complexity must surely be counter-intuitive for learning theory (which reduces learning to the mental labor of the learner on brief occasions when knowledge is transmitted, internalized, or tested) and even for the social analysis of education (which often ignores learning altogether). Marx is specifically critical of the distanced and privileged attempts of classical theorists to pretend away the alienated character of social life and, as a result, to capture it only in a mystified way that conceals the real social processes that produce it. This overcoat certainly fits a critique of learning theory.

2. Alienated learning is so situated in the social system of production that it is hard to find, describe, and confront: Economic categories are troublesome if allowed to refer to abstract entities when instead, says Marx, their very existence, or better, their function in the organization of experience, is fragile, dependent, situated, contextual, emergent (all that is easy enough to say), and (and here's the rub) estranged, alienated, and mystified in the relations among people and their activities in the political economy. We can say the same for categories of learning, which, by current practice, are treated institutionally as objects – a stockpile of objects, really: attention, memory, problem solving, higher-order skills, and so on – and not as activities well tuned to the relations among people and their world. So we say, over and against the mainstream, that learning is dependent, situated, contextual, and emergent; all this has not been easy enough to say and must still be said, relentlessly so. But it is only the first half of a critique of learning theory as currently institutionalized. A second half can use Marx to stretch even theories of situated learning into theories that (and here's the rub) confront learning and its market place as estranged, alienated, and mystified, that is to say, confront learning and even its apparent absence as two versions of a single educational commodity on sale.[19]

[19] "There is an absence, real as presence," warns the poet, John Montague (1984). An absence real as presence: yes, made up, but consequential; made up, but requiring a hero to confront

3. Quick and partial solutions are distorting: Marx takes to task the impulse to produce an immediate or literal remedy. The poverty of labor, for example, cannot be fixed up by a simple increase in wages.

An enforced *increase in wages*... would therefore be nothing but *better payment for the slave*, and would not win either for the worker or for labor their human status and dignity. (paragraph 61; emphases by Marx)

Similarly, in a system in which success is defined by the failure of others, in a system in which everyone has to do better than everyone else, there is no way for everyone to achieve school success (Varenne and McDermott, 1998). In a now-classic analysis of a balanced equilibrium for keeping the people on the bottom from ever climbing too high, Berg (1970) gave us a picture of the race between groups from the bottom of the social hierarchy doing well in school on the one hand and ever-increasing demands for school success as a criterion for access to jobs on the other; every achievement on the school front, says Berg, has been countered by an equal measure of unattainable requirements for employment.

Similarly, calls for more "authentic" curriculum and learning activities for school learners often leave the world unchanged relative to what children either have to learn in school or at least show off as having learned in school in ways that employers can use (Cuban, 1993). Systematically complex and contradictory relations between the school worlds of children and adult workplaces underscore Marx's skepticism about cosmetic fixes for the systemic ills of wage labor.

Marx honors his own prescription in "Estranged Labor" to stick squarely focused on relations of labor (learning) to understand how their practices produce the sphere of political economy in all its multiple structures, relations, and complexities. Just as Marx (paragraph 59) says of political economy, that it:

... starts from labor as the real soul of production; yet to labour it gives nothing, and to private property everything,

So we can say of the school theory of learning that it:

... starts from learning as the real soul of education; yet to learning it gives nothing, and to professional education everything.

it; made up, but in a world defined by what we are not, alienated what it takes away. The poor are too often defined by what they cannot do, by what they do not know, by what they cannot say (McDermott, 1988; Ranciere, 1991). The poor are forced to carry their alienation not only in their wallets, but in their heads and on their tongues. Apparent learning and its absence make each other real and consequential.

Rereading "Estranged Labor" insists that we notice that relations of learning are as thick and complex as relations of labor.

### PART IV. ALIENATED DISTRIBUTION

In the last half of the essay, Marx turns from an analysis of the concept of alienated labor to consider how the "concept must express and present itself in real life" (paragraph 43). At the same time, he begins to look at the same relations, until now understood as *internal* to the concept of alienated labor, as they inhere in the relation *between* labor and private property, between self-alienation and the way this un-free activity is produced in the service or dominion of others, between workers and men of means.

When we began rewriting "Estranged Labor," we left the main theoretical terms of Marx's analysis alone and found that even this minimalist approach yielded interesting ideas about learning under conditions of formal education. But toward the end of "Estranged Labor," Marx challenges the reader to develop new categories of political economy built up analytically from a base of alienated labor and private property.

Just as we have derived the concept of private property from the concept of estranged, alienated labor by analysis, so we can develop every category of political economy with the help of these two factors; and we shall find again in each category, e.g., trade, competition, capital, money, only a definite and developed expression of these first elements. (paragraph 65)

If we start with a critique fashioned from the perspective of alienated labor and its ties to private property, promises Marx, we might be able to pursue "a definite and developed expression" of alienated learning in educational production, distribution, exchange, and consumption.

We could explore the relations of learning in any one of the concepts of political economy and education, though "Estranged Labor" itself is not a powerful auger: The essay focuses overwhelmingly on relations of production. Exchange is mentioned four times (only in the introductory paragraphs), consumption once, and distribution not at all. Curiosity suggests the last holds promise. A more serious consideration is that modern state school systems have made distribution of learners' futures their primary concern, if not analytically or even rhetorically, then experientially and symptomatically.

Care is required. Marx had something more profound in mind than taking on distribution or any other political economic relation out of context, one at a time, or in a simple sequence (as learning theories seem disposed to arrange in line: pregiven knowledge, then transmission, then internalization followed by learning transfer). In the essay, "Introduction to a Critique of Political Economy," he dismisses as "a sequence, but a very superficial one" the political economists' conceit that:

Production, distribution, exchange and consumption . . . form a proper syllogism; production represents the general, distribution and exchange the particular, and consumption the individual case which sums up the whole. (1857: 130)[20]

He shows us how trivial the sequence is by promptly scrambling its order (in a fashion still agreeable to the classical political economists):

Production is determined by general laws of nature; distribution by random social factors, it may therefore exert a more or less beneficial influence on production; exchange, a formal social movement, lies between these two; and consumption, as the concluding act, which is regarded not only as the final aim but as the ultimate purpose, falls properly outside the sphere of economy. . . . (1857: 130)

The *force* of the 1857 essay lies in Marx's argument that production and distribution, production and consumption, the other relations in pairs, and all of them together, are deeply interrelated in multiple ways and mutually constitutive of one another.

Charged with understanding distribution in terms of alienated learning and private property, we are reminded that distribution and production are formative of one another, that the division of productive labor is a distributed part of the production of wages, goods, and profits (to be distributed). We can now sharpen our project to reflect this view: How is it, we may ask, that alienated learning, and stocks of knowledge and other property of the education establishment, find definite and developed expression in the laborious production of educational distribution?

It is not a new idea to approach the analysis of schooling in terms of basic political economic concepts. It has been done with sophistication as a matter of exchange and with great rhetoric as a matter of consumption. Exchange first: Two notable ethnographic accounts of learners in high schools, one in England, one in the U.S., locate a central relation between the students and teachers as a relation of exchange. Willis (1977: 64) explores clashing expectations over the exchange of respect by students for knowledge from teachers. Eckert's (1989) analysis of a high school in the Midwest hinges on the exchange of students' compliance to reasonable scholastic demands from teachers in return for the right to configure their social life in the school setting away from the family purview.

Now consumption: It is fashionable of late for educational policy to style students as consumers. Signs are everywhere. A recently appointed

[20] In 1857, Marx wrote an introduction to a planned six volume work that he would never finish (the three volumes of *Capital* being less than his plans for a first voume). In English, the "Introduction to a Critique of Political Economy" appears as an Afterward to *A Contribution to the Critique of Political Economy* (1859) and as an Introduction to the *Grundrisse* (1857–58). In both cases, it carries the title of its content: "Production, Consumption, Distribution, Exchange (Circulation)."

superintendent in an upscale California district gave her place in the system to a local newspaper:

I'm like the CEO of a company, and the company I'm running is education. Her teachers produce education, and the children consume it. Her job is quality control: You can never stay on status quo – it's either moving up or down. I want to continue the cycle and build on success.

At the other end of the cycle of success are parents who can sue the school system if the proper education (positively assessed knowledge and displays of success) are not delivered in time for the children to move up and out. In education, the consumers are organized.

That brings us to distribution, or rather, to an educational establishment view of education as distribution. Recall that, in Table 6.1, when we summed up initial word shifts from political economy to education, we replaced private property with standardized knowledge, curriculum, assessments, and inherent intelligence. We replaced the products of Marx's "men of means" – their political economy and its theory – with the educational establishment and its learning theory. Derived from a privileged position, we would expect a mystified account of alienated learning and indeed that is what they produced. In the hands of educational theorists, distribution is treated as a simple, abstract, uncontested process. "Naturally" access to education is differently distributed, just as inherent intelligence is assumed to be distributed. Schooling in a meritocracy helps sort and distribute its alumni into previously constituted social categories of class, race, ethnicity, etc. For some, this is the purpose of education, to distribute the right persons to the right places. For others, it is the beginning of a critique. Either way, distribution dominates most every consideration in educational institutions. Consider "special" education, aimed at nurturing people at both ends – disabled and gifted – of every continuum of assessed performances. Or consider Latour's critical analysis that links common assumptions about the dissemination of science with the necessity, inside such a diffusion (distribution) theory, for a first generator, a genius discoverer or inventor (1987, 1988; Fujimura, 1996). Schools for children and research laboratories are alike in their attention to the production of distributions of "knowledge." The *differences* in their practices contribute to the importance of distribution in educational theory and practice. To cite crucial phrases in "Estranged Labor": each "takes for granted what it is supposed to explain" (paragraph 2) and treats the distribution of educational excellence – no, make that the distribution of the *attribution* of educational excellence – as the "*necessary, inevitable and natural consequences*" of birthright and hierarchies of access and not the necessary, inevitable, and natural consequences of their own activities in relation to production, distribution, exchange, and consumption.

Further, as this theory goes, "real learning" is distributed on the other side of a divide that segregates schools from "real life" (a mystified claim that hides alienated everyday school practices while attesting to them). Perhaps the most mystifying and in the end the most alienated and alienating assumption is specifically a matter of distribution. This is a widely and deeply felt distinction that separates the production of official knowledges (e.g., science, literature, national curricular frameworks), always elsewhere, from their distribution throughout school practices. "The production of knowledge stocks" is carefully distinguished from what boils down to their apparently non-generative, unchanging distribution as they are "transmitted" through schooling, "learned," and "transferred" beyond. These renderings of learning and distribution do not heed the admonition to fix the investigative eye on learning, and they do not lend themselves to a *relational explanation* of processes of alienation, understood as learners' alienated learning labor and its mutually constitutive ties to distributive practices.

For a reticular, relational view of distributive practices, we can try, instead, to develop a conception of learning and schooling as a matter of the production (or labor) of distribution under conditions of alienated learning. Relations of distribution take on different – greater – significance in this context. Where we begin with a conception of learning as alienated, its distribution loses the abstract appearance of smooth circulation, or simple transportation. It no longer stands as a neutral process of allocation, transmission, or diffusion, as if according to a necessary and natural plan. We begin to think more of distributive practices that alienate, estrange, and appropriate learning, the products of learning, processes of learning, and learners themselves.[21] This makes it possible for us to think more systematically about how alienated learning participates in the self-valorization of capital.

In short, the distribution of alienated learning is at heart a matter of *political* economy. The organization of distribution partly defines working lines of power and contestation and how they lie in relation to alienated learning, including: estrangement, appropriation, struggles to keep, struggles to take away (variously: children, credentials, knowledge – and learning), attempts to "impart," and official processes of assessment. Once viewed as alienated, distribution is a matter of political struggle over societal "stocks of knowledge," credentials, gene pools, genius stocks, brains, and minds, all laid down in unequal relations between what Marx calls those of means and those without.

Further, the social relations that allow the translation of "private property" into educational establishment terms as "societal stocks of knowledge" depend on, as well as shape, the alienated character of distribution processes. *The institutionalization of predefined and fixed stocks of knowledge available for transfer and assessment both depends on and produces the estrangement of learning*

---

[21] Such an analysis could be read alongside Foucault (1975) and Rose's (1990) theories of normalizing disciplinary practices and schooling as a distributional endeavor.

*from learners in institutional settings.* If schools did not insist that learners engage in day-to-day competition to acquire what is called the core curriculum, the basics, cultural literacy, etc., it would not be possible to sustain the illusion of inherent intelligence, credentials to be earned, and a societal stock of knowledge to be transmitted. Its distributional potential is the defining feature of every item placed in the curriculum and especially on tests. School lessons are the sites for exercising stock options in a system of assessed "learning." If it is not assessed, it does not count in the distribution wars. The alienated learning of children in school and the propertied illusion of official knowledge make each other. *Learning-for-display in a world of positions distributed up and down a hierarchy of access and privilege is the more salient issue for participants to keep in focus.* That is why learning "in its relation to truly human and social property" (paragraph 69), just like labor, is hard to keep in view, and hard to keep at the core of education as its "real soul."

Institutionalized education cannot afford to keep learning in view, for it has always the more pressing task of reproducing what alienated men of means must guard as, and believe in as, the societal stock of knowledge and expertise. Alienated labor and learning produce and protect the alienated concept of private property and society's knowledge. Together, they produce the material and intellectual wealth of the established order. This is why children must go to school not to learn, but to not get caught not knowing required parts of standardized knowledge. Estranged learning is estranged because it is always done for others who use it for their own purposes. We know now what those purposes are. They use it to keep themselves (and their children) in place in a hierarchy of others, a hierarchy held together in part by a theory of learning that denies the relevance of the distribution system while making each participant's placement its most important product. Such circumstances of learning are caught up in what we have come to think of as a teaching crisis in which teachers and other "haves" are impelled to extract, distract, appropriate, and take on themselves the learning of learners who thereby are deprived of that relation themselves.[22]

The exercise Marx proposed at the end of "Estranged Labor" has brought us from a critique of production by way of alienated labor to a confrontation

---

[22] Margaret Mead long ago reminded us that not all societies live with a teaching crisis:

> Miscarriages in the smooth working of the transmission of available skills and knowledge did occur, but they were not sufficient to focus the attention of the group upon the desirability of teaching over and against the desirability of learning. Even with considerable division of labor and with a custom by which young men learned a special skill not from a father or other specified relative but merely from a master of the art, the master did not go seeking pupils. (1943)

> Similarly, a quick look at people in contemporary states learning languages, technologies, games, and job skills shows that most learning problems are created by schools in the service of the political economy.

with distribution by way of alienated learning. We like to think that Marx might have said the same thing about teaching and learning, and we get some confirmation from the short quote we offered from *Capital*. A longer version of that quote and our rewrite move us closer to what Marx might have said:

Capitalist production is not merely the production of commodities, it is, by its very essence, the production of surplus-value. The worker produces not for himself, but for capital. It is no longer sufficient, therefore, for him simply to produce. He must produce surplus-value. The only worker who is productive is one who produces surplus-value for the capitalist, or in other words contributes towards the self-valorization of capital. If we may take an example from outside the sphere of material production, a schoolmaster is a productive worker when, in addition to belaboring the heads of his pupils, he works himself into the ground to enrich the owner of the school. That the latter has laid out his capital in a teaching factory instead of a sausage factory, makes no difference to the relation. The concept of a productive worker therefore implies not merely a relation between the activity of work and its useful effect, between the worker and the product of his work, but also a specifically social relation of production, a relation with a historical origin which stamps the worker as capital's direct means of valorization. To be a productive worker is therefore not a piece of luck, but a misfortune.... (1867: 644)

Here is our translation into the sphere of alienated learning and distribution:

*Learning under capitalist production* is not merely *about* the production of *knowledge; it* is, by its very essence, *about* the production *and distribution of assessed knowledge.* The *learner* produces not for himself, but for *his or her place in the system.* It is no longer sufficient, therefore, for him simply to *learn.* He must produce *knowledge appropriate to_his situation.* The only *learner* who is productive is one who produces *test scores* for the *school,* or in other words contributes towards the self-valorization *and redistribution* of the *educational hierarchy.* If we may take an example from outside the sphere of material production, *students and* teachers are productive when, in addition to belaboring their *own* heads, they work themselves into the ground to enrich the owner of the school. That the latter has laid out his capital in a teaching factory instead of a sausage factory, makes no difference to the relation. The concept of a productive *learner* therefore implies not merely a relation between the activity of *learning and its useful effect, between the learner and what is learned (and can be shown to have been learned),* but also a specifically social relation of *education,* a relation with a historical origin which stamps the *learner* as the *school's* direct means of valorization. To be a productive *learner* is therefore not a piece of luck, but a misfortune....

*Observation*: One reason for publishing this exercise develops from our effort to understand how to conduct research and to teach in ways that squarely reflect our understanding of "learning." This practice of "reading" has given one answer: It does not treat scholarly work as a stock of knowledge property, nor reading as a means of acquiring it or transmitting it, but rather as a way to work generatively with it. This is surely a form of appropriation, but one that cannot lose sight of the producer of the work so appropriated and the continuing relation between them. The duty to text, and the respect referred to earlier, are neither first and foremost competitive relations nor ones that should intensify alienation from scholarly colleagues, thus, the pleasure of such engagements.[23]

This leads, however, to another point. If we allow ourselves this pleasure but call it scholarship and not learning, we reveal the alienated position we occupy in a world in which we insist there is no relation between our labors and the labors of learners in schools (between something called "knowl-edge production" or "high culture" and something called "schooling" or "training," or "the reproduction of knowledge"). This insistence is in one sense correct – it affirms (and in doing so participates in) divisions under contemporary capitalism between an elite cultural establishment and the institution of schooling. It affirms divisions between elite practices of re-search, expertise, and management and the activities of "lay people," or those so managed, including learners in school. But it is incorrect as an analysis of learning as a "life-engendering life" practice (paragraph 30), of learning "in its relation to truly human and social property" (paragraph 69), which would surely include scholarly practices in the same theoretical sweep as learning everywhere else. We may now ask, what does the analysis of alienated learning tell us about scholarly processes of reading and vice versa?

## CONCLUSION

If Marx is correct that the very contents of our minds are working against us, where can we get new materials to reshape them and, because it is never enough simply to change minds, to put them back into the fray, into the reorganization of the society of problems to which we adhere? A conceptual undertow relentlessly threatens to pull us back to the mainstream, where children are primarily minds ready to be filled according to capacity, where teachers are transmitters of what everyone knows must be known, and where schools are a neutral medium for sorting out the best and the brightest according to fair tests, the same for one and all. Reinforced by our ethno-graphic work, we have long known that children are innocent players in a world of competing forces, that teachers are good people trying to work

---

[23] Calling attention to the constitutive importance of reading as part of scholarly practice and as a major mode by which academics, among others, relate to the work of colleagues past and present, contrasts with the alienated, commodity-oriented character of critical diagnoses over the last fifteen years of the ailments of ethnographic writing. Reducing traditional anthropology to the illusion of writing authoritative ethnographies reduces it to its most commodified moment and remains silent about the complexities of practices that reveal the interdependent relations of fieldwork, writing, reading, and rereading that are the generative basis of any new learning.

around those same forces, and that schools – a significant portion of the gross domestic product of modern nation states – are only a possible tool in the reform of those forces. To stay alive to these alternative formulations, and to give them analytic rigor and political punch, we must constantly develop new materials and procedures.

Working our way through "Estranged Labor" has given us an account of estranged learning. We have developed a new momentary place to stand and a new set of tools with which to confront mainstream assumptions. It has allowed us a conceptual advance, namely, to see, once again but in a new way, not just learning, but the nation's very ideas about learning as part of a wider system of cultural, political, and economic forces that organize and define education and its problems. Good for us, and hopefully we can find ways to make the insights cumulative. But the method also has us excited. Work with good texts, like work with records of human interaction, like ethnographic fieldwork, if done carefully, if done slowly and visibly, can be an endless source for confronting and restaging the contexts of learning.

Most texts cannot withstand the kind of scrutiny we have paid to "Estranged Labor," and few texts have enough internal energy and complexity to deliver messages to concerns far from their defined topics. Those that can make the reach are worth working with over and over. Every time we thought we had finished our analysis of "Estranged Labor," a new use and a new lesson seemed to emerge.

We can close with a final example. We wanted to write a conclusion in which we said why we had continued to work with Marx's text. As happened often over the months of putting this rewriting together, after an hour of discussion, we returned to the text to read again how Marx ended his essay. He did it twice, once in the penultimate three paragraphs and again in a last line, and we can use them both. The penultimate three paragraphs, with a little rewriting, can give us our conclusions.

First it has to be noted that everything which appears in the worker as *an activity of alienation, of estrangement,* appears in the non-worker as a *state of alienation, of estrangement.* (paragraph 71)

Our first instinct was to rewrite the paragraph, substituting learner for worker and teacher for non-worker. Good enough, and it makes the case of the paper once again. But there is a stronger ending in it, for we are often non-workers, busy non-workers, of course, but intellectuals and liable to fall into "*a state of alienation, of estrangement.*" We cannot trust ourselves to think our way to the ideas we need to change our lives. We need help. One kind of help is to work on rich texts that force us systematically to relocate our work with the work of others, the work of teachers with the work of learners, the work of people alienated in one way with the work of people alienated in other ways.

The next paragraph is no less helpful to our conclusion.

Secondly, the worker's real, practical attitude in production and to its product (as a state of mind) appears in the non-worker confronting him as a theoretical attitude. (paragraph 73)

This time, substitute learner for worker and researcher for non-worker, and we can make the point of the paper again. The learner going to school faces not only difficult learning tasks, but a theoretical attitude – a theory of learning – that can turn the learner into a problem. The next substitution makes the point of our conclusion. We are the researchers, and it is difficult to escape the theoretical attitude that pays our salary as well as turning others into learning problems. We need help. In this case, it came from hard work with "Estranged Labor." In our earlier research, it came from hard work with films of children in school or tailors learning their trade in Liberia. There is order everywhere – in texts, in human interaction, in various cultures – and although these orders are always symptomatic of various problems, they can always be used as well to reorder our theoretical attitudes and the relations that support them.

The third paragraph of Marx's first conclusion pushes us further in our attempt to say why we have worked so long on "Estranged ~~Labor~~/Learning."

Thirdly, the non-worker does everything against the worker which the worker does against himself; but he does not do against himself what he does against the worker. (paragraph 74)

It is time for us to do to ourselves part of what is done to learners all the time. It is time to submit ourselves to a theoretical attitude that can knock us off our moorings and show us where we stand in relation to others. It is time to locate ourselves in the alienated learning we have been hawking around the world. Rewriting "Estranged Labor" has subjected our own work, and our learning, to the larger critique Marx developed in 1844. It is not all that we have to do, but it has been reorienting. For a final comment, we cannot do better than to repeat Marx's last paragraph:

Let us look more closely at these three relations. (paragraph 75)

# 7

# "Our Working Conditions Are Our Students' Learning Conditions"

## A CHAT Analysis of College Teachers

### Helena Worthen and Joe Berry

### INTRODUCTION

"Our working conditions are our students' learning conditions." This claim has been made again and again by contingent (adjunct, part-time, temporary, non-tenure track, or non-"regular") faculty in adult and higher education in the United States, usually in the course of some part of a union organizing or bargaining campaign. It is both a protest against working conditions that undermine effective teaching and a declaration of intent to organize to improve those conditions.

It also indicates that, from the point of view of contingent faculty, the interests of the faculty lie increasingly with their students rather than with the institutional management that has command of those conditions.

This distinction between the interests of faculty and of institutional management, as we will explain, has emerged progressively over the last thirty years as the adult and higher education workforce has undergone a shift from majority tenured and tenure-track to majority contingent. However, this distinction is invisible to many. Furthermore, this invisibility is itself promoted, asserted, and promulgated, often in the name of "quality." The argument goes that the interests of the institution and of faculty, meaning both tenured and contingent faculty, are identical because institution and faculty alike are committed to offering the best possible educational "quality" experience to their students. The key is that what "quality" means depends on what purpose one is serving.

Penetrating this invisibility is not a simple task. Faculty, both tenured and contingent, carry out their work in a single workplace; they deal with a single student body; they work under a single calendar; they teach from a single course catalog, and often teach the same courses and syllabi; a single set of criteria applies to students moving through the institution, whether

Note: A previous version of this article appeared in *Labor Studies Journal*, 27(3), 2002.

they are enrolled in classes taught by full professors or adjuncts. In many, if not most, cases, students themselves are unaware of what the employment status of their teachers is. Nevertheless, the difference between the working conditions of tenured and tenure-track faculty and contingent faculty is vast. This transformation of the faculty is a manifestation of different class interests at work within the institution.

This chapter focuses on these evolving and increasingly severe contradictions having to do with employment in the adult and higher education industry. It demonstrates the use of the cultural–historical activity theory (CHAT) to distinguish, on the basis of consciousness and purpose, between conflicting activity systems that, on the surface, appear to be a single system. Using CHAT to work backward from a moment of crisis for a contingent worker in an adult education program in the Chicago City Colleges, we sort out the key documents, division of labor, and ultimately the measures of "quality" by which a teacher's work is valued to reveal that, in one institution, two strikingly different goals are being contested. What is at stake in the short term is the teacher's job. What is being contested in the long term is the purpose of adult education.

We also argue that higher education policy discourse generally, as wielded by management, uses the word "quality" to mask differences. This in turn confuses the opportunities created by the conflict. As more and more workers in this industry are hired as insecure contingents, more power in the bargaining process accrues to the management side as a result of this confusion. We use this analysis to account for the experience of frustration, anger, and despair – and sometimes extraordinary courage and dedication – of contingent workers in adult and higher education. We argue that the transformation of the higher education industry through the employment of contingents who now constitute the majority of higher education faculty requires the surfacing and acknowledgment of these differences combined with strategic organizing, both within the contingent faculty cohort and across the largely working-class communities that they serve.

## READING THE CHAT MODEL

CHAT provides a framework upon which it is possible to lay out relationships among the multiple factors that contribute to a complex situation and address them in a systematic way. The essential premises of this framework are that action (in the context of *activity*, as in *activity theory*) is purposeful; that purpose informs and animates consciousness; that all activity is ultimately collective, even when being carried out by an individual person; that purposes engage with each other and against each other; and that all activity has historical (both in the material and ideological senses) dimensions, is socially constructed, and is mediated by the socially constructed *tool of tools* we call language.

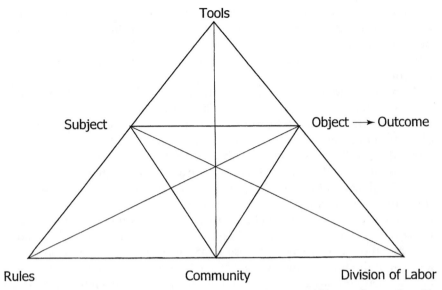

FIGURE 7.1. The mediational structure of an activity system (Engeström, 1987: 78).

These premises are expressed in a model. This chapter is not the place for a complete explanation of the CHAT model; suffice it to say here that we intend to use the model familiar to people who have encountered CHAT before, Engestrom's mediational structure of an activity system (Engeström 1987: 78). Numerous articles have been written proposing modifications to this model or suggesting other labels for its elements, especially for *object* and *outcome*, which are often read as *goal* or *purpose*. For our purposes, this version suffices in its basic form. The way we use it is like the way that Paulo Friere describes using other abstractions in *Pedagogy of the Oppressed* (1992). The abstraction, says Friere, serves as a code that is decoded by moving back and forth between the reality and the abstraction:

In the event, however, that men perceive reality as dense, impenetrable, and enveloping, it is indispensable to proceed with the investigation by means of abstraction. This method does not involve reducing the concrete to the abstract (which would signify the negation of its dialectical nature) but rather maintaining both elements as opposite which interrelate dialectically in the act of reflection. (Friere, 1992: 95)

The outcome of this dialectical process is, we would hope, "the supersedence of the abstraction by the critical perception of the concrete, which has already ceased to be a dense, impenetrable reality" (p. 96). Because our work (that is, the work of the authors both day-to-day and in writing this chapter) is part of a labor-side education program, we emphasize developing a "critical perception."

The model we are using is shown in Figure 7.1. We find it useful to read this model quite literally, attempting to identify how each element relates to some factor in the situation we are focusing on. We are also looking to see how many points on this model are, in our example, defined differently depending on the standpoint from which they are being viewed. When being used this way, the model operates as something between a diagram and a flow chart; that is, some of the lines on it express fixed reciprocal relationships and some express process.

Here is how we read the model in this case. We begin with the baseline: Rules-Community-Division of Labor. This is the fundamental social unit: a community that has certain rules and that through some process breaks out different roles for its members, people doing different kinds of work or holding different positions. Although all three of the elements along this baseline simultaneously relate to the elements higher in the model labeled Subject and Object-Outcome, we would read the model to say that the Subject (that is, the person or people whose activity we are studying) is selected, or generated, or emerges from the community through some process of division of labor according to some set of rules. To look ahead at our case study: The instructor whose activity we will focus on (his response to a threat of discipline, which we will argue is the administrative reaction to a conflict between two activity systems) has been chosen from his community (the faculty at his college) through a process of division of labor. This division is twofold, prefiguring the two conflicting activity systems. First, he and his fellow adult educators are separated from other faculty by their contingent status. They were hired as contingents and work as contingents. Second, he has emerged from among the adult educators because he has been elected as a union leader. This official role and his own personal identity in that role have a reciprocal developmental relationship. Thus, the element *community* is revealed as contested, something that is open to question. Is he really part of the overall community of faculty, or is he (and by extension, all the other adult educators) only part of the community of adult educators?

Returning to the model, the subject – in this case the instructor – has a purpose. He is trying to be a good teacher. We can match that with the labels *outcome* or *object* on the opposite side of the model. Much of his story will turn on what is meant by "good teacher." This instructor teaches math, history, reading, and writing. His students are typical adult education students: men and women of all ages, but over 18. These are people who did not complete high school and are trying to earn a General Education Diploma (GED) or learn English as a foreign language. Many of them work, but many are looking for work. Many are immigrants, not all documented. It is highly likely that those who are working are among the 21.3% of workers in Illinois who were making poverty-level wages in 2001 (Mishel, Bernstein, and Boushey, 2003: 386). Norton Grubb, who studied 32 community colleges and interviewed over 300 faculty and administrators in his 1999 survey of community college teaching practices, identifies this level of teaching as "one of the most difficult teaching challenges" (Grubb and Associates, 1999: 174) and says that how to meet that challenge is "one of the central debates within the open-access college. But it's not openly debated," he acknowledges, "at least not in the realm of practice..." (p. 173). The efforts that this instructor makes are signs of his commitment to his purpose, to meet this challenge.

At the top of the CHAT model is the label *tools*. We read this label very broadly to mean anything that is used to support the activity (the purposeful effort) of the subject trying to accomplish the object or outcome, with the important caveat that we must keep in mind that any tool, whether it is a hammer, a forklift, a computer, a gun, a dictionary, an Internet search engine, or a telescope, involves the use of symbolic communication, that is, language of some sort, whether it is words, computer code, icons, math symbols, musical notation, or oral speech. Money and other resources are also tools. The tool on its own may not engage in communication, but its use always does. The sheer fact of the engagement in symbolic communication in the use of any tool underscores the socially embedded nature of tools because language itself is a socially generated phenomenon. Following this, we can see that key documents are tools in this sense: A textbook may be a tool in a classroom, as a set of by-laws can be a tool for an organization. Similarly, and here we once again move from the abstract model to the concrete situation, a contract, in this case the collectively bargained employment contract governing the instructor in our case study and his relationship to the Chicago City Colleges, is a tool that plays a key role in this activity system. Not surprisingly, this contract, negotiated by the local union of the American Federation of State, County, and Municipal Employees organization on behalf of the contingent adult educators, is not remotely similar to the contract negotiated on behalf of the tenured and tenure-track faculty in the same Chicago City Colleges by the American Federation of Teachers (AFT) local union, which incorporates much higher wages, benefits, and, above all, long-term job security and job protections. Both tools – both contracts – of course address money and resources. This tool, then, embodies many of the differences between the two activity systems that co-exist and often conflict within the City Colleges.

We have now spoken to enough of the elements of the CHAT model to assert that what we have going on in the City Colleges, as in most institutions of adult and higher education in the United States today, is two activity systems. Although the institutional object (teaching, producing education) may appear to be the same whether one is an administrator or faculty member, contingent or tenured, enough of the other elements are different or contested so that we have to doubt whether the institutional object is not also different or contested.

We will now turn to the element at the lower left corner of the model: rules. We read "rules" to mean all the norms, customs, guidelines, and standards that govern the activity systems we have in focus. In an employment relationship within an educational institution we may find these rules in state-mandated guidelines, fiscal requirements, policy manuals, or union contracts, but we will also find them in internal institutional measures that shape the product, that is, education and the educational process. If the instructor is viewed as a worker who is hired to produce education, then his or her work will be evaluated by these measures. Similarly, the institution will be evaluated by these measures. The measures themselves express values.

Here follows a list, undoubtedly not complete, of these measures: graduation rates and totals; rates of student placement in employment and pay rates; rates of student placement in further education; scores on standardized tests; efficient use of resources; timely reporting and written accountability or "paperwork"; accessibility of education to all those who can benefit from it; class size and faculty/student ratios; evaluations based on teaching; development of student abilities to apply new learning in practice (outside classroom); encouragement and facilitation of lifelong pursuit of learning; professional development opportunities for faculty; usefulness of learning to the students; development of skills and habits of active citizenship; development of critical consciousness; creation of a collective, respectful, and reciprocal learning environment among students and teachers; and security of academic freedom of discussion for both students and faculty, among others.

Mixed together in this list are measures that reveal the quality of an institution as defined by, at one extreme, the value of administrative efficiency, and quality as defined by the value of student learning at the other. Combined, these measures might present an image of an ideal institution. Grubb (1999) describes such a hypothetical institution:

As educational leaders rather than (or in addition to "bean counters"), administrators would be responsible, with the faculty, for creating a culture that supports teaching – that recognizes its complexity in every subject, that respects its collective nature, and that communicates those beliefs to faculty and students consistently. The power and authority in most colleges would become less hierarchical and authoritarian, to facilitate institutional decisions about teaching and to eliminate the deep hostility between administrations and faculty that now exists. (Grubb and Associates, 1999: 362)

This ideal situation does not prevail in the Chicago City Colleges. Furthermore, given the current situation of accelerated de-funding of public education with consequent incentives to privatize, some measures compete strongly against others. In collective bargaining, the measures are selected that serve the interests of the stronger party. This is experienced by those who live and work under a contract negotiated in such a context as differences that cut to the quick of their lives as teachers. This is just as true in colleges where contingents have no union representation. Even in colleges where the power relationships are so unequal that no vocal opposition is evident, these issues are boiling under the surface.

By laying out the specifics of this situation on the framework of activity theory, we are able to bring to the surface, past the distracting "quality" discourse, the concrete conditions under which this instructor (and the hundreds of others in the City Colleges of which he is an example) is trying to do the work of teaching. The model indicates where we should look for the roots of the problem. Are all teachers one faculty? How did their working conditions get to be so different, then? It exposes how the rules may be different for one group compared with another (measures that promote the values of administrative efficiency versus the measures that support the values of student learning). It helps us see that there are really two activity systems in place here and directs us to expect conflict between them, conflict that will be mediated by the tool (the contract) that the instructor's union has negotiated for the purpose of protecting him and people like him should this conflict ignite.

We now briefly provide some background to the "quality" debate. Then, we turn to the situation in Chicago, to our case, reported through documents against the background of a narrative.

## THE "QUALITY" DISCOURSE IN THE CONTEXT OF HIGHER EDUCATION AND LABOR RELATIONS

The "quality" debate has emerged as the adult and higher education work-force has polarized as the numbers and percentages of non-tenure track faculty have increased since the 1970s. The literature reporting this steady increase includes Abel (1984), Barker (1998), Dubson (2001), Gappa and Leslie (1993), Nelson (1997), Schell and Stock (2001), Wallace (1984), Worthen and Berry (1999), Worthen (2001), and many pieces published by the academic unions, American Federation of Teachers (AFT), National Education Association (NEA), and American Association of University Professors (AAUP). The quantitative data, usually based on U.S. Department of Education National Center For Educational Statistics (NCES) surveys, clearly shows that most current faculty are contingent, especially if graduate employees and adult educators are included. One of the consistent threads in all of these reports, whether quantitative or qualitative, has been the felt and actual individual powerlessness of most contingent faculty vis-à-vis their employers. Although Gappa and Leslie advocate reforms mainly from the point of view of managers, some of the literature speaks directly from the frustrations of the contingent faculty themselves. These frustrations and their specific objects, as divided by Worthen and Berry in 1999, can fall into categories of "cost/overhead" (equity in pay and benefits, professional development funding, office and support, paid office hours, etc.) and "professional status" (choice of books and materials, academic freedom, hiring procedures, job security, access to permanent status, evaluation, access to professional development, etc.). The majority of contingent faculty, even the unionized minority, has been unable to gain most of these conditions, a fact that the existing literature richly documents. Many of the conditions in both categories directly relate to issues of quality in higher education and parallel the measures of quality listed in the previous section.

A number of authors address the changes in the political economy of higher education, especially in colleges and universities as workplaces. They include Aronowitz (2000), Hirsch and Luc (1999), Martin (1998), Moser (1999), Nelson (1997), Slaughter and Lesley (1997), Soley (1995), White (2000), and University of Maine (1999), as well as (again) multiple publications by the major U.S. unions of academic labor, AFT, AAUP, and NEA. There is a remarkable absence of dissent among them on a few descriptive aspects of the changes taking place, though they take different views on evaluation of these changes and recommendations for action. The observations they generally agree upon include: the increasing influence of private business, and its perceived needs and methods, in higher education; the greater administrative priority being placed upon economic efficiency in a competitive market; the greater drive for administrative flexibility, and the potential for new technology to be a major part in the radical restructuring of higher education and faculty work. All of these correspond to certain of the measures of "quality" listed earlier, quality from the management point of view.

Finally, any discussion of collective bargaining in higher education must be informed by Gary Rhoades' *Managed Professionals* (1998), which is based upon the most extensive study of faculty collective bargaining agreements yet published. His key theses are that academics are managed, not independent, professionals and that they are becoming an increasingly stratified group. Of particular importance to this chapter is his discussion of the growth of part-time and other contingent faculty labor, who usually have much lower levels of contractual protection, even if they are covered by collective agreements. This means that their power to bargain for a faculty definition of "quality" is minimal.

Despite this, there has been a push within academic labor management relations to accept "quality" as an umbrella under which the entire adult and higher education workforce could unite. Part of the argument in favor of this shift is that it would lower the level of adversarialism between administrators and especially the unionized contingent faculty. This debate has broken into the open within and among the academic unions and their close intellectual advisors. Both the AFT and NEA (1998) leaderships have put forward similar recommendations for bargaining strategies. These recommendations have been partially based upon the very influential work of Charles Kerchner and his collaborators. This work began with a focus upon K-12 unionism, but has been directly extended to higher education unionism as well (Kerchner and Mitchell, 1988; Kerchner and Koppich, 1993; Kerchner, Koppich, and Weeres, 1997; Kerchner, 1999). The core of the recommendations are two related propositions: one, that unions must begin to more energetically bargain issues of quality in education and, two, that the interests of both academic labor and management coincide in this area. Therefore, a strategy of labor-management collaboration for "quality" is recommended.

It is this strategy, of attempting to bring together contingent and non-contingent faculty and management under the umbrella of a common commitment to "quality" that we argue is misguided. As we can see from even our brief analysis discussed earlier, the definition of quality depends on standpoint: what measures of quality one prioritizes and whose purposes one is serving. The power to impose that definition depends on one's resources. We point to a different strategy: The creation of a healthy educational institution, we argue, would require more power, not less, in the hands of the contingent faculty at the bargaining table. After all, reduced adversarialism does not imply satisfaction. In fact, as our example will show, even in difficult situations, some people and some groups of faculty will resist. The struggle to maintain the faculty definition of quality, in the face of highly unequal power relationships, puts individual faculty in an often intolerable position and the collective faculty in what may appear to be a hopeless position (Wilson, 2001). But it may be that resistance has inherent rewards that make it just a little less intolerable than cooperation.

### THE CASE STUDY: A TEACHER ACCUSED OF NEGLIGENCE

This particular case came to our attention through a network of faculty who have been engaged in these issues for many years. Upon hearing about it, we interviewed the teacher involved. Then we examined the documents involved (memos, union contract, union bargaining flyers). We interviewed some of this teacher's colleagues for general background and document interpretation. We came to understand that the struggle between this teacher and his Acting Dean was woven into a process of institutional change that would use the "quality" issue to justify privatization of broad institutional functions. We then became involved with City Colleges of Chicago employees active in the Committee United Against Privatization (COUP), in which contingent faculty, non-contingent faculty, and staff participated. Finally, we have relied upon the experience of our combined forty years in higher education, part of that as contingent faculty and union activists in community colleges in three states (including in the City Colleges of Chicago themselves).

Although the adversarialism revealed in this example may seem extreme, it is not an aberration. We argue that we can see here in microcosm the conflicts at work in the Chicago City Colleges system generally: urban, unionized, under financial stress, closely linked to the machine politics of the city, and one of the largest community college systems in the country. As we note in our conclusion, the system is rapidly transforming itself and in a direction that can be understood using the two versions of "quality" that we contrast.

The situation we are looking at took place recently in one of the adult education programs of the Chicago City Colleges system. Adult education programs are places where most students attend to study for the GED and to learn basic skills and English as a second language. The documents that tell this story are a memo from an Acting Dean, relevant sections of the union contract, a response from the teacher who is being accused, and, finally, the relevant items that the union is currently trying to bargain.

We begin with the memo from an Acting Dean:

TO: Teacher X
FROM: Acting Dean Y
RE: Late Student Attendance Report

Date: May 25

It has been brought to my attention that you have just turned in your Student Attendance Report [SAR] for SP (Spring) yesterday, May 24. It was due on May 10. The End of Term Reports were run over the weekend; consequently, none of the attendance hours for your class will be counted or reimbursed. The grades will simply be entered into history.

This negligence on your part shows a lack of responsibility and commitment to the program. Your [sic] were given a "Records Day" on April 29 in order to get the majority of your paperwork completed. There were no classes during the weeks of May 10 through 20, so there was time to complete the SARs and you were on campus. You were assigned two days of registration only, so you had two other days to complete your paperwork, prepare lessons, or put cabinets in order. There were reminders posted in the ALSP office with the due date for tuning in SARs, so you could not have been unaware that they were due. You have been in the program for twenty years, so by now you should know grades and attendance are due when classes end. I can only conclude that you are irresponsible.

Also, this is not the first time you have been late. I understand you almost always turn in your SAR four or five days after the due date. This is the first time, however, that you have turned it in after the End of Term Reports have been run.

In the future, you are to adhere to all the due dates for turning in you [sic] SAR, midterm and final. If you do not, your negligence will result in disciplinary action. These two registrations cannot be added to your class at the end of the term. The registration forms should have been turned in at midterm when the students did not appear on you (sic) SAR. They have been in your class unregistered for the entire eight weeks which is against policy.

cc:     Personnel File, union

A letter like this, copied to the teacher's file and the union, is an official warning. Warnings constitute part of "progressive discipline," leading to possible termination. Therefore, a warning like this is a serious matter. Right away, we want to ask: Is it true? And, does it tell the whole story? But first we need to consider why the warning comes in this form.

## THE POWER OF PAPERWORK

As we saw in our earlier list, "paperwork" is one of the measures of quality. Warnings like this, in colleges like this, are often generated by paperwork. We should consider why this is so. After all, paperwork is not the primary criterion by which the quality of a teacher's work should be judged. But information about other aspects of teaching is not readily available to most administrators. Empirically, this appears to be widespread. Grubb notes:

Almost universally, faculty report that administrators are uninvolved in teaching issues. They don't visit classrooms, they don't know what's going on in classrooms, and – apparently – they don't care. (1999: 304)

All the administration knows about a teacher is her credentials at the time of hiring, attendance or sick day use, student or staff complaints, informal news that may be picked up during the course of spontaneous conversation, test scores and other quantifiable outcomes of students, and, yes, paperwork. Of course, another aspect of the teacher's work that the administration will be aware of is union activity.

So when an administrator wants to mount an effective complaint about a teacher, in practice, he or she has only a few possible strategies. One is to prove that the teacher is not qualified (i.e., properly certified or legally acceptable) and should not have been hired or assigned to, or retained in, a particular job in the first place. Another is to show that he or she is grossly negligent in keeping to a schedule. The third is to show that the teacher generates complaints. The last is to claim that the teacher is careless about paperwork. Remember that in most situations, unlike this one, contingent faculty have no union contract and are completely at-will employees. (Without a union, the administration does not have to mount a complaint at all – just decline to re-employ the teacher for the next term.)

To understand how the Acting Dean's attempt at discipline will affect this teacher, let us look at the contract that covers him with regard to his relationship to his workplace and employer.

## WEAK PROTECTIONS IN THE CONTRACT

The contract is one of the *tools* that can be used to protect the instructor in carrying out his effort to make a living teaching. It is itself an outcome of the activity system of which he is the subject (and here he is clearly a collective subject, as it covers him and all other instructors in his bargaining unit). But the degree of protection that it provides is a function of the "tools" and resources that his union brought to the table, as well as a function of the rules of bargaining and, most important, a function of the interaction of this activity system with the activity system against which (or with which) they were bargaining – that is, the City Colleges of Chicago administration. The balance of power during those negotiations was unequal and has led to weak protections for the instructor.

There are two sections of the contract that set out how a non-probationary employee can be terminated. These are Section 1(b) of Article VIII, Continued Employment, and Article IX, Discipline. Article VIII invokes a sort of administrative counseling, followed by an appeals process. In Article IX, the discipline – termination, for example – is imposed "as soon as practicable" and "shall be imposed in a confidential manner." The first, Section 1(b) of Article VIII, looks like the one that the Acting Dean is building a case under:

Article VIII – Continuous Service, Section 1: Continued Employment (b) Non-probationary employees who have not continued to perform satisfactorily shall be noticed in advance of their performance deficiency and counseled periodically [at least three (3) times during a period of at least (5) weeks] in ways to improve. If such employees continue to perform unsatisfactorily they shall be terminated.

The contract does not set out who does this counseling, what its content should be, or how the outcome of the counseling is evaluated. No time limit is set, so an employee who relapses five or ten years after an incident might be considered to "continue to perform unsatisfactorily." No consideration must be given to the possibility that an instructor may have a reason for his or her performance that stems from a professional concern. True, the terminated employee can request a review from the president of the college. But a negative decision by the president may only be appealed to a personnel review committee, which consists of two members appointed by the Board and one appointed by the union. Then the procedures of the Committee "shall be informal and no statement of rules or procedures shall be required or issued" [Section 2(b] and, most important, there is no appeal from this committee:

(iii) Neither the Union nor the employee shall have the right to appeal any decision under this subsection through the grievance procedure or to arbitration.

The other contract article that deals with termination is Article IX, Discipline. This article simply provides for firing a teacher on the spot and doing so secretly – "in a confidential manner."

In other words, it turns out that, although he has been working virtually full time in this program for twenty years, this teacher is in practice a contingent employee – a worker who has no job security. If the administration is in consensus about getting rid of a teacher, there is no way to balance this decision with faculty participation in the decision. The lack of effective opportunity to agree or disagree means that, with regard to terminating teachers, the faculty has no formal power at all, through the union or through other means, and the administration has all the power.

Imagine if the situation were reversed. Imagine what it would be like if a faculty leader could, as a response to late submission of paperwork by an administrator, set in motion a process for dismissal of that administrator that could not be effectively interfered with by any of her peers. Consider the difficulty of recruiting someone who would work under those conditions.

While we are looking at the contract, let us turn to the part where we find out what kind of wages this teacher, who has been teaching in the program for twenty years, is earning. Article XI, Wages and Benefits, gives us the answer: after fifteen years (the top of the scale), teachers in this college are making $22.85 per class hour. The maximum number of teaching hours that a teacher can be scheduled for per week is twenty-four, to a maximum per year of 1,152 hours. This means that a teacher with over fifteen years of employment, scheduled to work the maximum number of hours, can make $26,323.00 before taxes. In addition, $900 per year is allowed for class preparation (this works out to about seventy-eight cents per classroom hour). Benefits are a buy-in program, completely paid for by the employee with no employer contribution.

So this teacher, who is accused of "negligence" and "lacking commitment to the program" has been working for twenty years without job security in a job that pays at most $26,323 without benefits. Now let us turn to the teacher's response.

## THE TEACHER'S DEFENSE

The teacher, who is also the chief steward in his union, draws on the tools that he has learned to employ through his union experience. Rather than respond with anger or incoherence, he treats himself as a grievant whom he is representing and responds. That is, he chooses to define himself as part of a collective. He takes up the earlier questions, "Is it true? Is it the whole story?" Although the teacher's entire letter is reproduced here, it is broken out into paragraphs to enable an ongoing commentary.

TO: Acting Dean Y
FROM: Teacher X
RE: Your memo of May 25

Date: May 27

Your memo is inaccurate and misleading. I will begin with errors of fact.
1. The two registrations you mention in your final paragraph were not being added to my class for SP N2. They are registrations for the SU 99 term. The SU date is marked in the appropriate box on the forms.

If this teacher had in fact allowed two students to be in his class for an entire term without registering them, it would have lent considerable weight to an attempt to fire him. However, the teacher had marked the registration forms

SU (summer), not SP (spring) so they were timely after all. The administrator had misread them. But in a process without appeal, the administrator's mistake might never have been revealed.

The teacher continues:

2. While I regret, of course, that the attendance hours for my classes will not be counted or reimbursed, I cannot be held responsible for this. I submitted my SAR May 20, not May 24, that is, prior to the date on which End of Term Reports [ETRs] were run. In fact, I submitted my SAR initially on May 18. (Name omitted), the clerk who took them, returned them to my box with the note that I had miscalculated some of the attendance hours. I corrected these at the next available opportunity, Thursday, May 20th, and returned them to his box about 5 PM that same day.

Luckily, the clerk conscientiously kept a log of who submits SARs and when. The clerk, who has some job security through his union, does not fear getting in the middle of this kind of dispute. He is protected by the *tool* of his own union contract, which he undoubtedly has in mind when he sticks his neck out like this. Why the SARs were not passed along to the proper person in time to be included in the weekend run of End of Term Reports ETRs is not clear. However, they were out of the teacher's hands on Thursday, May 20.

The teacher then elaborates:

3. The language of your memo exaggerates the amount of available time that instructors have to complete SARs. You did note that teachers have other responsibilities during the time mentioned, including lesson preparation and "putting cabinets in order." In fact, I used about 1 1/2 hours of the April 29 Records Day to do records, including my SAR, but I did not complete it at that time. To have completed them would have meant lying about attendance for the following week. Then, as you know, the entire week of May 10 was filled with required activities. I did complete my SARs, along with other paperwork and class preparations, on the first day available for such work, Tuesday May 18. As I noted above, that was the day I turned them in to [the clerk], who checked them and turned them back to me for corrections.

A few things in this paragraph need clarification. First, the April 29 Records Day is a day in which teachers have the option of canceling classes for all or part of the day to do paperwork. The students, of course, do not have a choice if the teacher cancels class; they lose instruction. For many teachers, cutting instruction time is an undesirable choice. (Obviously, this is an example of a "quality" issue.) Second, April 29 is before the close of the term, so teachers have to "project" attendance if they want to complete SARs and then sign them as legal, subpoenable documents.

The memo now moves to another level:

I am sure that you are aware that one of the demands the union has made in current negotiations is for adequate time for paperwork; this episode makes a strong case for our demand.

The Acting Dean has not referred to this at all, but this is an important part of the "whole story," the context in which this event is occurring. To make this connection – between the teacher's individual situation and the contingent cohort's collective situation – is an aggressive and brave move by the teacher who is already in trouble. But teachers have been working without a contract for nearly a year. There is no question that the Acting Dean is aware of the situation regarding these negotiations. One of the contract demands is for five hours per term paid paperwork time – time to do the very work the teacher is accused of failing to do on time. In addition, by broadening the dispute to include bargaining, the teacher is reminding the Acting Dean that under labor law, union activity (including bargaining) is protected activity. Although this is a stretch, it is a strategic move.

4. Your charge that I "almost always turn in your SAR four or five days after the due date" is not true. This is not the sort of charge that you should make unless you can back it up. Saying "I understand," indicating that someone told you this about me, is not good enough. To place this charge in a memo that is copied to my personnel file without having evidence to support it is unacceptable.

One of the ways in which power is displayed, of course, is when one party is free to address the other party in a way that may be neither reciprocated nor acknowledged. This teacher deliberately responds to the administrator as if they were on an equal plane:

Finally, I need to address the tone of your memo. Language like "negligence," "lack of responsibility and commitment to the program" and "irresponsible" is inflammatory. You start with false allegations and proceed to label me with offensive terms that insult my twenty years of dedication to this work. Unchallenged, your memo could have serious consequences to my work here in this program, as you are well aware.

"Unchallenged" indicates that the teacher is aware that, given the lack of protection in the contract, he could simply be fired at once on the basis of being "negligent" and "irresponsible," whether these charges were true or not.

A third party, not knowing that your allegations are false, might take these offensive terms at face value.

An example of such a third party would be the Personnel Review Board (PRB). However, because the proceedings of the PRB are not "formal" and do not have to be made public, this teacher might reasonably expect that the PRB would take the administrator's allegations at face value.

Finally, the teacher's memo concludes:

Your actions, in other words, are unfair and malign me. In addition, I cannot overlook that this memo has appeared at a moment when our union is involved in difficult, drawn-out negotiations with the district over, among other things, this very issue of paid time to complete paperwork. As you know, I am not only on the negotiating team but am also the building site steward and the person most frequently called to resolve problems between teachers and administration. Therefore, attacks which undermine my credibility as a teacher have the double effect of undermining my effectiveness as an elected union representative. Our contract expressly forbids interfering with such duties. Your memo, for all the above reasons, should be withdrawn immediately.

CC:      Personnel file, union

The fact that this teacher is an elected steward means that, at the very least, he is well known among his peers. An attack on him has the multiplier effect created by his reputation among faculty, and if the attack is successful, it will chill faculty union activism for a long time. Someone who is doing his elected duty – whose union leadership could be legally sued, charged with failure to carry out duties of fair representation if he shrugs them off – acquires a history within an institution as time passes and evolves into the personal, individual embodiment of the relationship which, though masked by an appearance of compliance, is deeply adversarial. If we think of the contingent faculty as outsiders who observe the functioning of the college but have no power to influence it – anonymous faces at a window – he is among these faces at the window looking in, but, in his case, his face becomes recognizable. It reappears year after year, where no face should appear, an opposition where there is, theoretically, no opposition – reminding the administration that, in fact, the teachers, who comply mainly because they fear for their jobs, do know that there are other ways to run a college, better ways.

In this context of general powerlessness, any teacher who has been picked out from the rest of the faculty and represents a position that is not explicitly in agreement with the powers above inevitably appears to be a lone adversary, a situation most people will intentionally avoid at all costs. The ideal, of course, is to *engage in concerted activity* with others – the actual language of the U.S. National Labor Relations Act (U.S. Government, 1935, sec. 7). This is why, after all, unions exist in the first place, even in the fundamentally conservative environment of education. But the courage required to pursue creative, strategic activity under these conditions cannot be overestimated.

## QUALITY ISSUES THAT SOME FACULTY CONSIDERED WORTH STRIKING OVER

In fact, the teacher's situation was even worse than this. One of the reasons this situation was so aggravated was because the union had been attempting to negotiate issues that spoke directly to educational quality and also pulled some power back into the hands of teachers in the sense of writing into the contract measures of value that teachers consider important – for example, evaluations based on classroom teaching, opportunities for professional development, and – yes! – paid time outside of class time for paperwork. Negotiations had not been going well. At the time of these memos, faculty at several district sites covered by this contract had taken a strike vote, and the vote was in favor of striking, five to one. Add to this the fact that the administration had eliminated nearly forty percent of the jobs in this program over the past few years, and many of the remaining faculty were angry and increasingly militant. This teacher was visibly involved in the local leadership, which was spearheading the pressure to strike. That means that this memo came from administration at a time when this teacher was in the middle of a tense situation. The administration knew about this: Meetings around the strike vote were no secret. There was every reason to think that the memo, especially because it was based on flimsy if not trumped-up charges, had been timed strategically to isolate this teacher at a time when he knew he needed support going into this possible strike.

And what is it that some of the faculty had voted to strike over? Here are the actual demands that the administration management was resisting and that the teachers considered striking to get. The first four are clearly quality issues, purely professional items that will improve the quality of teaching of individual instructors and institution-wide.

- Evaluations based on classroom teaching, not on unpaid, non-teaching assignments;
- Extra paperwork pay – five hours per semester, so that instructors will not have to cancel class to complete paperwork;
- Prep time – one hour paid for every four hours taught;
- Professional development opportunities – $13,000 per year total for the district for outside tuition (allowing up to twenty-six teachers to take courses at colleges other than within the district they are teaching in, for which they already get tuition waivers); $500 per person maximum.

The last five of these items are typical union demands for conditions found at most organized workplaces: employer contributions toward benefits, paid sick leave, and pay increases.

- Paid sick days – nine per year for teachers working twenty-four hours per week;
- Retention deferral (Partial pay for four weeks unpaid layoff) one week after one year, with up to four weeks pay for those with seven years' seniority;
- Health Insurance – fifty dollars per month employer contribution for those working sixteen or more hours per week;
- Bereavement pay – one week, for immediate family as defined in the contract;
- Pay increases totaling five to ten dollars per hour, averaging six percent per year with step increases every two years.

Here is a union, trying to bargain for quality. Evaluations, prep time, paperwork time, professional development – what kind of institutional leaders would fight these?

## CONSEQUENCES: WHO WINS IF THE UNION LOSES?

To answer this question, let us think about what is at stake for each side. If management loses, what will be lost – who will suffer? If the union loses, what will be lost? Who will suffer? "Losing" this struggle will mean very different things to the two parties. When the union loses (that is, gives the administration what it wants), the faculty lose the means by which they can do their jobs adequately. When management "loses" in these negotiations (that is, gives the union what the faculty wants), the quality of the teaching institution may actually improve. Teachers, like the one whose situation we have been looking at, would, for example, be able to produce good teaching evaluations as evidence in favor of keeping their jobs, when charged with late paperwork. Charges of late paperwork will be less frequent if teachers had paid time to complete paperwork. But management will lose some – not much, but some – power.

The interaction illustrates several themes that constitute the relationship between teachers and administration, even when it is less inflamed:

- The influence of the administration's view of teaching, as expressed in the collective bargaining agreement. This administration holds a view of teaching as occurring in isolation, inside the black box of the classroom, rather than as an institution-wide practice that emerges from a culture of interaction among teachers and students. One way that this view is expressed is through the lack of institutional support for non-classroom activities, including prep time and paperwork.
- The dearth of information about teaching and teachers' work, which encourages administrators to rely on criteria like paperwork processing for evaluations of teachers' work;
- The impact of at-will employment on the balance of power between teachers and administrators;
- The demands placed on faculty leaders when they take on the quality issue in an environment of unequal power relationships.
- The limitations of faculty power over not only their own working conditions, but also their power to represent the basic interests of their students.

The problem of how a conflict like this can move toward resolution needs to be answered on a scale greater than one single teacher in one college in one district. More power for the union does not mean just that the total power of the institution is shared differently. It may mean that the institution plays a different role in the city and community. For example, the faculty definition is, we would argue, close to the likely perspective of an adult student. Evidence of this is the claim, "Our working conditions are our students' learning conditions." Students and faculty should be allies in this confrontation. To the extent that they prevail, the total power of the institution, and all the students, employees, and others connected to it, may become greater vis-à-vis the city or the state or the entire society if the union wins.

Our example is clarified by the use of CHAT in the following way: The actions being taken in this study are the operations of two separate activity systems. Each activity system is based on the point of view of the main actors (the teacher and the Acting Dean) as representatives of the groups from which they have emerged. Although the people who populate these two activity systems work in the same building, breathe the same air, and get paid by the same employer, they are different in purpose and consciousness, interpret the goals of their activities differently, and therefore are different in rules and values, resources, and power.

Because this case study comes from the workplace and is an example of a difference along a class divide, this makes it particularly illustrative of the Marxist roots of CHAT. One central tenet of Marxism is that the relation of exploitation (the worker giving up and the employer taking part of the value produced by the workers' labor power) results in different views of the work process in particular and the world in general – that is, different consciousnesses. This example, drawn from the educational workplace, is a sample of that difference in consciousness.

## "QUALITY" ISSUES ON A DISTRICT-WIDE SCALE: TARGETS FOR PRIVATIZATION

Taken together, the above themes illustrate the barriers that stand between faculty unions and the goal of collaborative bargaining with administrations if faculty unions agree to bargain under the umbrella concept of "quality." Clearly, the response, necessarily collective, to these barriers must be informed by a serious assessment of the differential powers and interests at play. This is no time for wishful thinking, but neither is it a time for despair nor for a union retreat from the reality of what, finally, amounts to class differences inside higher education.

We believe that subsequent events, since this case study was originally written, bear out our conclusion. Individually, this teacher was not fired. Later, he was elected to a top union office. Though a strike was not called, some small gains were made on the issues teachers raised. But a matter of months after the settlement, the administration initiated a process of examining many functions of the college district for possible privatization and outsourcing. One function already contracted out was *all* central financial operations, which have been handed over to the American Express Corporation, an action seemingly unprecedented in the history of U.S. public higher education. Also on the list for possible privatization are custodial services, computer services, library services, some counseling, and, again unprecedented if implemented, some instructional programs, including computer instruction, some business courses, and the very adult education program from which this case study is drawn.

One of the preparatory actions taken by the administration and board of the Chicago City Colleges district has been to call for "quality reviews" of selected programs, with very short timelines. Many employees fear that this is merely a cover for targeting potentially profitable aspects of the colleges for privatization. The adult educators' union has passed a resolution to this effect. The administration's choice of the rhetoric of "quality" to motivate this process would appear to sustain our contention of necessary adversality on this issue.

In fact, workers in the colleges have drawn just this conclusion and have created, both through bottom-up initiatives and the cooperation of some of the leaderships of the multiple unions in the district, the first city-wide employee and student coalition, across craft and status lines, in many years. The Committees United against Privatization (COUP) has made the City Colleges' privatization drive, conducted under the rhetoric of quality, a major issue. COUP has also sparked an increase in rank-and-file activism in some of the unions and among the sizable number of unrepresented employees, with unprecedented coalition mass meetings and demonstrations. Front-page stories in the daily commercial press testify to their success making this a civic issue (Dodge, 2001; Strzalka, 2001).

We would argue that these events suggest that the total power and influence that exists in an educational institution, such as a community college system, is not a zero-sum game. More power for employees, including faculty and their unions, does not just rearrange the power relations within the institution, though it certainly does do that. This power shift in the direction of workers can allow for the redefinition of quality in education and spur the assembly of coalitions that can actually increase the total power and influence of the institution and its educational services in the community. In CHAT terminology, this would mean expanding and redefining the community base of the teaching activity system. Whether that will occur in Chicago is yet to be seen, but enough has happened to suggest that the path of coalition with other educational workers and students, rather than with administrators, is the way to assemble the power necessary to bargain for the sort of quality in education that serves the interests of the working-class majority.

SECTION III

# WORK

# 8

## Contradictory Class Relations in Work and Learning

*Some Resources for Hope*

### D. W. Livingstone

**INTRODUCTION**

Antagonism between ruling classes and labouring classes has animated so-cial change in most historical societies. The miserable conditions of the peasantry and other labouring classes in feudal Russia and the terribly coercive rule of the tsars were breeding grounds for the 1917 Russian revolution and "the fantastically stimulating atmosphere of an active, rapidly changing society" (Luria, 1979: 1) in which a cultural–historical activity theory of learning initially developed. The massive concentrations of economic power in corporate capitalist hands in global capitalism today are associated with growing economic polarization, mounting misery in the "third world," and increasingly coercive efforts by imperial powers, most obviously the U.S. capitalist class and it allies, to strengthen their hegemonic position and attack the condition of their own labouring classes at the same time as they undermine allegiance of many of these workers to these regimes. Class antagonisms can hardly explain all social change but neither can they be ignored if we hope to understand the dynamic processes of lived experience, working, and learning in advanced capitalism (see Seccombe and Livingstone, 1999).

Marxist theories of learning were first systematically developed by Vygotsky and his followers in the wake of the Russian revolution, stagnated under Stalinism, and have subsequently been further developed in both the East and West as variants of cultural–historical activity theory (CHAT). However, class relations in the learning process have remained largely underdeveloped in this research. Some contemporary non-Marxist theories of learning, notably Pierre Bourdieu's theory of cultural capital, attend more explicitly to class relations but in a one-sided manner that also obscures working-class creative capacities. There is an evident need for Marxist theories of learning, and of activity theory in particular, to pay more concerted attention to contradictory class relations in the learning process. This chapter offers a brief critical review of the development of Vygotsky's perspective, suggests some useful additional conceptual tools, and provides a few relevant empirical findings. In particular, I suggest an expanded conception of forms of labour (including paid and unpaid labour) and forms of learning (including informal non-taught learning, informal education and training, organized non-school education, and formal schooling) in capitalist societies. The learning process is posited to be significantly shaped and driven by class relations in all of these forms of activity. From a working-class standpoint, the use-values and exchange-values implicated in learning activities are suggested as motivating forces in different actual learning practices. Findings from recent case studies with unionized workers are used to illustrate this argument. Greater attention to indigenous working class learning stimulated by use-value and socialization of the forces of knowledge production is suggested.

Lev Vygotsky deserves great credit as one of the first and most significant contributors to the development of a Marxist theory of learning. During the early years of the Soviet initiative to create a socialist state in Russia, he and his research team applied dialectical methods of investigation to more fully comprehend the movement of concepts and processes involved in human development, especially child development. In a similar fashion to Marx's critique of classical political economy in the development of *Capital*, he conducted an extensive critique of the conventional psychologists of his time as a means of formulating a more dialectical understanding of the relations between thought/speech and action from the most elementary to the development of higher psychological process. He took the classical Marxist view that "being determines consciousness" in the sense that the psychological makeup of individuals depends on the development of forces of production and the structure of social groups of particular societies. In highly developed societies with complex class structures, the relationship between base and psychological superstructure was understood to be mediated by many material and spiritual factors, but even here ". . . human beings are created by the society in which they live and . . . it represents the determining factor in the formation of their personalities" (Vygotsky, 1930/1994: 176). The central features of this approach were that it was instrumental, cultural and historical: instrumental in that all higher psychological responses to environmental stimuli are mediated by auxiliary stimuli or cues; cultural in that higher-order processes entail the social organization of tasks and relevant tools, most notably language; and historical in that these tools, such as writing and arithmetic, have expanded the powers of human knowledge and contributed to different organization of higher cognitive processes (see Vygotsky, 1978; Luria, 1979).

Vygotsky's research team carried out a series of experiments to identify the origins of higher forms of conscious behaviour in relations with the external world. The most dramatic of these experiments were conducted with peasant people of central Asia who were emerging from pre-literate feudal conditions into collectivized farming and modern schooling. Marked differences in modes of thought were found, with increasing dispositions toward voluntary attention, active memory, and abstract argument, all associated with experience of collectivization (Luria, 1979); related studies were conducted with rural and homeless youths. Extensive laboratory studies were carried out with young children and people with language disorders. This corpus of research can now be recognized as one of the first systematic and empirically tested theories of the social construction of learning and, in spite of its suppression during the Stalinist era, much of the research reported in this book testifies to its continuing relevance.

However, the many conceptual developments and empirical studies inspired by Vygotsky have largely focused on small group processes and activities such as the development of shared meanings, individual and distributed cognition, speech, and other skill formation in classroom, family, or paid workplace settings. As Elhammoumi (2001a) has observed, at much of this research has tended to overlook the larger institutional relations, such as forms of social control and power, distribution of wealth, and divisions of labour and social class, that form the bases of the structures and meanings in such particular settings. At the same time, most of the associated research has paid little attention to the fundamental contradiction in capitalist social structures that represents the most significant source of creative learning among subordinated classes, namely the contradiction between continuing socialization of the forces of production (especially knowledge production) and privatized relations of ownership of the means of production. Without sustained attention to the central contradictory social relationships serving to reproduce capitalist societies and generating the potential for their transformation, the basic objectives of Marxist inquiry are missed.

## MODES OF PRODUCTION AND HUMAN DEVELOPMENT

In an essay he wrote in the midst of his research, Vygotsky (1930/1994) espoused a clearly Marxist understanding of human consciousness as dependent on the development of the forces and social relations of production. The peasant studies of stark changes in modes of thought with collectivization probably helped to confirm this view. He was also in accord with Marx's view of the increasingly differentiated and fragmented historical development of human personality with the growth of capitalist industrial society. All classes in the division of labour experienced one-sided development through the instruments of their activities and associated training: the production worker chained to the dismal and exploitative monotony of specific fractional operations, the petty bourgeois to his capital and urge for profit. But Vygotsky also concurred with Marx that forces and conditions were developing within capitalist industry to overcome these exploitative and one-sided forms and facilitate fully developed individuals:

If in the beginning [of the capitalist period] the individual was transformed into a fraction, into the executor of a fractional function, into a living extension of the machine, then at the end of it, the very requirements of manufacturing require an all-round developed, flexible person, who would be capable of changing the forms of work, and of organizing the production process and controlling it. . . . [T]he growth of large-scale industry contains within itself hidden potential for the development of the human personality and . . . it is only the capitalist form of organization of the industrial process which is responsible for the fact that all these forces exert a one-sided and crippling influence, which retards personal development. (p. 180)

Caught up in the rapidly changing conditions of the Russian revolution, he also professed a faith that this development was imminent:

This general contradiction between the development of the production forces and the social order which was in correspondence with the level of development of these production forces, is being resolved by the socialist revolution and a transition to a new social order and a new form of organization of human relationships. *Alongside this process, a change in the human personality and the alteration of man himself must inevitably take place.* (pp. 180–81)

Whereas in his mature works Marx took a working class standpoint, both in terms of his engagement with the International Workingmen's Association and a focus on exploitative class relations, Vygotsky and his co-researchers focused closely on the interplay of social practices and speech patterns among their experimental subjects with little apparent attention to contradictory class relations. There were undoubtedly compelling reasons for this limited focus in the context of the strident optimism about proletarian liberation and the deadly ideological struggles that prevailed in the U.S.S.R. during this period (Gielen and Jeshmaridian, 1999). But the consequence was that little research attention was devoted to the actual differentiated conditions of class existence and consciousness that still dominated people's lives, even in the continuing studies of Luria and Leontiev, the co-researchers who long outlived Vygotsky.

With the demise of the Soviet Union and increasing global reach of the capitalist system, the central contradiction between continuing socialization of the forces of production and privatized relations of ownership of the means of production becomes more stark and presumably more relevant to human consciousness and learning.

## GLOBAL CAPITALISM AND THE KNOWLEDGE SOCIETY

The extension of capitalist commodity relations of production is now virtually global. Since the economic stagnation of the 1960s, the spatial and temporal mobility of capital has led to significant gains over organized labour around the globe. Many of the labour accords of the Fordist era have disintegrated as closures, mergers, automation, downsizing, and outsourcing are used to produce increasingly insecure labour forces. Of course, paid workplaces in capitalist economies have always been characterized by continual change as enterprises compete with each other for commodity markets, employers negotiate with employees over maximizing profits and/or creating fulfilling working conditions, and new technologies are adopted to aid all of these objectives. Throughout the twentieth century, capital intensification in extractive and manufacturing industries put an increasing premium on human mediation of expensive machinery. The rise of the service sector was contingent on the selling of labour-intensive services rather than material goods. The recent proliferation of information technologies has made a wider array of work tasks dependent on the self-monitoring use of workers' minds. In short, there has been a gradual trend for the motives and learning capacities of the workforce to play a more strategic role in the capitalist labour process. The dominant discourse of management theory has also shifted from advocacy of scientific management of workers' bodily movements through extrinsic rewards to promotion of *learning organizations* designed to enable continuing learning and enhance worker motivation to share their knowledge (see Boud and Garrick, 1999).

So, at the same time as capital intensification has produced pervasive unemployment and strategic hiring advantages over labour, the capitalist labour process per se demands more highly qualified workers to operate the tools of production. A major consequence is the proliferation of underemployment. That is, people seek higher and higher qualifications to compete for jobs whereas the availability of decent jobs diminishes. The cumulative knowledge and skill of the workforce increasingly exceed the requirements of the capitalist job structure. Empirical assessments of the changing occupational class composition of the employed labour force and of specific vocational preparation requirements for the aggregate array of jobs in countries like Canada and the United States have found only very gradual net upgrading of the actual skill requirements of jobs at best over the past few generations (Lavoie and Roy, 1998; Leckie, 1996; Barton, 2000; Handel, 2000). Conversely, rates of completion of post-compulsory schooling and participation in further education courses have grown exponentially during the same period (Livingstone, 2001). So, rates of underemployment – in terms of structural unemployment, involuntary reduced employment, and educational attainments exceeding job requirements – have grown significantly during this period (Livingstone, 1999). Dominant claims for the emergence of a *knowledge-based economy* remain suspect in terms of the restricted power most workers have to develop their knowledge and skill in capitalist workplaces, but most potential workers appear to be making concerted efforts to develop them nevertheless.

The socialization of the forces of knowledge production (especially through the availability of free voluntary forms, such as public libraries, trade union schools, and now electronic information networks) is a major source of potential autonomous cultural production by subordinate social groups. The increasing availability to working class people of such socialized forces of knowledge production represents a continual challenge to private capitalist efforts (via conglomerate ownership of mass media, commodified information packages, etc.) to control the social relations of knowledge production. It is probably true that if asked, "How are you doing in terms of investments?" most people would now probably reflect the capitalist fixation with exchange relations and profits and give a common initial response referring to money and other commodities. But most working class people invest substantial time, energy, and thought in unpaid activities primarily oriented to practical utility outside commodity circuits; they also exercise wide discretion in their alternative consumption uses of acquired commodities, and public accessibility of diverse information sources is increasing. This opposition between socialized forces and privatized relations of knowledge production is the *fundamental contradiction of knowledge development and learning in advanced capitalist societies* (see Livingstone, 1999).

### THE LIMITS OF RECENT EDUCATIONAL RESEARCH

There has been a very substantial corpus of empirical research on class and schooling as well as on workplace learning in the past few generations, and these studies have been increasingly informed by the cultural–historical activity theory approach. I will not review the features of such studies in any detail here (see Livingstone, 1995), except to note some of their common limitations in relation to the central contradiction of knowledge development and learning in advanced capitalist societies.

Among the most influential contemporary theoretical contributions on class and learning are the cultural reproduction theories of Pierre Bourdieu and Basil Bernstein.[1] Both of these eminent scholars have drawn lightly on the Marxist tradition in developing their conceptions. Bourdieu and Passeron's (1977) notion of cultural capital was developed by analogy with Marx's analysis of capital as an accumulation and reproduction process, whereas Bernstein's notion of restricted and elaborated language codes was partly inspired by the work of Vygotsky. A great deal of contemporary learning theory takes a class-blind and individualist perspective, but both of these

---

[1] This account of the work of Bourdieu and Bernstein is largely drawn from Livingstone and Sawchuk (2004). Among Bourdieu's wide array of writings, the most pertinent mature works are Bourdieu (1984, 1991). In Bernstein's narrower corpus, see Bernstein (1990, 1996). For some of the most extensive and insightful critiques, see Fowler (1997) and Swartz (1997) on Bourdieu and Sadovnik (1995) on Bernstein.

scholars have developed structural models of class differences grounded in cultural sensibilities and linked them to differential social effects of schooling processes. A critical appreciation of their contributions is needed to move beyond the limits of cultural capital theory. In both Bourdieu and Bernstein, the primary emphasis is placed on the general cultural knowledge, sophisticated vocabularies, and precise information on how schools work, which children from higher status origins acquire from their families. The possession of these cultural tools leads to their greater success in school relations than working class kids. Such cultural theories offer considerable insights into the discriminatory schooling conditions faced by working class people. In Bourdieu's case, as in human capital theories generally, an analogy is made between capital assets and human learning capacities. Children of the affluent classes, who have acquired familiarity with bourgeois cultural forms at home (through exposure to their parents' knowledge and manners, as well as linguistic forms) are seen to possess the means of appropriating similarly oriented school knowledge relatively easily. Working class kids, in contrast, find their unfamiliarity with these cultural forms to be a major obstacle to successful school performance. Bernstein makes similar arguments primarily in terms of language codes, with upper middle class children considered to possess more elaborated codes for abstracting and generalizing from school curricular materials. Both scholars, with the aid of teams of colleagues, have done extensive empirical verification and refinement of their models, deepening both their complexity and their insights into the discriminatory cultural processes that operate against the working class in most schools. Both theorists expose the dominance side of cultural reproduction in excruciating detail. At least in this limited sense, their contributions are comparable to those of feminist and anti-racist scholars who have critically exposed the dominant codes and structures of patriarchal and racist cultural forms (e.g., Spender, 1980; Said, 1993).

But Bourdieu and Bernstein have been preoccupied with delineating the cultural reproduction of inequality within fixed institutional forms. Thus, their accounts remain one-dimensional, functionalist descriptions of the status quo rather than real explanations of it. Bourdieu's and Bernstein's theories of class cultures have ignored a central rule of sociological investigation promulgated by one of the founding fathers of sociology they both build on, Emile Durkheim: To understand any social fact, we must study it through the full range of its variation. They never comprehend the creative cultural practices, independent education and learning activities, or collective cultural agency of the organized working class.

As Collins (1993: 134) concludes in one of the most nuanced critiques of Bourdieu's class-specific research on language and education:

[Bourdieu's] dialectic of subjective action and objective conditioning.... lacks a sense of the primacy of contradiction, however, and we are left with an account of conditioned strategies for action that overrides the conflictual creativity of interaction-based agency.... [T]he discursive always seems deducible from, reducible to, in a word, determined by something else: class conditions, capital composition, habitus, field effects. There is a truth in this determinist argument, but it is one-sided.... We need to allow for ... creative, discursive agency in conditions pre-structured, to be sure, but also fissured in unpredictable and dynamic ways.[2]

Working class people are always presented as reactive and marginalized in these perspectives, even in the more recent, empirically grounded works (Bourdieu, 1993; Bernstein, 1996). For example, as Fowler (1997: 11) observes, Bourdieu has exaggerated the cultural dispossession of the masses and excluded any popular art in his category of consecrated culture, constructing a canonical closure that is too complete and that blinded him to the existence of authorship within these popular art forms. Similarly, Pearl (1997: 143) argues that Bourdieu's central concept of *habitus*, which refers to humans' situated cognitive functioning and sense of possibilities, underestimated shifts in expectations and aspirations among different groups. He thereby developed a highly sophisticated defense of deficit theory (i.e., the limited capacities of lower class and other subordinated groups) whereas ostensibly aligning himself on the side of equity and social justice.

Socio-cultural theory-based research on education that builds more substantially on Vygotsky's work has experienced a resurgence in the current generation (e.g. Moll, 1990; Kozulin et al., 2003). Much of this research has followed Vygotsky's own preoccupation with delineating processes of shaping children's development and learning in relation to their general social environment. Some studies have offered more differentiated accounts of learning by children from distinct class origins. But most of these studies have tended to assess children's learning capacities from the standpoint of an established (middle class) educative process (e.g., Hautamaeki, 1986; Panofsky, 2003) or with very young children (Rojo, 2001). There are also recent ethnographic accounts that are more cognizant of changing social relations of schooling in response to extreme economic restructuring in predominantly working class communities (Packer, 2001). Such ethnographic studies can hardly avoid taking some account of working class kids' resistance and may register the lack of agency in conceptions of working class learning such as Bourdieu's (see Packer, 2001: 202–206, 296, and passim). But working class learning capacities continue to be viewed in limited terms

---

[2] Bohman (1999: 135) makes a similar critique of Bourdieu's general conception of human agency:

Actors are, in effect, "cultural dupes" to their habitus as they were judgmental dupes to Parsonian norms....Bourdieu needs to be clearer that even shared means are subject to constant interpretation and reinterpretations, often in ways that contest current identities and practices.

of either adaptation or resistance to upper middle class constructions of knowledge.

More generally, one of the most striking conditions of working class knowledge in capitalist societies appears to be the systemic refusal to permit any significant recognition of it in dominant institutional settings. I have alluded to the multiple dimensions of *underemployment* and their disproportionately high incidence among working class people earlier. Versions of this theme of wasted knowledge and denied recognition of working people's skills and learning capacities are now widespread. As a young woman public sector worker expresses it:

My friends are all underemployed. People from my generation, 20 to 35, we're all underemployed. People with university degrees, but they're maids or waitresses. Everybody I know. If not degrees, they have incredible intelligence and are good at a lot of things, but.... Education and the work world need to be re-thought. (Livingstone and Sawchuk, 2000: 140)

It is equally striking that the proponents of cultural capital and socio-cultural theories of education have virtually ignored the problem of underemployment. We suggest that this is primarily because their conceptions of knowledge and learning processes have focused almost exclusively upon aspects of knowledge that are easily quantified or expressed in commodity exchange relationships. Most versions of human capital theory rely heavily on an analogy with financial capital. The Marxist distinction between exchange-value and use-value is highly pertinent here. It is only from a working class standpoint that the use-value of much of working people's knowledge that is not officially credited in school and labour market exchanges becomes visible and valorized. But even if working class learning is conceived in the extraordinarily narrow terms of the labour market exchange value of school credentials, the underemployment of working people's knowledge in capitalist workplaces should now be seen as an endemic social problem. In any case, in contrast to cultural capital theory and current applications of socio-cultural theory to schooling, researchers' sustained engagement with working class-learners and organizations begins to generate an alternative perspective on their cultural sensibilities and learning capacities.

### FORMS OF WORK AND FORMS OF LEARNING

An inclusive understanding of relations between learning and work in capitalist societies requires expanded conceptions and careful consideration of the "underlayers," that is, unpaid as well as paid forms of work, and informal learning as well as the institutionalized formal education that people experience. As Figure 8.1 outlines, there are at least three distinguishable forms of work (paid employment, housework, and community volunteer

| Forms of Work | | | Forms of Learning |
|---|---|---|---|
| Paid Employment | ← | → | Formal Schooling |
| Housework | | | Further Education |
| Community Volunteer Work | | | Informal Training |
| | | | Non-Taught Informal Learning |

FIGURE 8.1. Forms of work and forms of learning.

work) and four forms of learning (initial formal schooling, further adult education courses, informal training, and non-taught informal learning).

"Work" is commonly regarded as synonymous with "earning a living" through *paid employment* in the production, distribution, and exchange of goods and services commodities. But most of us must also do some household work, and many need to contribute to community labours to reproduce ourselves and society. Both housework and community volunteer work are typically unpaid and under-appreciated, but they remain essential for our survival and quality of life (see Waring, 1988). *Housework*, including cooking, cleaning, childcare, and other sometimes complex household tasks, has been largely relegated to women and only gained some public recognition as women have gained power through increased participation in paid employment. As community life has become more fragmented with dual-earner commuter households, time devoted to *community work* to sustain and build social life through local associations and helping neighbours has declined, and the productive importance of this work has been rediscovered (Putnam, 2000). All three forms should be included in any thorough accounting of contemporary work practices.

"Learning," in the most generic sense, involves the gaining of understanding, knowledge, or skill anytime and anywhere through individual and group processes. Learning occurs throughout our lives. The sites of learning make up a continuum, ranging from spontaneous responses to everyday life to highly organized participation in formal education programs. The dominant tendency in contemporary thought has been to equate learning with the provision of learning opportunities in settings organized by institutional authorities and led by teachers approved by these authorities. *Formal schooling* has frequently been identified with continuous enrollment in age-graded, bureaucratically structured institutions of formal schooling from early childhood to tertiary levels, ignoring other types of instruction in bodies of traditional knowledge in subordinate groups (see Illich, 1971). In addition, *further education* includes a diverse array of further education courses and workshops in many institutionally organized settings, from schools to workplaces and community centres. Such continuing education is the most evident site of lifelong learning for adults past the initial cycle of schooling. But we also continually engage in informal learning activities to acquire understanding, knowledge, or skill outside of the curricula of institutions providing educational programs, courses, or workshops. *Informal education or training* occurs when mentors take responsibility for instructing others without sustained reference to a pre-established curriculum in more incidental or spontaneous situations, such as guiding them in learning job skills or in community development activities. Finally, all other forms of explicit or tacit learning in which we engage either individually or collectively without direct reliance on a teacher/mentor or an externally organized curriculum can be termed *non-taught self-directed or collective informal learning*. As Allen Tough (1978), a leading adult education researcher, has observed, informal learning is the submerged part of the iceberg of adult learning activities. It is at least arguable that, for most adults, informal learning (including both informal training and non-taught learning activities) represents our most important learning for coping with our changing environment. All of these forms of learning overlap and interact. But no account of "lifelong learning" can be complete without considering people's informal learning activities as well as their initial formal schooling and further education through the life course.

It should be noted here that socio-linguistic research conducted outside of school settings, with black working class youths, for example, has found much greater expressive capacity than Bernstein's imputed language codes (Labov, 1966, 2001). In terms of the dynamics of linguistic change through popular culture, it appears that some of the most creative current sources may be found in marginalized working class communities – consider dub poetry and hip hop music. In addition, some comparative community-based ethnographies have found complex capacities of black and white working class kids to shift between "standard" and more particular language traditions (Brice-Heath, 1983).

In contrast to most research on schooling, empirical studies of workers' employment-related learning based on cultural–historical activity theories have also been more attentive to specific creative and often informal practices in learning at work (e.g., Engeström, 1999a). Studies of problem solving in the realm of everyday activities, such as shopping, have discovered even more creative learning capacities among people with little schooling (Lave, 1988). The significance of such studies lies in their attention to the standpoints of subordinated people and the learning practices that they find relevant to solve problems they themselves identify and control. In Marxist terms, use-value in everyday life is the primary objective rather than capitalist exchange-value. The main reason discovery of such creativity is surprising is that recognition of working class capacity in advanced capitalist society continues to be highly devalued in exchange relations and dominant ideologies (compare Freire, 1970; Sharp, Hartwig, and O'Leary, 1989).

There is a compelling need for more extensive research into the realms of use-value, the forms of unpaid work, and informal learning that remain more substantially within the discretionary everyday control of working class

people. Of course, the use-value and exchange-value of activities are not simply dichotomous but exist in dialectical tension, whereas learning and work
are also overlapping spheres of activity. Although the dialectical forms and
overlapping character of learning and work activities remain seriously underdeveloped in cultural–historical activity theory to date, CHAT retains
great potential to aid understanding and overcoming of these forms and
relations. But most fundamentally, it is working class application of the
increasingly socialized forces of knowledge production in realms where
they retain the most discretionary control that can have the greatest potential for developing their capabilities, in Vygotsky's (1994: 180) terms, the
"hidden potential for the development of the human personality." Without this development, the actual liberation of exploited classes remains
illusory.

### PROSPECTS FOR CHANGE

As Gramsci (1994: 9,10,12) observed:

[E]very revolution has been preceded by a long process of intense critical activity,
of new cultural insight and the spread of ideas through groups of men [sic] initially
resistant to them, wrapped up in the process of solving their own, immediate economic and political problems, and lacking any bonds of solidarity with others in the
same position.... [T]here is no reason why the proletariat ... should not know how
and why and by whom it has been preceded, and how useful that knowledge can
prove.

The contradictions of capitalism continually provoke critical activity by exploited classes. In this period of global capitalist hegemony and diminished
strength of organized labour, sites more removed from exchange relations
become more important sites of critical learning activity. But this is not to suggest that the capitalist labour process ever becomes fully dominated by capital. Even in the most highly automated production processes, machine operators retain significant uncaptured control. The informal training provided
by more experienced operators remains essential to any novice wanting to
perform the job. For example, a young rolling mill operator in a unionized
steel mill, now on the job for several years, describes his experience:

Reading the tolerances in molten steel is *all* eyeball because we burn wood against it,
it makes an impression, and each mark on the impression dictates what you need to
do. That was the hardest part about the job, learning how to read that wood. The first
time I saw this guy stick a piece of wood against the bar flying by him I thought "He's
just doing that for the hell of it." [Laughs.] But that's the learning process, figuring
out what the steel is doing, or what grade, or what your tolerances are, and how it
reacts with different types of wood.... The guy who trained me is *absolutely* a super
guy. A pain in the ass to get to know. He told me that *sound* would save my life there
one day. And I wear earmuffs, and I wear earplugs. And when I was there for the first

couple of weeks, I just looked at him like he was from outer space, because I had no idea what he was talking about. I hear things now that I shouldn't hear. . . . That Mill, when it changes speed, I know. I know where it changed speed, if the bar is loose somewhere I can hear it, if it breaks out somewhere – the sound plays that much of a role. . . . Basically I learned the job like he did . . . a senior guy said, "Come with me, shut up, sit down, watch what I do." . . . I think I'm probably a year away from proficiency, to the point where I'll never be questioned ever again [by supervisors] on what I do.[3]

Many working class employees retain some discretionary control over their jobs, although seldom to this extent. Indeed, the most automated and computerized labour processes may depend more directly on some monitoring mediation by workers' minds and thereby enhance the potential collective economic power of the diminishing numbers of directly productive labourers (compare Mallet, 1975). In any case, the process of paid labour should never be dismissed as a strategic source of both dependent and autonomous development of working class capacity.

Indeed, case studies conducted at employment sites in cooperation with labour unions have discovered that many assembly line workers have developed informal learning networks to teach themselves how to use personal computers. Some of these workers have become competent computer programmers, even though they have no employer encouragement and no immediate opportunities to use these skills in their jobs (Sawchuk, 2003). Recent survey research finds that, although industrial and service workers are generally less formally schooled than corporate executives, managers, and professional employees, they are just as likely to devote time and energy to both informal job-related learning, ranging from computer literacy to health and safety, as well as unpaid work and general interest-related informal learning (Livingstone, 2001). Although much of this general knowledge may be irrelevant from the immediate objective of enhancing current job productivity, it is directly applicable in other socially useful and fulfilling household and community work and, potentially, in jobs redesigned to more fully use workers' growing repertoire of skills.

It is also probably the case that labour unions remain the most sustainable community sites for the development of collective critical insights about the capitalist system among working class people. A young assembly line worker in a large unionized auto plant describes his main informal learning activities:

I'll spend time learning anything to be better, music, computers, but the *union* is the big passion for me, like I feel like that's the thing where I can have the most opportunity to do things. For me, it's like that's what I want to do, you know . . . But with the union, there's so much potential to change and to do things and let's face

---

[3] Interview with rolling mill operator, local steel mill, Toronto, May 2004.

it, the pendulum has swung back. You know, I think we made a lot of progressive gains and it's swung back the other way where we're getting stripped of things that we bargained for. We're losing things that we achieved forty and fifty years ago and those things are being challenged, and the movement is an exciting place to be right now. Let's face it, because we haven't, you know, we've had struggles, like, no question all the way through. But now we're at a real pivotal point where the corporations are really saying to hell with the trade union movement, let's go global. Let's set up shop some place in the Pacific Rim where the human rights are ignored. . . . I mean, it's horrible. When you think about it, I mean, how can you support a system like that?. . . . You've got to understand. If there's an agenda that you want to put across to people and you want to build a movement, you have to have some knowledge on what the issues are. You have to be able to explain them on the shop floor if you want the support because as a union we're only going to move forward or push an agenda if we have the support of the people. . . . We're going to have to pave the road before they'll drive down it. It's a dirt road and they're not ready to drive down some of these roads yet, but they will, or we're going to lose. We're at a bit of a crossroads. We have to change. We can't stay the same, but we can't forget our past and we can't give up the gains we've made. So this means new ways of fighting for things and sometimes the new ways of fighting things are going back and doing the old way. For example, young guys who've never been on strike have to learn how to picket and how prior strikes contributed to increased workers' and civil rights. (Livingstone, 2002: 224, 230)

Labour unions exist in many forms in advanced capitalist societies and opportunities for worker-centred learning vary widely; they are hardly exclusive sites for the development of the working classes in capitalism (see Livingstone and Sawchuk, 2004). But they continue to represent the most sustainable organizational sites for collective development of independent working class consciousness. Recent in-depth studies of the paid and unpaid labour practices of unionized workers in large-scale industrial settings have found that their expressions of oppositional working class consciousness are far greater than workers in general (Seccombe and Livingstone, 1999).

As both Marx and Vygotsky both asserted, the relations between consciousness and material conditions in developed societies with complex class structures are increasingly complicated. The proletariat in Marx's sense represents a diminishing portion of the labour force, whereas both intermediate class positions and marginalized underclasses more dependent on advanced capitalism both increase (Livingstone and Mangan, 1996). There is no point in glorifying the unionized industrial working class or in romanticizing the current revolutionary potential of the working class in general – which currently exhibits even more limited class consciousness. Any democratically constituted transformation from capitalism would probably involve strategic alliances with other exploited classes and those discriminated against within this system more immediately on grounds of gender, race, age, and disability.

The capitalist mode of production has massively increased the commodification of everyday life over the past two centuries. Continual change is inherent in the system, and prospects for descent into barbarism persist. Resolution of the general contradiction between the development of the production forces that irresistibly make information and knowledge ever more accessible and the private capitalist social relations through which ruling classes obstinately try to restrict access for profit is unlikely to be imminent. But, if resolution through democratic transition to a new social order that nurtures fully developed human personalities is ever to occur, critical learning activities and bonds of solidarity among those highly exploited by this system remain an essential pre-condition. Those researchers who share Marx and Vygotsky's vision would be well advised to pay greater sustained attention to indigenous working class learning activities.

# 9

## From Labor Process to Activity Theory

Paul S. Adler

### INTRODUCTION

As new technologies and new organizational forms proliferate, work is moving back to the center of organizational research (Barley, 1996; Barley and Kunda, 2001). And as interest in work grows, so too does the corresponding theoretical challenge: How best can we apprehend the nature of work itself and its links to both the organizational structure and to the lived experience of work?

This chapter returns to the roots of one of the more prominent theories of work organization, Labor Process Theory (LPT; see Thompson, 1989; Wardell, Steiger, and Meiskins, 1999; Jermier, 1998). Inaugurated by Braverman's "classic" work (1974; classic according to Burawoy, 1996) and inspired by Marx, LPT has been a key influence on critical research on work around the world. Recently, however, LPT has been losing momentum in favor of post-modernist strands of theorizing, in particular, those building on the work of Michel Foucault, where the inspiration comes from Nietzsche rather than Marx.

I argue that one reason for LPT's loss of momentum has been its inability to deal with an increasingly discomforting anomaly. LPT is fundamentally incompatible with the growing consensus that capitalist development has been associated not with the *deskilling* trend predicted by Braverman, but with a trend toward the *upgrading* of worker skills and responsibilities. I argue that LPT's inability to accommodate upgrading is due to the one-sidedness of its reading of Marx. This chapter proposes an alternative, more dialectical reading of Marx that may help us better understand the changing nature of work.

The chapter begins with a brief recapitulation of labor process theory. I then outline the empirical case for skill upgrading and show the futility of LPT's efforts to deal with this anomaly. I then propose an alternative reading of Marx and explicate that reading using Activity Theory (as developed by

Engeström, 1987, 1990; and discussed by Blacker, 1993; Holt and Morris, 1993). The body of the chapter illustrates the potential fruitfulness of this alternative framework through a brief analysis of the case of the rationalization of software development. A discussion section suggests a number of implications of this activity-theoretic perspective for several other streams of work research. The conclusion looks toward the future.

## LABOR PROCESS THEORY, BRIEFLY

Inspired by Marx, labor process theory proposes that the key to understanding work organization lies in the structure of the broader society within which it is embedded, rather than in human psychology or in the dynamics of dyadic exchange. Social structure, in turn, is seen as fundamentally determined by the prevailing relations of production – the nature of property rights over productive resources. The relations of production characteristic of capitalist societies derive from the nature of the commodity (the *germ*, or core, of capitalist production: Marx, 1977: 163). The commodity is something produced for sale and, as such, has two contradictory aspects: its use-value – its value as something useful to the purchaser – and its exchange-value – its power to command money in exchange. As a system of commodity production, capitalist relations of production have two main dimensions. First, ownership of productive resources is dispersed among firms that confront each other as commodity producers in market competition: Call this the *capital relation*. Second, alongside those who enjoy such ownership is a class of non-owners who, lacking access to means of production, must sell their capacity to work (*labor power*) as if it were a commodity on the labor market: Call this the *wage relation*.

These features of the capitalist social structure have strong implications for the organization of work. Under the capital relation, and notwithstanding important variations across industries, regions, periods, and strategies, firms must reduce costs of production. Management responses include downward wage pressure, work intensification, work reorganization, technological change, and relocation, as well as efforts to align owners' and workers' financial interests. These responses in turn elicit reactions from workers. Under the wage relation, an incomplete contract, workers sell their capacity to work (labor power) at the going rate in exchange for the promise to do whatever they are asked within some zone of indifference, but it is management's challenge to extract effective work effort. (Piece-rate systems do not fundamentally change this, but merely change the form of the conflict at the heart of the wage-effort bargain; as elucidated by both Marx and Taylor.) Management responses to this pressure include closer supervision, financial incentives, work reorganization, technological innovations, and normative control. Firms might attempt to derive competitive advantage from collaboration with other firms and with their own employees; but the fundamentally competitive nature of capitalist, commodity-based relations of production – both among firms and between management and workers within firms – threatens constantly to undermine any such collaboration.

Whereas more traditional readings of Marx – as indeed many non-Marxist theories – give a key role to technological change as a driver of social change and determinant of work organization, many labor process theorists – along with other social constructionists – have been adamantly opposed to *techno-logical determinism*. Marking it as distinctively neo rather than traditional in its reading of Marx, LPT argues that attributing a basic causal role to technology would be to naturalize the socially constructed, historically specific, capitalist relations of production (e.g., Burawoy, 1979: 14ff, 220). Technology is itself shaped by these relations of production (Noble, 1986).

The net result for work organization, according to LPT, is that:

Control and cost reduction structure the division of labour, involving the design of work and the division of tasks and people to give the most effective control and profitability. This is sustained by hierarchical structures and the shaping of appropriate forms of science and technology. (Thompson and McHugh, 2002: 367)

Alongside these broad structural features of capitalist work organization, LPT acknowledges that empirically observed situations will also reflect a host of local factors specific to firms, markets, institutional contexts, the ideologies of the various actors, and the history of their interrelations. LPT does not deny the importance of these local factors, but argues that this variation is shaped by the deep structure of capitalist relations of production and that our theories therefore should acknowledge the layered causality involved.

## THE UPGRADING CHALLENGE TO LABOR PROCESS THEORY

From its inception, LPT has been critical of those who claim to see upgrading trends in work and the emergence of "new paradigms" in work organization (e.g., Bell, 1973; Touraine, 1969; Piore and Sabel, 1984; Kern and Schumann, 1984; Mathews, 1994). The first wave of LPT, based on the reading of Marx just summarized, argued that capitalist imperatives of control and cost reduction led inexorably to "deskilling" – fragmenting jobs, reducing skill requirements, and replacing worker autonomy with management control. Numerous studies compellingly described cases of deskilling in various occupations (e.g., Zimbalist, 1979). Over the years, and confronted with conflicting examples and arguments, its proponents have nuanced their positions – retreating to an increasingly narrow programmatic "core" (see Lakatos, 1970). Backing away from deskilling, some labor process theorists embrace a polarization view, according to which some occupations might be upgraded, but others, presumably representing the larger number of workers, are deskilled; and others went further, to a contingency view according to which skill outcomes are dependent on the state of the

TABLE 9.1. *Evolution of the U.S. Occupational Structure*

| Year | 1900 | 1970 | 2000 |
|---|---|---|---|
| **Clerical** | **0.03** | **0.18** | **0.16** |
| **Professional, technical** | **0.04** | **0.14** | **0.16** |
| Service workers, excl. private household | 0.04 | 0.11 | |
| Private household workers | 0.05 | 0.02 | |
| **Total service, incl. private household** | **0.10** | **0.13** | **0.14** |
| **Salesworkers** | **0.05** | **0.07** | **0.12** |
| Operative and kindred | 0.13 | 0.18 | |
| Laborers, excl. farm and mine | 0.13 | 0.05 | |
| **Total operatives plus laborers (excl. farm)** | **0.26** | **0.23** | **0.12** |
| **Managers, administrative, proprietors** | **0.06** | **0.08** | **0.11** |
| **Craftsmen, foremen** | **0.11** | **0.14** | **0.12** |
| Farmers | 0.20 | 0.02 | |
| Farm laborers and foremen | 0.18 | 0.01 | |
| **Total farmers plus farm laborers** | **0.38** | **0.03** | **0.04** |

*Source:* U.S. Bureau of the Census (2000). Author's imputation for 1900 and 1970 based on Statistical Abstract. Census data after 1970 combine operatives and laborers, do not distinguish private household workers, and do not distinguish farm laborers from farmers and farm managers. Bold font indicates main categories; regular font indicates sub-categories.

class struggle. Most recently, LPT has been challenged by an ascendant foucauldian post-modernism that has abandoned both references to Marx and efforts to identify long-term trends in skill (e.g., Covaleski, Dirsmith, Heian, and Samuel, 1998; Ezzamel and Willmott, 1998; Knights and Willmott, 1989; see neo-Marxist critiques by Thompson and Smith, 2001; and Tinker, 2002). This new approach has shifted focus from the broader structural features of capitalism to a richer portrait of subjective work experience.

One reason, I submit, for the loss of momentum of LPT and of the credibility of its Marxist premises is the *prima facia* implausibility of its central claim of deskilling. On the neo-Marxist view outlined earlier, it is inconceivable that, over the longer term and in the aggregate, job characteristics could have trended upward. Yet, not only are upgrading counterexamples common in the literature, but accumulating evidence points in the direction of an overall, albeit modest, upgrading of average skill requirements (Form, 1987; Attwell, 1987; Spenner, 1988).

Consider, first, the evolution of the occupational distribution of the workforce. Table 9.1 shows data on the case of the United States over the twentieth century. There are, of course, many difficulties in interpreting these data, but it is hard not to see in this mutation of the occupational structure an important upgrading, notably in the massive contraction of the unskilled farm and non-farm laborer category, the more recent contraction of the operative category, and the growth of the professional and technical category.

(We might note, too, that many people classified in the growing category of managers and administrators have very little managerial authority and arguably belong to the working class broadly construed.) The fact that the corresponding industry structure has shifted dramatically, first from agriculture to manufacturing and then from manufacturing to service, does nothing to save the deskilling thesis because this thesis is formulated at the level of the labor force as a whole.

How do Marxist-inspired labor process theorists respond to data such as these? Braverman (1974:20) anticipated the most common responses. He suggested that we simply ignore such occupational data because (a) they do not recognize the experience-based skills of farmers and farm laborers; (b) commentators often inflate the skills of manufacturing operatives, classifying them as semi-skilled merely because they work with machinery, whereas classifying laborers as unskilled merely because they do not; (c) the data ignore the class difference between middle-class professional/technical categories and the working class narrowly construed; and (d) they mask the dilution over time of skills in the craftsmen category.

Although there is arguably some truth to all these objections, it nevertheless takes a huge effort of imagination to see the shift registered in these statistics as compatible with an aggregate deskilling story. Deskilling within each of the occupational categories in Table 9.1 would have had to be pervasive to outweigh the upgrading effect of the compositional change traced in the table – where in fact the evidence points toward upgrading within most occupations, too. Where scholars have been able to use independent measures of skill, such as the Dictionary of Occupational Titles, none have found evidence of aggregate deskilling; a modest upgrading trend is the almost universal conclusion (see the comprehensive review of U.S. studies by Spenner [1988]).

Second, consider the average education level of the workforce – arguably an important indicator of skill requirements: It, too, has increased dramatically. The fraction of U.S. seventeen-year-olds who had completed high school grew from six percent in 1900, to fifty-seven percent in 1950, to over eighty percent by the end of the century. Braverman (1974) suggests we ignore this evidence too, because (a) it reflects the demands of urbanization rather than industry; (b) it is biased by the inclusion of non-working-class categories; (c) school is a way to keep unemployed youth off the streets; and (d) many workers' education is underutilized.

Again, these points all have some validity; however, despite this huge increase in the supply of more educated labor, high school and college education has continued to yield a sizable positive economic return in the labor market (Goldin and Katz, 1999), and this result is difficult to understand unless at least some of this increase in education levels reflected increasing skill requirements rather than pure screening and credentialism (Abramowitz and David, 1996). As Goldin and Katz write, the most plausible explanation for this pattern is that "technological change and capital deepening have both served to increase the demand for more skilled labor over the long run" (1999: 25–26). A considerable body of economic research has consistently found that capital equipment and worker skills are complements rather than substitutes (Goldin and Katz, 1998).

Faced with evidence such as this, it is not surprising that neo-Maxist LPT has shifted away from the strong version of the deskilling thesis advanced by Braverman. A somewhat weaker version is expressed in the polarization thesis. Braverman (1974: 425) invoked polarization to show that his deskilling thesis was compatible with an increase in average skill levels by arguing that the categories that were upgraded were not truly working class: "The mass of workers gain nothing from the fact that the decline in their command over the labor process is more than compensated for by the increasing command on the part of managers and engineers" (1974: 425). Later writers allowed that some working-class categories too might experience upgrading, but still wanted to argue that the mass at the bottom of the skill distribution was growing in size and was further degraded in skills. However, the data cited earlier on the evolution of skills within occupations does not support any such polarization stories. To restrict our vision to manufacturing for a moment, polarization is difficult to reconcile with Steiger's (1999) finding that the proportion of skilled workers among production workers increased between 1950 and 1990 in sixteen of nineteen manufacturing industries.

The final refuge of LPT has been a retreat from any broad trend generalizations, toward a contingency view. Summarizing the contingency view, Smith and Thompson write:

LPT is not dependent on deskilling or Taylorism as the characteristic form of the capitalist labor process. Its core theory merely recognizes that competitive relations compel capital to constantly revolutionize the labor process and that within that framework, capital and labor will contest the character and consequences of such changes. (Smith and Thompson, 1999: 211)

Compared with the deskilling or polarization arguments, such a contingency view is easier to reconcile with the data just summarized – but it is harder to reconcile with LPT's ostensible Marxist grounding. It is one thing to argue that workers sometimes succeed in forcing management to upgrade jobs and in forcing government to provide greater access to education. But the idea that the balance of class power should be so favorable to workers over such large aggregates and over such a long period is difficult to reconcile with any theory that claims a Marxist lineage. If the data do show a long-term, aggregate upgrading trend, any Marxist theory must attribute primary causality to capitalist industry's need for skilled labor, not to dominance of workers in their struggle against capitalists.

To date, those who have seen in the data evidence of broad upgrading trends have usually distanced themselves from Marx. Exceptions to this generalization are rare: Hirschhorn (1984), Kenney and Florida (1993), and Engeström (1987; 1990) are exemplary. Much of the upgrading literature has often simply ignored the scandalously large mass of low-skilled workers that still anchors the bottom of the occupational skill distribution. Many write about the upgrading trends they claim to discern as if this mass were about to disappear overnight. Some recent champions of the "knowledge society," for example, write as if we will all shortly be "symbolic analysts," whereas, in reality, low-skilled, routine jobs continue to proliferate (Reich, 1991; U.S. Bureau of Census, 2000: 419).

We thus have on the one side a utopianism that ends up masking a scandal and on the other side a polemical denunciation of this scandal that seems unable to acknowledge some basic facts. There is, however, a version of Marx – one I call *paleo-Marxist* – that is easy to reconcile with *both* a broad pattern of upgrading *and* a multitude of counter-examples of deskilling. I call this view paleo not to signal any pejorative connotation – on the contrary, I will argue that it is the more fruitful interpretation – but simply to signal the fact that it was common prior to World War I but was subsequently eclipsed by neo-Marxism. This essay explicates that paleo point of view, arguing that capitalism progressively upgrades work as part of the process that Marx called the socialization of the forces of production.

## READING MARX

LPT, like other theories that take inspiration from Marx, takes as its starting point the proposition that: "the development of the contradictions of a given historical form of production is the only historical way in which it can be dissolved and then reconstructed on a new basis" (Marx, 1977: 619).

The term "contradiction" is here used in a Hegelian sense, to designate incompatibilities between real forces rather than merely between logical propositions. For LPT and other neo-Marxists, class struggle is the motor of history, and the development of the contradictions of capitalism consists of intensified worker struggles in reaction to exacerbated exploitation and misery. The more traditional reading of Marx – the paleo-Marxist view – sees the basic contradiction as being between the forces and the relations of production. The forces of production are composed of technology in the form of instruments and materials, and workers' productive faculties; the relations of production, as discussed earlier, are the relations of ownership and control over the productive forces.

The paleo-Marxist reading accepts all of the elements of labor process theory laid out in the earlier exposition – with the exception of the dismissal of technology as an important causal factor and, as a result, comes to a different conclusion regarding the vector of change in work organization. (My exposition of the paleo reading is based on G. A. Cohen's [1978] presentation of Marx's theory of history. Cohen's version of Marx has been criticized by, amongst others, Levine and Wright [1980] and J. Cohen [1982]; see G. A. Cohen's [1988] reply, also Wright, Levine, and Sober [1992]. This essay takes G. A. Cohen's interpretation from the general societal plane into the production process.) On the paleo view, the long-term path of development of the class struggle is determined by the evolution of the underlying contradiction between the "socialization" tendency of the forces of production and the persistence of private-property-based relations of production (Marx and Engels; 1959: 95).

Socialization is commonly construed as the process whereby people new to a culture internalize its norms: Marx's use is broader. Marx's discussion of the socialization of the forces of production (e.g., Marx, 1973: 705; 1977: 1024; as distinct from his arguments in favor of the socialization of property relations through nationalizations) suggests that this psychological internalization is just one form of a more general phenomenon: The forces of production are socialized insofar as they come to embody the capabilities and constraints developed in the larger society rather than only those that emerge from isolated, local contexts.

The "objective" socialization of the forces of production is visible at the societal level in the complexification of the social division of labor – the specialization of industries and regions, and their increasing global interdependence (see also Van der Pijl, 1998, Sohn-Rethel, 1978; Engels, 1978). At the enterprise level – where society's forces of production are instantiated as specific labor processes – objective socialization was characterized by Engels (1978: 702) in these terms:

Before capitalist production. i.e. in the Middle Ages. [...] the instruments of labor – land, agricultural implements, the workshop, the tool – were the instruments of labor of single individuals, adapted for the use of one worker [... The bourgeoisie transformed these productive forces] from means of production of the individual into *social* means of production, workable only by a collectivity of men. The spinning-wheel, the hand-loom, the blacksmith's hammer were replaced by the spinning-machine, the power-loom, the steam-hammer; the individual workshop, by the factory, implying the cooperation of hundreds and thousands of workmen. In like manner, production itself changed from a series of individual into a series of social acts.

To these objective dimensions of socialization corresponds a subjective dimension (to reprise the conventional meaning of socialization). When the effective subject of production is no longer an individual worker but the "collective worker," workers' identities change – workers are re-socialized. (Recall that in Marx's view, human nature is nothing but "the ensemble of the social relations"; Marx, 1975: 423.) Socialization in this subjective sense can be understood as the emergence of more *interdependent self-construals* (Markus and Kitayama, 1991). The civilizing mission of capitalism is not only to stimulate enormously the quantitative development of the objective components of the forces of production, but also to take a decisive step in the realization of humankind's fundamentally social nature: "When the worker cooperates in a planned way with others, he strips off the fetters of his individuality, and develops the capabilities of his species" (Marx, 1977: 447).

The *Communist Manifesto* is eloquent on this interweaving of objective and subjective aspects of socialization:

> The bourgeoisie, historically, has played a most revolutionary part. The bourgeoisie, wherever it has got the upper hand, has put an end to all feudal, patriarchal, idyllic relations. . . . In place of the old local and national seclusion and self-sufficiency, we have intercourse in every direction, universal interdependence. . . . And as in material, so in intellectual production. The intellectual creations of individual nations become common property. National one-sidedness and narrow-mindedness become more and more impossible . . . The bourgeoisie . . . has rescued a considerable part of the population from the idiocy of rural life. . . . The bourgeoisie cannot exist without constantly revolutionizing the instruments of production. . . . [W]ith the development of industry, the proletariat not only increases in numbers; it becomes more concentrated in greater masses, its strength grows, and it feels that strength more. . . . Thereupon the workers begin to form combinations (trade unions). . . . Now and then the workers are victorious, but only for a time. The real fruit of their battles lies not in the immediate result, but in the ever-expanding union of the workers. The union is helped on by the improved means of communication that are created by modern industry and that place the workers of different localities in contact with one another. . . . The advance of industry, whose involuntary promoter is the bourgeoisie, replaces the isolation of laborers, due to competition, by their revolutionary combination, due to association. . . . What the bourgeoisie, therefore, produces, above all, is its gravediggers. (Marx and Engels, 1959)

The development of the forces of production pulls workers out of what Marx and Engels call "rural idiocy." In the *Poverty of Philosophy*, Marx similarly celebrates the end of "craft idiocy." Marx's use of the term idiocy preserves both its colloquial sense and the meaning from the Greek *idiotes*, denoting an asocial individual isolated from the polis. At the opposite end of the spectrum from the *idiotes* – in the form of the unskilled worker or the craftsman – is the "social individual" described by the *Grundrisse* – in the form of the technician who accesses and deploys society's accumulated scientific and technological knowledge:

> to the degree that large industry develops . . . it is neither the direct human labor he himself performs, nor the time during which he works, but rather the appropriation of his own general productive power, his understanding of nature and his mastery over it by virtue of his presence as a social body – it is, in a word, the development of the social individual which appears as the great foundation-stone of production and of wealth. (Marx, 1973: 704–706)

Under capitalism, this socialization tendency is simultaneously stimulated, retarded, and distorted by the prevailing relations of production.

Competitive pressures force firms to break down parochialisms and to stimulate technological progress; but instead of a broadening association of producers progressively mastering their collective future, capitalism imposes the coercion of quasi-natural laws of the market over firms and the despotism of corporate bureaucracy over workers. The limitations on collective mastery that result from the dominance of the market over firms are visible in capitalism's inability to manage public goods and externalities. The limitations resulting from the despotic authority of managers over workers within firms is visible in the Sisyphean nature of corporate human resource management strategies – condemned to futility by the capitalist firm's need for workers who are simultaneously dependable and disposable (Hyman, 1987). These handicaps become increasingly intolerable fetters on social development with the increasing complexity of technology and the growing knowledge-intensity of the economy (Adler, 2001).

However, in the overall dynamics of capitalism, these various constraints must and do slowly cede to the overall progress of socialization. In modern industry, competitive advantage often flows from skill upgrading and from greater collaborative interdependence within and between firms. The pursuit of those sources of competitive advantage makes capitalists the "involuntary promoters" of socialization – to use the phrase quoted earlier from the *Communist Manifesto* (see Cohen, 1978; Levine and Wright, 1980). Amongst workers, the overall, long-term, aggregate effect – Marx's logic encourages us to conjecture – is to foster upgrading: greater intellectual sophistication and broader worldviews.

As a result of the persistence of capitalist relations of production, the path of socialization, both objective and subjective, is halting and uneven. Globalization integrates markets, but by whipsawing regions against each other. Management mobilizes the collective worker, but then finds profits dependent on savage downsizing and outsourcing. There is a long-term upgrading trend, but firms often find the low road of deskilling and super-exploitation too tempting. We should also note that, under capitalist conditions, even progressive change has social costs: As technologies advance and markets integrate, workers often bear the burdens of structural unemployment; old union craftsmen are often pitted against young non-union technicians; contracting out and globalization often undermine old solidarities.

In analyzing the evolution of skill and work organization, LPT has truncated this dialectic. According to Marx, the production process within capitalist firms has two aspects (reflecting the two aspects of the commodity): the *labor process*, in which workers, tools, and materials are combined to create new use-values, and the *valorization process*, in which these use-values appear in the form of exchange-values and in which the operative considerations are not technical but monetary – wages, capital, and profit (Marx, 1977: Appendix; Thompson, 1989; Bottomore, 1983: 267–270). How then should we understand the relations between these two aspects of production? Marx writes:

If capitalist direction [of work] is thus twofold in content, owing to the twofold nature of the process of production which has to be directed – on the one hand a social labor process for the creation of a product, and on the other hand capital's process of valorization – in form it is purely despotic. (Marx, 1977: 450)

Neo-Marxist LPT interprets this to mean that the historical development of capitalist work organization reflects above all the balance of class forces – despotism versus resistance. Paleo-Marxists, by contrast, recall that, in Marx's Hegelian discourse, content and form can be in contradiction with each other. The paleo reading of this passage thus highlights the growing contradiction between an increasingly socialized labor process (the content) and the barriers posed to further socialization by the persistence of valorization constraints (the form).

The following sections develop and deploy an Activity Theory framework for understanding the socialization of the labor process and its dialectical contradiction with capitalist property relations. My argument is that these paleo-Marxist Activity Theory lenses are useful for studying work and its history because they enable us to grasp the significance of a real but uneven trend of upgrading as a reflection of the deepest contradictions of capitalism. This viewpoint allows us to grasp the contradictions that beset capitalist management and to grasp them in a surprisingly intuitive way: On the one hand, management needs and cultivates the productive power of the collective worker, and, on the other, management limits this development due to pressures of corporate profitability.

## AN ACTIVITY THEORY FRAMEWORK

If our task is to understand work and its relation to organization structure and to lived experience, Marx's model of the labor process provides a fruitful starting point. The main elements of the labor process are, according to Marx, "(1) purposeful activity, that is work itself, (2) the object on which that work is performed, and (3) the instruments of that work" (Marx, 1977: 284). Like Cohen (1978: Ch. 3), I take the first element to refer more specifically to the worker's productive capabilities. I also make one further amendment by differentiating a fourth element: the community within which the worker works and which shares the object of that work. The resulting model is summarized in Figure 9.1. (It can be read as a stripped-down version of the model proposed by Engeström, 1987, 1990, and discussed by Blackler, 1993; Holt and Morris, 1993.)

Some comments will help situate this model. Taking as a baseline the more common schema in psychology, in which object and subject appear alone, as stimulus and response, note, first, that for Marx, human activity

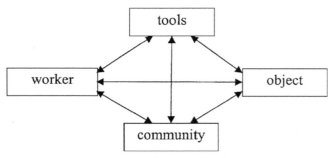

FIGURE 9.1. The structure of the labor process.

is tool-mediated activity – where tools include both material tools such as hammers and symbolic ones such as language and concepts (Vygotsky, 1962: 1978). Second, the appropriate unit of analysis for the study of work is not the quasi-automatic reflex *operation,* nor the discrete, goal-oriented, individual *action,* but rather the *activity* understood as a motivated collective endeavor and, in such collective activity, the subject's relation to the object is mediated not only by tools but also by community (Leont'ev, 1978). Third, in Marx's analysis, the "object" of work (in German, *Gegenstand*) includes both of the dictionary senses: the material on which the work is performed (in German, *Objekt*) and the intended goal of the activity. With this notion, Marx attempts to overcome both simplistic materialism – which accords insufficient place to intentionality in shaping the object – and classical idealism – which accords insufficient recognition to the obdurate nature of the object's materiality (Marx, 1959: 243; Engeström, 1987; Foot, 2002).

Figure 9.1 is a model of what Marx calls "production in general" (Marx, 1973: 85): It is trans-historical insofar as it does not acknowledge any more historically specific, "concrete" determinations. Because we are here trying to develop a theory of capitalist work organization, the most basic of these relevant to our present task are the determinations characteristic of the capitalist form of society. Of these latter, most fundamental is the contradiction between use-value and exchange-value of which the commodity is the germ. This contradiction is reflected in each of the elements of the labor process. The object of work is both the creation of useful things (use-values) and the generation of profit (exchange-value). Tools and community are both means of technical accomplishment and means of extracting useful labor from potentially recalcitrant labor-power. The worker is simultaneously a creative member of the collective worker and a disposable, variable-cost, budget item under another's control. More generally, viewed as use-value, each element participates in the socialization process; viewed as exchange-value, each is subordinate to the valorization process's profit imperative. In the neo-Marxist view, these contradictions are only virtual, because the use-value content disappears behind its exchange-value form; but in the paleo view, these contradictions are real, driving the evolution of work organization. The following section illustrates the potential fruitfulness of theorizing work organization though such lenses.

## A CASE: SOFTWARE DEVELOPMENT

As software has grown more complex over the past few decades, the software development process has slid into chaos (Gibbs, 1994; Lieberman and Fry, 2001). One 1994 survey of 8,330 projects in 365 firms in banking, manufacturing, retail, wholesale, health care, insurance, and government found that only 16% of projects were on time, within budget, and met originally specified requirements – only 9% in large companies. Some 31% of projects were "impaired" and eventually cancelled. Approximately 53% of projects were "challenged," and the average challenged project met only 61% of its requirements. The average impaired or challenged project was 189% over budget and 222% over schedule (Standish Group, 1994).

It is therefore not surprising that over this same period the software field has been the object of numerous rationalization efforts (Cusumano, 1991; Swanson et al., 1991; Griss, 1993; Weber, 1997; Friedman and Cornford, 1989). Examples include structured programming, project planning models, information engineering, and object-oriented programming. Currently, one of the most influential of these efforts is that based on the *Capability Maturity Model* (CMM) (see Software Engineering Institute, 2002). (I leave for another occasion discussion of other lines of evolution in the software field.)

The CMM owes its birth to the U.S. Department of Defense's increasing frustration with chaos in defense systems software development (Humphrey, 2002). The Department of Defense (DoD) funded the Software Engineering Institute (SEI), based at Carnegie-Mellon University, to develop a model of a more reliable development process. With the assistance of the MITRE Corporation and with input from nearly 1,000 industry people, SEI released the CMM in 1991. The model – summarized in Table 9.2 – distinguishes five successively more "mature" levels of process capability, each characterized by mastery of a number of Key Process Areas (KPAs). Level 1 represents an entirely ad hoc approach. Level 2 represents the rationalization of the management of individual projects. Level 3 characterizes the systematic management of its portfolio of projects. Levels 4 addresses the quantification of the development process. Level 5 addresses the continuous improvement of that process. The underlying philosophy of this hierarchy was inspired by Crosby's (1979) TQM approach to quality in manufacturing (Humphrey, 2002).

The CMM has become the basis for numerous software service organizations' improvement efforts in both the government and commercial sectors. Its diffusion has been driven in considerable measure by its use in sourcing

TABLE 9.2. *The Capability Maturity Model*

| Level | Focus and Description | Key Process Areas | Proportion of Appraised Organizations, 1998–2002 |
|---|---|---|---|
| **Level 1: Initial** | **Competent people and heroics:** The software process is ad hoc, occasionally even chaotic. Few processes are defined, and success depends on individual effort and heroics. | | 16.9% |
| **Level 2: Repeatable** | **Project management processes:** Basic project management processes are established to track cost, schedule, and functionality. The necessary process discipline is in place to repeat earlier successes on projects with similar applications. | * software configuration management <br> * software quality assurance <br> * software subcontract management <br> * software project tracking and oversight <br> * software project planning <br> * requirements management | 43.2% |
| **Level 3: Defined** | **Engineering processes and organizational support:** The software process for both management and engineering activities is documented, standardized, and integrated into a standard software process for the organization. All projects use an approved, tailored version of the organization's standard software process for developing and maintaining software. | * peer reviews <br> * intergroup coordination <br> * software product engineering <br> * integrated software management <br> * training program <br> * organization process definition <br> * organization process focus | 24.6% |

*(continued)*

TABLE 9.2 (*continued*)

| Level | Focus and Description | Key Process Areas | Proportion of Appraised Organizations, 1998–2002 |
|---|---|---|---|
| **Level 4: Managed** | **Product and process quality:** Detailed measures of the software process and product quality are collected. Both the software process and products are 7.3% quantitatively understood and controlled. | * software quality management<br>* quantitative process management | 8.0% |
| **Level 5: Optimizing** | **Continuous process improvement:** Improvement is enabled by quantitative feedback from the process and from piloting innovative ideas and technologies. | * process change management<br>* technology change management<br>* defect prevention | 7.3% |

*Source:* Software Engineering Institute, 2003

decisions by the DoD and other government and commercial-sector organizations. The first sourcing evaluations pressed suppliers to reach Level 2, but by the late 1990s, the bar had been raised to Level 3.

Accumulating evidence suggests that moving up the CMM hierarchy leads to improvements in product cost, quality, and timeliness (Clark, 1999; Harter, Krishnan, and Slaughter, 2000; Krishnan et al., 2000; Herbsleb et al., 1997). But many skeptics remain unconvinced (e.g., Crocca, 1992; Bach, 1994, 1995; Conradi and Fuggetta, 2002; Lynn, 1991; Ngwenyama and Nielson, 2003). Gains may be specific to the sampled organizations. They may be earned at the expense of developer morale and commitment, and given the importance of developers' attitudes to performance, any performance gains may therefore be ephemeral. Typical of opposition to such standardized and formalized methodologies is this assessment by two well-respected software management experts:

Of course, if your people aren't smart enough to think their way through their work, the work will fail. No Methodology will help. Worse still, Methodologies can do grievous damage to efforts in which people are fully competent. They do this by trying to force the work into a fixed mold that guarantees a morass of paperwork, a paucity of methods, an absence of responsibility, and a general loss of motivation. (DeMarco and Lister, 1987: 116)

Most LPT research on these kinds of efforts to rationalize software development has interpreted them as mechanisms of exploitative control (Kraft, 1977; Greenbaum, 1979; Friedman and Cornford, 1989; Prasad, 1998). Kraft (1977: 61) summarizes the analysis this way:

Canned programs, structured programming, and modularization are designed to make the supervision of software workers by managers easier and more like the supervision of other workers . . . Such managerial techniques have made possible the use of relatively less skilled programmers for what were formerly the most complex software tasks.

Some of the more recent LPT research on software has nuanced this analysis, moving closer to a contingency view (Greenbaum, 1998; Beirne, Ramsey, and Panteli, 1998).

To explore the impact of the CMM, I studied a large software consulting firm I will call GCC, conducting interviews with developers and managers in four programs (a program is an organizational unit devoted to a series of projects with a single large customer; see Adler, 2003). These programs all developed and maintained relatively large-scale systems for government clients. Two programs were at CMM Level 5: Program A, which had recently downsized due to changing client needs from 1,600 to 450 people, and Program C, with 450 people. Two sister programs were at Level 3: Program B with 215 people and Program D with 470. In late 1999, I interviewed between 15 and 22 people at various hierarchical levels and in various functions in each of these four programs. (Note: for simplicity, I will refer to all employees directly involved with software development – specifying customer requirements, programming, testing – as "developers," to distinguish them from support staff in Quality Assurance (QA) and other such functions, and from supervisors and managers.) Interviews lasted approximately one hour. They were tape-recorded and interviewees were assured anonymity. The recordings were transcribed, and edited versions were sent back to interviewees for review and correction. I also consulted voluminous internal documentation from each of these programs as well as documents from corporate entities supporting them.

### Socialization of the Development Process

Traditionally, at the lowest levels of process maturity, developers enjoyed considerable autonomy, task variety, and task identity. Greenbaum (1979: 64–65) quotes a veteran programmer thus:

I remember that in the fifties and early sixties I was a "jack of all trades." As a programmer I got to deal with the whole process. I would think through a problem, talk to the clients, write my own code, and operate the machine. I loved it – particularly the chance to see something through from beginning to end.

The labor processes within which developers worked were largely local. Kraft (1977: 56) writes of this period: "Programmers (and analysts) followed a logic and procedures which were largely of their own making." Being tacit rather than codified, tools were difficult to communicate across locales, and skills were not easily transferable. Working knowledge was in these senses private rather than social. As one of Greenbaum's interviewees put it:

No one knew what was going on – certainly not the managers. But even the programmers and systems analysts were confused. There were no standards for doing anything – coding, testing, documenting – they were all done the way each person felt like it, or in fact, they were not done at all. [...] Programmers never documented what it was their program was to do. It was the same with setting up testing procedures and test data. When the whole system was put together, we never knew if it really worked because nothing got written down. (Greenbaum, 1979: 73–77)

At higher levels of process maturity, developers were embedded in larger social aggregates, and encountered pre-specified methods that were the fruit of a complex, organized, large-scale process development effort. Tools, materials, community, and skills were no longer naturally emergent phenomena grounded in local experience. They were formalized and standardized. Developers were aware that their effectiveness was not only the result of their own individual effort and skill and of informally shared tricks of the trade, but also and increasingly the result of this social, rather than private, accumulation of working knowledge:

I came from a background in industrial process computers and the organization I worked for was much less structured in how they handled all this. The process was basically just define the requirements, write the code, then do a final test. Apart from that, you were basically on your own. Here the processes tell you a lot more about how to do the work. [...] Previously, it was more like a "hand-me-down" – you learned how to do your work with some help from other people on the job, or just by yourself. (B: development)

At first, this socialization took a form many developers experienced as alienating, coercive, bureaucratic authority. Discussing the Military Standards for software quality control that came into force in the mid-1980s, one veteran noted that: "[Military Standard] 2167A was supposed to make coding a no-brainer" (D: development manager). In the civilian Program A, too, the initial experience with process was top-down, oriented to conformance, and "most managers felt that it was just a matter of ensuring that people were implementing it" (A: program manager).

By the time of my study a decade or more later, the Level 5 Programs had pushed the socialization of the production process considerably further, both in its extent and its form. The term *software process* was now used to refer to a whole hierarchy of standard operating procedures, from Policies defining broad, corporate requirements down to Instructions defining individual tasks. The *granularity* of process at its finest levels can be gauged by the Instructions at one of the Level 5 programs, Program C. There were separate Instructions that covered high-level design, two types of low-level design, two types of code reviews, and one for testing, as well as Instructions for filling out Change Request Implementation forms and Root Cause Analysis forms. Each Instruction was several pages in length. They often included the specific forms to be completed as well as flow-charts detailing the sequence of associated tasks. Overall, the process documentation summed to some eight linear-feet of shelf space. In recent years, almost all of this documentation had been put online, along with a host of other management information and communication tools. Prescribed work-flows were being built into automated document routing systems.

If the documentation that developers were required to read was voluminous, so too was the documentation that they were required to write. In the words of one interviewee (perhaps exaggerating for dramatic effect):

I can write the code in two hours, but then I have to spend two days documenting it! It can be very frustrating. We have to document check-in and check-out, a detailed design plan, a development plan. We have to print out all the differences between the old and the new code. There's documentation for inspection and certification. There's an internal software delivery form. A test plan. And all these need to be signed. [...] I used to be an independent developer for about three years. I never even created a flow-chart of my work! The only documentation I needed was a "to do" list. So I had to change of lot of habits when I got here. (B: development)

Over the previous decade, the socialization of the development process had also taken a progressively more "enabling" form (Adler and Borys, 1996). Interdependence was no longer a function of bureaucratically imposed authority but experienced as collaboration within the collective worker:

Where I used to work before I came to GCC, the development process was entirely up to me and my manager. What I did, when I did it, what it was going to look like when it was done, and so forth, was all up to me. It was very informal. Here everything is very different. It's much more rigid. It's much more formal. A lot of people lay out the schedule, the entire functionality, and what I'm going to be accountable for – before I even get involved. [...]

When I got here I was kind of shocked. Right off, it was "Here are your Instructions." "So what does this tell me?" "It tells you how to do your job." I thought I was bringing the know-how I'd need to do my job. But sure enough, you open up the Instructions, and they tell you how to do your job: how to lay the code out, where on the form to write a change request number, and so on. I was shocked.

But I can see the need now. Now I'm just one of 30 or 40 other people who may need to work on this code, so we need a change request number that everyone can use to identify it. It certainly feels restrictive at first. They explained the Instructions and the whole Program C process to us in our orientation seminar, but it's hard to see the value of it until you've been around a while. Now I can see that it makes things much easier in the long run.

I hate to say it. As a developer, I'm pretty allergic to all this paperwork. It's so time-consuming. But it does help. You've got to keep in mind, too, that by the time we see the Instructions, they've been through a lot of revision and refinement. So they're pretty much on target. (C: development)

Socialization was visible in all four elements of the labor process, as discussed in the following sub-sections.

***Tools.*** Formalized process created a common vocabulary – a key tool for collaboration:

In a Level 1 organization, one without a common process, even one where there was a lot of goodwill between the functions, they wouldn't have the common vocabulary, or common definitions of key tasks, and everything would be subject to conflicting interpretation, so people would be fumbling in the dark. A common process greatly simplifies things. (C: project manager)

Memory had become objectified and collective, augmented by a growing stock of available tools:

Process gives people access to assets from prior work – for estimation, for standards and procedures, and for lessons learned. In our asset library, we keep the standards and procedures of all our projects, and project managers refer back to these to use as templates. We encourage people to share and borrow. (A: quality assurance)

Take for example our internal software delivery procedure. At first, developers thought that this was just more burdensome paperwork. But soon they found it was a great memory system. (B: quality assurance)

The formalized process was seen as an enabling tool to the extent it leveraged similarities across projects for more effective work:

[E]ven when tasks are more innovative, you can still get a lot of advantage from process. You need to sit down and list the features you want in the system, and then work out which are similar and which are different from your previous work. And you need to make sure the differences are real ones. You'll discover that even in very innovative projects, most of the tasks are ones you've done many times before. Then, for the tasks that are truly novel, you can still leverage your prior experience by identifying somewhat related tasks and defining appropriate guidelines based on those similarities. They won't be precise instructions of the kind you'll have for the truly repetitive work: but these guidelines can be a very useful way to bring your experience to bear on the creative parts of the work. (B: testing, formerly with Program A).

Statistical process control tools were used to systematically improve the process:

We used to be a group of hackers. If we'd have had to rebuild a system, we simply wouldn't have been able to do it because we wouldn't have had the documents. We've come a long way from that! Now we function according to a defined process and we collect data on ourselves so we can do defect causal analysis to drive continuous improvement. (A: quality assurance)

All four types of tools were distinctive in being the fruit of a socialized development process rather than locally emergent.

The CMM also functioned as a kind of tool. In Engeström's terminology, the CMM functioned as a "more advanced model" of software development that was used to guide improvement efforts. As such, the CMM represented a highly socialized tool, insofar as it was seen as an industry-validated approach rather than merely a local initiative:

The CMM is helping us move ahead. Just to take an example, even if the CMM didn't exist we would need a technology change management process [a Level-5 KPA]. Of our 450 people, we have about 50 people in CMM, QA, and data management. To move them from one process to another is sometimes like herding cats! The CMM helps us in that by providing an industry-validated approach. (C: program manager)

***Object.*** The object of work was brought into clearer focus and stabilized by the collective discipline of the process:

Our policies and procedures mean that I have better information on what we're trying to do because we have better requirements documents and better information on how to do it with Instructions, etc. At Level 5 versus Level 1, I'm more confident we're all playing to the same sheet of music. Looking across the organization, process also means that managers understand better the way the whole system works, so they are all playing the same game. (C: development manager)

The object was expanded socially and temporally to include other people who would work on the software:

I think that our process – and even the paperwork part of it – is basically a good thing. My documentation is going to help the next person working on this code, either for testing or maintenance. And vice versa when I'm on the receiving end. (C: development)

The object was also expanded technically: The process itself became an object of developers' work:

Perhaps the biggest change as we've become more process mature is that it makes everyone more interested in process improvement. Take an example: Now I'm working on a new software utility. Top management asked us to evaluate it, to see if we should all use it. So I've been facilitating a series of meetings with all the managers, where everyone is talking about the utilities they are using and the problems they're having. It's been great to see this kind of problem-solving work going on. That's the effect of having a defined technology change management process [a CMM Level-5 KPA]. CMM got this process going for us. (D: logistics)

**Community.** Process maturity also brought greater rationality, both formal and substantive, to the structuring of the collective worker, in three sets of relations: staff/line, horizontal, and vertical.

With process maturity, new staff functions, such as Configuration Management and Process Engineering, emerged, and new line/staff relations were created. QA illustrates the new relations. In the past, QA was often remote from the daily work of developers, arriving on the scene at the end of the work cycle to inspect the output. QA's role evolved with process maturity to (a) a greater focus on process quality rather than only product quality, (b) greater responsibility for infusing process rather than only auditing it, and (c) a closer and more collaborative relation with the line departments:

QA is not a policeman! QA is there to help the project identify the processes you need, tailor existing ones to your needs, learn that process, and do a check to see if you're using it. If I find a problem, it's my job to help the project work out how to address it and how I can help. (B: quality assurance)

In the community's horizontal relations, greater specialization went hand in hand with more systematic coordination and integration:

Process means that people play more specialized, defined roles, but also that these specialists get involved earlier and longer as contributors to other people's tasks. If we analyzed the way a coder uses their time, and compared it with comparable data from, say, 15 years ago, we'd find the coder doing less coding because of more automated tools. They'd be spending more time documenting their code, both as it was being built and afterwards in users' guides. They'd be spending more time in peer reviews. And they'd be spending more time in design meetings and test plan meetings. As for testers [...] now the testers are more involved in system concept definition and requirement definition activities. (A: quality assurance)

Organization-wide processes of coordination were made more visible:

A well-defined process gives you a kind of map of the whole enterprise. (B: quality assurance)

The overall process is more intelligible now. All the organization charts, the people, the processes and documents, and the minutes of various groups are on the Web site. (C: program manager)

The collective worker expanded to encompass the client organization:

There's a great focus now on "accountability" all through the system. We are expected to be more aggressive in pushing back when things are inconsistent with our processes. And that goes down to our project managers. Instead of simply supporting our customer management counterparts, the project managers have to be willing to push back. That's changed the tone of some of our monthly unit review meetings with the customer. This culture change goes right down to the staff. In general, we try to buffer the staff from these issues, but if they get instructions that violate our processes, they have to push back too. (C: program manager)

In the community's vertical structuring, formalized process meant that the parochial concerns of subgroups and individuals and the resulting conflicts were drawn into the open. These concerns became the objects of collective scrutiny and thus were less covert:

We say it's important to document software errors, but that's hard to sell. Developers are used to just doing the corrections, and the testers hate the documentation too. But we try to sell the testers on this by explaining that this way they can get credit for the problems they find. And we try to explain to them that if we document the errors, we can track them, and if errors recur, we can find root causes. That will help us convince the developers, for example, that a given module has too many problems. When it's documented, it's less personal, and it helps the dialogue with the developers. But you also have to ensure that managers won't use the data punitively. (B: testing, formerly with Program A)

I think formalized process and metrics can give autocratic managers a club. But it also gives subordinates training and understanding, so it makes the organization less dependent on that manager: He can be replaced more easily. Before I came to GCC, I worked for one of the most autocratic managers you can find. It was always, "And I want that report on my desk by 5 p.m. today," with no explanation or rationale. Compared to that kind of situation, an organization with a more mature process leaves a lot less room for a manager to arbitrarily dictate how you should work and when work is due. And a more mature process also means that there are more formal review points, so any arbitrary autocratic behavior by a manager will become visible pretty quickly. (D: quality assurance)

At higher levels of process maturity, formal procedures were more numerous, but developers had more opportunity to participate in defining and refining them. Through a formalized Tailoring Cycle, software development standards and procedures ("S&Ps," of which there were over 100 at Program A) were modified for each project with the participation of the developers themselves:

People have to be a part of defining the process. We always say that "People support what they help create." That's why the Tailoring Cycle is so important. As a project manager, you're too far away from the technical work to define the S&Ps yourself, so you have to involve the experts. You don't need everyone involved, but you do need your key people. It's only by involving them that you can be confident you have good S&Ps that have credibility in the eyes of their peers. (A: project manager)

When S&Ps are chosen for a project, the rule is that they have to be sent out to everyone affected for review. And sometimes we give some pretty negative feedback! I remember I wrote on one draft, 'Hey, you've forgotten to tell us how to get out of bed in the morning and how to brush our teeth!' It was way too detailed and rigid. Those kinds of things get shot down pretty quickly. Over a period of years, people learned how to write procedures that were reasonable for our work environment. [...] When I managed software development on one of our bigger projects, I asked all our software developers to help me tailor our S&Ps. The GCC people knew the drill, but we also had some other contractors working on this with us [. . .] and they would say, "No, just tell me how you want us to do this." About a year into the project, I remember one of the contractors who had complained the most about this extra work coming to me to thank me, saying, "If you'd have written these, I would have just ignored them. But since I helped write them, I've felt duty bound to follow them." (A: development)

The Tailoring Cycle was not the only vehicle for participation in process definition. In Programs C and D, Software Engineering Process Groups (SEPGs) also served this purpose. In recent years, the SEPGs had put increasing weight on encouraging suggestions for process improvement from lower-level staff. Moreover, many departments in all four programs had process improvement teams. Whereas these teams were sparse and temporary in the two less mature programs, they were ubiquitous and on-going in the two more mature programs.

*Workers.* Process encouraged a shift from a traditional form of training – apprenticeship – toward something more systematic. Apprenticeship is a mode of learning that is appropriate and necessary when knowledge is the local, tacit, and private property of the artisan-craftsman (see for example Sacks, 1994; Lave, 1988). A more socialized production process relies on forms of knowledge that are more codified and on forms of training that can thus be more rationalized. Going back a couple of decades, this transformation began with the shift to formal university training requirements for development jobs; more recently, under the pressure of CMM, the transformation continued with the further rationalization of the acquisition of firm-specific skills:

We've developed a formal mentoring program. There's a checklist of the key processes everyone needs to understand, and every new person is assigned a mentor whose job it is to explain each of these in turn. The checklist is audited by QA. (A: testing)

We had an informal training and mentoring program, and when we got serious about the CMM, we wrote it down. Writing the process down has had some great benefits. It's made us think about how we work, and that's led to improvements. For example, formalizing the training program has helped bring some outliers into conformance. (C: training)

Through its multiple effects on the other elements of the labor process, process maturity led to a changed subjective identity among developers – toward a more interdependent self-construal (Markus and Kitayama, 1991). The collective worker was no longer merely objective, but now also a lived reality. What mattered to these professionals' self-esteem and identity was now not so much their individual efficacy as their collective efficacy (Bandura, 1997; Gibson and Earley, n.d.). In my interviews, "we" tended to replace "I" as the subject of work, because people increasingly saw themselves as part of a collective effort. The ratio of mentions of "we" to mentions of "I" in my interview notes was 1.83 in Program A and 1.95 in Program C (the two

Level-5 programs), and 1.29 in Program B and 1.44 in Program D (the two Level-3 programs). Interviewees expressed their experience of the shift thus:

Here, I'm just a small part of a bigger project team. So you don't do anything on your own. It's a collaborative effort. So there has to be a lot of communication between us. And the process is there to ensure that this communication takes place and to structure it. The process helps keep us all in sync. In a small organization doing small projects, you have a lot of flexibility, but there's not much sharing. You're kind of on your own. Here, I'm just a small part of a bigger project team. So you don't do anything on your own. It's a collaborative effort. (C: development)

Developers want above all to deliver a great product, and the process helps us do that. What I've learned coming here is the value of a well thought-out process, rigorously implemented, and continuously improved. It will really improve the quality of the product. In this business, you've got to be exact, and the process ensures that we are. You have to get out of hacker mode! (A: development)

Some programmers here used to be very isolated. We had one fellow who just sat in his cube all day from six in the morning till two in the afternoon. Many of us didn't even know his name! But the process here drew him into team meetings and into new conversations. Eventually we even got him helping with training. (B: development)

More concretely, this new self-construal emerged through a mix of adult socialization (e.g., Kohn and Schooler, 1983) and "attraction-selection-attrition" (Schneider, 1987). On the effects of the former, we have the testimony quoted earlier of "But I can see the need now" (C: development). In Program D, one interviewee described his experience in these terms:

I was not originally a believer in this process stuff. I remember seeing coding guidelines when I joined the Program D. I just threw them into a corner. But a year later, I found that my code didn't make it through the code checker, and that got me to reconsider. So I went to some CMM training a few years ago – and I've been converted! Most of the developers and leads are being dragged into process kicking and screaming. Any coder would rather just hack. (D: process engineering)

(See Conn, 2002, for discussion of the process of developer socialization in another software factory.) On the importance of attraction-selection-attrition, two excerpts are illustrative:

You won't fit in well here if you don't like structure, you prefer working by yourself, you don't like getting suggestions from other people, or you don't like taking responsibility for your work and for making it better. (A: testing, formerly with Program A)

We still have to deal with the "free spirits" who don't believe in process. [. . .] Most of them adapt, although some don't and they leave. (C: process engineering)

*A New Professionalism.* This more interdependent self implied a corresponding mutation in the nature of developers' notion of professionalism. Some aspects of professionalism were preserved, whereas some were significantly transformed – in a socialized direction.

On the one hand, process leveraged traditional values of professionalism, including the appeal to individual pride in the results of one's own work:

We appeal to people's sense of professionalism, saying something like, "We're all professionals. And as professionals, we're both pretty mobile *and* committed to high quality work. Since I may leave here at some point, even soon, it's my duty as a professional to give the organization the documentation it needs to continue serving the customer." (B: quality assurance)

Our process makes for better testing, which means earlier detection of problems, which in turn makes the life of the programmer a lot easier and avoids a lot of embarrassment. (B: department manager, formerly with Program A)

On the other hand, however, process seemed to encourage a broadening of professionalism, its socialization beyond the closed, "guild" form it has often taken. Whereas traditional conceptions of professionalism give great weight to the individual practitioner's judgment and thus to their autonomy – if not economic autonomy, at least technical decision-making autonomy (Freidson, 2001) – process maturity encouraged the emergence of a more collective professional subject. This mutation is particularly significant because it appeared to moderate the traditional tension between professional autonomy and bureaucratic authority:

Usually people run away from audits. But amazingly, recently we've seen several projects volunteering – they want to show off their accomplishments and process capabilities. (A: process engineering)

The Improvement Team's work [...] made everyone realize that there are real business benefits to sharing information – instead of just worrying about your own rice bowl. I'm your [internal] customer, so I need you to understand my requirements. And the effect has been to make people interested in improving their own operations on their own, even without management being involved or pushing them. (D: logistics)

Professionals tend to have strong ties to and identify with their occupational community (Gouldner, 1957; Van Maanen and Barley, 1984). Interviews suggested that the greater process maturity strengthened both developers' professional-cosmopolitan orientations and their bureaucratic-local orientations. Insofar as the object of their work expanded to include process, at least some developers read more industry journals and attended more conferences, in particular, those focused on process issues. Simultaneously, they were drawn into more discussions around these process issues with hierarchical superiors and with staff from other GCC units.

### Socialization Versus Valorization

The progressive socialization of the labor process in software development was simultaneously stimulated, retarded, and distorted by the valorization process. On the one hand, process improvement and CMM certification efforts were stimulated by senior management's conviction that these would help profitability; but on the other hand, progress was limited by (a) contradictions between the pursuit of technical performance (use-value) and profit (exchange-value), (b) the competitive rivalry between firms that undermined their collaboration, (c) the tension between corporate interests and the collective interests of its employees, and (d) the tension between the collective nature of work and the individualizing effects of the wage relation. In aggregate, the centrifugal effects of valorization appear to have been weaker than the centripetal effects of socialization, but the former were strong enough to make the progress of socialization halting and uneven.

***Technical Performance Versus Profit.*** Clearly, part of the CMM effort was "for show," responding to symbolic legitimacy pressures rather than technical performance pressures. As such, it sometimes led to a decoupling between formal process and daily practice (as described by Meyer and Rowan, 1977). Comments such as these were common in the two Level-3 Programs but rare in the two Level-5 Programs:

We do have written processes, but some are not always used consistently. They are not always being used by the developers. They are not always used by the program managers in their regular reviews. (B: process engineering, formerly with Program A)

The evaluation and CMM SCE [Software Capability Evaluation] forced us to update our documents. We didn't really change anything in how we work though. (D: development)

In part, this symbolic/technical tension reflected a deeper contradiction between use-value and exchange-value. Interviewees were often aware that their labor process improvement efforts were at risk of being overridden by a higher, valorization imperative:

One key challenge is maintaining buy-in at the top. Our top corporate management is under constant pressure from the stock market. The market is constantly looking at margins, but government business has slim margins. That doesn't leave much room for expenditures associated with process improvement – especially when these take two or three years to show any payoff. (C: process engineering)

As I see it, GCC is a corporation, and that means it's run for the benefit of the major stockholders. So top management is incentivized to maximize dollar profits. Quality is only a means to that end, and, in practice, quality sometimes gets compromised. I used to be a technical person, so I know about quality. But now I'm a manager, and I'm under pressure to get the product out – come what may. I just don't have time to worry about the quality of the product. I have a manager of software development under me who's supposed to worry about that. (D: development manager)

It's hard to convince people that improving the process will help us get or keep business. [Referring to the recent downsizing of Program A:] We had a world-class process, and look what happened to us! Jobs in an organization like this depend a lot more on the vagaries of contracting than on our process excellence. (A: department manager)

The contradiction between socialization and valorization was particularly visible to the interviewees in the form of missed opportunities for process improvement:

We could do better at capturing and using lessons learned. We have all the vehicles for doing it – presentations, newsletters, databases. But it takes time. And there are so many competing priorities. In the end, it's all about profit and meeting schedules! (laughs) (A: project manager)

We do ask project teams to do a Lessons Learned report at the end of the project. We post the results on the database. But there's no staff support for the process. (A: quality assurance)

This contradiction was also visible in the gap between the expanded object of work as a use-value and limited tools available to employees for tackling this new object:

All these forms have a valid purpose, but it takes so long to fill them out that it just doesn't seem very efficient. We really need a lot more automation in doing all this. (B: development)

There's no doubt that more process maturity means more paperwork. Some of it is good, and some of it is an impediment, especially from a productivity point of view. Unless we have the tools to automate this documentation, it has to slow us down. We still don't have the right tools. (C: project manager)

The key issue moving forward, I think, is that we still don't have the resources we need to devote to process. A program of this size should have a full-time staff dedicated to our internal process maintenance. (C: quality assurance)

***Collaboration Versus Competitive Rivalry.*** The weight of the valorization imperatives was also visible in tensions that disrupted collaboration with clients:

The biggest problem here has been the customer and getting their buy-in. At Program A, our customer grew towards process maturity with us. Here [at Program B], we started with a less mature client. Some of the customer management even told us that they didn't want to hear about QA or our quality management system – they saw it as wasteful overhead. When you bid a project, you specify a budget for QA and so forth, but if they don't want to pay, you have a resource problem. And once you get the contract, then you start dealing with specific project managers within the customer organization, and these managers don't necessarily all believe in QA or simply don't want to pay for it out of their part of the budget. On the Y2K project, the customer kept changing standards and deadlines. Basically, we were dealing with a pretty process-immature customer, and that made it difficult for us to build our process maturity. Things have improved considerably since then. (B: process engineering, formerly with Program A)

***Employees' Interests Versus Corporate Interests.*** GCC managers understood that process maturity required a high level of employee participation. But the vertical authority structure that expresses the wage relation created a constant risk that managers would veer off into coercion:

We didn't initially have any questions on the employee survey about your boss. Frankly, people were worried that managers might retaliate. But now we do, and we find the data very useful in surfacing management problems. The earlier rounds of the survey did show some big communications problems in some groups. Counseling often helped, and in some cases, we moved people out to other positions. (A: program manager)

***Collective Nature of Work Versus Individual Wage Relation.*** The contradiction between the collective and collaborative requirements of effective process (the use-value aspect) and the individual and competitive nature of the employment contract (the exchange-value aspect) was visible in concerns voiced by some interviewees about job security:

If you have a good process, then people become like widgets you can stick into it, and everyone knows what their job is. Obviously that's a big advantage for the organization. [...] On the other hand, it also brings some fear for job security. It does make my job as a programmer easier to fill. (B: department manager, formerly with Program A)

This contradiction also helps explain a certain disinterest and passivity on the part of some developers:

I follow the rules because they are there. (B: development)

By and large, people just accept the Instructions pretty passively. (C: development manager)

It's hard to scare up much process improvement effort from the troops. Almost all the process improvement activity comes from people assigned to that task. (C: training)

***Overall.*** The overall result of the socialization tendencies and valorization counter-tendencies was an uneven process of socialization – an unevenness visible in variation across individuals:

We still have to deal with the "free spirits" who don't believe in process. These are typically people who have worked mainly in small teams. It's true that a small group working by itself doesn't need all this process. But we rarely work in truly independent small teams: almost all our work has to be integrated into larger systems, and will have to be maintained by people who didn't write the code themselves. These free spirits, though, are probably only between 2% and 4% of our staff. We find some of them in our advanced technology groups. We have some in the core of our business, too, because they are real gurus in some complex technical area and we can't afford to lose them. And there are some among the new kids coming in, too: many of them need convincing on this score. Most of them adapt, although some don't and they leave. (C: process engineering)

## DISCUSSION AND IMPLICATIONS

This paleo-Marxist version of activity theory also has implications for a number of related themes in current research on work and organization:

### Tools

The paleo view highlights the tension between socialization expressed in the progressive differentiation and integration of tool makers and tool users and the persistent valorization pressures that encourage firms to design and use tools to coerce more effort from recalcitrant users. This perspective suggests that there is something terribly one-sided about the current fascination with tacit knowledge (see also Adler, 1996; see also Hedlund, 1994: 76; Zollo and Winter, 2002). In the most common construal (stemming from Polanyi), tacit knowledge is individual and private; in an alternative construal, tacit knowledge can be collective, the property of a community of practice; but in either case, tacit knowledge is essentially local, the antithesis of universal, socialized knowledge. Tacit knowledge is often illustrated by reference to the difficulty of articulating our knowledge of how to ride a bicycle. As I write this, the Tour de France has just concluded, and Lance Armstrong won for the fifth consecutive time. The amount of formal, articulated, engineering, and scientific knowledge that has been invested in perfecting his riding technique, his bicycle, his training program, his team's organization, and so forth, is massive. Clearly, there is a tacit dimension to Armstrong's performance; but just as clearly, theory should acknowledge the emergence of the whole field of sports science and the deep transformation of the structure of knowledge that is its corollary.

### Object

The basic object contradiction is between the progressive expansion and enrichment of the object viewed as a technical challenge and the narrowness and poverty of profit as an object. This tension is visible in numerous studies of Total Quality Management: management encourages workers to invest themselves in process improvement, but profit imperatives deter management from acting on the resulting suggestions. In part, the contradiction is captured in institutionalization theory (Scott, 1995; Powell and DiMaggio, 1991), as a tension between technical and legitimacy constraints; but institutionalization theory has not always been explicit about the deep ambiguity of "technical" constraints under capitalist conditions: It has often conflated the use-value and exchange-value aspects of the technical domain. As a result, even though institutionalization theory has identified the role of social construction in the symbolic legitimacy domain, it has tended to "naturalize" the technical-task domain.

### Community

The case sketch highlighted the persistent, contradictory co-existence of enabling and coercive features of modern organizational forms. This analysis sits uneasily with the broad architecture of current organization theory. Organization theory has long been split between "rational" and "natural" systems views, and within the latter, split between consensus and conflict approaches (Scott, 2003). Perhaps organizational research would advance more fruitfully if, instead of playing these perspectives off against each other as if they were incommensurable paradigms, we acknowledged that each reflects part of the whole picture and focused our research more systematically on understanding their interrelations. For example, research on teams in organizations might advance more fruitfully if teams were seen both as a high-performance organization design and as a form of normative and concertive control, and if the real, material contradiction between the two aspects were brought into focus as an object of study.

### Workers

The preceding case suggested that firms' attempts to strengthen collaboration and coordination have profound effects on workers' self-construals. Marx's linkage of objective and subjective socialization is developed and extended in Elias's (2000) discussion of "figuration," and this perspective is emerging as a fruitful avenue for organizational research (Van Iterson et al., 2002). Even though valorization pressures limit the trend, we see knowledge-intensive firms such as GCC encouraging the emergence of new forms of collectivism, ones that we might interpret as differentiated from traditional collectivism by their lower power-distance (Triandis and Gelfand, 1998) and/or by their coexistence with high individualism (Kagitcibasi, 1997). This suggests that our theories of motivation may also need expansion. When firms mobilize the collective worker to ensure a more effective labor process, and when workers respond by internalizing this community, then autonomy – whether of the individual or of the self-directed team – becomes less salient as a source of motivation in job design: Collaborative interdependence may activate more collectivistic sources of motivation.

### SOCIALIZATION AND SKILL IN HISTORICAL PERSPECTIVE

In conclusion, let us return to the starting point: the future of critical research on work organization. Others have criticized Braverman and the earliest labor process theory research for ignoring factors such as class consciousness, the role of workers' power in shaping work and skill, the limited diffusion of scientific management techniques, and gender and other social and discursive forces in shaping the social construction of skill categories (for recent reviews of criticism and debate, see Wardell, 1999; Grugulis, Willmott and Knights, 2001). By contrast, the preceding discussion of the Census occupation data and the case sketch suggest a very different critique, one that demands a theory that accounts for both a long-run increase in average skill levels and a profound change in the form of skill.

The key to an effective response to this challenge lies, I have argued, in restoring the causal weight of technology – the forces of production – in our account. Whereas neo-Marxist labor process theory focuses on the role of capitalist relations of production in shaping work organization, the paleo-Marxist approach I have proposed situates skill and work organization at the intersection of the forces and the relations of production, influenced by both.

On the one hand, under the impact of the progressive socialization of the forces of production, tasks become on average more complex, and there is a progressive differentiation of roles and increasing collaborative interdependence at various levels: between workers (team work), work units (process management), hierarchical levels (employee involvement), specialized functions (cross-functional teams), and firms (supplier partnerships). Yes, the autonomy and nobility of traditional crafts are trampled underfoot in this process; but the larger mass of workers often find the complexity of their tasks increased and their work relations broadened. Increasing proportions of men and women are drawn into mixed-gender, interdependent work relations. Workers are drawn from local isolation into the web of globalization, which (*pace* neo-Marxist theories of dependency) also tends to increase work complexity and broaden relations in developing countries (as in the paleo-Marxist account offered by Warren, 1980).

On the other hand, and in contrast, the persistence of capitalist relations of production has a fundamentally ambiguous effect. The capital relation of competition sometimes stimulates the advance of the forces of production, but sometimes obliges firms to sacrifice long-term for short-term gains, and systematically obliges them to privilege owners' private benefits over broader social benefits. Tentative moves towards inter-firm collaboration are both stimulated and undermined by competitive rivalry. The wage relation privileges owners' interests over workers'. As owners' agents, managers sometimes find it profitable to upgrade workers' skills, but sometimes find it more profitable, if only in the short term, to deskill work, manipulate teamwork to create peer pressure, let horizontal specialization degenerate into adversarial rivalry, and use hierarchy for command and control. These effects should not be ignored as mere "noise" in the data: they reflect the deep structure of property relations under capitalism. It is therefore appropriate that scholars should highlight and criticize them as reflecting an important, imminent tendency of capitalism.

What can we say about the relation between these two sets of forces in the overall evolution of work and skill? The neo-Marxist interpretation offered by LPT gives little causal efficacy to the forces of production (e.g., Burawoy, 1979: 14ff, 220) and argues that capitalist development, insofar as workers' struggles have not been able to counteract capitalist pressures, leads to increasing misery, including the deskilling and degradation of work. When Marx and Engels write in the *Communist Manifesto* that capitalism develops its own "gravediggers," neo-Marxist LPT takes this to mean that capitalism creates a class with so little left to lose that it has no alternative but to revolt – workers will have nothing to lose but their chains.

On the paleo-Marxist view, the development of capitalism is profoundly shaped by the progressive socialization of the forces of production. Over the long run, the overall effect is to create a working class that is increasingly capable of taking on successfully the task of radically transforming society and of assuming the leading role in a new form of society. This task is made progressively easier by the gradual socialization of relations of production even within the womb of capitalism itself, notably in the form of the increasing concentration and centralization of capital and the growing role of government in the economy. (Whether workers are *motivated* to undertake this historic, revolutionary mission – as distinct from being *capable* of undertaking it – depends on distinct, socio-political, super-structural factors.)

Marx's writings themselves are ambiguous on the relation of the two sets of forces. Elsewhere (Adler, 1990), I have argued that this is because these writings, even *Capital*, mixed the analysis of long-term and shorter-term trends, and combined objective analysis with polemical advocacy. The paleo interpretation was nevertheless dominant until World War I. Ideologically, it went hand in hand with a sense of the historical inevitability of socialism and a great self-confidence on the part of the major working-class parties.

Since around World War I, the more radical parts of the left have argued that the paleo-Marxist view concedes too much continuing legitimacy to capitalism. The objection would appear to be that if capitalism continued to foster the development of the forces of production and the working class's capabilities, it would be difficult to justify radical hostility to it. But on the paleo view, there are plenty of fundamental, and increasingly compelling, reasons to doubt that capitalism is the "end of history" (*pace* Fukuyama, 1992). Even if the aggregate, long-term trend in work organization is toward upgrading, the unevenness of this process is a scandal that is increasingly resented. More generally, capitalism seems unable to eliminate its "savage inequalities" (in Kozol's, 1991), its persistent un- and underemployment, its recurrent economic crises and wars, and its ecological irresponsibility. The paleo view allows critical scholars to advance this critique whereas acknowledging the progressive aspects of capitalist development. The neo view turns the critique into shrill polemic.

We need a robust theory of work. A paleo-Marxist version of activity theory provides a promising starting point. Empirically, it provides us with a surprisingly intuitive way of grasping the everyday contradictions of the capitalist firm. Theoretically, it allows us to characterize the fundamental limitations of capitalism and how these limitations conflict with a long-term socialization trend. And politically? In the short term, prospects for radical change due to this escalating conflict may seem dim, but the socialization thesis puts history on the side of radical change.

10

# Values, Rubbish, and Workplace Learning

Yrjö Engeström

## THE VALUE DILEMMA

In psychology and education, values are usually understood as personal preferences or subjective orientations toward the world. In other words, values are firmly located *inside the individual subject's mind*. Although this may correspond to much of our everyday experience, there is also a very different, if not diametrically opposite, way of locating value. This alternative way is illustrated by a bitter letter to the editor, signed by the pseudonym 'A long-term unemployed with three degrees', recently published in the leading Finnish newspaper *Helsingin Sanomat*.

I would like to finally utilize the education I have received and the experience I have collected through my life, but for both public and private sector employers, *my value* in the labor market seems to be full zero [italics added].

The author of these lines talks about his or her value in the labor market. In other words, the value is primarily *in the object* – in this case, in the person trying to sell his or her labor power in the market. There is still a subjective element involved, namely, the fact that the value of the object is assessed by the employers. But value is definitely not just a personal preference or subjective orientation of an employer; it is something more objective and societal.

In both profit-oriented management guidebooks and critical studies of organizations, work-related values are typically treated as mental and textual constructs of ideology, used primarily for purposes of motivating employees, gaining their commitment, or achieving control. Two books that share the same title, *Values at Work* (Cheney, 2002; Henderson & Thompson, 2003), are a case in point. Cheney's book is a critical analysis of the clash between cooperative and market values in the Mondragon cooperative; Henderson & Thompson's book is a guide for managers for building 'threads between people, performance and profit'. Despite their opposite ideological points

193

of departure, both books treat values essentially as mental and discursive constructs. Paradoxically, even critical organizational studies of value seem at least as mentalistic and subjectivist as traditional psychology of values (see also Barker, 1993). As Thevenot (2002: 52) puts it, they suffer from a 'lack of material embedding of political and moral grammars'.

From the point of view of cultural – historical activity theory (Engeström, Miettinen, & Punamäki, 1999), this point of departure is misguided. In an activity-theoretical view, values at work are embedded in the object of the activity. Objects are contradictory unities of use-value and exchange-value, generated materially, mentally, and textually. In this view, values are also inseparable from motives. Thus, in medical work, the use-value of illness as object generates the motive of healing, whereas the exchange-value of illness generates the motives of treatment-for-profit and cost-cutting.

Being embedded in multiple activity systems simultaneously and successively, objects have lives of their own and resist goal-rational attempts at control and prediction. Negotiations of objects are always also negotiations of values and motives – not just of 'what' but also of 'why', 'for whom', and 'where to'. The doctor and the patient necessarily negotiate not only the diagnosis and treatment but also the consequences (use-value) and the expenses (exchange-value) of care, for both parties. Such negotiations are highly value-laden, whether their value aspect is openly articulated or not.

The articulation, questioning, and expansive transformation of values can eventually only succeed at the level of collective activity systems. Problem solving and reflection-in-action at individual or dyadic levels will not suffice. This requires special kinds of learning actions. In particular, these actions include facing and questioning 'worthless' or 'useless' objects in negotiations and boundary encounters between actors with different power and hierarchical positions.

To get a firmer grip of values, we must first develop a framework for understanding the dynamics of objects as they move through different steps in their life cycles.

### THE LIFE OF THE OBJECT: RUBBISH THEORY

Recent critical discussions on the importance of objects for organizational and social theorizing almost invariably emphasize the mobility, restlessness, and continuous transformations of objects. Although exciting, this rejection of static notions of object is also somewhat troubling. In recent literature, there seems to be no way to systematically capture and analyze the precise nature, paths, and steps of movement and transformation of objects.

Appadurai's (1986) and Kopytoff's (1986) suggestions of studying the 'cultural biographies of things' were largely limited to the spheres of exchange and consumption, and the movement itself was reduced to the opposite processes of 'commoditization' and 'singularization'. Latour's (1996) suggestion of framing the movement in terms of 'localization' and 'globalization' is intriguing but very vague. Attempts to use models of activity systems for analyzing steps in the movement of objects (see Engeström, 1996) have thus far remained anecdotal.

We have to go twenty-five years back in time to find a rigorous and imaginative attempt to analyze step-by-step the movement of objects. This is Michael Thompson's (1979) book *Rubbish Theory*. Thompson's insight is that, with time, objects lose their value and turn into rubbish. Rubbish, however, is not always the end point of an object's life. Out of rubbish, durables emerge. For example, the value of a car decreases each time it is sold, until it no longer appeals to any buyer and becomes rubbish. However, if this rubbish car is for some reason not destroyed but put away and left in a barn for another twenty or thirty years, a connoisseur may find it, and it may instantaneously become a durable collector's item with a high value attached to it.

Thompson calls the object in circulation *a transient*. There are two possible steps of qualitative transformation in the life of an object in circulation: (1) a transient becomes rubbish, and (2) rubbish becomes *a durable*. Rubbish, the necessary middle point, is largely invisible, kept out of sight.

For Thompson, individual actions of buying and selling are not themselves particularly interesting (as they might be for Appadurai and Kopytoff). They represent only *quantitative* reductions of the object's value. What is interesting is the *qualitative* step from transient to rubbish or from rubbish to durable.

Thompson's basic scheme focuses on circulation, or exchange. This is its basic weakness. Thompson does acknowledge that the spheres of production and consumption are equally important, but he fails to characterize in detail (indeed, even to name) the transitions of the object connected to those spheres. This is clear when one looks at the basic diagram in which Thompson summarizes his theory (Figure 10.1).

## OPENING UP PRODUCTION AND CONSUMPTION

I suggest that the spheres of production and consumption can very well be opened up for analysis at the same level of detail that Thompson devoted to exchange.

In Thompson's model (Figure 10.1), the bottom element of the exchange or circulation sphere consists of transients, publicly visible objects that are actively manipulated by selling and buying. One might characterize this part of the model as the *layer of public manipulation*. In the sphere of production, this layer is occupied by raw materials (including parts or whatever ingredients the producer needs to put together a finished product). Raw materials are actively and publicly manipulated as they are turned into marketable products. In the sphere of consumption, this layer is occupied by objects in use – products being actively consumed by their so-called 'end users'.

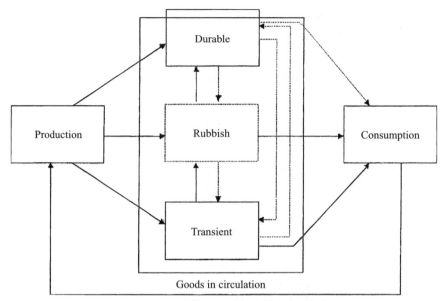

**Consumptive production and productive consumption**

FIGURE 10.1. Thompson's basic model of transitions in the life of an object. Continuous lines represent 'possible transfers'; dashed lines represent 'impossible transfers' (Thompson, 1979: 113).

In Figure 10.1, the middle element in the sphere of circulation consists of rubbish – invisible, poorly controlled, and surprising.

But of course the fact that the boundary between rubbish and non-rubbish is not fixed but moves in response to social pressures means that new elements may suddenly appear within his [the economist's] field, whilst others may suddenly disappear in an equally distressing and inexplicable manner. (Thompson, 1979: 12)

This middle part of the model may be called the *layer of invisible resistance and emergence*. In the sphere of production, this layer is occupied by products in repair, those products that have been returned to the producer from circulation or consumption because they have been found faulty or broken down before their warranty has expired. The producers are not keen on disclosing and discussing these troublesome items, yet they have to deal with them all the time as if in the shadows. In the sphere of consumption, this layer is occupied by objects being serviced or maintained. Here, the users themselves have to engage in the fixing and servicing of their objects to keep them usable. Again, this is not the favorite aspect of consumption we consumers like to discuss, except when engaged in the discourse of complaining.

The top element of circulation in Figure 10.1 consists of durables with increasing value. Durables are definitely public, but they are typically not supposed to be actively manipulated after they reach their status as durables.

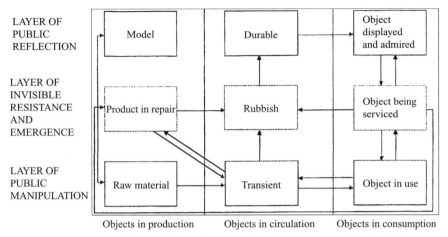

Consumptive production and productive consumption of objects

FIGURE 10.2. Spheres, layers, and states in the life of an object.

In effect, they are supposed to sit still and let their value grow as people observe, reflect, discuss, and speculate about them – until the price is right and another exchange takes place. This top part may be called the *layer of public reflection*. In production, this layer is occupied by models that represent and guide the creation of the future products, in reflective dialogue with manipulative actions on raw materials. In consumption, this layer is occupied by objects displayed and admired, such as collectibles in galleries.

I will now put forward a diagram that completes the work started by Thompson (Figure 10.2). Each cell in the diagram may be understood as a distinctive state of the object.

## ACTIONS ON THE OBJECT

It is not enough to identify the spheres, layers, and states of the object. The main task is to identify the transitions, or actions, that take place as the object moves between the different states.

As Figure 10.3 shows, I have identified sixteen possible actions that change the state of the object. To elaborate on the potentials of the framework, I will now briefly examine these actions.

As a concrete case, I will examine transformations in the life of a set of objects encountered on a daily basis in medical work in primary health care settings. This set of objects consists of patients and health problems increasingly 'dumped' on primary care clinics, at least in Finland. These include cases of alcohol and drug abuse, chronic pain, dependency on medications, chronic mental health problems, and more generally cases of multiple simultaneous chronic illnesses, especially in elderly patients. This

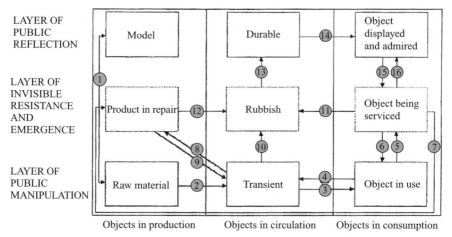

FIGURE 10.3. Possible actions that transform the object.

vaguely defined and ill-bounded set of objects is sometimes characterized as 'difficult patients', 'demanding patients', or 'complex patients', but there is no general agreement or theory about what exactly makes them 'difficult', 'demanding', or 'complex'.

The first action in Figure 10.3 is the naming of the object, which in medicine takes place by means of diagnosis and testing. More generally, this first action may be called *stabilization*. It involves separating the object from its background, giving shape to and defining the object as an identifiable entity. In medicine, accepted stabilizing names are listed in official classifications of diseases. These classifications are oriented to specific singular diagnoses based on biomedical data. They are notoriously useless for the characterization of cases in which multiple biomedical conditions, or worse yet, biomedical, social, and psychological issues are intertwined. Thus, the very first action on these objects tends to be taken in a fragmenting mode, isolating one or more biomedically acceptable diagnoses from the messy totality of the patient's condition.

If the patient is diagnosed with a medical condition that needs hospitalization, the object will be immediately placed in its appropriate Diagnosis Related Group (DRG). The DRG framework is defined as 'a system for classifying patient care by relating common characteristics such as diagnosis, treatment, and age to an expected consumption of hospital resources and length of stay; its purpose is to provide a framework for specifying case mix and to *reduce hospital costs and reimbursements and it forms the cornerstone of the prospective payment system*' (Agency for Healthcare Research and Quality). In other words, the DRG system puts a price tag on the object. The price is based on statistical data on average costs of cases in the same DRG category (for a profit-oriented discussion of the DRG system, see Block & Press, 1986; for a critical study of the same phenomenon, see Geist & Hardesty, 1992).

Mean length of stay is calculated by dividing the sum of inpatient days by the number of patients within the DRG category. Mean total charge is calculated by dividing the sum of patient charges by the number of patients within the DRG category. Total charges represent the dollar amount charged for the hospitalization rather than the amount paid or the actual costs to provide the care. Patients who are more seriously ill tend to require more hospital resources than patients who are less seriously ill, even though they are admitted to the hospital for the same reason. Recognizing this, the DRG grouper splits certain DRGs based on the presence of secondary diagnoses for specific complications or comorbidities.

The use of the DRG system exemplifies the second action in Figure 10.3, the entrance of the object into the sphere of circulation and exchange. Although this event is mundanely called selling or buying, I call this the action of *commoditization*. The object enters the sphere of circulation and exchange with a price tag on it. This action is brought to conclusion when the patient, or whoever represents the patient, is for the first time charged or billed for the care. That is when the disease truly becomes a transient.

From the point of view of the patient, his or her condition is not any-more just his or her personal source of discomfort, suffering, and fear. It has become a package where the illness and the care are inseparably inter-twined and constitute each other. How does this object enter the sphere of consumption?

As the patient receives care from the care provider, he or she typically begins to consume the care immediately. This is most obvious in the taking of medicine – a central action in almost all medical care. But even the less tangible aspects of care, such as instructions for diet and physical exercise, must be actively used and implemented to produce an effect. The notion of 'productive consumption' is indeed very appropriate here. The third action in Figure 10.3 may simply be called *using*.

Often, the patient's condition and medication need to be checked and assessed regularly. When this requires a visit or some other billable trans-action with a care provider, the object returns to the sphere of exchange and appears as a transient once again. In a way, the value of this particular illness case is reassessed. For lack of a better term, I call this fourth action *consumption-initiated recommoditization*.

Of course, not all actions of care require a re-entry to the sphere of exchange. In chronic illnesses, a large amount of service work is done by the patient on him- or herself. These are examples of the fifth and sixth actions in Figure 10.3. The fifth action may be called *maintaining*. The sixth one is typically tightly coupled to the fifth one and may be called *reusing*.

When a patient's condition deteriorates significantly, often through the appearance of new, related diseases, the object typically re-enters the sphere of production. In a way, all chronic illness is riddled with continuous product recalls. After a while, the prescribed care regime proves insufficient, so new diagnoses and care regimes are needed (Wiener et al., 1983). This re-entry to production may be initiated from consumption, that is by the patient him- or herself (action seven), or from exchange, that is by a care-giver orgranization (action eight). I call these actions *consumption-initiated* and *exchange-initiated restabilization*, respectively. Action nine in Figure 10.3 represents the *production-initiated recommoditization* of the object.

Two major questions remain. How do these patient cases become rubbish? And how might they become durables?

There are three ways in which a disease may become rubbish. The first (action eight) is pretty obvious: the patient is so poor and the medical insurance arrangements are so weak or non-existent that the patient's care is not anymore billed, which means that the patient is not anymore given care or receives care as a charity only. The second alternative (action nine) is that the patient becomes so old and/or weak that the care providers begin to see the care as useless or too costly for the limited benefits gained. The third alternative is the most subtle and very possibly the most common one. The patient's illness may become a trivial routine or disturbing nuisance and abuse of medical servies for the medical care providers, which leads them to see the object as rubbish, to be avoided and sent away as soon and with as little expense as possible.

The third alternative has been extensively studied by Mizrahi (1986) in her perceptive book, *Getting Rid of Patients*. On the basis on extensive ethnographic fieldwork in a hospital, Mizrahi describes the invisible classifications at play.

Within the house staff culture there were two major systems of social classification. The first depended on the disease of the patient – 'interesting' versus 'uninteresting' – with the latter category predominating during the house staff's graduate medical training. This system of categorization is basically devoid of reference to the external social structure and to some degree independent of the personal and social characteristics of the patient. It is almost solely determined by professional criteria related to diagnosis; that is, the symptoms are the primary basis of valuation, and outcome of the disease – whether it is curable – is the secondary basis.

The second system of social classification begins with the ideal patient and ends with the despised patient. The ideal patient is described in terms such as 'clean', 'articulate', 'cooperative', and so forth – most of which closely conform to external systems of social status. Despised patients are defined as abusers – of themselves, the system, house staff – and as such are subject to counterabuse. (Mizrahi, 1986: 70)

However, the final determinant of rubbish is economical: the 'bottom line' in patient calculation, as Mizrahi points out.

When the house staff did raise the issue of costs, it was almost always in regard to patients who were wasting taxpayers' money by inappropriate use of the medical or hospital facilities. This assessment of patients who 'abused' the system clearly supported their desire to GROP [get rid of patients] those who, in their estimation, were costing the taxpaying public millions of dollars for unwarranted care. (Mizrahi, 1986: 79)

Here is a poignant quote that concerns diabetes, taken from an interview with one of Mizrahi's subjects.

We get tired of it . . . if it's the fifty-seventh [hospital] admission for somebody who is diabetic who gets drunk and doesn't take insulin and then has to be intubated in the intensive care unit. . . . Everybody says along the way, 'Why are we spending all this money on this guy who is trying to kill himself?' (Mizrahi, 1986: 80)

Figure 10.3 shows that an object may enter the state of rubbishnes through three actions (ten, eleven, and twelve). The first route (action ten) is through an exchange in which a transient is found to possess minimal or no value. In medicine, this might happen when a care provider tries to hand over a patient (such as the one described by Mizrahi's informant in the quote cited earlier) to another care provider. The second route (action eleven) is initiated in a maintenance effort, when an object in consumption is found hopelessly worn out and thus discarded as rubbish. This might be what the patient in Mizrahi's quote had actually done to his own illness and to himself. Finally, the third route (action twelve) is initiated in a repair effort within production, when repair of the product is found too costly. If the care prodvider in Mizrahi's example simply abandons the patient for all practical purposes, it performs this action. I call these three actions *devaluation in exchange, devaluation in maintenance,* and *devaluation in repair,* respectively.

Now what about diabetes becoming a durable? In medicine, objects become durable when they are hailed and immortalized as breakthroughs. It used to be that after heart disease had progressed beyond a certain point, it was considered incurable and became, in effect, rubbish. When Christiaan Barnard performed the first open-heart transplant surgery in 1967 with great international press coverage, certain variants of heart disease rubbish became objects of heroic breakthrough medicine. The event, the technique, and Barnard himself became durables, standard icons in medical history texts.

Few people remember that the first patient to receive a heart transplant was Louis Washkansky, a 55-year-old man suffering from diabetes and heart disease. Of course, diabetes did not reach the echelons of durability. It remained a sidetrack of the story that may be retrieved from the rubbish dumps of medical history.

The thirteenth action in Figure 10.3, the transition from rubbish to durable, may be called the action of *revaluation.* When a durable is placed into the sphere of consumption (action fourteen), the action may be called *freezing*. Finally, when a frozen object – such as the iconic representation of Barnard and his transplant surgery – needs maintenance (e.g., the forthcoming celebration of the 50th anniversary of the first open-heart transplant in the year 2017), the actions of *retouching* (action fifteen) and *refreezing* (action sixteen) are initiated.

## HOW VALUE IS SHAPED

The life of the object is also the life of value. In the production sphere, the object takes its shape and acquires its value by virtue of being transformed by human labor. The amount and kind of labor invested in the production of the object represents the foundational 'hard core' of value. The action of commoditization (the second action in Figure 10.3) is the anticipatory definition of the exchange value of the object. This is a critical step, as observed by Leont'ev.

The doctor who buys a practice in some little provincial place may be very seriously trying to reduce his fellow citizens' suffering from illness, and may see his calling in just that. He must, however, want the number of the sick to increase, because his life and practical opportunity to follow his calling depend on that. This dualism distorts man's most elementary feelings. Even love proves capable of acquiring the most ugly forms, not to mention love of money, which can become a veritable passion. (Leont'ev, 1981: 255; see also Rodwin, 1993, for a recent collection on physicians' conflicts of interest)

In the sphere of exchange, the object is sold and bought. One might say that the sphere of exchange is the sphere of negotiated value, where fluctuation and situational factors play an important role. But at the same time, there is something fatefully pre-determined in the evolution of value in the sphere of exchange. In the longer run, each resale of the object is tendentially a step further toward becoming rubbish. The eventual critical action of devaluation (action ten in Figure 10.3) involves some kind of conclusive declaration of the worthlessness of the object. Becoming rubbish has thus a sense of finality. When a person is declared 'chronic', or 'disturbed', or 'alcoholic', or 'uninsured', or 'troublemaker', the stigmatic definition is very difficult to eliminate or transform. In terms of exchange-value, this status means that there are very few or no buyers: The expenditure of dealing with rubbish is considered greater than any possible gain or revenue. In this sense, rubbishness is a state of inaction, of decaying in a limbo. Only very few lucky objects find their way into revaluation and durability.

The 'softness' and malleability of value is revealed in the sphere of consumption. Each user of the object finds it easy to decrease its value: just use it, or easier yet, just let it sit and become old. This eating away of value in consumption seems innocent enough as long as the user does not have to face the fateful transition of the object into rubbish.

Now these observations have an uncomfortably deterministic sound. They may help us see critical steps in the formation of object and value, but they also seem to exclude the possibility of reversals and deviating courses of action. This is why I think the theory is severly incomplete and biased in the form presented thus fur. The task of the next section is to show how this bias may be corrected.

## THE INTENTIONAL RESHAPING OF VALUE

Consider physicians, nurses, assistants, and receptionists working at a primary care health center responsible for providing health care services to the local population for no or a nominal fee. A very significant portion of their clients are the types of 'complex' or 'demanding' patients described earlier. By now, it should be clear that these are patients who are either already declared or rapidly becoming rubbish.

In fact, it seems clear that dealing with these rubbish or near-rubbish cases is the characteristic that distinguishes this type of public health center from other medical providers, such as private clinics or hospitals. These professionals are doomed to deal with rubbish as the core object of their activity.

For neoliberal ideologists, politicians, and enterpreneurs, the decline of public health into a marginal rubbish dump is of course welcome. On the other hand, among practitioners, it evokes various reactions of denial, defense, and escape.

Expanding on the theory presented in this chapter makes it clear that there are much more optimistic and exhilarating alternative courses of action available for practitioners.

The theory, as presented thus far, depicts the state of rubbishness as the inevitable end point of most objects. The only alternative to rubbishness is the equally final and closed end point of becoming a durable. Both rubbish and durables are essentially dead ends, domains of inaction and immutability. This leaves nature – understood as resources not yet molded by humans – as the only source of new raw materials for objects. Human activity looks like an endless process of exploiting nature, of turning natural resources into artefactual objects and eventually into useless rubbish.

There are three types of significant actions that are not accounted for by this limited version of the theory. First, there are actions of *playful conversion*, which basically search for and pick up rubbish to turn it into newly defined raw materials (action seventeen in Figure 10.4). Second, there are actions of *caring revitalization*, which pick up rubbish and turn it into newly conceptualized transients (action eighteen in Figure 10.4). Finally, there are actions of *engrossed appropriation*, which turn rubbish into enjoyable objects in use (action nineteen in Figure 10.4). I briefly examine each one of these three expanded action types.

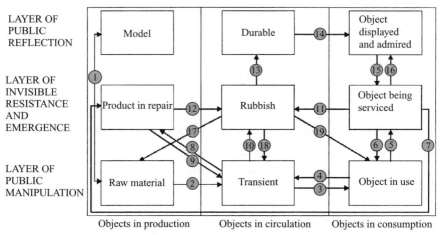

FIGURE 10.4. Expanded model of actions on the object.

Actions seventeen, eighteen, and nineteen are peculiar in that they do not seem necessary for standard rational-choice economics, yet they undeniably take place all the time. Let us first take a look at action seventeen, playful conversion.

It is well known that inventors and artists look for and use pieces of rubbish as raw material for their works, sometimes with astonishing results. Children and teachers of the innovative educational practices of Reggio Emilia in Italy use items of rubbish and convert them into toys for productive play. The most obvious case of conversion is the recycling movement in its different manifestations, from local voluntary efforts to nationwide programs promoted and administered by states and municipalities. What is playful about all these examples, including recycling, is the idea that useless junk may be converted into something unexpectedly useful, even beautiful.

How could this action apply to rubbish patients in public health care? How might complicated or demanding patients be converted into raw materials for something quite different?

There is a relatively simple answer to this. Many of the patient groups mentioned earlier are in fact left in the shadows of medical research, so that there is actually very little knowledge and understanding of the nature of their problems and needs. Patients with multiple overlapping medications – and potential dependencies on medications – are a case in point. Excessive medication is clearly an economic and medical problem. To tackle it effectively, we need more in-depth knowledge from the field. Few would be better equipped to generate this knowledge than the general practitioners working at public health centers. Rubbish patients, such as those with excessive medications, and their stories may thus be converted into ethnographically grounded research knowledge, which in turn will serve as raw material for designing new tools, policies, and practices for changing the situation. What is playful about this kind of conversion is that it involves experimenting with new genres of research, for instance, bringing together practice-bound case narratives, locally grounded theorizing, and statistical generalizations.

The second new action depicted in Figure 10.4 is caring revitalization (action eighteen). This action implies turning rubbish back into transients within the sphere of exchange. In everyday life, we witness such salvaging actions all the time. The typical scenario is the following. A person throws away or abandons an object as rubbish. Another person sees the object and exclaims: 'Please, don't throw it away, give (or sell) it to me, I can still find good use for it!' The object changes hands and – simultaneously – returns from the abyss of rubbishness to the land of living transients. What is caring about such an action is that it necessarily involves compassion for something already condemned. What is revitalizing about it is that it literally gives new life, a new hope, to the object. This typically happens by means of reconceptualizing the object. The new user has a slightly (or radically) different idea for the use of the object: the object is about to receive not only new life, but also a new identity.

Again, how could this action apply to rubbish patients in public health care? How might difficult or demanding or hopeless patients be redefined as interesting transients?

The very act of changing hands may offer a key to an answer. The treatment of patients in a busy health center typically takes place in dyadic form, between the individual physician (or nurse) and the individual patient. Practitioners seldom have a chance to look at their colleagues' cases. And it is even more rare that patients get the chance to discuss each others' problems and care. To make space for actions of caring revitalization, collaborative reconceptualization sessions between multiple practitioners – and eventually multiple patients – might be an effective way to go. For a start, each practitioner might simply select a difficult or hopeless case, put together the data available on the case, and present it in a joint session of the practitioners at the center. A more demanding step would be to involve the patient him- or herself in such a session. The most demanding format would bring in multiple patients who have been similarly categorized.

The potential of such sessions lies in the shifting and cross-breeding of perspectives. At the same time, such sessions represent a new type of caring. The patient is taken as a person who has a voice that is worth listening to.

The third new action depicted in Figure 10.4 is engrossed appropriation (action nineteen). This action involves turning rubbish into enjoyable objects in use. This implies a concept of consumption and pleasure very different from neoliberal notions.

When market theorists think about a pleasurable, rewarding experience, the root image they have in mind seems to be eating food ('consumption') – and not in the context of a public or private feast, either, but apparently, food eaten by oneself. The idea seems to be of an almost furtive appropriation, in which objects that had been parts of the outside world are completely incorporated into the consumer's self. (...) one need only imagine how different the theory might look like if it set off from almost any other kind of enjoyable experience: say, from making love, or from being at a concert, or even from playing a game. (Graeber, 2001: 260)

An everyday example of the action of engrossed appropriation is that of listening to a story told by an unlikely narrator who opens up a window into his or her world of the downtrodden. This is the simple secret behind the influence of entire genres of books and films, from Franz Fanon to Studs Terkel, from Luis Bunuel to Aki Kaurismäki.

It is not too difficult to see the implications of this for the care of rubbish patients in public health care. Eliciting and listening to the patients' stories is of course easier said than done. Time pressure and output demands are heavy. Therefore, it seems necessary to combine the actions of engrossed appropriation with the actions of caring revitalization and playful conversion discussed earlier. Together, these three actions represent a significant new component to be introduced into the work of primary care practitioners. This component consists of research, listening, and collaborative reconceptualization. Such a reflective component of work will eventually generate new diagnostic categories and new methods of care. Such a component is worth fighting for. It requires administrative and political recognition and allocation of appropriate resources in terms of time, space, and tools.

### THE LEARNING CHALLENGE

Coping with rubbish or, more exactly, revaluing rubbish, is a challenge to workplace learning. It does not concern only public health care. In our studies of postal work, we witnessed very similar contradictions when mail carriers discussed their relation to 'junk mail' (Engeström et al., 1996). The same phenomenon appeared in a study of firefighters facing the increasingly prevalent 'useless calls' from people with non-serious emergencies (Mankkinen, 2002). And it came up again recently in our study of investment managers in a bank, discussing what they called the 'unproductive mass' of relatively passive clients (Engeström et al., 2004). To condense, the challenge consists in turning rubbish into gems. The gems are not to be understood as dead durables, but as live raw materials, transients, and enjoyable objects in use.

The three expansive actions identified earlier – playful conversion, caring revitalization, and engrossed appropriation – are actually demanding actions of learning. They expand the 'normal' life process of the object, adding a reflective and creative layer to it. This is the very meaning of learning actions (see Engeström, 1999b).

My central thesis is that value is embedded in objects. Objects, in turn, are not fixed and frozen entities. They live, move, and change in complex cyclic ways. I took Thompson's (1979) rubbish theory as my point of departure to analyze this movement.

But I needed to expand Thompson's theory in two major steps. First, I went beyond Thompson's preoccupation with exchange and opened up the spheres of production and consumption. Secondly, I rejected the idea that rubbish and/or durables are final, closed states in the life cycles of objects and values. I opened up the possibility of actions of intentional reshaping of value, of turning rubbish into gems.

Overall, the expanded rubbish theory of value developed in this chapter is itself a learning challenge to critical research and emancipatory interventions in at least three senses.

The first challenge is to open our eyes to rubbish as a huge reservoir of potential novelty. Talk about values is typically very noble and uplifting – and it typically leads to very little practical results. The expanded rubbish theory asks us to look downward, into the invisible and abandoned. In studies of organizational change and work-related learning, this means that attention should be directed to the wastelands of unpleasant or useless tasks, actors, objects, and clients, as well as to failures, mistakes, and dead ends usually forgotten.

The second challenge is to cross-breed the conceptual framework of value-related actions put forward in this chapter and Marx's concept of commodity as the contradictory unity of exchange-value and use-value. Clearly, the actions of intentional reshaping of value are to a large extent actions of rediscovering use-value in what the market has doomed as worthless, that is, as possessing minimal exchange-value. Are these actions merely playing with marginal residues, like those of die-hard golddiggers who reopen mines long ago abandoned by large corporations as unprofitable? Or are there real new dimensions of use-value to be discovered by recycling, recombination, and reconceptualization?

The third challenge is to develop and acquire tools for the reflective learning actions of playful conversion, caring revitalization, and engrossed appropriation. These actions are not well understood, and there is little support in work organizations for their implementation. Perhaps careful nurturing of these learning actions will give new meaning to the notion of 'human resources'.

# EVERYDAY LIFE

# 11

## Education as Mediation Between the Individual's Everyday Life and the Historical Construction of Society and Culture by Humankind[1]

Newton Duarte

> What is man? This is the primary and principal question that philosophy asks. How is it to be answered? (...) Reflecting on it, we can see that in putting the question "what is man" what we mean is: what can man become? That is, can man dominate his own destiny, can he "make himself," can he create his own life?
>
> (Gramsci, 1978)

### INTRODUCTION

Since the later 1980s, I have been undertaking study and research directed at the elaboration of a Marxist theory of education. These studies encompass works written by Marx himself as well as by more contemporary authors and include a wide range of fields of knowledge, from philosophy to psychology, passing through sociology, history, and economy (Duarte, 1993, 1996, 2000a, 2000b, 2000c, 2002a, 2002b, 2003a, 2003b, 2003c). In these studies, I have touched upon a complex set of mediations that connect the critical analysis of contemporary capitalist social reality to the debates in the field of pedagogical ideas. However, taking into account the limited space of a chapter, it will not be possible to approach here this complex set of mediations. Some simplification will become inescapable and providing a somewhat schematic character in my argumentation. Being conscious of the limits of this chapter, I have proposed the task of holding here the position on an articulation between activity theory and the theory of everyday life from the point of view of Karl Marx's philosophical anthropology.

### KARL MARX'S PHILOSOPHICAL ANTHROPOLOGY

The thesis that there is an inner connection between Karl Marx's historical materialism and his anthropological philosophy was already the purpose of

[1] This chapter was translated from Portuguese by Maria Silvia Cintra Martins, Ph.D. (UNESP, Brazil).

a study by George Markus in his book *Marxism and Anthropology* (Markus, 1978), where he analyses the concept of *human essence* in Marx's work. Markus shows that Marx's concept of human essence is constituted of five categories: work, sociality, consciousness, freedom, and universality. A good deal of the considerations that I develop here concerning Marxian philosophical anthropology rest on this analysis elaborated by Markus. I do not intend to present a survey of Markus's book, as this would be beyond the objectives of this chapter, but I want to note that I consider this book an excellent introduction to the study of Marxian philosophy and, thus, it may provide a meaningful contribution to the understanding of the philosophical fundament of the psychology developed by Vygotsky, Leontyev, and Luria. It is worthwhile considering, in this sense, the very great affinities between this book by George Markus and A. N. Leontyev's book entitled *Problems of the Development of the Mind* (Leontyev, 1981).[2]

In *Marxism and Human Nature*, Sean Sayers (1998) discusses a matter similar to the one present in Markus's book, when he analyzes the relations between Marx's historicism and the category of human nature. I certainly agree with Sayers when he affirms that human nature is, for Marx, essentially historical and that this conception outreaches both the idea of an unchangeable human nature that would be independent of social conditions and the post-modern complete relativism that rejects any attempt at constituting a unified vision of humankind as a whole.

The starting point of Marxian philosophic anthropology is labor activity understood as the metabolism between human beings and nature, that is, the transformation of nature by human activity, which produces and reproduces the socio-cultural reality that differentiates human beings from other animals. This point is made particularly clear in *Economic & Philosophical Manuscripts* (1844), as well as in *The German Ideology* (1846), in *Grundrisse* (1857–1858) and, finally, in the first volume of *Capital* (1867).

When affirming, according to Marx's philosophy, that human historicity, engendered by work, differentiates qualitatively social reality from the purely biological natural reality, I do not aim to establish a rigid opposition between the world of nature and the social world. A human being is, first of all, a living being, that is, a being whose existence can never occur without the indispensable biological basis. By no means do I intend to claim that human life or the learning process takes place in a way completely independent of natural processes. However, the recognition of the

---

[2] Regarding the study of the Marxist philosophical fundaments present in Vygotsky's, as well as in Leontyev's and in Luria's works, I cannot avoid calling attention to the importance of the works developed by the Soviet philosopher Evald Vasilyevich Ilyenkov (1924–1979) in what concerns Marxist dialectics, such as *The Dialectics of the Abstract and the Concrete in Marx's Capital* (Ilyenkov, 1982), *Dialectical Logic, Essays on its History and Theory* (Ilyenkov, 1974), *The Concept of the Ideal* (Ilyenkov, 1977), and *Leninist Dialectics and the Metaphysics of Positivism* (Ilyenkov, 1979). Considering, however, my objectives with this chapter, I'd rather present my interpretation of Ilyenkov's studies in further work.

indispensable relation between nature and society as an ontological fundamental principle in Marxian philosophic anthropology must come with an equal recognition of the fact that social reality has its specificities when compared with nature. In other words, this means that, in historical terms, there has been a *moment* in which there occurred a leap in the evolution of life in our planet, the leap from purely biological evolution of species toward human social history (Lukács, 1980). This leap did not establish a break, but constituted the beginning of a qualitatively new ontological field, the one belonging to socio-historical reality.

In Marx's theory, the fundament of his philosophic anthropology is also the fundament of his conception of history. Marx and Engels thus made this point clear in *The German Ideology*:

Men can be distinguished from animals by consciousness, by religion or anything else you like. They themselves begin to distinguish themselves from animals as soon as they begin to produce their means of subsistence, a step which is conditioned by their physical organization. By producing their means of subsistence men are indirectly producing their actual material life. (...) The first historical act is thus the production of the means to satisfy these needs, the production of material life itself. And indeed this is a historical act, a fundamental condition of all history, which today, as thousands of years ago, must daily and hourly be fulfilled merely in order to sustain human life (...) The second point is that the satisfaction of the first need (the action of satisfying, and the instrument of satisfaction which has been acquired) leads to new needs; and this production of new needs is the first historical act. (Marx & Engels, 1975: 31)

Why should the "first historical act" be the production of the means for satisfying human needs and, at the same time, the production of new needs? The answer to this question calls for the understanding of the meaning, in Marx's work, of the dialectical relation between the processes of objectification and of appropriation. Such a dialectical relation is at the core of the Marxian conception of labor, at the core of the historical process of production and reproduction of human culture. Appropriation emerges, above all, in the relation between human beings and nature. In this relation, the human being, by means of his transforming activity, appropriates nature, incorporating it to social practice. Simultaneously, there also occurs the process of objectification, once the human being produces and reproduces an objective reality bearing socio-cultural characteristics, accumulating thus the activity of the many human generations. This brings about the need of another form of the process of appropriation, not any longer only as appropriation of nature, but as the appropriation of cultural products of human activity, appropriation of the objectifications of human species,[3] that is, of the cultural objects in which are objectified the preceding social activity.

---

[3] In Duarte (1993, 1996), I worked with a differentiation between *human species* and *human genus*. In this differentiation, I have restricted the concept of human species to the biological characteristics that are transmitted by human genetic code and have adopted the concept of human genus with the meaning of the set of human characteristics constructed along

To assure his subsistence, the human being accomplishes the first histori-cal act, the fundamental historical act, that is, he produces the means that allow the satisfaction of vital needs. This implies that human activity, since its basic forms, aimed at the creation of conditions of survival, is differentiated from animal activity. The latter is characterized by consumption of what is found in nature and that may satisfy immediately some vital need, such as a fruit, for instance, that satiates hunger. Concerning human beings, however, between the need and the object that may satisfy it there is the mediation of the activity of production of tools, that is, the activity of production of means of subsistence.

The production of such means of subsistence transforms nature, being therein included in the transformation of human nature itself. Humaniza-tion, in the light of this perspective, is a historical process of production, re-production, transformation, and enlargement of the essential human forces, which exist objectively in the culture of all humankind, even when, in a society divided into social classes and centered on private property, such essential forces are not always within reach for appropriation on the part of the great majority of human beings. In this case, we are before the process of alienation that implies, in its primary form, the separation between the increasing material and intellectual riches produced by human labor on one hand and the extremely poor and reduced life that has been characterizing the existence of the major part of people on the other hand. I shall return later to the question of alienation. For now it is necessary to resume the analysis of the dialectics existing between the processes of objectification and appropriation.

The difference between animal activity and human activity is clearly man-ifested when one analyzes, for instance, the production of tools.[4] A tool represents not only something a human being utilizes in his action, but also something whose function (or functions) is not given by nature, but rather determined by social activity.

When a natural object is transformed into a tool, what happens is that something previously resulting only from natural forces (natural causality) is now transformed as a result of intentional human activity (teleology).[5] Human social activity creates a new meaning for the object. Such creation, however, does not take place inside an arbitrary form, that is, the new mean-ing of the object does not derive only from a subjective desire, nor even

---

socio-cultural history. In English, however, the expression human genus is seldom used, and I have preferred to use the expression human species, comprising both the human characteristics determined by genetic code and those produced and reproduced culturally.

4 Although I give the example of the production of tools, it is important to remark that ob-jectification is not restricted to physical objects, resulting, as well, in non-material products, such as language, relationship among human beings, knowledge, etc.

5 Lukács (1980) analyzes the way labor generates the relation between teleology and causality in social reality.

from a mere convention established by a group of persons. The production of a tool is above all an objective process that imposes the characteristic of objectivity to human thinking and action, first, because it is necessary to know the nature of the object in order to equate it to the purposes of human action. In order that the object may be inserted into the logic of human action, it is necessary for the human being to appropriate the logic of nature, at least in what refers to the object at issue. Second, the transformation of an object into a tool cannot be arbitrary, because an object can only be considered a tool when it possesses a function inside social practice.

Thus, to be able to transform a natural object into a tool, the human being must take into account, that is, must know the natural characteristics of the object, at least those directly related to the functions the object will have. Here it does not matter which kind of knowledge is considered, either being scientific knowledge of the natural properties of the object, or merely empirical knowledge, resulting from generalizations based on practice. In either case, a certain level of knowledge of the natural object by itself (is indispensable), that is, of what the natural object is, independent of its insertion into human activity. Both the production and the use of a tool are connected to the knowledge of the functions such a tool has inside social activity and to the knowledge of the objective properties of the objects onto which is directed the action mediated by such a tool. According to Leontyev (1981):

The making and use of tools is only possible in connection with consciousness of the objective of the labour action, but use of a tool itself leads to consciousness of the object of the action in its objective properties. The use of an axe not only corresponds to the objectives of a practical action but at the same time objectively reflects the properties of the object, i.e. the object of labour, onto which its action is directed. The blow of an axe subjects the material that constitutes this object to an unfailing test; it makes a practical analyses and generalization of the objective properties of objects according to a certain attribute objectivised in the tool itself. It is thus the tool that is the carrier or vector of the first real conscious, rational abstraction, the first real conscious, rational generalization. (p. 215)

At the beginning, the elaboration of objective knowledge was the result of the practical production and utilization of tools but, along with the historical development of social structures and institutions, and with the appearance of science, of philosophy and of art, knowledge started to acquire a relative autonomy in relation to the immediate necessities of everyday practice. Natural sciences, for instance, allow, more and more, knowing nature in its own inner legality, a legality that, in its origin, was not a result of any kind of conscious act. Such sciences produce what Agnes Heller (1984: 100), as well as her master Georg Lukács, called *de-anthropomorphization*, referring to the vision the human being has about nature.

Getting back to the example of production and use of tools, the fact is that the appropriation of a natural object that is transformed into a human tool can never be achieved in absence of the original objective conditions of such an object, even when it suffers enormous qualitative transformations as a result of human activity, provoking phenomena with no precedent in natural history. The object, therefore, is not totally separated from its natural logic; such logic is inserted into the logic of social activity. The object in its natural state is the result of the action of physic-chemical and biological forces. In the condition of a tool, it becomes also a result of social and conscious activity.

When creating a new function for a natural object (such a creation can take place, initially, in a non-intentional form, i.e., accidentally) the human being intends, through his/her activity, to make the object assume the desired functions and characteristics. In other words, there exists a process inside, in which the object, when transformed into a tool, becomes an objectification (as a product of human activity), once the human being has objectified himself in it, transforming it into a humanized object, that is, a *carrier* of human activity. This fact does not only mean that the object has been subjected to human action, but also that it has started to have new functions, it has become a synthesis of social activity, a synthesis that will be an object of appropriation of all human beings that come to incorporate such an objectification to their individual activity.

Some explanation becomes necessary concerning the word objectification, which is sometimes used with a negative meaning that is altogether different from the meaning it has in Marxian philosophy. Marx used the German word *Vergegenständlichung*, which is translated into English as objectification or also as objectivation. The first form has become more usual, and it is the one adopted by me in this text, except for some quotations in which the second form is used. More important, however, than the choice of one or another of these two words, is distinguishing neatly objectification from alienation (or estrangement), a distinction that is quite clear in Marx's writings. George Lukács, in the preface of the 1968 edition of *History and Class Consciousness*, explains that alienation is a historically surmountable phenomenon, which gets superseded with the supersession of class society, that is, of capitalist society, by socialism. Objectification, in its turn, is a phenomenon inherent in human activity:

If we bear in mind that every externalization of an object in practice (and hence, too, in work) is an objectification, that every human expression including speech objectifies human thoughts and feelings, then it is clear that we are dealing with a universal mode of commerce between men. And in so far as this is the case, objectification is a natural phenomenon; the true is as much an objectification as the false, liberation as much as enslavement. Only when the objectified forms in society acquire functions that bring the essence of man into conflict with his existence, only when man's nature is subjugated, deformed and crippled can we speak of an objective societal condition of alienation and, as an inexorable consequence, of all the subjective marks of an internal alienation. (Lukács, 1968: xxiv)

At the risk of being redundant, I should still add that, according to this perspective, the concept of objectification is completely distant from a certain meaning it has acquired nowadays, that is, as the process by which a person treats people as if they were mere objects.

Returning to the dialectical relation between objectification and appropriation, another important point for Marxian philosophical anthropology is that, through such dialectical relations, there emerges (are objectified) new forces and new human needs, as a result of the new actions generated by the enrichment of human activity. There would not exist historical development if human beings, that is social activity, just required the use of a closed set of human forces and the satisfaction of an also closed set of human needs. Historical development is rendered possible exactly by the fact that the dialectics between objectification and appropriation present in the process of production and reproduction of a cultural object generates, in human activity and consciousness, new needs and new forces, faculties, and capacities:

Only due to the fact that man lives in such a humanized world, that the human abilities and needs, evolved in the past, confront him from his birth on in a ready material form, and so he has at his disposal, in this objectified fashion, the results of the whole preceding social development, it is only because of all this that he is able not to begin anew, but to continue this development at the point reached by the earlier generations. In the process of "appropriation" (Aneignung) of humanized objects (which constitutes one of the main dimensions of socialization) the individual transforms into living-personal needs and skills the historically created social wants and abilities objectified in the elements of his milieu – and in this way a *material-practical transmission* of tradition is realized in society, which constitutes the basis of historical *continuity* and at the same time renders social *progress* possible. So it is only work as objectification of human essence that creates the possibility of *history* as such. (Markus, 1978: 8)

That is why I consider the dialectics between objectification and appropriation as constituting, in Marxian philosophical anthropology, the fundamental dynamics of human historicity: Each process of appropriation and objectification generates the need for new appropriation and new objectification.

It would, however, be wrong concluding from this analysis that the relation between objectification and appropriation only appears when a human being creates something totally new. In the example concerning the production of tools I analyzed earlier, the mistake this conclusion would lead to can be easily detected. The repetition of the production of an already existing type of tool is also a process of objectification, as well as of appropriation. Moreover, it is very difficult, in history, to separate in an absolute way repetition from creation, production from reproduction. Often enough, when reproducing something already existing, new aspects are discovered that will lead to its development and even to the creation of something new. The same thing may happen with the discovery of new forms of utilization for something already existent. In my previous works, I have been support-ing the thesis that to develop creativity schooling does not need and does not have to be understood as something incompatible with the reproduc-tion of already existent culture. The dichotomization between reproduction and creativity, between reproduction and autonomy results, among other causes, from the fact that one does not understand that the dialectics be-tween objectification and appropriation in social history also implies the dialectical character of reproduction of society and culture.

In the educational milieu, the word reproduction has acquired a com-pletely negative connotation. This has been in part a consequence of the diffusion of the ideas derived from the so-called theorists of reproduction, like Bourdieu & Passeron, Althusser, Boudelot & Establet, Gintis, and oth-ers. It does not matter here whether such diffusion has done justice to these authors' theories. The fact evidenced here is that the diffusion of ideas, mainly in the field of sociology of education, originated from the theorists of reproduction and has contributed to an essentially negative vision of the role of schooling in social reproduction. As a Marxist theorist of schooling, I could, in no case, ignore the alienating character schooling often has, repro-ducing the alienation generated by capitalist social relations. What I discuss, however, is the absence of a dialectics in the analysis of the reproductive role of school. If school is part of the reproduction of capitalist society, then it is part of the reproduction of the contradictions of the capitalist society. One of such contradictions, analyzed by Marx, resides between the development of productive forces and the capitalist relations of production. So, I ask: Is not the diffusion of knowledge by means of schooling located exactly in the field of the development of productive forces, especially nowadays, when capitalist society depends so much on the advance of knowledge? If knowl-edge is part of the means of production, then, when we fight for the real socialization of knowledge (that cannot be confused with mere acquisition of information) through schooling, would not we be fighting for the social-ization of the means of production, that is, for the destruction of the private ownership of means of production typical of capitalist society?

Another origin of the negative character assigned to the word repro-duction derives from the field of psychology of education and of didactics, with the theories of learning centered on individuals' spontaneous activity. Such theories remount to *Emile* by Rousseau, passing by Froebel, Pestalozzi, Montessori, Claparéde, Ferriere, Dewey, Piaget, and others, coming to irra-tional extremes today, as is the case of the "radical constructivism" by Ernst von Glasersfeld and followers. I have been calling such theories "learning to learn" pedagogies, once they have in common the defense of four principles: (1) everything people can learn by themselves has a greater educative value than what they can learn by means of transmission from other people; (2) the process of acquisition of knowledge has more educative value than the knowledge previously produced by humankind; (3) learning that occurs as a response to needs emerging within the individual's everyday activities has more educative value than learning resulting from a school curriculum with previously established contents and a deliberate systematic teaching method; and (4) school learning must aim at the formation of individuals prepared for an intense and permanent adaptation to the new social demands, which means, in reality, the adaptation to the demands of capitalism.

Such "learning to learn" pedagogies regard in a quite negative way the word reproduction in what is referred to as the pedagogical process, that is, their view is that education should not represent the transmission of socially accumulated knowledge, but rather a process of "learning to learn" and learning by doing. My question concerning such pedagogies is that they produce the impoverishment of the conventional contents usually included in schooling. They lead to the devaluation of the acquisition of classical knowledge, of the higher forms of knowledge produced by human history. They ignore, thus, a fact that had already been revealed by Marx in the nineteenth century, that is, that human subjective richness is only brought into being and develops by means of objective richness:

Only through the objectively unfolded wealth of human nature can the wealth of subjective human sensitivity – a musical ear, an eye for the beauty of form, in short, senses capable of human gratification – be either cultivated or created. For not only the five senses, but also the so-called spiritual senses, the practical senses (will, love, etc.), in a word, the human sense, the humanity of the senses – all these come into being only through the existence of their objects, through humanized nature. The cultivation of the five senses is the work of all previous history. Sense which is a prisoner of crude practical need has only a restricted sense. For a man who is starving, the human form of food does not exist, only its abstract form exists; it could just as well be present in its crudest form, and it would be hard to say how this way of eating differs from that of animals. The man who is burdened with worries and needs has no sense for the finest of plays; the dealer in minerals sees only the commercial value, and not the beauty and peculiar nature of the minerals; he lacks a mineralogical sense; thus the objectification of the human essence, in a theoretical as well as a practical respect, is necessary both in order to make man's senses human and to create an appropriate human sense for the whole of the wealth of humanity and of nature. (Marx, 1992: 353–354)

Paradoxical as it may sound, if the richness of human subjectivity is formed by means of the appropriation of the richness objectified in human works, then even creativity is formed and develops in human beings by means of reproduction of the creativity historically developed by humankind. There does not exist, therefore, a conflict between the reproduction of historically produced knowledge and the valorization of creativity and of intellectual and moral individual autonomy inside the educative process.

The second aspect of Marxian philosophical anthropology I must approach here, though in a brief and abridged way, concerns the dialectical relation between humankind development (humanization) and the alienation produced by capitalist society. In such a society, the appropriation of objectified labor assumes the form of private property, that is, of capital accumulation. Labor (objectifying activity) produces richness; on the other hand, such production assumes the form of capital reproduction. Marx, however, was not a romantic; he did not feel nostalgic about pre-capitalist societies. His vision concerning the historical role of capitalist society was deeply dialectical, and the supersession of capitalism was understood by Marx as a passage from the private appropriation of richness produced by human labor to its appropriation on the part of all human beings. Objectification is also transformed with the supersession of capitalism. Once it is no longer dominated by the aim of producing surplus-value, it no longer involves alienating labor; it becomes, rather, the simultaneous wealth of the laborer and of the society that benefits from the products of such labor. As Marx wrote in *Grundrisse*:

In fact, however, when the limited bourgeois form is stripped away, what is wealth other than the universality of individual needs, capacities, pleasures, productive forces etc., created through universal exchange? The full development of human mastery over the forces of nature, those of so-called nature as well as of humanity's own nature? The absolute working-out of his creative potentialities, with no presupposition other than the previous historic development, which makes this totality of development, i.e. the development of all human powers as such the end in itself, not as measured on a predetermined yardstick? Where he does not reproduce himself in one specificity, but produces his totality? Strives not to remain something he has become, but is in the absolute movement of becoming? In bourgeois economics – and in the epoch of production to which it corresponds – this complete working-out of the human content appears as a complete emptying-out, this universal objectification as total alienation, and the tearing-down of all limited, one-sided aims as sacrifice of the human end-in-itself to an entirely external end. (Marx, 1993: 488)

This excerpt exemplifies Marx's dialectical approach about capitalist society. From the *Economic and Philosophical Manuscripts of 1844* to *Capital*, Marx always analyzed capitalism as an essentially contradictory society: Capitalism historically created the necessary conditions for free and universal development of humankind; this was realized by means of the process of capital reproduction and of market universalizing, a fact that results in the creation of the deepest objective and subjective forms of alienation humankind has ever known. Marx regarded the great challenge for the construction of a communist society the supersession of the alienation produced by capitalism without retrograding in relation to the development produced by it. Two attitudes were considered ridiculous by Marx: the first consisting in nostalgia for pre-capitalist societies, and the second implying the belief that humankind would have to be content with the complete emptiness to which we are reduced as human beings in capitalist society; an emptiness that is the consequence of the mediation of social relations by commodity exchange-value.

The concise commentaries on Marx's philosophical anthropology presented previously certainly do not do justice to the richness of the Marxian conception of human essence (Markus, 1978) or of human nature (Sayers, 1998), or even of human individuality (Duarte, 1993). Anyway, it would represent an inopportune pretension believing it to be possible to synthesize such conception in a few paragraphs. My objective here was only to register the importance, within philosophical anthropology, of the dialectical relations between objectification and appropriation, and between humanization and alienation. Such relations are fundamental for us to understand how A. N. Leontyev analyzes the human individual's formation as a process of appropriation of social accumulated experience.

## INDIVIDUAL'S FORMATION ACCORDING TO
## A. N. LEONTYEV'S PSYCHOLOGY

In his book *Problems of the Development of the Mind*, A. N. Leontyev (1981) analyzed in a deep and detailed way the relations between phylogeny and ontogeny in human species, showing us the differences existing between human development and the development of other animal species. Leontyev's analysis of the relations between human phylogeny and ontogeny is explicitly rooted in the philosophical anthropology of Marx and Engels. This fact is particularly evident through the centrality the process of "appropriation of the socio-historical experience" acquires in the analysis of the formation of human individuals:

The spiritual, mental development of individual men is thus the product of a quite special process, that of appropriation, which does not exist at all in animals, just as the opposite process does not exist in them either, viz., that of objectifying their faculties as objective products of their activity. (Leontyev, 1981: 295)

Unfortunately, such processes have seldom received the attention they deserve in the field of activity theory. As yet, the consequences of the thesis concerning human individual formation, by means of the appropriation of cultural objects, as reproduction of essential human forces embodied in such objects, have not been duly explored in terms of research on learning processes.

It is important to point out that for Leontyev the psychological theories according to which the human individual formation is analyzed as a process of adaptation are wrong:

Despite capitalist psychological notions of man's ontogenetic development, however, as "adaptation" to the environment, his adaptation to it is not a principle of his development at all. Progress in man's development can consist, on the contrary, in his leaving the limitedness of his immediate milieu, and not at all in adaptation to it, which, in those circumstances, would only have impeded the fullest possible expression of the wealth of truly human traits and capacities. That is why to speak of man's adaptation to his social environment is at least ambiguous – in both social and ethical respects. (Leontyev, 1981: 299)

This passage is of the utmost importance for understanding the social and educational consequences of a psychology devoted to the analysis of appropriation of cultural objects by individuals. Dealing more directly with schooling, it is not difficult to notice that Leontyev's conception concerning the human individual's formation as the appropriation of social experience is not compatible with the idea that individuals should learn at school only the range of knowledge easily inserted into the immediate cultural environment of such individuals. On the contrary, it would be rather desirable for human individuals to appropriate, by means of schooling, the richest intellectual works of mankind, which were created during social history, even when (maybe it would be more adequate to say "mainly when") such works may seem distant from the pragmatic reality of students' everyday life. Schooling should not aim at students' adaptation to their immediate social environment; just as schooling proper ought not to be adapted to such an environment. Instead, schooling must try to transcend such limits in what refers to the formation of individuals' conscience.

Although I am specifically going to deal with Agnes Heller's theory of everyday life in the next section of this text, it is worth saying beforehand something that is directly related to the paragraph above. Even though Heller (1984), in her book *Everyday Life*, affirms that alienation is not a phenomenon essential to everyday life, that is, the existence of a non- alienated everyday life is considered possible, the author equally affirms that in class societies, and especially in capitalist society, everyday life is predominantly alienated and alienating. When everyday life is impregnated with alienation, one of the characteristics of everyday thought is anthropomorphism, that is, people tend to make the "analogous projection of their experiences in their immediate environment and their everyday activity on to the world in general" (Heller, 1984: 53). Such a characteristic of alienated everyday thought is connected to other characteristics belonging to this same thought, such as pragmatism and superficiality. Considering such a problematic context, the analysis of the real possibilities for school educational practice in the light of a Marxist perspective has become a great challenge, that is, the construction of a critical pedagogy has become a great challenge, because such a pedagogy needs, above all, to think about schooling as a process of the fight against alienation with which everyday life in contemporary society is impregnated. At this point, I tend to disagree with a good portion of what has been supported by left-wing educators, especially when they oppose to school knowledge everything that comprehends popular cultures, or the culture of oppressed groups, or the culture of the working class, etc. Often enough, such educators eventually defend a resistance to school knowledge, which is identified as bourgeois culture and as something inevitably connected to the interests and to the ideology of the ruling class. Different from this kind of conception, my vision of what may be a Marxist pedagogy is that political struggle for the supersession of capitalism toward socialism should include among its strategies: (1) the political fight for the existence, in every country, of a national system of schooling, from kindergarten to university, that should be maintained by the State, that is, a public and free school system, so that the right to the access to knowledge is effectively assured to everyone; and (2) the ideological fight for the elaboration and diffusion of a kind of pedagogy in which schooling's main task is the transmission of the best existing products in terms of human intellectual culture, in the fields of natural sciences, social sciences (human sciences), art, and philosophy. A Brazilian Marxist educator, Dermeval Saviani, has thus defined the tasks, that is, the challenges confronting such pedagogy:

a) Identification of the most developed forms through which objective and historically produced knowledge is expressed, recognizing the conditions of its production and understanding its main manifestations, as well as the present tendencies of transformation; b) conversion of objective knowledge into school knowledge, in such a way as to make its appropriation by students possible within school space and time; c) providing the means necessary for the students not only to appropriate the results of objective knowledge, but also to appropriate the process of its production, as well as the tendencies of its transformation. (Saviani, 1997: 14)

In other words, it is a pedagogy that defends the socialized appropriation of intellectual riches, once intellectual riches are also part of the means of production. Capital is, according to Marx, the private ownership of means of production. Struggling against capital is struggling for the collective appropriation, that is, for socialized appropriation of the means of production. Knowledge, that is, intellectual culture, is part of the means of production, today more than ever. In contemporary capitalist society, knowledge continues to represent private property, in spite of every ideology concerning the existence of a post-industrial society, knowledge society, or learning society. Struggling for the socialized appropriation of knowledge is a necessary part of the struggle for socialism and for communism.

Returning now to the analysis of individual formation in Leontyev's psychology, let us see how he explains the three principal characteristics of the process of appropriation of cultural objects by individuals.

First, for the appropriation of the cultural object to occur, the individual must carry out activities that are adequate to the social characteristics of such an object. The grade of adequacy of the individual's activity to the social characteristics of the object will depend on the concrete circumstances in which appropriation occurs, but at any rate the individual will have to reproduce in his activities the main characteristics of the social experience relating to that object.

Another characteristic of appropriation is that:

It is a process that has as its end result the individual's *reproduction* of historically formed human properties, capacities and modes of behaviour. In other words it is a process through which what is achieved in animals by the action of heredity, namely the transmission of advances in the species' development to the *individual*, takes place in the child. (Leontyev, 1981: 422)

The processes of objectification and of appropriation constitute the mediation between the history of humankind and the individual's formation. Whereas in other species, the genetic code is responsible for the mediation between the species and the individual; in human species, the genetic code is not sufficient to propigate such mediation, because a very relevant part of a human being's characteristics is historical, that is, is objectified in the culture up until now constructed by the ensemble of human beings.

The process of cultural objectification of human species is historically cumulative. When making this affirmation, I do not ignore that such an accumulation is far from being linear and homogeneous; I do not ignore either that there exist historical losses resulting from the destruction of the culture produced by certain societies. Nevertheless, I consider a Marxist vision, that is, a critical and materialistic vision of the history of construction of human culture does not imply the negation of the cumulative character, that is, the character of progress inherent in human history. I remember here something I have already commented on previously, about the dialectical vision Marx had of the historical role of capitalist society. As a consequence of post-modern relativism and of the undeniable destructive capacity developed by capitalist society, the idea of a historical progress of humankind has been facing strong rejection within the contemporary academic milieu. The idea of progress is associated with a naive ethnocentric evolutionist perspective, and Marxism is often accused of defending such a perspective. I totally disagree with this kind of analysis, which has as an effect of weakening of the struggle for the supersession of the contradictions produced by capitalism. Paraphrasing Gramsci (1978: 358), I affirm: "in this situation attacks on the idea of progress are very tendentious and interested-motivated."

The cumulative character of human history is not manifest in any simple way. It is manifest in each of the cultural products. In the social meaning of an object or cultural phenomenon is accumulated the historical activity of many generations. This is a decisive point for a historical and dialectical conception of the human individual's formation: When appropriating a cultural object, the individual appropriates the activity condensed in such an object, that is, he appropriates structures, operations, and mechanisms of thought and action. That is why Leontyev affirms that the mechanisms of individual culture appropriation are "mechanisms of the forming of mechanisms" (Leontyev, 1981: 305). This fact keeps in check the old and ever-so-repeated idea that the transmission of knowledge produces intellectual passivity and impedes the development of autonomy and creativity. It is worth questioning which kind of transmission of knowledge we are talking about. If the subject matter being taught and learned constitutes, in fact, the essence of the cultural object, that is, the human activity objectified in it, then such a transmission will be reproducing in the individual certain processes on whose basis he will be able to develop his creativity. According to this perspective, the individual's development:

... is a product of transmission and assimilation by individuals of the achievements of socio-historical development and the experience of preceding generations. Any creative advance of thought that man subsequently makes independently is only possible on the bases of mastering this experience. (Leontyev, 1981: 314)

At the risk of being tedious, I shall, however, insist on this matter. Quite frequently, when people criticize the idea of transmission of knowledge at school, they oppose transmission to autonomy and creativity without having carefully analyzed what is in fact transmitted. If they stopped and reflected more cautiously on this question, they would find that, in most of contemporary school situations, what is at play does not include knowledge transmission, but, rather, the transmission of scattered and superficial pieces of information. Of course, such a situation cannot contribute to the development of anyone's creativity and autonomy. However, when a real transmission of knowledge occurs, students appropriate mental activity objectified in such knowledge. Leontyev makes this question quite clear when mentioning the example of the formation of logical thought in individuals:

A capacity for logical thought can only result from mastering *logic*, i.e. this objective product of mankind's social practice. Processes of logical thinking cannot form in a person who has lived from early childhood without contact with objective forms embodying human logic, and without contact with men, even though he may, on countless occasions, encounter problem situations, the adaptation to which would require the formation of just this capacity. (Leontyev, 1981: 296–297)

The third characteristic of the appropriation process, signaled by Leontyev, is that such a process is always mediated by relation between human beings and is, thus, a process of transmission of social experience, that is, an educative process in the broad sense of the term. The individual's formation always implies an educative process, and it can be direct or indirect, intentional or non-intentional, accomplished by means of practical activities or through oral explanations, etc. I shall return later to this subject to analyze what differentiates schooling from the other kinds of processes by means of which a society educates individuals.

To finalize this item about the individual's formation from the point of view of Leontyev's psychology, I will approach briefly the theme of alienation.

First, alienation is understood by Leontyev as a social process, typical of societies that are divided into classes and particularly acute in the historical context of capitalist society. In such a context, alienation occurs primarily as the separation between the life of individuals and the human material and intellectual riches accumulated throughout history. In other words, the great majority of human beings are impeded, because of capitalist social relations, of appropriating the human experience objectified in the culture produced by humankind. When people cannot appropriate such material and intellectual richness, what occurs is an enormous reduction of the possibilities of their individual development, which remains well below the levels already socially attained by humankind. An abyss is created that keeps the life of the majority of individuals away from the essential human forces:

> Throughout the history of class society the embodiment of the advances of mankind's joint activity and of the totality of human capacities in the development of separate individuals has been one-sided and partial. Only abolition of the supremacy of private property and of the antagonistic relations engendered by it will create conditions such as will eliminate the necessity of this one-sidedness of individuals. The conditions will thereby be created in which the main principle of man's onto-genetic development, viz. reproduction in the characteristics and capacities of the individual of these all-round ones that have been moulded in the course of the socio-historical process, will have full scope to develop for the first time. (Leontyev, 1981: 300–301)

Besides this analysis of the phenomenon of alienation as a social process of private appropriation of human richness and consequent limitation of the possibilities for the appropriation of the same richness on the part of the majority of human beings, Leontyev also analyzes another form through which alienation gets manifest in capitalist society, namely the "disparity between the objective result of man's activity on the one hand, and its motive on the other" (Leontyev, 1981: 252). Using the example of labor alienation in capitalist society, Leontyev demonstrates that there is a separation between the *objective meaning* of the laborer's activity and the *personal sense* this activity has for him (Leontyev, 1981: 253). The first one, that is, the objective meaning, is formed by the content proper of the activity accomplished by the laborer who certainly has the due conscience of such content, or else he would not be able to carry out the activity. Yet, the personal sense the labor activity has for the laborer is not determined by its content, but rather by the wage value for which the laborer has sold his labor force. The value of such a wage determines the material conditions of the laborer's life, and this is the sense the labor activity acquires for him. It is important to remark that such alienation is above all the result of capitalist society and not a mere question of attitude or of mentality. I emphasize this point because it is not a question, in the light of the perspective of the Marxist analysis made by Leontyev, of a problem that may be surmounted in the purely subjective plane, that is, with "consciousness," on the part of the laborer, about the social value of his labor or with the adoption of enterprise administration strategies that seek to create an ambience for the laborer's involvement, individually and collectively, in the enterprise objectives or other initiatives of the same nature. It is not a question that might be solved in terms of changes in the style of enterprise management. This process of alienation analyzed by Leontyev can only be eliminated with the supersession of capitalist relations of production, that is, with the supersession of capital (Mészàros, 1995). It remains, however, beyond the objectives of this chapter to develop a more detailed analysis of the consequences of such dissociation between meaning and sense in what concerns both the activity and the consciousness of human beings in contemporary society. I only want to register my impression that part of the present studies in the field of the theory of activity devoted to workplace learning has not as yet given due attention to the phenomenon of alienation. Sometimes these studies seem to neglect even the important theoretical contribution of Leontyev in this field.

### AGNES HELLER'S THEORY OF EVERYDAY LIFE AND SCHOOLING AS MEDIATION BETWEEN EVERYDAY LIFE AND THE "SPECIES-ESSENTIAL OBJECTIVATIONS FOR ITSELF"

The point of departure of Agnes Heller's theory of everyday life is continuity of historical process, that is, continuity of human life. To say the same thing in other words, the question is about the process of the continuous reproduction of human species. For such reproduction to occur, it is necessary for people to be reproduced and for society to be reproduced. When activities are prominently directed toward people reproduction, that is, toward the continuity of each human being's life, such activities constitute, according to Heller, the sphere of everyday life or, simply, the everyday. When the activities are prominently directed toward reproduction of society, they constitute the non-everyday spheres of human life or, simply, the non-everyday.

Thus, for Heller, an everyday activity is not an activity that is necessarily carried out every day and, inversely, a certain activity may be carried out every day without pertaining to the everyday life sphere. For example, an activity that I, as an individual, need to accomplish for my individual reproduction is going to the supermarket to buy food, cleaning products, etc. This is, therefore, one of my everyday life activities, though I do not go to a supermarket more than two or three times a month. When, on the other hand, I write an essay or a book, I may carry out such an activity almost every day until I finish what I am writing. Can, however, such an activity be considered an everyday activity according to Heller's criterion? Certainly not, because this is an activity I carry out as a researcher, that is, an activity I perform for society because the reproduction of contemporary society needs people devoted to research. Both these examples already show that there is not an absolute separation between the everyday and the non-everyday character of an activity. In the case of the supermarket, when buying the commodity it sells, I participate in the reproduction of capitalist economy, that is, I participate in social reproduction. In the case of my writing activity of essays and books, this is a part of my work as a professor, work for which I earn an income that determines the material conditions of my individual reproduction.

The concept of everyday life proposed by Agnes Heller cannot be confused with the concept of social practice, either. In the academic world, such identification is quite common and is based on a very inaccurate and vague distinction between the world of theory (generally identified with the academic world) and the world of social practice. However, if we identify everyday life with social practice, we will be faced with the following problem: Is not the theory world, or academic world, part of social practice? The formulation of the question per se points out the nonsense inherent in this kind of conception. The idea of social practice itself is very vague; after all, when we consider the human being as an essentially social being, which kind of practice would not be social? What is the criterion for considering the activity of elaborating a theory as something that is not a social practice?

Another mistaken idea about everyday life concerns the identification between the everyday and the real. Thus, the attempt at understanding an everyday activity would represent the attempt at abandoning the field of mere ideas and the setting out toward reality. If we identify the everyday with the real, then that which does not belong to the everyday will not be given a real existence, that is, everything that is real belongs to the everyday. However, this kind of conclusion is tricky because it broadens too much the concept of everyday that would thus comprise almost everything, becoming a concept without any value.

Such comments on inaccurate, and inconsistent notions concerning the concept of everyday life are necessary for us to understand the concept proposed by Heller in a correct way. The best way to understand such a conception, however, is not, in my personal opinion, the purely logical abstract way, but, rather, by means of the historic-genetic explanation of human reality. In the second section of this chapter, when analyzing Marx's philosophical anthropology, I have already approached the question concerning labor activity as the point of departure of human history, that is, of the differentiation between the human being and the other animals. Georg Lukács, in his unfinished work entitled *Esthetics*[6] (Lukács, 1982), developed a genetic-systematic analysis of art as one of the spheres of objectification of human species, a sphere that, as the sphere of science, would have its

---

[6] As far as I know, an English version of this work of Georg Lukács does not exist. I utilize here the Spanish version published in 1982 in four volumes.

historical genesis in the sphere of everyday life, more specifically in labor as considered a vital human activity. Agnes Heller has started from this philosophical reflection of Lukács to develop in her book *Everyday Life* a theory of the spheres of objectification of human species. Therefore, to understand such a theory, we need, above all, to understand that labor is the ontological fundament of human existence, as well as the conceptual basis for the analysis of the different forms of objectification of the human being. It was not by chance that in his last and also unfinished work, *The Ontology of Social Being*, Lukács takes the category of labor as the one on which lie all the other categories of analysis of human reality:

All those determinations which we shall see to make up the essence of what is new in social being, are contained in labour. Thus labour can be viewed as the original phenomenon, as the model for social being, and the elucidation of these determinations already gives so clear a picture of the essential features of social being that it seems methodologically advantageous to begin by analyzing labour. (Lukács, 1980: 67)

Labor, this fundamental anthropological unity, was, historically, the common ground on the basis of which the sphere of everyday life developed, as well as the other spheres of human objectification that emerged and got a progressive autonomy in relation to the everyday life sphere, namely, art, science, philosophy, politics, and moral. That is why Heller defines labor as an activity that is directed both toward individual reproduction, that is, an everyday activity, and toward the society reproduction, that is, a non-everyday activity. As I have shown earlier, Leontyev also explores such a double aspect of labor where alienation is referred to as a break in the relation between the social meaning of labor and its personal sense.

From the historical point of view, however, labor must be initially considered as an activity inherent in everyday life, once it was, in the primal times of our species, devoted to human beings' immediate survival, by means of tool reproduction used for obtaining food and protection. From the beginning, it was a joint activity, which produced the development of both the relationship and the communication between human beings. Thus, we already have in this genesis of human social existence three kinds of objectification: the production of instruments, the production of forms of relation and the production of language. Such basic forms of objectification of human species, without which even the most primitive culture cannot exist, Heller calls species-essential objectivations in itself. Why "in itself"? Because they emerge and develop in a socially spontaneous way, that is, they are produced and reproduced without the necessity of the human being's reflecting about their existence. They are simply given in people's immediate reality and are reproduced by means of the activities people carry out. It is the case of speech. A child acquires speech simply by living together with other people. Parents, when a child is born, do not put in question the way he/she will acquire speech. On the contrary, such questioning only appears if a spontaneous learning does not occur, that is, such spontaneous reproduction of speech.

The species-essential objectivations for itself (science, art, philosophy, moral, and politics) emerge historically from the everyday life sphere but, little by little, they become spheres that are relatively autonomous in relation to everyday life; they get more and more distant from the heterogeneity inherent in everyday life activities and homogenize into spheres with characteristic features. Historically, there existed societies without such objectifications, but their appearance and development eventually incorporated them to human essence, that is, the development of human species is no longer possible without the participation of the "species-essential objectivations for itself."

The everyday life theory developed by Heller explores intensely both the dialectics between objectification and appropriation and the dialectics between humanization and alienation. At each moment of her book, Heller makes the distinction clear between phenomena resulting from alienated social relations, and that may, therefore, be superseded historically, and those phenomena that, though having appeared inside alienated society, constitute decisive advances for human essence and must be considered universal values to be preserved in a society superseding capitalism, that is, inside a socialist society.

Concerning the everyday life sphere, Heller is quite insistent when affirming that it is not necessarily alienated, that is, the characteristics inherent in "species-essential objectivations in itself" and in the kind of relation people establish with such objectivations in their everyday life do not necessarily produce alienation. It is possible, in principle, to have a non-alienated everyday life. Yet, the struggle against alienation cannot be limited to the sphere of everyday life, though it constitutes a very rich ground for the dissemination of alienation, the origin of alienation derives from the social relations of production, that is, the supersession of alienation calls for the revolutionary change that may lead to the abolition of capitalist relations of production. If, on one hand, this book of Heller's postulates a vision of socialism that is not restricted to changes in wider economic and political structures, that is, it defends a vision of socialism in which the humanization of everyday life is also an essential part, on the other hand, such socialism is quite distant from the typically post-structuralist idea of the substitution of collective and unified political struggle against capitalism for the fragmentary individual or at best group resistance to the micro-powers diffused in a capillary way inside the social tissue. Here I confine myself to this book of Heller's, I will not discuss her change in political perspective and her abandoning socialist perspective in later work. Yet, the important fact I point out here is that her theory concerning everyday life, articulated to Marxist theory on alienation and on its supersession, is very distant from the post-modern thesis on the end of meta-narratives or grand narratives. The meta-narrative giving sense to the theory of everyday life is Marxist philosophy of history.

Resuming the question regarding Heller's theories of objectification, another aspect to be detached is that despite the fact that the emergence and historical development of the species-essential objectivations for itself constitute a meaningful conquest for human essence, Heller never loses sight, of the fact that the spheres "for itself" are not immune to alienation. For example, the existence of science is a decisive historical conquest; this fact, however, does not in the least imply that specific contents of science might not be charged with alienation. In present times marked by a strong influence from post-modernism, it is necessary to stress time and again that, according to Heller's theory, science in fact means objective knowledge of reality, and it is in fact possible to refer to forms of knowledge that are more advanced and more perfect than others. At the same time, Heller's theory shows that when pragmatism, characteristic of everyday life, invades other spheres of human objectification, such as science, we face the process of fetishism of everyday life structure and of its expansion over the spheres that, when assuming a structure strange to them, also become alienated and alienating. This is a complex and quite contradictory process that I will not have space for analyzing here. Objectivation inside the spheres for itself may require a high degree of consciousness in relation to what is produced and to how it is produced; in the conditions of capitalist society, however, this may occur inside a process of subordination of such production to the logic of capital reproduction and to the diffusion of the dominant ideology.

A *theory of human individuality* is also part of everyday life theory. For Heller, the formation of every human being begins in everyday life, where the first appropriations of cultural objects occur, that is, the basic learning of anyone's life. The complete development of a human being will, however, be extremely limited if the activities integrating such a person's life are limited to everyday activities. This means that Heller considers the appropriation of the species-essential objectivations for itself indispensable for individual formation. It is part of the process by which an individual may become the subject of her or his life, may surmount the spontaneous hierarchy of everyday life, and may construct a conscious hierarchy of activities, guided by freely chosen values. It is worth calling attention here to Leontyev's criticism of the psychologies that envisage individual formation as a process of adaptation to the immediate environment where the individual lives. Heller, as well as Leontyev, also holds in the book I am referring to the position that the individual must go beyond his immediate environment so that his life is not limited to the alienated reproduction of its particularity.

That is why I have been working on an educational theory for which school is considered an institution whose task consists of propitiating the mediation between everyday life and the "species-essential objectivations for itself." According to this theory, school is not a place where individuals may only do things that give them pleasure or that they desire to do. School does not aim to satisfy the immediate needs of individuals' everyday life, but, rather, to produce higher needs in them, certain needs that lead to the enrichment and development of such individuals:

Education is not something merely pleasurable. On the contrary, it may well be disturbing and upsetting – indeed, perhaps it should be so. The study of philosophy, for example, is and ought to be responsible for encouraging doubts and problems where none were felt before. It should lead people to criticize and question their beliefs; it should introduce difficulties and a certain kind of discontent. Similarly, good literature and art rarely present the most comforting or pleasant picture of life. However, despite this discontent – *through* it, indeed – both philosophy and art can be avenues towards higher – richer and fuller – forms of experience, fulfillment and happiness. (Sayers, 1998: 18)

The kind of schooling I have been defending in my works would aim at producing in individuals the process Lukács and Heller call the process of "homogenization," compared with the heterogeneity that characterizes people's activities and thought in everyday life. By reason of such necessary heterogeneity of everyday life activities, individuals hardly have the opportunity to transcend the superficial ties with such activities and do not manage to get engaged in them with their entire personality. They need to save time, energy, and thought when carrying them out, so that they can be up to everyday life as a whole. Yet, if on one hand this kind of attitude is necessary for the course of everyday life, on the other it quite limits the possibilities of richer objectifications of the individual as a conscious member of human species. In other words, it is very difficult to leave one's individual mark in the human world when one needs to split attention, time, and energies into a great and heterogeneous quantity of activities. This is one of the great obstacles to the relationship with the species-essential objectifications for itself, once the latter require the surmounting of such heterogeneity:

Homogenization is the criterion of "emergence" from the everyday, and – it must be emphasized – not a subjective criterion. Everyday life could not be reproduced without the heterogeneous human activities, and neither could the objectivation "for itself" be reproduced without the homogenization process. The homogeneous spheres and objectivations themselves require homogenization for their reproduction. If a society has a positive legal system, then it also needs citizens who spend their lives or at least part of their lives "working themselves into" the homogeneous structure of the law, to learn legal thinking. If a society needs natural science, it also needs individuals able to appropriate the homogeneous structure of the scientific disciplines, and learn how to "operate" therein, thus bypassing both everyday life and everyday thinking. (Heller, 1984: 58)

What are, however, the characteristics of the process of homogenization, that is, what is necessary for the emergence from the everyday to occur?

First, a *direct relation* between the individual and a homogeneous sphere of species-essential objectifications for itself is necessary. Second, the *active and conscious relation* of the individual with such a sphere of human objectivation is necessary, that is, it cannot be a spontaneous relation similar to the one existing between the individual and the species-essential objectivations in itself in everyday life activities.

The school educative process, in the light of the perspective of the mediation between everyday life and the species-essential objectivations for itself aims exactly at forming in individuals such a direct intentional and active relation with such objectivations. Let us take the example of science. The individual may, in his everyday life activities, appropriate some knowledge derived from the scientific field. Most commonly, however, what occurs is that such appropriation will be an indirect result of some activity with different purposes. The appropriation of such knowledge is, in this case, an indirect result. In the case of educative activity, the relation with scientific knowledge, that is, its appropriation by the individual is a result pursued in a direct, intentional way.

Third, for homogenization to occur, it is necessary for the individual to concentrate on a sole task, that is, in the course of the interval of time when he performs a task in one of the spheres of the species-essential objectivations for itself, it is necessary for him to interrupt the dispersion that characterizes the multiplicity and the concomitancy typical of everyday activities. Also in this case, schooling may play a decisive role in the formation of the individual. Often enough, educational fashions tend to disvalue important characteristics of schooling, as is the case of the concentration and discipline necessary for intellectual activity. Such behavior has been often criticized as characterizing authoritarian pedagogical attitude, but the fact is that intellectual activity calls for concentration, attention, and discipline. How can anyone enjoy the pleasure of playing a melody by Beethoven or Tom Jobim on the piano if she has not undergone the process of dedicating hours on end to the learning of music, which requires concentration, training, and discipline? When analyzing the partiality that characterizes most criticism made about traditional methods of teaching, Gramsci (1978) wrote:

...it will always be an effort to learn physical self-discipline and self-control; the pupil has, in effect, to undergo a psycho-physical training. Many people have to be persuaded that studying too is a job, and a very tiring one, with its own particular apprenticeship – involving muscles and nerves as well as intellect. It is a process of adaptation, a habit acquired with effort, tedium and even suffering. (p. 42)

The fourth criterion of the homogenization process is that the individual particularity must be subjected to the broader social requirements of the sphere of objectification in which the activity is carried out. As Heller (1984) explains:

This may involve the suspension of all particular motivation (as in the case of moral activity on the generic level), it may be the suspension of a particular viewpoint (as in the case of artistic or scientific activity) or it may be simply the suspension of certain particular aspirations which run counter to "being absorbed" into the given objectivation (as in the work-process). (p. 58)

Also in this case, the importance of schooling is outstanding. Let us take the example of the necessity for the suspension of a particular viewpoint in scientific activity. It is not the case here that the individual loses his personal point of view, but, rather, that he becomes capable of getting distant from such personal perspective and of looking at the world assuming an external standpoint. Without it, scientific objectivity would not exist. There is no space here for presenting my interpretation on how this fact also occurs in art, but I mention that, according to the Lukacsian conception presented in the work *Esthetics* (Lukács, 1982), the artist surmounts his individual particularity in the process of construction of the particularity of the work of art. The work of art is always a unique, particular work, it always represents a unique particular world, but it is not a direct portrait of the artist's individual particularity. Similarly, though the reception of a certain work of art is always unique for each individual, we can say that, through such reception, because it is truly artistic, the individual surmounts (without eliminating) his particular viewpoint and places himself inside the universe constituted by the work of art. Such a procedure, in the case of science as well as in the case of art, does not occur without a long learning process. The same thing can be said about particular motivations. Studies in the field of the formation of morality, carried out by researchers within distinct and even conflicting approaches, tend to converge on one aspect, that moral development requires an attitude that implies surmounting personal motivations. Such an attitude, however, does not occur spontaneously; it needs to be intentionally formed in individuals by means of educative processes directly designed for this objective. This is particularly true in a society that produces deep forms of alienation as is the case of contemporary capitalist society. Heller thus concludes the analysis of the process of homogenization:

Finally, we must mention the criterion provided by the generalization of our personalities, our thoughts, our experiences, our aspirations, our capabilities. (Exactly which of these we generalize, depends to a large extent on the specific sphere on which our homogenization process is centred.) And here it must be pointed out that we may transcend everyday life without necessarily transcending everyday thinking; and, vice versa, ability to rise above, to emerge from everyday thinking does not necessarily imply leaving behind the intention of everyday life. From all of this it is clear that the process of homogenization – depending on the objectivation and the degree of the homogenization – is indeed a process. And we cannot always label all the types of activity we engage in as either 'everyday' or 'non-everyday'. 'Everyday' and 'non-everyday' are ideal types of activity, and empirical overlapping does not impair the validity of the homogenization criterion. (Heller, 1984: 58–59)

The importance of such a process of homogenization in everyday life theory is directly linked to the analysis of the category of person, which is divided into *particularity* and *individuality*. Any "human being" whatever, that is, any person whatever, is unique. Singularity is one of the characteristics of the concept of person. In spite of the fact that all people are unique, they can only exist in their uniqueness as cultural social beings, that is, by means of the appropriation of cultural objects, as we have already seen in Leontyev. Yet, cultural objects as well as the essential human forces objectified in them are generalizations. It is worth repeating here the excerpt in which Leontyev shows us that the actions with tools are actions containing generalizations:

The blow of an axe subjects the material that constitutes this object to an unfailing test; it makes a practical analyses and generalization of the objective properties of objects according to a certain attribute objectivised in the tool itself. It is thus the tool that is the carrier or vector of the first real conscious, rational abstraction, the first real conscious, rational generalization. (Leontyev, 1981: 215)

Every person realizes, therefore, his singularity by means of generalization and not in opposition to generalization. Every person is unique as a social being, that is, is unique in his sociality. Marx wrote in *Grundrisse* (Marx, 1993: 84) that the human being is "not merely a gregarious animal, but an animal which can individuate itself only in the midst of society." That is why Heller (1984) affirms that:

Man's uniqueness, his non-repeatability, is an ontological fact. But this is not to say that real communication between men is impossible, nor that man is closed off in his uniqueness; nor does it mean that this uniqueness, in and for itself, constitutes the essence of man. In the first place, man's uniqueness and non-repeatability are only realized in his objectivized world. Without self-expression there can be no self-determination or self-preservation for the human being; and self-awareness as the synthesis of consciousness takes shape as the world becomes objectivized – primarily in work and in language. Only he who generalizes can have self-awareness, awareness of his particularity. Work is such a generalization, and so is even the most primitive form of linguistic exchange. Where there is no generalization, where there is no promulgation of human species-essentiality, there is no human particularity. (p. 9)

Nevertheless, in the society founded upon social division of labor and private property, that is, in alienated society, the formation of the person tends to hypertrophy the particularity, that is, tends to transform it into the center of life and, simultaneously, it determines narrow limits for such a life. Heller uses the term particularity both to characterize the uniqueness of every human being and to refer to the person whose life, as a result of alienated social relations, has his activity and his subjectivity centered on the reproduction of particularity.

As long as an immediate identification with the self and an equally immediate identification with we-awareness characterize man – average man, civilization will nourish and foster particularity. According to Marx. the human essence develops via an 'emptying-out' of individual existence, the efflorescence of human wealth proceeds *pari passu* with the impoverishment of persons. It is this process of alienation which has nourished particularity. Particularity is the subject of alienated everyday life. (Heller, 1984: 15)

To an everyday alienated life corresponds an alienated subject: the particularity. Such alienation impedes the development of individuality. We have seen in the philosophical anthropology of Marx that labor, as an objectifying activity, is the source of the social development of human essence. In this sense, labor is the essential human activity, that is, the activity that makes human essence develop. Labor should also be the source of the development of individuality. A true, rich individuality is that which objectifies itself in a universal and diversified form, a fact that requires the appropriation, as we have seen, of the objectifications fuller of contents, that is, the richest objectifications ever produced by humankind. However, as we have seen earlier, according to Leontyev, in capitalist society, the alienation of labor provokes a break between the social meaning of an activity and its personal sense. Because of alienated labor, instead of leading to the development of human essence in individual activity, that is, instead of being the realization of a truly human life, the labor activity becomes only a means for survival. According to Marx, in alienated labor:

Life itself appears only as a means of life. The animal is immediately one with its life activity. It is not distinct from that activity; it is that activity. Man makes his life activity itself an object of his will and consciousness. He has conscious life activity. It is not a determination with which he directly merges. Conscious life activity directly distinguishes man from animal life activity. Only because of that is he a species being. Or rather, he is a conscious being, i.e. his own life is an object for him, only because he is a species-being. Only because that is his activity free activity. Estranged labour reverses the relationship so that man, just because he is a conscious being makes his life activity, his essence [Wesen], a mere means for his existence.[7] (Marx, 1992: 328)

Thus, for the subject tied to alienated everyday life, activity no longer leads to the development of individuality, no longer leads to the development of human essence in individual life; instead, it gets transformed into a mere means for the guarantee of subsistence. The guarantee of subsistence, however, should be only the point of departure, only the means for attaining the end, which should be the fulfillment of the individual as someone representing human species, that is, a participant in the development of humankind as a whole. That which should only be a means (subsistence, reproduction of particularity) becomes an end in itself.

So, as a result of alienation, as far as the average person living in society is concerned, man's consciousness, i.e., his species characteristics, becomes a means of discrediting his own species-essence by making that essence a means of his existence. This is the particular, the alienated person. But every man need not necessarily without

[7] The German word *Wesen* was translated as "being" in the edition I refer to. However, along with George Markus and Ágnes Heller, I consider "essence" as the best translation in this case.

exception carry out this transposition of ends and means. There can be, and indeed always are, those who win through to seeing the species in the person, and who relate to themselves as to species-beings: who see themselves – from the point of view of species-being, from the point of the actual stage reached in the development of the species at a given time – as objects, who see that they should not be identified with the needs of their own existence. and that they should not make their being, the forces of their being, nothing more than a means of satisfying the needs of their existence. So, we give the name of 'individual' to the person for whom his own life is consciously an object, since he is a conscious species-being. (Heller, 1984: 17)

Heller, thus, opposes the concept of individuality to the one of particularity. In class society, no person is immune to alienation, exactly because all of us, in one way or another, participate in the reproduction of alienated social relations. Heller did not divide society into two groups: the one including particularistic persons and the other one including individualities. For Heller, individuality, that is, its formation is, above all, a process:

No person is without particularistic motivation, nor is there any person who never in any way whatever, transcends, in some degree, his own particularity. No hard and fast line can he drawn between the particularistic person, on the one hand, and the individuality on the other. Individuality is a development; it is the coming-to-be of an individual. This coming-to-be takes different forms in diferent ages. But whatever form concrete individuality, or its ideal, takes in a given age, individuality is never complete but is always in a state of flux. This flux is the process of transcending particularity, the process of 'synthesization' into individuality. (Heller, 1984: 15)

According to my point of view, a Marxist theory directed at schooling must have such a concept of individuality as a reference for the education of new generations. This means that a Marxist theory of education cannot be satisfied with a school concerned with the formation of individuals adapted to the narrow limits determined by the alienated everyday life of capitalist society. Heller (1984: 17) affirmed that, at each historical moment, the highest limit for the development of individuality is "that level to which the human generic essence has objectively developed in the given society." This must be our reference for the education of new generations. This is my horizon, both a political and an educational horizon: a society in which every person may develop up to the level already historically reached by human essence.

12

# Activity and Power

*Everyday Life and Development of Working-Class Groups*

## Peter H. Sawchuk

> What is abstracted in orthodox sociology as 'socialization' is in practice, in any actual society, a specific kind of incorporation. Its description as 'socialization', the universal abstract process on which all human beings can be said to depend, is a way of avoiding or hiding this specific content and intention. Any process of socialization of course includes things that all human beings have to learn, but any specific process ties this necessary learning to a selected range of meanings, values, and practices which, in the very closeness of their association with necessary learning, constitute the real foundations of the hegemonic ... Specific communities and specific places of work, exerting powerful and immediate pressures on the conditions of living and of making a living, teach, confirm, and in most cases finally enforce selected meanings, values and activities.
>
> (Williams 1977: 117–118)

### INTRODUCTION

Certainly, human learning as a process of socialization constitutes a foundational element of the hegemony of advanced capitalism. In many ways, the concept of learning speaks to those core relations that have informed and continue to inform the sociological enterprise: agency/structure, micro/macro, change/order. However, understanding learning as a generalized 'socialization' process is deeply problematic: It is inherently normative, often unknowingly so; it is ahistorical; it presumes the form of relation between individuals and society; in short, it obscures more than it reveals. In sociology, those applying (or, more often, simply presuming) notions of socialization leave relations amongst human development, mental life, and the conflict specific to life under and beyond capitalism, neatly beyond the purview of discussion.

I begin with this general assertion as a way of situating the fact that in opposition to this prominent mode of sociological thinking, during the early

238

days of socialist transformation in Soviet Russia, there emerged the potential for a radical alternative rooted in the work of L. S. Vygotsky and colleagues. As others in this volume have noted, this new opening offered the possibility of a new standard for understanding human agency: an understanding that is mediated as well as historicized and materialist, which admits agency as *both* individual *and* collective social action. Taken together, this approach describes a historical materialist dialectical approach to human learning summarized by the concept of *activity*.

Scholars dealing with the concept of activity have understood for some time the need to overcome the dichotomies related to individual *and* environmental explanations of learning, with considerable success. Moreover, although the concept of activity and the Cultural Historical Activity Theory (CHAT) tradition have provided a tenable starting point for understanding the learning dimensions of capitalist hegemony, in Sawchuk (2003) I identified a series of lacunae requiring attention. Among these are the need to better assess the everyday lives of subordinate social groups empirically; the need for a more explicit mapping of one of Marx's central foci, class struggle; and the need for more than simply referential commentary on the 'political-economic' dimensions of activity as embodied in the analysis of the role played by contradictions inherent within capitalism's 'commodity form'. I suggested at the time that several of the keys to addressing these issues already rested within CHAT itself, but went on to show that concepts from the fields of sociology and cultural studies – specifically those that illuminate 'everyday life' – can provide a useful supplement.

The significance of my preoccupation with everyday life, however, requires some further explanation (cf. Duarte, this volume). In earlier work, I and others have argued that the plurality of human learning practice shines brightest as our analytic lens moves further from organized, state, or employer-based learning forms. This is because of the normative closure of these institutional forms. Livingstone, in the present volume, adds further detail to this argument. Suffice it to say here that, when comparing subordinate and dominant social groups on the issue of learning, something like parity emerges only in the realm of informalized, everyday knowledge production, storage, and transmission. Against this, we see that modern, compulsory schooling has consistently expanded its inclusion of citizens while maintaining vastly differentiated outcomes (Livingstone, 1999). Thus, I claim that it is when we look beneath the radar of normative closure, 'scriptural imperialism' or the 'disciplinary gaze' – that is in the realms of everyday life (within and beyond schools) – that we can hope to most clearly see learning as individual and collective human historical development under and beyond capitalism.

In this chapter, I look at the various forms of practice that both bar and develop the individual and collective capacities of subordinate class groups to engage in social change. I begin by describing the social significance of this investigation with reference to the claim that, as a feature of advanced capitalism, these capacities for change have been continually under attack. I call this a tendency toward the 'evisceration' of working-class communities. Turning the dominant logic on its head in some ways, I go on to argue that ideologies of the 'knowledge economy' or 'learning society' are more a response to this evisceration, rather than simply a natural result of changes to work processes, knowledge/skill requirements, communications processes, technological change, or globalization. This, despite or perhaps in addition to the fact that the working class of the industrialized West is now more formally 'educated' than at any other time in the history of the world. I then proceed to analyze two defining principles of the relation amongst learning, knowledge, and class power. For these purposes, I highlight contributions of Michel de Certeau, Henri Lefebvre, and Pierre Bourdieu that, in distinct ways, address the everyday. Finally, in the latter half of the chapter, I apply the concepts through concrete, empirical illustrations. Here, I apply CHAT principles to identify three specific modes of knowledge activity in terms of class domination, resistance, and transformation, concluding with important questions relating to the role of class consciousness and revolutionary development. Forms of political consciousness do not, I argue, simply appear as socialization models might suggest. They emerge from uniquely human labour processes, the processes through which human beings make themselves vis-à-vis a process of 'expansive learning' defined by the progressive resolution of activity system contradictions.

## THE EVISCERATION OF WORKING-CLASS COMMUNITY

As a means of both contextualizing my argument and explaining its social and political significance, I want to begin by posing the question: What came first, the erosion of traditional knowledge production capacities of working-class communities or the clamouring need for an apparently new 'knowledge economy'? I suggest that this is far more difficult to answer than mainstream pundits would have us know. To address the question critically, it is crucial to situate the current status or health of working-class communities. Of course, international generalizations are always tenuous. Nevertheless, a host of sources have documented in agonizing detail the forces of dissolution and fragmentation of such communities. One of the most penetrating, recent examinations of working-class life in England goes a long way toward capturing the essence of this trend in terms of collective cultural life. It is worth quoting at some length:

[D]escribing the nature of working class people in an age of such fragmentation and atomization, especially where so many are so uncertain, is not straightforward . . . For the working class, themselves, for whom the economically marginal and socially excluded are family members and neighbours, they have had to deal in the most palpable way with the decline of their own economic role and social position. Since the 1980's, the gradual decline of the culture of the working class has been one of the most powerful, telling developments in British society... The task of trying to capture the voices of working class people, emphasized the gradual effacement of a way of life based around a coherent sense of the dignity of others and of a place in the world. Those around forty have a coherent way of describing their lives and a sense of what has happened to the working class, but as one comes down through the generations, one moves away from the efficacy of any narrative of the social, away from the co-ordinates of class and encounters an arid individualism devoid of personal embedding in something beyond the ego. The coherence of a spoken common understanding based upon mutual respect and shared sources of value, becomes more and more infrequent until, among the very young, understanding and value seem impossible. An inescapable conclusion of the work seems to be that the most dispossessed individuals understand their lives the least and are certainly the least able to articulate their existence... During a period of mass unemployment, in which work has become more atomized and more precarious, insecurity has become the condition of too many. Elementary solidarities of family, work and place, once consolidated by the culture of the trade union and tertiary education, have been washed away by the corrosive cleansing of *laissez-fraire* economic practice.... (Charlesworth 2000: 1–5)

Under such conditions, so prevalent in advanced capitalist countries around the globe, it is not hard to understand that amongst the casualties is knowledge production capacity. This chapter is no place for a full exploration of the damage to the traditional knowledge production capacities of working-class communities beyond noting that political economic factors, socio-cultural activity, learning, and subordinate class standpoints find themselves deeply enmeshed within this process of decline. Certainly stagnation, crisis, destruction, re-settlement, resumed economic growth, and so on have been the hallmark of capitalism from the beginning (e.g., Maddison, 1982), having both distinct and shared elements across different national contexts. Nevertheless, it becomes increasingly difficult to argue that this current phase of advanced capitalism has not ushered in something unique in terms of the new freedoms felt by capital: to move, to contract, to search for profit, and to 'freely trade' across the planet. Beyond establishment of 'free trade zones' and the general rise of neo-liberalism over the last four decades, clearly the rooted-ness of economic production in any one specific physical location has fallen. The results are new levels – I suggest qualitatively different conditions of – economic atomization, turbulence, and fragmentation for the vast majority (Hewitt, 1993; Menzies, 1996). Taken as a whole, it can easily be argued that working-class communities and their historical knowledge production capacities are under siege.

The capacities of working-class groups, particularly unionized ones, can, must, and still do stubbornly resist these forces of evisceration, particularly where there are additional stabilizing forces (e.g., strong welfare state, strong labour laws, workers' political parties, significant social capital, and so on).

However, capital has clearly eroded the conditions through which workers' traditional knowledge was created and largely controlled through the practices inherent to the working-class community itself. Indeed, ethnographic studies of work confirm that, in the past, workers often had significantly greater control over learning processes, including all the elements that constitute it such as the mediation of assignments and career development, the storage and transmission of (often tacit) knowledge and skill, and even the evaluation of production. In many ways, these facts are confirmed through the bitter and variegated struggles for work process control that characterized work in the late 19th and 20th centuries (e.g., Zimbalist, 1979; Montgomery, 1987). The fact is that the capacities for a rich, culturally based form of everyday knowledge generation was present more abundantly under the great working-class communities of old, associated with Fordism and, in North America, what has been called the 'golden era' of the immediate post-World War II period.

## THEORIES OF RELATIONS BETWEEN SUBORDINATION, LEARNING, AND THE EVERYDAY

With this brief summary of class struggle and learning as a backdrop, I submit that today subordinate social groups have fewer 'legitimate' spaces in the world of knowledge production – save for the places they can make themselves. In other words, their knowledge, as a feature of advanced capitalism, is more systematically and effectively denied, denigrated, or ignored. In this section, I wish to take a moment to reflect on why and how this is the case. To do this, I focus on the relations between class subordination and knowledge, that is, to my mind, it remains relevant to recognize that people do *learn to learn* in the sense that they interiorize not simply specific knowledge and skill content, but also a generalized sense of the relations between knowledge and their lives.

In this discussion, the institutions of schooling and formal pedagogy cannot be ignored. To begin, it is important to recognize that the correlation of social class and schooling achievement from childhood through to adulthood represents one of the strongest, most enduring social scientific axioms of the last century (e.g., United Kingdom Adult Education Committee, 1919; Bowles and Gintis, 1976; Courtney, 1992; Livingstone 1999). Myriad analyses exist addressing the contexts of most advanced capitalist countries; most explore the class reproductive capacities of schooling systems. A recent contribution by Richard Hatcher (2000) nicely summarizes this literature by conceptualizing the origins of class reproduction in the relationship between subordinate groups and knowledge itself. He points out that central to this subordination mechanism are the processes of, first, *objectification* and *decontextualization* of knowledge and, second, the process of 'entering into knowledge', which is 'only possible if the subject installs himself or herself in the relationship to the world which the constitution of this knowledge pre-supposes'. In contrast, to dominant class groups, according to Hatcher, for working-class students, knowledge is contextualized in terms of 'the family and the street, and based on personal involvement' (pp. 189–190).

Recognizing these processes forms a prelude to a broader dialectical analysis of the relationship between subordination, learning, and knowledge into adulthood; and, as in schooling, the reproduction of differentiated and differentiating outcomes rests on the appearance of 'learning' as a natural, neutral, and universally available social experience from which different class (as well as racial and gendered) outcomes emerge. Here and elsewhere, I contend that the appearance of the neutrality and openness of learning is akin to the social mechanism that Bourdieu (1984) described as 'distinction', where an apparently universal cultural aesthetic (i.e., taste) is in fact a highly differentiating and differentiated, class process. In keeping with this perspective and paralleling Hatcher's analysis, in the first few chapters of *Distinction*, Bourdieu discusses the idea of 'mental distance' and its role in the development of the dominant aesthetic judgment (cf. Duarte this volume pp. 233 – 234). According to Bourdieu, the creation of mental distance is linked with the ability/inability to separate one's practice from the immediacy of its accomplishment. Closely related to the development of mental distance is the tendency to presuppose alternative characterizations of the activity. In terms of a basic CHAT analysis, this type of process pre-supposes the capacity, always socially achieved, to generate alternative 'goals' and 'motives' loosened from the conditions shaping operational levels of activity. Clearly, this relates to Bourdieu's discussion of one's 'distance from necessity'. This type of distance is associated with the ability to foreground form rather than content as well as one's competence in certain linguistic forms (also associated with success in schooling), but at its most basic, for working people, the persistent linkage of learning to function and the inability to presuppose alternative goals and motives of activity form the foundation of the tendency against the generation of the 'mental distance' necessary to name one's life as a *life-long learning* process. Simply put, although human agency and discretion can be generated in a host of unexpected places and unpredictable means, where it is scarce – under conditions of communal evisceration – people's relation to knowledge and with it their ability to engage in self-conscious 'learning' is severely muted. Thus, similar to Bourdieu's notion of 'distinction', we see that an apparently universal human process, that is, learning, is in fact a class-power process dependent upon a naturalization of specific cultural and material practices and conditions. What emerges from this type of realization is a social mechanism whereby certain features of practice are naturalized to produce a hierarchical order of ability or lived capacity.

I suggest that central to both explaining as well as de-stabilizing this process is the adoption of a fundamentally different lens through which 'learning' is understood. As introduced, CHAT offers such a lens by allowing broad forms of culturally and materially mediated social participation to move centre stage in analysis of learning practice. In other words, CHAT allows everyday social practice to move to the fore as a defining feature of learning. However, although people from all class groups obviously engage in everyday learning, for subordinate groups, the relation between this type of knowledge activity is unique. From a working-class perspective, traditionally the relation between informal and formalized learning emerges from the standpoint of a 'cultural outsider,' a feature of experience defined by one's position within the institutions of capitalism.

According to Leont'ev (1978), Vygotsky initiated the development of a structured approach to learning understood as historically, culturally, and materially mediated participation. From this starting point, Leont'ev, Luria, and others came to think of learning as a social practice defined by dynamic transformations, contradiction, change, and interrelations with other social systems. At the same time, however, it is worth noting that Vygotsky's writings also outlined a clearly discernible faith in the progressive nature of formal schooling, a faith that Van Der Veer and Valsiner, for example, critique as a type of imagined *educational utopia* (1994: 6). However, as outlined creatively by McDermott and Lave (this volume), the goal of the activity in formal education is rooted in the commodification of knowledge acquisition. In this sense, within schooling, the primary contradiction of the commodity form is not a problem to be resolved but a fact to be yielded to, if not celebrated. Importantly, for my argument here, *expansive learning* as understood by Engeström (1987), predicated as it is on the resolution of contradictions in activity systems, thus can never be fully achieved in the current institutional form of capitalist schooling (noting also its intimate linkage with capitalist labour markets). Moreover, given that market exchanges in the context of the capitalist accumulation process tend to, in relative terms, impoverish rather than liberate the masses, we're presented with a Gordian knot akin to the economic participation of workers in a capitalist economy, identified by Marx, which assures that with greater participation there is ever greater subordination. Following Hatcher and others mentioned earlier, formal learning produces effects that are exclusionary (even as it actively incorporates more and more people). This is accomplished by the de-legitimation of human practice that begins from and expresses a perspective incongruous with learning as commodity production. Thus, it is true that the creative and transformative working-class practices tend to appear in the crevices – or 'interstitial spaces' – of legitimate institutional life.

An analysis of subordination and knowledge, however, is incomplete without a recognition of the points of resistance and revolt. At the centre of this recognition is an analysis of the accumulation of scarce discretionary time, the pooling of scarce material resources, and the collective development of knowledge and skill that recognizes – indeed positively expresses – working-class standpoints. These are, in fact, some of the important needs that are met by everyday learning networks (Sawchuk, 2003). These networks offer a powerful antidote to the dominant (and dominating) ideologies that surround people's ideas about learning and their orientation to knowledge. Membership in working-class networks produce the potential for the legitimisation of a field of participation that is denied and delegitimised elsewhere. In the 'learning life-history interviews' I conducted in my research, the challenge of establishing alternative forms of legitimate peripherality (Lave and Wenger, 1991) in the context of class society played a major role in the production of the distinctive learning patterns reported (Sawchuk, 2003). Levels of stability are rooted in the distribution of material resources in society and thus under capitalism must be understood as heavily influenced by class processes. Equally important beyond the material barriers that these networks help to overcome, they also produce a form of 'proletarian public sphere' (Negt and Kluge, 1993) where learners find their social standpoints positively acknowledged and their past experiences of schooling and the difficulties they have experienced accepted and developed upon. In this way, we see how cultural and material stability – the stability once offered by the great working-class communities discussed earlier in the chapter – are key mediating factors in understanding patterns of social learning amongst working-class adults.

## ON THE EVERYDAY: NEW CONCEPTS FOR ANALYZING ACTIVITY AND CLASS POWER

To this point, I've summarized relatively well-trodden ground across sociology of education on the one hand and CHAT on the other. What is missing thus far – in fact, what has been missing traditionally from the work of critical scholars on the matter of class reproduction and learning – is an explicit theory of how this mechanism of differentiation works in terms of mental life, subordinate cultural forms, and human agency. I suggest that responding to this gap requires careful, dialogic incorporation of key concepts from sociology as well as cultural studies, each brought under the rubric of CHAT. Specifically, the challenge demands conceptual tools able to address how everyday life is saturated with power relations and how these relations are actively produced, reproduced, and, occassionally, transformed. Certeau, Lefebvre, and Bourdieu are important starting points for my analysis, despite the fact that only one explicitly considered himself Marxist. What they share, however, is what sociology refers to as a conflict perspective that shapes their highly sensitive and detailed understandings of the relations between social structures and individual agency in the realm of everyday life.

Michel de Certeau's own depiction of the basic relations between legitimized education and the various everyday responses to it (what he referred to as 'uses of it') appears as follows:

The presence and circulation of representation (taught by preachers, educators and popularizers as the key to socioeconomic advancement) tells us nothing about what it is for its users. We must first analyze its manipulation by users who are not its makers. Only then can we gauge the difference or similarity between the production of the image and the secondary production hidden in the process of its utilization. (Certeau 1984: xiii)

It is in this same way that mainstream educational thought tends to ignore everyday learning. Indeed, Certeau's conceptualization of everyday life emerges from a multi-disciplinary reflex to explore (across sociology, anthropology, history, socio-linguistics, and philosophy) 'the scientific literature that might furnish hypotheses allowing the logic of un-self-conscious thought to be taken seriously' (Certeau, 1984: xv). Indeed, it can also be argued that Certeau's formulation of the everyday and what he refers to as 'tactical responses' emerge from sensitivities similar to those we associate with CHAT, including concerns for historicity and, in particular, the process of mediation.

This type of approach opens a space for a re-configuration of our analyses of knowledge production amongst both dominant and subordinate class groups. That is, we can identify relations amongst 'strategic' knowledge production and 'tactical' knowledge production. Certeau understands the difference in this way:

I call a 'strategy' the calculus of force-relationships which becomes possible when a subject of will and power (a proprietor, an enterprise, a city, a scientific institution) can be isolated from an 'environment'. A strategy assumes a place that can be circumscribed as proper and thus serve as the basis for generating relations with an exterior distinct from it (competitors, adversaries, 'clienteles', 'targets', or 'objects' of research). Political, economic, and scientific rationality has been constructed on this strategic model. I call a 'tactic', on the other hand, a calculus which cannot count on a 'proper' (a spatial or institutional localization), nor thus on a borderline distinguishing the other as a visible totality. The place of a tactic belongs to the other. A tactic insinuates itself into the other's place, fragmentarily, without taking it over in its entirety, without being able to keep it at a distance. It has at its disposal no base where it can capitalize on its advantages, prepare its expansions, and secure independence with respect to circumstances. The 'proper' is a victory of space over time. On the contrary, because it does not have a place, a tactic depends on time – it is always on the watch for opportunities that must be seized 'on the wing'. Whatever it wins, it does not keep. It must constantly manipulate events in order to turn them into 'opportunities'. (Certeau 1984: xix)

For Certeau, perhaps the prototypical expression of tactical practice is *la perruque*, for example:

. . . the worker's own work disguised as work for his employer. It differs from pilfering in that nothing of material value is stolen. It differs from absenteeism in that the worker is officially on the job. *La perruque* may be as simple a matter as a secretary's writing a love letter on 'company time' or as complex as a cabinetmaker's 'borrowing' a lathe to make a piece of furniture for his living room . . . [T]he worker who indulges in *la perruque* actually diverts time (not goods, since he uses only scraps) from the factory for work that is free, creative, and precisely not directed towards profit . . . whose sole purpose is to signify his own capabilities through his work and to confirm this solidarity with other workers or his family through spending his time in this way. (Certeau 1984: 25–26)

I not only argue that the analysis of both strategic and tactical forms of knowledge production benefits from a CHAT approach, but that the proper analysis of the tactical, given its amorphous nature, may in fact *require* analytic frameworks such as CHAT to be adequately grasped as a concrete, historical human process. A CHAT analysis suitable to tactics, however, requires particular forms of emphasis. The focus here becomes *contradiction, multivoicedness* (a point I address in terms of social standpoints), and Engeström's notion of 'expansive' vs. 'contracted' learning.

To continue to develop third-generation CHAT for a critical analysis of class-power and activity, however, some further tools are required. First, we must address basic materialist elements of space and time. What can we make of the points made by both Certeau and Lefebvre that the practices of the powerful are characterized by the victory of 'space over time' whereas the practices of the weak are characterized by the victory of 'time over space'? To be sure, these can be dealt with in a number of ways. In my own work, I've chosen to think in terms of the interrelation of two concepts: *fragmentation* and *interstitiality*. Fragmentation, in this context, represents the victory of space over time, a force against which all subordinate groups grapple. It is a force of de-mobilization and domination. In turn, fragmentation tends to create, dialectically, practices of interstitiality – the hidden practices, *la perruque*, within the gaps of institutional life – that represent creative and developmental resistance to such conditions.

Certeau's work on the everyday, although providing important observations, does not unfortunately include a particularly coherent conception of capitalism per se. As such, there is much that goes under-recognized. In this context, it makes a good deal of sense to look toward the work of Lefebvre: the cultural theorist whose work, when taken as a whole, contains particular emphasis on the commodity-conditioned forms of everyday life as understood in the Marxist tradition. Indeed, Lefebvre persistently argued that everyday life should be at the center of a critical Marxism:

The extension of capitalism goes all the way to the slightest details of everyday life . . . A revolution cannot just change the political personnel or institutions; it must change *la vie quotidienne* which has already been literally colonized by capitalism. (Lefebvre, 1988: 79–80)

Along with the theme of alienation, Lefebvre discusses fragmentation explicitly, against which he privileges the concepts of resistance understood

by the term *le detournement*. *Le detournement* or 'diversion', a term borrowed from the French Situationalists, refers to a re-appropriation of space.
Important similarities are to be found here to Certeau's concept of the
tactical.

Empirically, Lefebvre's preoccupations leaned toward the realm of leisure
but always as an activity inter-connected to other systems of activity (the
home, community, work): a dialectical refusal to submit casually to dominant
institutional divisions. Emphatically, Lefebvre felt that the everyday contained the most important seeds of stark social criticism and social change,
elements I illustrate in the next section of the chapter. Like Certeau, the basic materialist elements of time and space were central to Lefebvre's analysis.
In particular, space and its re-appropriation, both culturally and materially,
in opposition to the violence of capitalist law and property, were central.
He understood time as both a means and a goal of such actions. A key
inflection of Lefebvre's work, summarized in his essay 'The Everyday and
Everydayness' (1987), is that prospects for liberation were to be located
in our consciousness of alienation in everyday life, that is, liberation and
socialist transformation were rooted in making strange and alien the very
experience of alienation itself. This process, in fact, describes specific forms
of transformation in the structure of activity. His connection to this chapter,
in this sense, is to further reinforce the political importance of recognizing and analyzing everyday learning as a distinctively class process. Both
Lefebvre and Certeau's specific contribution to the analysis of everyday life
lie in their understanding of relations of fragmentation and interstitiality,
complete with moments of determination as well as freedom, creativity, and
human agency. Thereby, they open up for analysis all the more widely the
potential for CHAT to critique, understand, and change the processes of
commodification and alienation endemic to capitalism, and learning life
under and beyond capitalism specifically.

However, neither Certeau's nor Lefebvre's work, on their own, provide
a workable model of how subordinate standpoints come to be interior-
ized and, in turn, result in dominated, accommodative as well as resistant and revolutionary practice. Interiorization or turning, from a CHAT
perspective, is part of a historical materialist analysis of mental life and
activity, a central achievement of the work of Vygotsky (e.g., Graham,
1972). However, CHAT approaches to date have not adequately addressed
class-cultural dispositions, as either a historical dimension of activity or
as a central mediating artifact. To introduce this into a CHAT analysis
of activity and class-power, I propose looking toward the work of Pierre
Bourdieu.

I argue here and elsewhere that activity, as a differentiated and differentiating mode of social practice, contains within it cultural–historical mechanisms that can be understood through the use of Bourdieu's concept of
'habitus': a central component of the Bourdieuian sociology of position

and disposition, a politicized science of the schemata of perception and appreciation. The habitus is a,

... generative and unifying principle which retranslates the intrinsic and the relational characteristics of a position into a unitary lifestyle, that is, a unitary set of choices of persons, goods, practices. Like the positions of which they are a product, habitus are differentiated, but they are also differentiating. Being distinct and distinguished, they are also distinction operators, implementing different principles of differentiation or using differently the common principles of differentiation. (Bourdieu, 1998: 8)

The habitus thus represents a form of artifact prior to, or rather more fundamental than, the semiotic: a master artifact that is social, yes; symbolic, yes; and yet fundamentally distinct from language per se (cf. Jones's, 2002, discussion of the Vygotsky 'sign-centrism' debates).[1] In at least one sense, the habitus concept fits relatively comfortably in recent, critical discussions of 'personality' in the CHAT tradition (e.g., Rey, 2002) as a concept related more to 'sense' (as opposed to meaning) that is not describable as consciousness on the one hand nor tacit practice on the other. It is arguable that the concept of habitus speaks to Vygotsky's concern over the relations between thought and the 'motivating sphere of consciousness, a sphere that includes our inclinations and needs, our interests and impulses, and our affect and emotion [which] stands behind thought' (Vygotsky, 1987: 282). Indeed, in Sawchuk (2003), I argue that patterned forms of participation rooted in the unique cultural and material contexts of working-class standpoints provide evidence of a working-class 'learning' habitus. At the same time, we should be quick to note that Bourdieu's focus was the field of 'cultural production' – based on *presumptions* of participatory processes rather than actual *analyses* of them directly. Indeed, the dialectic of class position and class disposition that the likes of Bourdieu (e.g., 1984) and followers such as Charlesworth (2000) describe so well is perhaps best understood – if it is to avoid the appearance of mechanical pre-determination (a charge often levelled at Bourdieu) – as a process of cultural–historical activity.

However, in terms of an appropriation of Bourdieuian concepts, we should not proceed much further without an explanatory note of caution. For Bourdieu, a person's habitus is closely connected to its realization in a specific *field* of activity. The concept of field is meant to refer to a scope of relevancy for interaction complete with specific roles, logic of operation, history, and so on, a rough equivalency to the idea of a normative institution. In other words, the concept of 'field' assumes a normative, highly structured

[1] In this regard, I have some sympathy for the concerns of Rubinstein and Brushlinsky who suggest that acquisition of speech is based on a more general process that shapes attention and relevance, though I reject the broader tenor of their argument. Nevertheless, Bourdieu's "habitus" outlines such a process while also rejecting the conflation of such a process with notions of 'thinking', 'meaning', or 'consciousness' per se.

arrangement of forms of *capital*. My point here is that I and others (e.g., Calhoun, LiPuma, and Postone, 1993; Dreyfus and Rabinow, 1999) feel that one needn't take on the 'structuralist baggage' of 'field' to make good use of the concept of habitus. In other words, habitus is a conceptual means of explicating the type of physically, culturally, and historically embodied set of dispositions that shape, but do not determine, the participatory roles that are available to people, which vis-à-vis their habitus they would be interested in taking up in the first place.

Taking the concepts of each of these three scholars into account, we now find ourselves in the position to pose some important questions to the current third-generation CHAT approach. For example, we might ask how CHAT would begin to address *la perruque* or *le detournement*; how might it analyze class standpoints, via the use of *class habitus* or some other conceptual means, to trace different developmental forms of activity; and on what bases might it more adequately address power relations, conflict, and political significance of mundane activity? The starting point for this type of appropriation is, in my view, their relation to the dialectical concept of contradiction. It is this mode of abstraction that allows us to see the inner conflict, for example, in the commodity form, and the dual realities of practice within activity systems through time. It is in the context of such considerations that what I shall refer to as the 'projected orientations' toward use-value and exchange-value exchange gain their significance.

## ASCENDING TO THE CONCRETE: SOME EMPIRICAL ILLUSTRATIONS

At this point, I hoped to have established both the need for and means of paying close attention to the issues of class-power in activity. It is worth emphasizing again, because it is sometimes a point of confusion, that this type of approach to the everyday *does not* claim that *everyday learning* is the sole domain of subordinate groups, but rather that the everyday takes on distinct social significance (as well as patterns) for subordinate groups. At the center of this distinction are the relations of *legitimate* and *illegitimate* social standpoints. What is meant by legitimacy and illegitimacy? Legitimacy is a socio-political notion and a function of communities of interest ratified through their linkages with one or more legitimate societal institution. To the degree that subordinate groups are divested of their own communities, there is no legitimate space for them to occupy positively *as who and what they are*. For example, in schools, the taken-for-granted standpoint of the middle- or upper-class student is legitimatized; that is, entry into activity in these terms (complete with prior familial experiences with the institution of schooling and surplus of time, space, and parental energies) is the starting point for successful forms of 'legitimate peripheral participation' (Lave and Wenger, 1991). The working-class student, in contrast, cannot legitimately find a mode of participation *as a working-class student* within the structure of school-based activity. This example gives an idea of the complexity with which CHAT must (and can) cope: Legitimate activity systems and modes of participation exist dialectically with alternative, illegitimate ones.

To elaborate on this point, at the heart of this definition of the legitimacy/ illegitimacy relation is, of course, the primary contradiction of all activity systems under capitalism, i.e., the contradiction between use- and exchange-value within the commodity form. Thus, use-value orientations (i.e., activity governed in the last instance by the production of 'use-value') as opposed to exchange-value orientations (activity involving use-value but governed in the last instance by the production of 'exchange-values') offer a unity of opposites, parallel, mutually constituting but opposing dimensions of human development. Activity systems governed by use-value production are, on the whole, illegitimate under capitalism. Use-values such as comfort, sustenance, social justice, solidarity, mutual need, and even democracy, to the degree they truly govern (as opposed to merely accompany) an activity system, are illegitimate at either the goal or motive levels of activity. They are ignored, discounted, denied relevance, and, in some cases, directly attacked by capital. Of course, under capitalism, use-value production, as governed by the production of exchange-values, is absolutely necessary. Furthermore, if we accept, as I do, that ultimately expansive learning is defined by the progressive resolution of systemic contradictions, then paradoxically one can engage in processes of expansive learning by resolving a range of more peripheral contradictions only to the point of the most primary contradiction, that of use-exchange value. To move beyond this point is the dividing line between epochal and truly historical – that is, revolutionary – activity. Recovering the point I made in the previous section, one of the points I wish to emphasize here is that the realm of the tactical, *la perruque, le detournement*, and what is called the 'triumph of time over space' is the appropriate topic of investigation for use-value governed activity systems under capitalism.

Activity whose goal revolves around learning is, following the detailed works of those like Galperin and Davydov, unique. Learning, in this sense, is not activity but rather *knowledge activity*. Illegitimate knowledge activity is itself an achievement and the necessary starting point for social transformation. Drawing on Certeau, it describes the transformation from the tactical to the strategic; in Bourdieu's terms, it is the bridging of content and form, and entails the establishment of 'mental distance.' This is the movement from the many small 'triumphs of time over space' toward the 'triumph of space over time' in which 'what is won can be kept' and accumulated; where the subordinate social standpoint itself (e.g., the working-class subject) becomes valorized in a community that comes to increasingly govern its own mode of objectification (i.e., artifact creation), its own mode of appropriation (i.e., artifact-mediation), and ultimately its own reproduction (i.e., through historically expansive learning).

I cannot, in this space, offer data that is anything more than illustrative. Related here is a point made nicely by Ilyenkov (1982) regarding the importance of connecting theoretical analysis to the concrete via empirical work:

[t]he dialectical materialist method of resolution of contradiction in theoretical definitions thus consists in tracing the process by which the movement of reality itself resolves them in a new form of expression. Expressed objectively, the goal lies in tracing, through analysis of new empirical materials, the emergence of reality in which an earlier established contradiction finds its relative resolution in a new objective form of its realization. (Ilyenkov 1982: 263)

Following, I structure the analysis in terms of three types of concrete working-class development. The types are derived from careful qualitative study of workers' lives in Canada (see Sawchuk, 2003; Livingstone and Sawchuk, 2004). Emphatically, in terms of any one person's actual life, these three types are *not* mutually exclusive: They can and do co-exist.

In this typology, the first type, *domination*, involves knowledge activity governed by an exchange-value orientation. Such activity systems rarely resolve internal contradictions. More often than not, for the working-class they result in contracted or degenerative modes of activity system development. In many ways, they exemplify the processes of 'evisceration' outlined earlier in the chapter. The type of knowledge activity outlined later as *resistance* offers an analysis of working-class learning that skirts the line between use-value and exchange-value orientations. As my interview data focus on the employed and unionized working-class in Canada – what in Livingstone and Sawchuk (2004) we call the 'most powerful of the least powerful' – these types of activity were not uncommon. In these cases, the evisceration of working-class communities has been slowed. Scarce cultural and material resources still persist and can still be pooled, distributed, and developed. Here, we see enormous complexity in people's knowledge activity. The forces of fragmentation encourage the development of tactical responses within interstitial spaces, dispersed across a range of locations where working-class groups still exercise bits and pieces of individual and collective discretion. So, it is in these 'stolen' moments – during the breaks and gaps within the labour process, in the truck on the way home after a shift, in the easy chair in front of the television where one would otherwise simply rest one's body, around the kitchen table with family members or friends, in the pub where networks of workers, neighbours, friends, and, in the case later in this chapter musicians, gather – that people can cobble together a semi-coherent and ongoing mode of knowledge development. It is not coincidental that it is through these processes that workers first begin to politicize their own knowledge and learning. The third type of knowledge activity, *transformation*, suggests the rudimentary formation of not simply a 'class in itself' but a 'class for itself'. Illegitimate activity passes toward a form that, in the community of workers that mediates it, becomes legitimized. Thus, workers begin to re-assess their lives and their learning, from which emerges distinct forms of education and development. The central vehicle, in the case of my data set, is of course the trade union. In this third type of knowledge activity, people create systems of activity with developmental trajectories that run parallel to – occasionally violently intersecting with – the dominant exchange-value oriented structures of education, training, work, and politics.

One of the points I wish to demonstrate across the three types is that there are important transformations that occur regarding the structure of knowledge activity and habitus. The content of the habitus undergoes change, but perhaps more important, as part of this process the structural location of the working-class learning habitus shifts within the different forms of knowledge activity system as well. One can note, for example, that the working-class learning habitus tends to mediate practice at the operational level of activity in the first two types, whereas under the third we see what Engeström (e.g., 2000) calls a significant *re-instrumentalization* of activity. The habitus becomes a central tool and sometimes an object of activity. As we shall see in turn, this is also an important explanatory resource regarding what Marxists understand as class consciousness.

### Type 1: Domination

Epochal activity, that is activity confined to its own historical epoch, is defined under capitalism as activity that has as its motive structure (and often its goal orientation) the production of exchange-values. This may be the production of goods or services for one's employer. It can mean the obtainment of an educational credential for the purposes of exchange on a labour market. It might also mean learning applied to the service of an employment contract, the gaining of a promotion, and so on. Of course, I use the term 'exchange' in a particular way; it does not encompass all forms of social exchange. Rather, it refers to *capitalist exchange*; that is, exchange modeled on (if, for the working-class, never realizing for itself) the appropriation of surplus value, rational maximization, accumulation, and profit (what, in *Capital* [Volume 1], Marx described in terms of the classic M-C-M' exchange chain). According to a Marxist approach, this is the realm – what Marx called the 'inner most secret' – of class domination. As participants in a capitalist economy, workers must engage in these forms of exchange for a wage, in organizations that engage in even more elaborate forms of these types of exchange. In terms of knowledge activity systems, or learning, a typical description of this from my research is as follows: 'I engage in education and training to learn something else and to make myself more marketable' (Clerical Worker). We might note how this describes participation in a system of activity systems overlapping a number of social spheres (e.g., schooling, work-based training, and labour market participation) all in a way governed by exchange-value production.

It is important to note, however, that a growing majority of workers in advanced capitalist countries, in fact, cannot apply their knowledge to the 'legitimate' spheres of exchange processes. This is itself an expression of the underlying contradiction of capitalism that many analysts are loath to recognize. Indeed, against the growing levels of credentials and significant accumulation of informal skills and knowledge, the vast majority of work-places, simply put, have not kept up (e.g., Berg, 1970; Livingstone, 1999). In Canada, as in most Western industrialized countries:

[L]arge numbers of employees perform work that is low-skilled and requires less education than they have. More than 20 percent of employees feel overqualified for their jobs... For instance, there is a surplus in computer literacy in this country. In 1994, over two-thirds (68 percent) of the employed were computer literate, but only half of all employees (and even fewer self-employed people) actually used a computer in their work. More generally, job structures often deprive workers of opportunities to use their education and talents. (Lowe, 2000: 170)

In interviews with people such as this chemical worker, the structure of know-ledge activity systems that produce these types of results becomes clearer:

R:[2]   Sometimes they ask you your opinions on things, what do you need, how do you do this, how much space do you need, but in the end it's all their call right. I remember one time we told them that in this one situation we were getting these sparks coming off, so they told us to start using Nitrus and we told them that we didn't think it was going to work, it's not strong enough to clear the tanks, and then what happens, the guy goes to take the hose off and he gets covered in chemical. We said, it just didn't have enough pressure, it wasn't going to work, blah, blah, blah, but they just do what they want anyways. They're the ones with the formal schooling. They're the ones with the high-paying jobs, so they're the ones who know better than us on the floor.... These are lab technicians telling you to do things but they don't know. They don't know that there are tricks to the trade. These people with their prestigious jobs don't want to listen to some grunt.

I:      So, what's that make you think about the value of what you do?

R:      Can't complain you know. The cash is good and money talks in this day and age. You could do worse, but if the money wasn't there I wouldn't stay.... Like would I say that I'm interested in the job I'm doing? No. I'm doing it because the money's good. There's a lot things that I could do that might only pay $10 an hour and the interest is there.... You know it's like somebody says to you, 'I hear your job pays $25 an hour. Well what do you do there?' I say, 'I don't know really – it's $25 an hour man – who the fuck cares what I do!' (Chemical Worker)

The types of peripheral contradictions described – left unresolved un-der this type of dominating knowledge activity system that are all too

---

[2] In the following excerpts, 'R' refers to the respondent; 'I' refers to the author/interviewer.

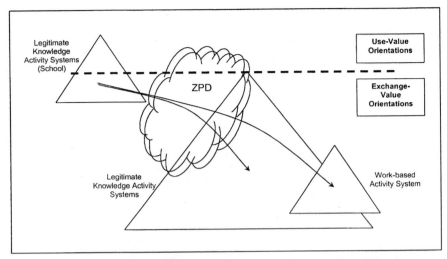

FIGURE 12.1. Class domination in knowledge activity systems and work development. *Note:* Zone of Proximal Development (ZPD).

frequent – result in vast wasted potential and resources, and notably severe alienation and frustration. Such knowledge activity systems can be represented in a modified version of Engeström's (1987) basic triangular graphic in Figure 12.1.

Such diagrams as I use them here are (as is typically so) largely heuristic and metaphoric. They do not, on their own, represent a detailed analysis, as such. Nevertheless, Figure 12.1 does capture, in broad strokes, the tenor of this type of knowledge activity system. The modifications over the Engeströmian triangular graphic include the addition of the use-value and exchange-value dashed line, which is meant to indicate the overall governance or orientation of the activity system. Though it is far from a perfect way to represent, dialectically, this dimension of activity, we can nevertheless note, for example, that the legitimate knowledge activity system (school) straddles this dashed line. This is because, arguably, it does provide some opportunities in both realms: Education can and does serve the needs of humans directly as valuable 'in itself' at the same time it serves the capitalist economy. Further, however, we can note that legitimate knowledge systems identified flowing forward in time into adulthood are positioned below the dashed line, firmly in the realm of exchange-value orientation within this type of system. My claim is that when relegated to this realm, activity can never truly be *expansive* because it can't (without exiting this realm) resolve the primary use-value/exchange-value contradiction of the commodity form that marks the transition from capitalism to another societal form. Work-based activity systems are a subset of larger societal *legitimate*

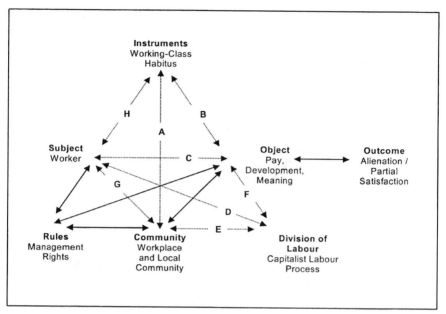

FIGURE 12.2. Unresolved contradictions and weak mediations in work-based activity systems from a working-class standpoint.

*knowledge activity systems* and thus occupy a position embedded in them, again largely governed by exchange-value production.

A slightly more detailed examination of working-class standpoints in work-based activity systems is shown in Figure 12.2. This figure typifies the unresolved contradictions with an emphasis on the weak mediations (represented by dotted lines), which tend to assure this lack of resolution. For example, workers in my research whose learning seemed to best exemplify this dominating type of knowledge activity systems detail the weak mediations resultant from the classic Taylorist, assembly-line style, division of labour (i.e., lines D-F-C in Figure 12.2). Distinct from but, of course, implicated in the workplace is the underdevelopment of the working-class habitus. This is represented in Figure 12.2 by the isolated subject without strong mediational connections to culturally or materially stable communities. These are depicted as weak mediations (lines G-A-H), mismatches between conditions and artifacts.

Of course, the workplace is not the only source or site where we find structural limitations to worker knowledge activity system development. Third-generation CHAT correctly notes the importance of analysing overlapping activity systems. How does paid work dove-tail with home and community life? The garment home-worker who follows gives us a clue combining in the process both class and gender effects of subordination in which the woman is expected to take primary responsibility for child and home-care:

We have to take care of children and work at home at the same time, so we don't really have much spare time to learn other leisure activities. Maybe when our kids grow up we'll have more time to take up on these leisure activities. Sometimes I have to work until late at night. Therefore I dare not register [for any courses]. Time is really a crucial factor. . . . As a working class, we must be more interested in learning the practical things, rather than those purely leisure activities such as floral arrangement, cosmetics or aerobics. Those are for the richer people who have more leisure time. (Garment Worker)

Another woman, this time an autoworker, gives us a slightly more elaborate picture emphasizing the 'cramped' time and spaces in which learning, if it is to be engaged in at all, must be shoe-horned:

I have a really cramped time, so many things I love to do, but I have the children, I get up at 5 am, don't get home until 5 pm, so by the time supper's cooked, and I've played with kids, and get 8 hours sleep, I'm really squeezed for time. I have to read on the bus. . . . [For women] to continue our education in the evening is such an inconvenience for everyone – we're suffering with guilt, the children are sick, he's not a great caregiver. I'm wondering if he's looking after the little one with a fever. I'm studying for exams. No cooperation from my partner . . . For a lot of women, they need that support from a partner, or if they have workplace training, especially workplace training, if workplaces would just squeeze some time in and allow the employees to learn, or take a day off and allow them to learn, or have more options for Saturday trainings, it would be a great help. Especially for women. (Autoworker)

*Type 2: Resistance*

In an insigtful article, Häyrynen (1999: 115–132) speaks about resistance as follows:

. . . coercion does not eliminate the mass inventiveness or silent argumentation of the people (Billig, 1991), though it forces this argumentation to take capillary forms similar to those that power assumes. (p. 125)

In this context, resistance tends to be reproductive of power relations. More broadly, CHAT as formulated by Leont'ev defines goal-directed actions as conscious, whereas both operations (related to local conditions of practice) and the broader motive of activity (related to institutional, social, and political economic contexts) are typically beyond the self-conscious attention of participants. These three levels of activity are important for understanding working-class learning, but activity systems, as we know, are not as self-contained as Leont'ev originally suggested. So, in third-generation CHAT analysis, we might ask: What do overlapping systems of activity look like in relation to working people's knowledge activity? The following excerpt from an interview with a woman who works as a batch processor in a chemical factory provides a typical illustration of how learning, spread across different spheres of activity, allows the pooling of scarce material resources as well as the pooling of scarce experiences of discretionary control over the learning process. As I've indicated, elite and professional groups combine experiences across spheres of activity as well; however, in working-class households, the premises, purposes, and patterns of this overlap have a unique social significance; they define a response to domination and fragmentation, tactical practices of interstitiality.

R:  I used the computer a lot at the [my former job at a] steel mill when I worked certain departments...So the kids wanted to know what I wanted for Christmas one year, so the kids bought [a computer] for me. So I worked at it a little bit and [my daughter] had this word processor on it. And my daughter's got the booklet and she showed me how to do it because she knows how to do it. [My partner] has to do it on his job too, and he has things to do at home too so he said 'We've *got* to sit down and we've got to learn how to do it, more often than what we do.'...[Like] we used to go down to the pub every Saturday night – there used to be a whole group of us you know – and then this guy that used to have his own band he used to get people up to sing. And we used to do two or three songs and you know then after doing that for a couple of years he said well come on, we'll get you up every set to do three or four songs. So I kept on doin' that for a long time. And then I started taking music lessons – like playing guitar right?....And then there was learning all the different songs. I mean I have to sit down there and learn the songs. And then if they're not easy songs you can't expect the other ones to pick it up, so I mean if you want to sing it they have to sort of know it basically, so you hopefully give them the tape and they have the time to learn it. [Learning when you're an adult] is not like one person teaches all the time. It's a group of people. It's not like the way school sets things up. You're doing it with a group of people.

I:   And that's different than how you learn things in the school system?

R:  I think so, yeah. Because when you're in the school system, I mean, you sit in the classroom and the teacher teaches you things, like you know, after that you're sort of on your own to do your own work. You can't say, 'These four kids get together and do our homework', or, 'Let's get our answers together.'...But when I've had a job like, you work with people...

I:   What do you remember about learning during that period? How would you describe yourself as a student in the school. Did you like the work?

R:  The only thing that I can say that I didn't enjoy doing, and I think that's when I got into really goin' to high school, and I think that was probably when I started takin' algebra. Man! That to me, that didn't click in my brain at all! It looked so easy!

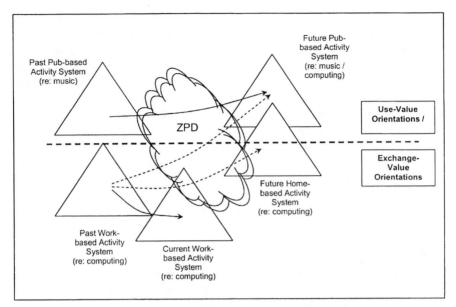

FIGURE 12.3. Fragmentation/interstitiality of music/computer learning.

I:  Didn't click in mine either!
R:  It looked so easy when they showed you on the blackboard. And I thought, 'That's easy,' give you a question on paper and I thought 'Oh, god, how do you do this?' (laughs) 'Where do you start' 'where do you finish?'. There was no way. It didn't click . . . That's just my own respects and I never think that I'm smart enough to learn anything. And that's why people always say to me 'Why do you say that? You're not stupid. Why do you always call yourself down?'. Because I say 'That's just the way I am.' Like you know, I never think I'm going to learn anything, or I never think I'm good enough in anything. (Chemical Worker)

This woman makes it clear that, from a working-class standpoint, there are important distinctions to be made regarding the knowledge activity systems of everyday life and the legitimized knowledge activity systems of schooling, though in this example, such distinctions are not yet politicized. Moreover, she provides an account of how processes of fragmentation and interstitiality play out across the working-class knowledge activity systems. Many systems need to be represented here to grasp the combination of the chemical worker's home and work-based computer learning in combination with her other learning interest, her music. In Figure 12.3, I include representations of the woman's past computer learning in the steel mill as more advanced than her current work-based learning signaling a contracted knowledge activity system (i.e., the transformation arrow moving down and to the right).

However, I also include, as linked to the woman's past work experiences, a form of expansion (up and to the right) as her activity shifts toward linkages to the family and home as well as to the pub activity system where she plays music with a community of others. Finally, I note a transition from exchange-value orientations (activity triangle place below the dashed use/exchange value line) toward computer knowledge activity that is partially oriented toward exchange-value and partially toward her life as an amateur musician, which is governed by use-value production. Her account claims that her learning in music and computers has developed extensively. Figure 12.3 suggests this is because she, along with the other participants in the home and pub-based activity systems, is resolving contradictions leading toward expansive learning. To the degree that she diverts her experiences in the realms of exchange-value toward the purposes of her life as an amateur musician, she is also engaging in a relatively complex form of Lefebvre's *le detournement*.

To further demonstrate the complexity of the practice within this second type of knowledge activity system, we can take the following example. An autoworker outlines his novice attempts at learning about computers. It is firmly motivated by his insecurity in the labour market, which characterizes the motive structure of his activities. This knowledge activity is highly fragmented; any coherence it develops is related to its overlapping development across a series of (spatially and temporally) interstitial gaps in his daily life. It represents an accumulation of the small 'triumphs of time over space':

I:    Do you get any information from TV?
R:    Yeah, actually a radio program about the e-line or what do they call it, e-mail and all that stuff, all through your computer now, how you go about it and you sort of, as you're driving along, say 'Oh yeah. Well I'll write that down'. That's how I pick it up.
I:    So if you happen to hear something on, you'll sort of perk your ears up?
R:    Even the television has that, I'll be flicking through just trying to relax, especially when that new system came out for Windows, I was taping it off the television and it was like 'Oh Geeze! I didn't realize computers could do that.' ... [But] it's something that probably in the next two years I'll get [a computer] depending how far my little boy is into it, because and I think the wife has a little bit of knowledge about it. ... And we'll probably use friends, because we have close friends who have just gotten [a computer]. ... Oh yeah, actually [there's a] guy at work. I would definitely talk to him. And he just went into it not that long ago, I can remember him talking about it at work. (Auto Worker)

Based on this short excerpt, we can begin to sketch the development of computer-based knowledge activity systems in Figure 12.4. Again, we see that for the working-class subject, there is a specific type of complexity that is unique to subordinate subjects in that it is heavily resisted, rather than

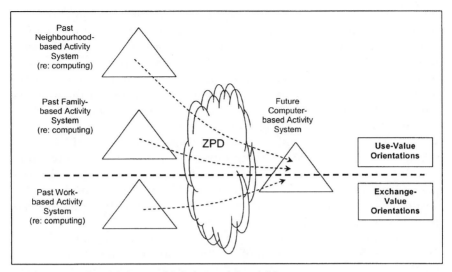

FIGURE 12.4. Combining multiple interstial activities.

supported, by the institutional structures that surround it on all sides. We can see that knowledge activity systems governed by both use- and exchange-value combine and allow for multiple interpretations. Work-based computer learning experiences provide the possibility of expansion whereas neighbourhood-based activity with friends and family-based activity (though contributing to the expansion of the work-based learning) may actually contract as the introduction of 'exchange-value orientation' foment rather than resolve core contradictions in these systems.

The activity analyzed in this example of type 2 is not 'strategic' in Certeau's terms because it does not rest on the significant control over either time or space. It is largely interstitial. Coherence, which in the case of this worker is something like a pre-strategy, is generated in terms of auto worker's ability to re-key the primary frames[3] of 'driving home listening to the radio', 'relaxing by the television', and even parenting (i.e., with a focus on his boy's learning) as something more than isolated and separate activities. This worker frames/keys these instances largely for the purposes of the interview and more broadly as the rudiments of a computer 'learning project', accentuating (bringing to the level of conscious goal-oriented action) the skill/knowledge development dimension. This process of re-interpreting experience and finding new ways to understand and mediate experience through the use of cultural networks (none of which depends upon conscious, goal-directed actions) counters the fragmentation of discretionary control that subordinate people experience. To use the language of CHAT,

---

[3] I use the terms 'keying' and 'framing' in the sense of Erving Goffman's work.

these unplanned practices were not recognized as learning in themselves because they were not situated within an activity system that had *learning* as its goal. In general terms, this type of transformation occurs through a process that has been described as the co-creation of a collectively meaningful object of activity. However, this co-creation of learning as a meaningful object of activity, on an ongoing basis (beyond the frame of the interview encounter) is highly influenced by material resources, namely, the distribution of discretionary time and energy. A critical perspective on activity such as the one I'm proposing allows us to better understand the complex relationships between these systems of activity that are partially broken up and dispersed. And, it is these patterns of arrangement that gives rise to particular responses, elaborated over time to form dispositions that define a working-class learning habitus; the object of domination, the means of partial resistance, or otherwise.

Across these illustrations we see a general pattern of coping and resistance. We see a general erosion of the hegemony of standard 'educational ideology' and an indirect challenge to the notion of legitimate/illegitimate learning. Workers, in this sense, begin to displace this discourse, which never matched well their own *working-class learning habitus.* Through this act of displacement, they begin to strengthen the 'weak mediations' seen under the first type of knowledge activity system I analysed. In other words, a semi-conscious sensitivity to class struggle approaches the horizon of activity.

### *Type 3: Transformation*

The account of a chemical worker that follows provides us with a sense of an approaching horizon that defines the transition between knowledge activity systems types 2 and 3. It can be understood as a form of *la perruque* in the classic formulation, though it is something more as well. Work-time 'owned' by the employer is diverted by the two workers in the excerpt toward the opportunity to teach and learn to weld. More than this, the worker notes that these skills were never accepted as legitimate (for promotion) in the eyes of the company. Finally, in the last portion of the excerpt, the worker provides an account of how – collectively, in everyday exchanges – certain contradictions of the work-based activity system rise to the surface.

R:  I was doing just some basic maintenance and cleaning and it turned out an old guy taught me how to weld. And it just happened that a job came up for maintenance and you gotta know a lot of stuff like welding and I had a lot of stuff but I remember [the company] wouldn't accept the welding that I'd learned from him.... One of the guys from the maintenance shop who I was working with and he was supposed to build this railing system, and I was cutting all this tubing for him and we were talking and he says to me, 'Have you ever done any welding?' And I said, 'No', and he said, 'Oh well I'll teach you'. So I just started with some tack welding and I went from there.... So that's the thing about learning for me. But like now, I pay a lot of attention to health and safety because you know somebody really has to learn a lot about it or the workplace won't be safe. At first how it was is you would just learn from other workers all the different rights you have, your obligations. And gradually I started taking courses on my own ...

I:  So, what do you think about the company's courses generally? Good, bad, okay?

R:  Good and bad. They teach you just what they want you to know. They'll put something on and teach you, but as far as sticking to it they don't. That's why a lot of people now don't bother, they feel they're wasting their time.... As far as following through on a course, the company follows through on it when it's feasible for them, if it's not feasible, forget it.... I'll give you another example of how people learn. I'm working with a guy, and he turns to me one day and says, 'You couldn't get a better place to work, this place treats you like gold'. I said 'Yeah', and I laughed, 'All you are is a number. They don't know you by name. When you're time comes up, all they see is a number. They don't feel sorry for you', and he's looking at me as if I didn't know what I was talking about. So he was trying to get his cousin in one time and they wouldn't hire him and he was all mad because he goes, 'Look at all the good work I've done!' And I said to him 'They don't know you from Adam man. They don't know how much stuff we each put out and they don't really care. I get paid the same as you. The paycheck won't change.' But he's coming around I think. He's kind of iffy, now, you know he's only had that one experience, sometimes it takes a couple of experiences before you learn. (Chemical Worker)

Figure 12.5 attempts to highlight stronger mediations (signaled by thicker mediation lines), a new instrumentality, new objects/goals, and the potential for new developmental trajectories of activity. These are elements responsible for the transition toward expansive (working-class) knowledge activity development understood as activity that challenges the elements of the primary contradiction.

It is worth noting here that in Chapter 2 of Engeström's (1987), we find a treatment of the work of Zinchenko, which may have some loose connection to the notion of habitus. It deals with different practices of memory in the CHAT tradition. These different practices include conscious/voluntary as well as less conscious/involuntary memory. Both are expressions of how the specific object of memory is positioned within the structure of activity. A class-habitus, by comparison, might be thought of as a less conscious and involuntary type of memory within the type 1 and 2 activity systems already outlined. However, in type 3, there emerges a self-conscious appreciation of the character of one's habitus. Importantly, this signals a shift in the structural position of the habitus within an activity system, in a sense, retrieved

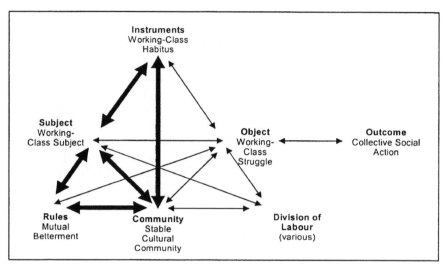

FIGURE 12.5. Re-instrumentalizing knowledge activity and the emergent horizon of working-class struggle.

from the level of operations (cf. discussion of Asmolov in Chapter 3). Specifically, this shift becomes possible through individual involvement in forms of social organization that develop and express a working-class standpoint positively and openly. Participation in organized labour offers a key example of a social structure through which this type of shift can occur under advanced capitalism, giving the study of this and other forms of social activism particular significance for critical perspectives on activity. In all cases, involuntary memories of sensibilities, dispositions, comportment, and tastes become articulated as shared objects for the mediation of future practice.

Building on this significance, take for example the role of participation in the trade union for the following interviewee attempting to learn about his life and his position within a particular political economic context. Participation in the trade union activity system, for him, brings forth for conscious articulation one's class position, to affect ongoing participation in a whole host of settings. In effect, it shifts what was otherwise background, 'seen but unnoticed' subordinate tracks of interaction into focus.[4]

Education? I don't have any, I don't believe in it. I left school when I was 15. Never stayed on further than I had to.... My real learning came when I joined the Miner's strike. You learned what the state apparatus is, keeping people in order, protecting the issues. That was my education... [In fact] the trade union's role as I see it is to highlight what knowledge we actually do have and how we attain it. How we actually do learn things, and I'll give you an example a quick example. [Workers I

---

[4] Again, drawing on the sense of these terms in the work of Erving Goffman.

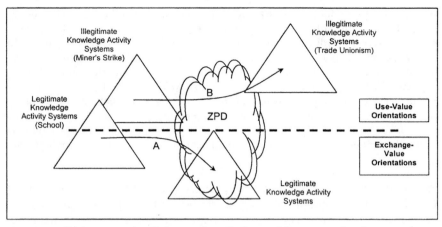

FIGURE 12.6. An example of phase 3 knowledge activity system development.

know] learned about health and safety the hard way. They learned about workers' compensation the hard way. Only through their experience. They never went to any course – they learned it when the employer screwed them and then they had the time to sit down and say, 'Why'd they do that to me – after all I've given them.' And that's the best, unfortunately it's the hardest as well, the best experience a worker can get because it cuts through all the nonsense because it hits you directly, it gives you time to think and to read and ask questions and start understanding what it's all about. (Chemical Worker)

Graphically represented, we see this system of knowledge activity in Figure 12.6.

This chemical worker, a union activist, outlines the role of an existing, culturally and materially stable community of workers as well as the organizational form offered by the union, which produces a shared object of inquiry fore-fronting conflictual class relations. The content of the habitus changes. A radicalized form of the working-class habitus emerges but, importantly, also comes to increasingly mediate knowledge activities generally. When structurally located within the activity system as a prominent mediating cultural artifact, it accounts for class reflexes, the fabric of what is often thought of as working-class culture. When structurally located within the activity system as object/goal, we see something that we might call *class consciousness*. Type 3, transformation, is marked by these structural re-locations rooted, first and foremost, in specific social movements.

## CONCLUSION

It would be foolish for me to claim that class consciousness was simply the result of growing up poor and living the life of a poor kid and then the life of a hard-pressed young husband and father. There are many people with similar backgrounds who developed a very different set of ideas about society. And there are many others, whose early lives were much different from mine, whose world-view was close to mine. . . . In the light of such experiences, traditional dogmatic 'class analysis' cannot remain intact. But as dogma disintegrates, hope appears. Because it seems that human beings, whatever their backgrounds, are more open than we think, that their behaviour cannot be confidently predicted from their past, that we are all creatures vulnerable to new thoughts, new attitudes. While such vulnerability creates all sorts of possibilities, both good and bad, its very existence is exciting. It means that no human being should be written off, no change in thinking should be deemed impossible. (Zinn, 2003: 4)

Reflecting on his own life growing up, these comments from radical American historian Howard Zinn suggest important questions that analyses of class-power and activity can begin to answer. Indeed, I believe at this point there are few approaches better suited to the task. Forms of political consciousness do not, obviously, simply appear as the socialization models I began this chapter with seem to suggest. They are a uniquely human labour process, the process through which human beings make themselves; they are, in the sense provided by the CHAT, learned. They can be learned across schooling, work and, as I've argued here, everyday life. Indeed, learning occurs whenever cultural mediation exists and the contradictions of activity systems are resolved. Truly expansive learning demands the resolution of contradictions, especially those inherent in the commodity form. Given the difficulty of addressing this primary contradiction within schooling, the workplace, and most other institutions deemed legitimate under advanced capitalism, there emerges a special significance to studies of everyday life.

In this chapter, I've explored the various forms of practice that develop the individual and collective capacity of subordinate class groups to engage in social change rooted in the learning process. I argued for the social significance of this interest early on when I briefly outlined how these capacities and the various, nationally specific cultural worlds of working-class communities are being challenged under advanced capitalism. I went so far as to say that it is the erosion of these capacities that have in fact given rise to the terms *knowledge economy* and *learning society*. I went on to examine the general relation between learning, knowledge and class-power. This led to a claim that a better, more critical and more politicized understanding of everyday life was necessary. Finally, I attempted to apply the ideas developed in the first half of the chapter to several pieces of interview data.

My three-type model of the relations between class-power and activity confirms, if nothing else, the political significance to be found in the mundane, hidden, and taken-for-granted world of working people's everyday lives. The appropriation of various concepts from sociology and cultural studies were an important means of sensitising and opening up fresh ground under the CHAT rubric. Beyond all of this, however, is the finding that taking into account issues of legitimate/illegitimate participation, knowledge forms, and social standpoints within a CHAT framework confirms the importance of tactical resources that allow interstitiality to develop in response to the fragmentation and evisceration of working-class communities.

One of the most important points that hopefully will have become evident by now is that across this model important differences are understandable vis-à-vis CHAT in relation to, on the one hand, the hidden and tactical practices that emerge when we apply the concepts of Certeau and Lafebvre as well as Bourdieu in terms of the class habitus specifically. The habitus undergoes a double transformation in terms of content *as well as* structural position within the knowledge activity systems. The working-class learning habitus tends to mediate practice at the operational level of activity in the first two types (i.e., domination and resistance), whereas under the third type we see what Engeström (e.g., 2000) calls a significant *re-instrumentalization* of activity. The habitus becomes a central tool and, at points, an object of activity. As I explained, tactical victories through small triumphs of time over space, *la perruqe, le detournement,* cannot be kept and accumulated. These types of activity systems are adequate for 'learning to cope.' They are not sufficient for anything like historical transformation. For this type of shift, there is required the building of social movements that express and develop the standpoint of the particular social group.

# References

Abel, E. (1984). *Terminal degrees: The job crisis in higher* education. New York: Praeger.

Abramowitz, M., and David, P. A. (1996). Technological change and the rise of intangible investments: The U.S. economy's growth part in the twentieth century. In *Employment and growth in the knowledge-based economy* (pp. 35–60). Paris: Organization for Economic Cooperation and Development.

Adler, P. S. (1990). Marx, machines and skill. *Technology and Culture*, 31(4), 780–812.

Adler, P. S. (1993). The learning bureaucracy: New united motors manufacturing, Inc. In B. M. Staw and L. L. Cummings (Eds.), *Research in organizational behavior, Vol. 15* (pp. 111–194). Greenwich, CT: JAI Press.

Adler, P. S. (1996). The dynamic relationship between tacit and codified knowledge: Comments on Nonaka's 'managing innovation as a knowledge creation process. In G. Pogorel and J. Allouche (Eds.), *International handbook of technology management* (pp. 110–124). Amsterdam: North-Holland.

Adler, P. S., and Borys, B. (1996). Two types of bureaucracy: Enabling and coercive, *Administrative Science Quarterly*, 41(1), 61–89.

Adler, P. S., Goldoftas, B., and Levine, D. I. (1997). Ergonomics, employee involvement, and the Toyota production system: A case study of NUMMI's 1993 model introduction. *Industrial and Labor Relations Review*, 50(3), 416–437.

Adler, P. S., Barbara Goldoftas, and Levine, D. I. (1998). Stability and change at NUMMI. In R. Boyer, E. Charron, U. Jürgens, and S. Tolliday (Eds.), *Between imitation and innovation: The transfer and hybridization of productive models in the international automobile industry* (pp. 128–160). New York: Oxford University Press.

Adler, P. S., Goldoftas, B., and Levine, D. I. (1999). Flexibility versus efficiency? A case study of model changeovers in the Toyota production system. *Organization Science*, 10(1), 43–68.

Adler, P. S. (2001, March–April). Market, hierarchy, and trust: The knowledge economy and the future of capitalism. *Organization Science*, 214–234.

Adler, P. S. (2003). *Practice and process: The socialization of software development.* Unpublished manuscript, University of Southern California.

Afonso, A. J. (2002). Políticas contemporâneas e avaliação educacional. In A. J. Afonso, and L. C. Lima (Eds.), *Reformas da educação pública: democratização, modernização, neoliberalismo* (pp. 111–127). Porto, Portugal: Afrontamento.

Agency for Healthcare Research and Quality (2005). *AHRQ Home.* http://www.ahcpr.gov

American Association of University Professors. (1999).*Graduate students today: Working for academic renewal; A kit for organizing on the issues of part-time and non-tenure track faculty; Faculty rights; AAUP guidelines to protect nontenured faculty rights* (pamphlets). AAUP: 1012 14th Street NW, Suite 500, Washington DC, 20005–3465.

American Association of University Professors. (2001). Uncertain times: The annual report on the economic status of the profession. *Academe* (April–May) 25–98.

American Federation of Teachers. (1994). *Part-time faculty issues.* Item #607. Washington, DC.

American Federation of Teachers. (1996). *Statement on part-time faculty employment.* Item # 640. Program and Policy Council Task Force on Part-Time Employment (L. Stollar, M. Hittleman, and K. Schermerhorn) AFT: 555 New Jersey Avenue, NW, Washington, DC 20001.

American Federation of Teachers/National Education Association. (1998). Shaping the profession that shapes the future. Speeches from the AFT/NEA Conference on Teacher Quality, (September 25–27) Washington, DC.

American Federation of Teachers. (1998). *The vanishing professor.* Item #587, (July) AFT Higher Education Department, AFT: 555 New Jersey Avenue, NW, Washington, DC 20001.

Anderson, K. (1999). Marx on suicide in the context of his other writings on alienation and gender. In E. Plaut and K. Anderson (Eds.), *Marx on suicide* (pp. 3–28). Evanston, IL: Northwestern.

Appadurai, A. (1986). Introduction: Commodities and the politics of value. In A. Appadurai (Ed.), *The social life of things: Commodities in cultural perspective* (pp. 3–63). Cambridge, UK: Cambridge University Press.

Arce, A. (2002). *A pedagogia na 'era das revoluções'; Uma análise do pensamento de Pestalozzi e Froebel.* São Paulo, Brazil: Editora Autores Associados.

Aronowitz, S. (1997). Academic unionism and the future of higher education. In C. Nelson (Ed.), *Will teach for food: Academic labor in crisis* (pp. 181–214). Minneapolis, MN: University of Minnesota Press.

Aronowitz, S. (2000). *The knowledge factory: Dismantling the corporate university and creating true higher learning.* Boston: Beacon.

Asmolov, A. G. (2001). *Psychology of personality; Principles of general-psychological analysis.* Moscow: Smysl.

Asmolov, A. G. (2002). *Beyond consciousness; Methodological problems of nonclassical psychology.* Moscow: Smysl.

Attewell, P. (1987). The deskilling controversy. *Work and occupations*, 14(3), 323–346.

Babson, S. (Ed.). (1995). *Lean work: Empowerment and exploitation in the global auto industry.* Detroit, MI: Wayne State University Press.

Bach, J. (1994) The immaturity of CMM. *American Programmer*, 7(9), available online at: http://www.satisfice.com/articles/cmm.htm.

Bach, J. (1995). Enough about process: What we need are heroes. *IEEE Software*, 12(2), 96–98.

Bandura, A. (1997). *Self-efficacy: The exercise of control.* New York: W. H. Freeman.

Barker, J. (1993). Tightening the iron cage: Concertive control in the self-managing organization. *Administrative Science Quarterly*, 38, 408–437.

Barker, K. (1998). Toiling for piece-rates and accumulating deficits: Contingent work in higher education. In K. Barker and K. Christensen (Eds.), *Contingent work: American employment relations in transition* (pp. 195–220). Ithaca, NY: IRL/Cornell University Press.

Barley, S. R. (1996). Technicians in the workplace: Ethnographic evidence for bringing work into organization studies. *Administrative Science Quarterly*, 41 (3), 404–441.

Barley, S. R., and Kunda, G. (2001). Bringing work back in. *Organization Science*, 12(1), 75–94.

Barton, P. E. (2000). *What jobs require: Literacy, education and training, 1940–2006.* Princeton, NJ: Educational Testing Service.

Beamish, R. (1992). *Marx, method, and the division of labor.* Champaign: University of Illinois Press.

Beck, C. (1994). Postmodernism, pedagogy, and philosophy of education. In Andrey Thompson (ed.) *Philosophy of education 1993* (pp. 1–13). Urbana, IL: Philosophy of Education Society.

Becker, A. L. (1995). *Beyond translation.* Ann Arbor, MI: University of Michigan Press.

Beirne, M., Ramsay, H., and Panteli, A. (1998). Developments in computing work: Control and contradiction in the software labour process. In P. Thompson and C. Warhusrt (Eds.), *Workplaces of the future* (pp. 142–162). London, Macmillan Business.

Bell, D. (1973). The coming of post-industrial society. New York: Basic Books.

Berg, I. (1970). *Education and jobs: The great training robbery.* London: Penguin.

Bernstein, B. (1990). *Class, codes and control, vol 4: The structuring of pedagogic discourse.* London: Routledge.

Bernstein, B. (1996). *Pedagogy, symbolic control and identity.* London: Taylor and Francis.

Berstein, R. J. (1990). Rorty's liberal utopia, *Social Research*, 57(1), 30–72.

Berstein, R. J. (1997). One step forward, two steps backward: Richard Rorty on liberal democracy and philosophy, *Political Theory*, 15(4), 538–563.

Berstein, R. J. (1998). *Beyond objectivism and relativism: Science, hermeneutics, and praxis.* Philadelphia: University of Pennsylvania Press.

Bertelsen, O., and Bödker, S. (Eds.). (2000). Information technology in human activity. *Scandinavian Journal of Information Systems*, 12, 3–14.

Bhaskar, R. (1986). *Scientific realism and human emancipation.* London; New York: Verso.

Bhaskar, R. (1989). *Reclaiming reality.* New York: London: Verso.

Bhaskar, R. (1991). *Philosophy and the idea of freedom.* Oxford, UK: Blackwell.

Blackler, F. (1993). Knowledge and the theory of organizations: Organizations as activity systems and the reframing of management, *Journal of Management Studies*, 30(6), 863–884.

Block, L. F., and Press, C. E. (1986). *Building market strength through DRGs.* Chicago: Pluribus Press.

Blonsky, P. (1928). The subject of psychology and psychopathology from a genetic standpoint. *Journal of Genetic Psychology*, 35, 356–373.

Bohman, J. (1999). Practical reason and cultural constraint: Agency in Bourdieu's theory of practice. In R. Shusterman (Ed.), *Bourdieu: A critical reader* (pp. 129–152). Malden, MA: Blackwell.

Bottomore, T. (1963). *Karl Marx: Early writings*. London: Watts.

Bottomore, T. (Ed.). (1983). *A dictionary of marxist thought.* Cambridge, MA: Harvard University Press.

Boud, D., and Garrick., J. (Eds.). (1999). *Understanding learning at work.* London: Routledge.

Bourdieu, P. (1984). *Distinction: A social critique of the judgement of taste.* Cambridge, MA: Harvard University Press.

Bourdieu, P. (1991). *Language and symbolic power.* London: Polity.

Bourdieu, P. (1993). *La misere du monde.* Paris: Seuil.

Bourdieu, P. (1998). *Practical Reason,* Stanford, CA: Stanford University Press.

Bourdieu, P., and Passeron, J. C. (1977 [1970]). *Reproduction in education, society and culture.* London: Sage.

Bowles, S., and Gintis, H. (1976). *Schooling in Capitalist America.* New York: Basic Books.

Braverman, H. (1974) *Labour and monopoly capital: The degradation of work in the twentieth century.* New York: Monthly Review Press

Brice-Heath, D. (1983). *Ways with words: Language, life and work in communities and classrooms.* Cambridge, UK: Cambridge University Press.

Brown, J. F. (1936). *Psychology and social order.* New York: McGraw-Hill.

Brown, J. F. (1938). Freud vs. Marx: Real and pseudo problems distinguished. *Psychiatry,* 1(2), 249–255.

Brown, M. (1986). *The production of society.* Lanham, Md.: Rowman and Littlefield.

Browne, A. (1937). Psychology and marxism. In D. Lewis (Ed.), *The mind in chains* (pp. 167–184). London: Fredereick Muller.

Burawoy, M. (1979). *Manufacturing consent.* Chicago: University of Chicago Press.

Burawoy, M. (1996). A classic in its time. *Contemporary Sociology,* 25(3), 296–299.

Calhoun, C., LiPuma, E., and Postone, M. (Eds.). (1993). *Bourdieu: Critical perspectives.* Cambridge, UK: Polity Press.

Callinicos, A. (1989). *Against postmodernism.* Cambridge, UK: Polity Press.

Callinicos, A. (1991). *The revenge of history.* Cambridge, UK: Polity Press.

Certeau, M. (1984). *The practice of everyday life.* Berkeley: University of California Press.

Chaiklin, S. (Ed.). (2001). *The theory and practice of cultural-historical psychology.* Åarhus, Denmark: Åarhus Unversity Press.

Chaiklin, S., Hedegaard, M., and Jensen, U. J. (Eds.). (1999). *Activity theory and social practice: Cultural historical approaches.* Åarhus, Denmark: Åarhus University Press.

Charlesworth, S. J. (2000). *A phenomenology of working class experience.* Cambridge, UK: Cambridge University Press.

Chase, B. (1998). *'New unionism' in higher education.* Speech to National Center for Collective Bargaining in Higher Education, Baruch College, New York, NY.

Cheney, G. (2002). *Values at work: Employee participation and market pressure at Mondragón.* Ithaca, NY: ILR Press.

Clark, B. (1999). *Effects of process maturity on development effort.* Unpublished paper, available at http://sunset.usc.edu/~bkclark/Research.

Cohen, G. A. (1978). *Karl Marx's theory of history: A defense.* Princeton, NJ: Princeton University Press.

Cohen, G. A. (1988). Human nature and social change in the Marxist conception of history, *The Journal of Philosophy*, 85(4), 171–191.

Cohen, J. (1982). Review of G. A. Cohen, Karl Marx's theory of history. *The Journal of Philosophy*, 79(5), 253–273.

Cole, P. (1907). *Herbart and Froebel; An attempt at synthesis.* New York: Teachers College/Columbia University.

Collins, J. (1993). Determination and contradiction: An appreciation and critique of the work of Pierre Bourdieu on language and education. In C. Calhoun (Ed.), *Bourdieu: Critical perspectives* (pp. 116–138). Chicago: University of Chicago Press.

Conn, R. (2002). Developing software engineers at the C-130J software factory, *IEEE Software* (September/October), 25–29.

Conradi, R., and Fuggetta, A. (2002). Improving software process improvement, *IEEE Software* (July–August), 92–99.

Courtney, S. (1992). *Why adults learn: Towards a theory of participation in adult education.* New York: Routledge.

Covaleski, M. A., Dirsmith, M. W., Heian, J. B., and Samuel, S. (1998). The calculated and the avowed: Techniques of discipline and struggles over identity in Big Six public accounting firms, *Administrative Science Quarterly*, 43(2), 293–327.

Critchley, S. (1998). Derrida: Ironista privado o liberal público? In: Mouffe, C. (org.) *Desconstrucción y pragmatismo*, Buenos Aires: Paidós.

Crocca, W. T. (1992). Review of Japan's Software Factories: A Challenge to U.S. Management. *Administrative Science Quarterly*, 37(4): 670–674.

Crosby, P. B. (1979). *Quality is free.* New York: McGraw-Hill.

Cuban, L. (1993). *How Teachers Taught* (2nd ed.). New York: Teachers College Press.

Cusumano, M. A. (1991). *Japan's software factories: A challenge to U.S. management.* New York: Oxford University Press.

Davydov, V. V. (1988). Problems of developmental teaching. *Soviet Education* 30(8), 15–97.

Davydov, V. V. (1991). The content and unsolved problems of activity theory. *Interdisciplinary Newsletter for Activity Theory*, 7/8, 30–35.

Davydov, V. V. (1993). The perspectives of activity theory. *Interdisciplinary Newsletter for Activity Theory* 13/14, 50–53.

Davydov, V. V. (1996). *Theory of developmental teaching.* Moscow: Intor.

Davydov, V. V. (1998). The last speeches. Riga: Experiment.

Davydov, V. V. (1999). A new approach to the interpretation of activity structure and content. In S. Chaiklin, M. Hedegaard, and U. J. Jensen (Eds.), *Activity theory and social practice* (pp. 39–50). Aarhus: Aarhus University Press.

De Geer, H. (1982). *Job studies and industrial relations: Ideas about efficiency and relations between the parties of the labour market in Sweden, 1920–1950.* Stockholm: Almqvist & Wiksell International.

DeMarco, T., and Lister, T. (1987). *Peopleware: Productive projects and teams.* New York: Dorset.

DeNora, T., and Mehan, H. (1993). Genius: A social construction. In J. Kitsuse and T. Sarbin (Eds.), *Constructing the social.* Los Angeles: Sage.

Dickens, C. (1844). *Hard times.* New York: W.W. Norton.

Dodge, S. (2001). Students, faculty heckle city colleges board. *Sun Times* (May 4) Chicago, 22.

Dreier, O. (1993). Re-searching psychotherapeutic practice. In S. Chaiklin and J. Lave (Eds.), *Understanding practice* (pp. 105–124). New York: Cambridge University Press.

Dreier, O. (1997). *Subjectivity and social practice.* Aarhus: Institut for Filosofi, Aarhus Universitet.

Dreier, O. (1999). Personal trajectories of participation across contexts of social practice. *Outlines* 1, 5–32.

Dreyfus, H., and Rabinow, P. (1999). Can there be a science of existential structure and social meaning? In R. Shusterman (Ed.), *Bourdieu: A critical reader* (pp. 84–93). Oxford, UK: Blackwell.

Duarte, N. (1993). *The individuality for itself: Contribution to a historic-social theory to the formation of the individual.* Campinas, Brazil: Autores Associados.

Duarte, N. (1996). *School education and theory of the everyday life and the Vygotsky school.* Campinas, Brazil: Autores Associados.

Duarte, N. (2000a). *Vygotsky and learning to learn: Critique of neo-liberal and post-modernist appropriations of Lev Vygotsky's theory.* Campinas, Brazil: Autores Associados.

Duarte, N. (2000b). Human anatomy contains a key to the anatomy of the ape; The Dialectics in Vygotskian and Marxian theory and the question on objective knowledge in schooling. *Revista educação e sociedade,* 71, 79–115. (Available in Portuguese: http://www.scielo.br)

Duarte, N. (Ed.). (2000c). *About constructivism: Contributions to a critical analisis.* Campinas, Brazil: Autores Associados.

Duarte, N. (2002a). *Vigotski e o 'aprender a aprender': críticas às apropriações neoliberais e pós-modernas da teoria vigotskiana* (2nd edition). Campinas, Brazil: Autores Associados.

Duarte, N. (2002b). Who is Vygotsky? Epistemological issues and implications for debates. *5th ISCRAT Conference – The International Society for Cultural Research and Activity Theory* (June 18–22), Free University Amsterdam, Holland.

Duarte, N. (2003a). Tacit knowledge and school knowledge in teachers' education – why Donald Schön didn't understand Luria. *Revista Educação e Sociedade,* 24(83), 601–625. (Available in Portuguese: http://www.scielo.br)

Duarte, N. (2003b). Knowledge Society or Society of Illusions? *Four critical dialectical essays in philosophy of education.* Campinas, Brazil: Autores Associados.

Duarte, N. (2003c). A teoria da atividade como uma abordagem para a pesquisa em educação [Activity Theory as an Approach to Educational Research]. *Perspectiva,* 21(2), 279–302.

Duayer, M. (2001). Marx, verdade e discurso. *Perspectiva.* Florianópolis, 19(1) (January–June), 15–39.

Duayer, M. (2003). *Ontologia na ciência econômica: realismo ou ceticismo instrumental?* UFF: Niterói. Unpublished manuscript.

Duayer, M., and Moraes, M. C. M. (1997a). A ética pragmática do neoconservadorismo: Richard Rorty. In L. M. Huhne (Org.), *Ética,* Rio de Janeiro, Brazil: Uapê.

Duayer, M., and Moraes, M. C. M. (1997b). Neopragmatismo: A história como contingência absoluta. *Tempo,* Revista do Departamento de História, UFF, 2(4) (December), 27–48.

Dubson, M. (2001). *Ghosts in the classroom: Stories of college adjunct faculty and the price we all pay.* Boston: Camel's Back Books.

Eagleton, T. (1991). *Ideology.* New York: Verso.

Eagleton, T. (1999). Utopia and its opposites. In L. Panish and C. Leys (Eds.), *Necessary and unnecessary Utopias, Socialist Register.* London: Merlin Press.

Eagleton, T. (2003). *After theory.* London: Penguin Books.

Eckert, P. (1989). *Jocks and Burnouts Social Categories and Identity in High School.* New York: Teachers College Press.

Elhammoumi, M. (2000). *Lev Vygotsky: The Feuerbach of marxist psychology.* Unpublished manuscript.

Elhammoumi, M. (2001a). Lost – or merely domesticated? The boom in socio-historico-cultural theory emphasizes some concepts, overlooks others. In S. Chaiklin (Ed.), *The theory and practice of cultural-historical psychology* (pp. 200–217). Åarhus, Denmark: Åarhus University Press.

Elhammoumi, M. (2001b). The reception of Lev Vygotsky in South America: A fertile terrain for a materialist psychology. In M. Golder (Ed.), *Vygotsky: A radical psychologist* (pp. 51–66). Buenos Aires, Argentina: Ateneo Vigotskiano de la Argentina.

Elhammoumi, M. (2002). To create psychology's own capital. *Journal for the Theory of Social Behaviour,* 32(1), 89–104.

Elhammoumi, M. (2004). Is 'back to Vygotsky' enough? The legacy of socio-historico-cultural psychology. *Historical materialism: Research in critical marxist theory.* 12(3), 32–51.

Elias, N. (2000). *The civilizing process.* Malden, MA: Blackwell.

Elkonin, D. B. (1998). *Psicologia do jogo.* São Paulo: Martins Fontes.

Elkonin, D. B. (2000). *Toward the problem of stages in the mental development of children.* Available online at: www.marxist.org

Engels, F. (1890/1978). "Letter to Joseph Bloch." In H. Selsam and H. Martel (Eds.), Reade in Marxist Philosphy (pp. 204–206). New York: International Publishers.

Engels, F. (1978). Socialism: Utopian and scientific. In R. C. Tucker (Ed.), *The Marx Engels reader* (2nd ed.; pp. 683–717). New York: Norton.

Engeström, Y. (1987). *Learning by expanding: An activity-theoretical approach to developmental research.* Helsinki, Finland: Orienta-Konsultit.

Engeström, Y. (1990). *Learning, working and imagining: Twelve studies in activity theory.* Helsinki, Finland: Orienta-Konsultit.

Engeström, Y. (1996). Interobjectivity, ideality, and dialectics. *Mind, Culture, and Activity,* 3, 259–265.

Engeström, Y. (1999a). Activity theory and individual and social transformation. In Y. Engeström, R. Miettinen, and R.-L. Punamäki (Eds.), *Perspectives on activity theory* (pp. 19–38). New York: Cambridge University Press.

Engeström, Y (1999b). Innovative learning in work teams: Analyzing cycles of knowledge creation in practice. In Y. Engeström, R. Miettinen, and R.-L., Punamäki (Eds.), *Perspectives on activity theory* (pp. 377–404). Cambridge, UK: Cambridge University Press.

Engeström, Y. (2000). From individual action to collective activity and back: Developmental work research as an interventionist methodology. In P. Luff, J. Hindmarsh and C. Heath (Eds.), *Workplace studies: Recovering work practice and informing system design* (pp. 150–166). New York: Cambridge University Press.

Engeström, Y. (2001). Expansive learning at work: Toward an activity theoretical reconceptualization. *Journal of Education and Work,* 14(1), 133–156.

Engeström, Y., Miettinen, R. and Punamäki, R.-L. (Eds.). (1999). *Perspectives on activity theory*. New York: Cambridge University Press.

Engeström, Y., Toiviainen, H., Pasanen, A., and Haavisto, V. (2004). *Collaborative concept formation at work*. Paper presented at the Academy of Management Meeting, New Orleans, August 6–11.

Engeström, Y., Virkkunen, J., Helle, M., Pihlaja, J., and Poikela, R. (1996). Change laboratory as a tool for transforming work. *Lifelong Learning in Europe*, 1(2), 10–17.

Evangelista, O., and Shiroma, E. O. (2003). Um Fantasma ronda o professor: a mistica da Competência. In M. C. M. Moraes (org.), Iluminismo às avessas: Produção de Conhecimento e politicas de Formação docente (pp. 81–98). Rio de Janeiro: DP&A.

Ezzamel, M., and Willmott, H. (1998). Accounting for teamwork: A critical study of group-based systems of organizational control. *Administrative Science Quarterly*, 43(2), 358–396.

Fenichel, O. (1934/1967). Psychoanalysis as the nucleus of a future dialectical materialistic psychology. *American Imago*, 24, 290–311.

Ferrière, A. (1927). *The activity school*. New York: The John Day Company.

Fichtner, B. (1999). Activity theory as methodology: The epistemological revolution of the computer and the problem of its societal appropriation. In M. Hedegaard and J. Lompscher (Eds.), *Learning activity and development* (pp. 71–92). Åarhus, Denmark: Åarhus University Press.

Flores, A. (1938). Psychology and marxism: A bibliography. *Dialectics*, 4, 21–24.

Foot, K. A. (2002). Pursuing an evolving object: Object formation and identification in a conflict monitoring network. *Mind, Culture and Activity*, 9 (2), 132–149.

Form, W. (1987). On the degradation of skills. *Annual Review of Sociology*, 13, 29–47.

Fowler, B. (1997). *Pierre Bourdieu and cultural theory*. London: Sage.

Foucault, M. (1975/1977). *Discipline and punish*. New York: Vintage.

Fraser, S. (1991). *Labor will rule: Sidney Hillman and the rise of American labor*. New York: Free Press.

Freedman, B. (1939). Psycho-social repression and social-rationalization. *American Journal of Orthopsychiatry*, 9(1), 109–122.

Freedman, B. (1940). Amplifications of marxist psychoanalysis. *American Journal of Orthopsychiatry*, 10(2), 351–354.

Freidson, E. (2001). *Professionalism: The third logic*. Cambridge, UK: Polity.

Freire, P. (1969). *Pedagogy of the oppressed*. New York: Continuum.

Freire, P (1970). *Pedagogy of the oppressed*. New York: Herder and Herder.

Freire, P. (1992). *Pedagogy of the oppressed*. New York: Continuum Publishing.

Friedman, A. L., and Cornford, D. S. (1989). *Computer systems development: History, organization and implementation*. Chichester: John Wiley & Sons.

Froebel, F. (1887). *The education of man*. New York: D. Appleton.

Froebel, F. (1895). *The mottoes and commentaries of Friedrich Froebel's mother play*. New York: D. Appleton.

Froebel, F. (1917). *Pedagogics of the kindergarten*. New York: D. Appleton.

Fujimura, J. (1996). *Crafting science*. Cambridge, MA: Harvard University Press.

Fukuyama, F. (1992). *The end of history and the last man*. New York: Free Press.

Gappa, J. M., and David W. Leslie (1993). *The invisible faculty: Improving the status of part-timers in higher education*. San Francisco: Jossey-Bass.

Geist, P., and Hardesty, M. (1992). *Negotiating the crisis: DRG and the transformation of hospitals.* Hillsdale, NJ: Lawrence Erlbaum.

Geras, N. (1995). Language, truth and justice. *New Left Review,* 209 (January/February), 110–135.

Gibbs, G. G. (1994). Software's chronic crisis. *Scientific American* (September), 86–92.

Gibson, C. D., and Earley, P. C. (n.d.). *Work-team performance motivated by collective thought: The structure and function of group efficacy.* Unpublished manuscript, University of Southern California.

Gielen, U. P., and Jeshmaridian, S. S. (1999). Lev S. Vygotsky: The man and the era. *International Journal of Group Tensions,* 28(3/4), 273–301.

Giest, H. (2001). Education and media. *Paedagogica Pannonia,* 3, 7–46.

Goldin, C., and Katz, L. F. (1998). The origins of technology-skill complementarity. *Quarterly Journal of Economics,* 113(3), 693–732.

Goldin, C., and Katz, L. F. (1999). The returns to skill in the United States across the twentieth century. (Working Paper #7126). Washington, DC: National Bureau of Economic Research.

Gouldner, A. W. (1957). Cosmopolitans and locals: Toward an analysis of latent social roles, *Administrative Science Quarterly,* 2(3), 281–306.

Graeber, D. (2001). *Toward an anthropological theory of value: The false coin of our dreams.* New York: Palgrave.

Graham, L. R. (1972). *Science and philosophy in the Soviet Union.* New York: Knopf.

Gramsci, A. (1978). *Selections from the prison notebooks* (5th edition). New York: International Publishers.

Gramsci, A. (1994). Socialism and culture. In R. Bellamy (Ed.), *Antonio Gramsci: Pre-prison writings* (pp. 8–12). Cambridge, UK: Cambridge University Press.

Greenbaum, J. M. (1979). *In the name of efficiency.* Philadelphia: Temple University Press.

Greenbaum, J. M. (1998). The times they are a' changing: Dividing and recombining labour through computer systems. In P. Thompson and C. Warhusrt (Eds.), *Workplaces of the future* (pp. 124–141). London: Macmillan Business.

Griss, M. L. (1993). Software reuse: From library to factory. *IBM Systems Journal,* 32(4), 548–566.

Grubb, N. and Associates. (1999). *Honored but invisible: An inside look at teaching in community colleges.* New York: Routledge.

Grugulis, I., Willmott, H., and Knights, D. (2001). Special issue on the Labor Process Debate, *International Studies of Management and Organization,* 30(4) (entire issue).

Haack, S. (1997). *Evidencia e investigación, hacia la reconstrucción en epistemologia,* Madrid: Editorial Tecnos.

Hall, S. (1973). *A 'reading' of Marx's 1857 introduction to the grundrisse.* (Working Paper #1). Birmingham, U.K.: University of Birmingham, Center for Contemporary Culture Studies.

Handel, M. (2000). *Trends in direct measures of job skill requirements.* (Working Paper #301). Blithewood, NY: Jerome Levy Economics Institute.

Harter, D. E., Krishnan, M. S., and Slaughter, S. A. (2000). *Effects of process maturity on quality, cycle time, and effort in software development. Management Science,* 46(4), 451–466.

Hatcher, R. (2000). Social class and school: Relationships to knowledge. In M. Cole (Ed.), *Education, equality and human rights: Issues of race, sexuality, special needs and social class* (pp. 182–200). London: Falmer.

Haug, W. F. (2003). *High-tech capitalism; Analyses concerning mode of production, work, sexuality, war and hegemony*. Hamburg: Argument.

Hautamaeki, A. (1986). Activity environment, social class and educational career: development of mastery among 11–17-year-olds. *Scandinavian Journal of Educational Research*, 30(1), 1–16.

Häyrynen, Y.-P. (1999). "Collapse, Creation, and Continuity in Europe: How do People Change." In Y. Engeström, R. Miettinen, and R.-L. Punamäki (Eds.), *Perspectives on Activity Theory* (pp. 115–132). New York: Cambridge University Press.

Heaney, S. (2000). *Beowulf*. New York: Farrer, Straus and Giroux.

Hedegaard, M., and Lompscher, J. (Eds.). (1999). *Learning activity and development*. Åarhus, Denmark: Åarhus University Press.

Hedlund, G. (1994). A model of knowledge management and the n-form organization, *Strategic Management Journal*, 15, 73–90.

Heller, Á. (1984). *Everyday life*. London: Routledge & Kegan Paul.

Henderson, M., and Thompson, D. (2003). *Values at work: The invisible threads between people. Performance and profit*. Auckland, New Zealand: HarperCollins.

Herbsleb, J., Zubrow, D., Goldenson, D., Hayes, W., and Paulk, M. (1997). Software quality and the capability maturity model. *Communication of the ACM*, 40(6), 30–40.

Hewitt, P. (1993). *About time: The revolution in work and family life*. London: Rivers Oram Press.

Hirsch, W., and Luc, W. (1999). *Challenges facing higher education at the millennium*. Phoenix, AZ: Onyx Press and the American Council on Higher Education.

Hirschhorn, L. (1984). *Beyond mechanization*. Cambridge, MA: MIT Press.

Holt, G. R., and Morris, A. W. (1993). Activity theory and the analysis of organizations. *Human Organization*, 52(1), 97–109.

Holzkamp, K. (1991). Psychoanalysis and marxist psychology. In C. Tolman and W. Maiers (Eds.), *Critical psychology: Contributions to an historical science of the subject* (pp. 81–101). Cambridge, UK: Cambridge University Press.

Holzkamp, K. (1992). On doing psychology critically. *Theory & Psychology*, 2, 193–204.

Huarte, J. (1575/1946). *Examen de ingenios para las ciencias*. Buenos Aires: Esapsa-Calpe Argentina.

Humphrey, W. S. (2002). Three process perspectives: Organizations, teams, and people. *Annals of software engineering*, 14, 39–72.

Hyman, R. (1987). *Strategy or structure? Capital, labour and control, work, employment and society*, 1(1), 25–55.

Illich, I. (1971). *Deschooling society*. New York: Harper and Row.

Ilyenkov, E. V. (1974). *Dialectical logic, essays on its history and theory*. Moscow: Progress Publishers.

Ilyenkov, E. V. (1977). The concept of the ideal. In *Problems of dialectical materialism* (pp. 71–98). Moscow: Progress Publishers.

Ilyenkov, E. V. (1979). *Leninist dialectics and the metaphysics of positivism*. London: New Park Publications.

Ilyenkov, E. V. (1982). *The dialectics of the abstract and the concrete in Marx's capital.* Moscow: Progress Publishers.

Jacoby, S. M. (1983). Union-management cooperation in the United States: Lessons from the 1920s. *Industrial and Labor Relations Review, 37,* 18–33.

Jermier, J. M. (1998). Critical perspectives on organizational control. *Administrative Science Quarterly, 43*(2), 235–256.

Jones, P. (2002). The word becoming a deed: The dialectic of 'free action' in Vygotsky's tool and sign in the development of the child. In D. Robbins and A. Stetsenko (Eds.), *Voices within Vygotsky's non-classical psychology: Past, present, future* (pp. 143–160). New York: Nova Science Publishers.

Kagitcibasi, C. (1997). Individualism and collectivism. In J. W. Berry, M. H. Segall, and C. Kagitcibasi (Eds.), *Handbook of cross-cultural psychology* (pp. 1–49). Needham Heights, MA: Allyn & Bacon.

Kanigel, R. (1997). *The one best way: Frederick Winslow Taylor and the enigma of efficiency.* New York: Viking.

Kaptelinin, V. (1996). Activity theory: Implications for human-computer interaction. In B. A. Nardi (Ed.), *Context and consciousness: Activity theory and human-computer interaction* (pp. 103–115). Cambridge, MA: MIT Press.

Kaptelinin, V. (2003). UMEA: Translating interaction histories into project contexts. *Proceedings of the CHJ'95 Conference on Human Factors in Computimg Sciences,* Fort Lauderdale, Florida.

Kelly, J. E. (1982). *Scientific management, job redesign and work performance.* London: Academic Press.

Kenney, M., and Florida, R. (1993). *Beyond mass production: The Japanese system and its transfer to the U.S.* New York: Oxford University Press.

Kerchner, C. T. (1999). Knowledge workers: Trade unionism's new frontier. *Thought and Action.* (Fall), 11–17.

Kerchner, C. T., and Koppich, J. E. (1993). *A union of professionals: Labor relations and educational reform.* New York: Teachers College Press.

Kerchner, C. T., Koppich, J. E., and Weeres, J. (1997). *United mind workers: Unions and teaching in the knowledge society.* San Francisco: Jossey-Bass.

Kerchner, C. T., and Mitchell, D. E. (1988). *The changing idea of a teachers' union.* New York: The Falmer Press.

Kern, M., and Schumann, M. (1984). The *end of the division of labour?* Munich: C. H. Beck.

Knights, D., and Willmott, H. (1989). Power and subjectivity at work: From degradation to subjugation in social relations. *Sociology, 23,* 535–558.

Koch, D. (1982). Friedrich Froebel, o criador do Jardim de Infância, no seu bicentenário. *Convivium, 25,* 45–63.

Koch, D. (1985). *Desafios da educação infantil.* São Paulo: Loyola.

Kohn, M. L., and Schooler, C. (1983). *Work and personality.* Norwood, NJ: Ablex.

Kopytoff, I. (1986). The cultural biography of things: Commoditization as process. In A. Appadurai (Ed.), *The social life of things: Commodities in cultural perspective* (pp. 64–91). Cambridge, UK: Cambridge University Press.

Kornilov, K. N. (1930). Psychology in the light of dialectic materialism. In C. Murchison (Ed.), *Psychologies of 1930* (pp. 243–278). Worcester, MA: Clark University Press.

Kozol, J. (1991). *Savage inequalities: Children in America's schools*. New York: Crown.

Kozulin, A, Gindis, B., Ageyev, V., and Miller, S. (Eds.). (2003). *Vygotsky's educational theory in cultural context*. New York: Cambridge University Press.

Kraft, P. (1977). *Programmers and managers: The routinization of computer programming in the United States*. New York: Springer Verlag.

Krishnan, M. S., Kriebel, C. H., Kekre, S., and Mukhopadhyay, T. (2000). Productivity and quality in software products, *Management Science*, 46(6), 745–759.

Kunz, R. (1999). A espera dos escravos globais, *Folha de S. Paulo*, Caderno Mais!, June 13, http://www1.folha.uol.com.br/fsp/mais/Fs13069912.htm

Labov, W. (1966). *The social stratification of English in New York City*. Washington, DC: Center for Applied Linguistics.

Labov, W. (2001). *Principles of linguistic change Volume 2: Social factors*. Oxford: Blackwell.

Labriola, A. (1908). *Essays on the materialistic conception of history*. Chicago: Charles H. Kerr Publishing.

Lakatos, I. (1970). "Falsification and the Methodology of Scientific Research Programmes." In I. Lakatos and A. Musgrave (Eds.), *Criticism and the Growth of Knowledge* (pp. 91–198). New York: Cambridge University Press.

Latour, B. (1987). *Science in action*. Cambridge, MA: Harvard University Press.

Latour, B. (1988). *Pasteurization of France*. Cambridge, MA: Harvard University Press.

Latour, B. (1996). On interobjectivity. *Mind, Culture, and Activity*, 3, 228–245.

Lave, J. (1988). *Cognition in practice*. New York: Cambridge University Press.

Lave, J. (1988). *Cognition in practice*. Cambridge, UK: Cambridge University Press.

Lave, J. (1993). Introduction. In S. Chaiklin and J. Lave (Eds.), *Understanding practice* (pp. 3–34). New York: Cambridge University Press.

Lave, J. (1998). Teaching as learning, in practice. *Mind, Culture, and Activity*, 3, 149–164.

Lave, J., and Wenger, E. (1991). *Situated learning*. New York: Cambridge University Press.

Lavoie, M., and Roy, R. (1998). *Employment in the knowledge-based economy: A growth accounting exercise for Canada* (Research Paper R-98-8E). Ottawa, Canada: Applied Research Branch, Human Resources Development Canada.

Leckie, N. (1996). *On skill requirements trends in Canada, 1971–1991*. Ottawa, Canada: Human Resources Development Canada and Canadian Policy Research Networks.

Lefebvre, H. (1987). The everyday and everydayness. *Yale French Studies*, 73, 7–11.

Lefebvre, H. (1988). Towards a leftist cultural politics. In C. Nelson and L. Grossber (Eds.), *Marxism and the interpretation of culture* (pp. 75–88). Chicago: University of Illinois Press.

Lenin, V. I. (1908/1927). *Materialism and empirio-criticism: Critical notes concerning a reactionary philosophy*. New York: International Publishers.

Leontyev, A. A. (1997). *Fundaments of psycholinguistics*. Moscow: Smysl.

Leontyev, A. A. (1999). *Psychology of (social) exchange*. Moscow: Smysl.

Leontyev, A. A. (2001a). *The active mind*. Moscow: Smysl

Leontyev, A. A. (2001b). *Language and speech activity in general and educational psychology*. Moscow: Rossijskaja Akademija Obrazovanija.

Leontyev, A. A. (2003). *Educational system 'School 2100'; Pedagogics of healthy sense*. Moscow: Izdatel'skij Dom RAO.

Leontyev, A. A., and Leontyev, D. A. (2003). The myth about breakage: A. N. Leontyev and L. S. Vygotsky in 1932. *Psikhologicheskij zhurnal,* 24(1), 14–22.

Leont'ev, A. N. (1974). The problem of activity in psychology, *Soviet Psychology,* 13(2), 4–33.

Leont'ev, A. N. (1978). *Activity, consciousness, and personality.* Englewood Cliffs, NJ: Prentice Hall.

Leontyev, A. N. (1981). *Problems of the development of the mind.* Moscow: Progress Publishers.

Leontyev. A. N. (1994). The problem of activity in the history of development of Soviet psychology. *Philosophy of Psychology* (pp. 263–277). Moscow: Izdatel'stvo Moskovskogo universiteta.

Leontyev, A. N., and Zaporozhets, A. V. (1946). *Vosstanovlenie dvizhenij* [Rehabilitation of movements]. Moscow: Medicina.

Leontyev, D. A. (1999). *Psychology of sense.* Moscow: Smysl.

Leopoldo, E., and Silva, F. (1996). Ética e razão, In A. Novaes (Org.), *A crise da razão,* Sao Paulo, Brazil: Cia. Das Letras, Ministry da Cultura, Nacional de Arte.

Levine, A., and Wright, E. (1980). Rationality and class struggle. *New Left Review,* 123, 47–68.

Lieberman, H., and Fry, C. (2001). Will software ever work? *Communications of the ACM,* 44(3), 122–124.

Liebschner, J. (1992). *A child's work; Freedom and guidance in Froebel's educational theory and practice.* Cambridge, UK: Lutterworth Press.

Livingstone, D. W. (1995). Searching for missing links: Neo-marxist theories of education. *British Journal of the Sociology of Education,* 16(1), 53–73.

Livingstone, D. W. (1999). *The education-jobs gap: Underemployment or economic democracy.* Toronto: Garamond Press.

Livingstone, D. W. (2001). *Working and learning in the information age: A profile of Canadians.* Ottawa, Canada: Canadian Policy Research Networks.

Livingstone, D. W. (2002). Working class learning, cultural transformation and democratic political education: Gramsci's legacy. In C. Borg, J. Buttigieg, and P. Mayo (Eds.), *Gramsci and education* (pp. 219–240). Lanham, MD: Rowman and Littlefield.

Livingstone, D. W., and Mangan, J. M. (Eds.). (1996). *Recast dreams: Class and gender consciousness in Steeltown.* Toronto: Garamond.

Livingstone, D. W., and Sawchuk, P. H. (2000). Beyond cultural capital theory: Hidden dimensions of working class learning. *Review of Education, Pedagogy and Cultural Studies,* 22(2), 203–224.

Livingstone, D. W., and Sawchuk, P. H. (2004). *Hidden knowledge: Organized labour in the information age.* Toronto: Garamond Press.

Lobkowicz, N. (1967). *Theory and practice: History of a concept from Aristotle to Marx.* Lanham, MD: University Press of America.

Lompscher, J. (1994). Luria's contributions to developmental psychology. In W. Jantzen (Ed.), *Neuronal connections of the consciousness; On the topicality of Luria's neuropsychology* (pp. 61–88). Münster/Hamburg, Germany: Lit.

Lompscher, J. (2002). The category of activity as a principal constituent of cultural-historical psychology. In D. Robbins and A. Stetsenko (Eds.), *Voices within Vygotsky's non-classical psychology. Past, present, future* (pp. 79–99). New York: Nova Science Publishers.

Lompscher, J. (2004). *Learning culture of competence development from a cultural-historical point of view; Adult learning in the process of labor.* Berlin: Lehmanns Media LOB.

Lowe, G. (2000). *The quality of work.* New York: Oxford University Press.

Lukács, G. (1968). *History and class consciousness.* London: Merlin Press.

Lukács, G. (1980). *The ontology of social being: Labour.* London: Merlin Press.

Lukács, G. (1982). *Estética 1 – La peculiaridad de lo estético,* 4 vol. Barcelona, Spain: Grijalbo.

Luria, A. (1976). *Cognitive development: Its cultural and social foundations.* New York: Cambridge University Press.

Luria A. R. (1979). *The making of mind: A personal account of Soviet psychology.* Cambridge, MA: Harvard University Press.

Lynn, L. H. (1991). Japan's software factories (book review), *Sloan Management Review,* 32, 88–90.

MacKinnon, C. (1982). Feminism, marxism, method, and the state: An agenda for theory. *Signs,* 7, 515–44.

Maddison, A. (1982). *Phases of capitalist development.* Oxford, UK: Oxford University Press.

Mallet, S. (1975). *Essays on the new working class.* St. Louis, MO: Telos Press.

Mankkinen, T. (2002). *The historical construction of firefighters' activity.* Unpublished seminar paper. Helsinki: Center for Activity Theory and Developmental Work Research (in Finnish).

Markus, G. (1978). *Marxism and anthropology; The concept of 'human essence' in the philosophy of Marx.* Assen, The Netherlands: Van Gorcum.

Markus, H. R., and Kitayama, S. (1991). Culture and the self: implications for cognition, emotion and motivation, *Psychological Review,* 98, 224–253.

Martin, R. (Ed.). (1998). *Chalk lines: The politics of work in the managed university.* Durham, NC: Duke University Press.

Marx, K. (1844/1964). *The economic and philosophical manuscripts of 1844.* New York: International.

Marx, K. (1844/1964). Estranged labor. In *Marx Karl, The economic and philosophical manuscripts of 1844* (pp. 106–119). New York: International.

Marx, K. (1844/1963). *Karl Marx: Early writings.* New York: McGraw-Hill.

Marx, K. (1844/1975). *Karl Marx: Early writings.* New York: Vintage.

Marx, K. (1992). *Early writings.* London: Penguin Books.

Marx, K. (1845/1999). Peuchet on suicide. In E. Plaut and K. Anderson (Eds.), *Marx on suicide* (pp. 43–75). Evanston, IL: Northwestern University Press.

Marx, K. (1847/1995). *The Poverty of philosophy.* Amherst, NY: Prometheus Books.

Marx, K. (1857/1970). Appendix: Production, consumption, distribution, exchange (circulation). *A Contribution to the critique of political economy.* New York: International.

Marx, K. (1857–1858/1973). *Grundrisse.* New York: Penguin.

Marx, K. (1859/1900). *A contribution to the critique of political economy.* New York: International.

Marx, K. (1959). Theses on Feuerbach. In L. S. Feuer (Ed.), *Basic writings on politics and philosophy, Karl Marx and Friedrich Engels* (pp. 243–245). Garden City, NY: Anchor Books.

Marx, K. (1971a). *Psychology and marxism.* Paris: Union Générale d'Editions.

Marx, K. (1859/1971b). A *contribution to a critique of political economy*. Moscow: Progress Publishers.

Marx, K. (1860/2000). *Theories of surplus value*. Amherst, NY: Prometheus Books.

Marx, K. (1867/1986). *Capital, Volume I*. New York: Penguin.

Marx, K. (1881–1882/1972). *The ethnological notebooks of Karl Marx*. Assen, The Netherlands: Assen, van Gorcum & Comp.

Marx. K. (1977). *Capital. Volume 1*. New York: Vintage.

Marx, K. (1993). *Grundrisse foundations of the critique of the political economy*. London: Penguin Books.

Marx, K., and Engels, F. (1959). The communist manifesto. In L. S. Feuer, (Ed.), *Marx and Engels: Basic writings on politics and philosophy* (pp. 1–41). New York: Anchor.

Marx, K., and Engels, F. (1975). *Marx/Engels collected works, Volume 5*. Moscow: Progress.

Marx, K., and Engels, F. (1975). *The German Ideology*. New York: Lawrence and Wishart.

Mathews, J. A. (1994). *Catching the wave: Workplace reform in Australia*. Ithaca, NY: ILR Press.

McDermott, R. (1988). Inarticulateness. In. D. Tannen (Ed.), *Linguistics in context* (pp. 37–68). Norwood, NJ: Ablex.

McDermott, R. (1993). Acquisition of a child by a learning disability. In S. Chaiklin and J. Lave (Eds.), *Understanding practice* (pp. 269–305). New York: Cambridge University Press.

McDermott, R. (1997). Achieving school failure, 1972–1997. In G. Spindler (Ed.), *Education and cultural process* (pp. 110–135). Prospect Heights: Waveland Press.

Mead, M. (1943). Our educational emphases in primitive perspective. *American Journal of Sociology*, 48, 633–639.

Mehan, H. (1993). Beneath the skin and between the ears. In S. Chaiklin and J. Lave (Eds.), *Understanding practice* (pp. 241–268). New York: Cambridge University Press.

Menzies, H. (1996). *Whose brave new world? The information highway and the new economy*. Toronto: Between the Lines Press.

Mészàros, I. (1995). *Beyond capital*, London: Merlin Press.

Meyer, J. W., and Rowan, B. (1977). Institutionalized organizations: Formal structure as myth and ceremony, *American Journal of Sociology*, 83, 340–363.

Miettinen, R. (1999). Transcending traditional school learning. In: Engestrom, Y., Miettinen, R., and Punamaki, R. (Eds.), *Perspectives on activity theory* (pp. 325–344). New York: Cambridge University Press.

Mishel, L., Bernstein, J., and Boushey, H. (2003). *The state of working America 2002/2003*. Ithaca, NY: Cornell University Press.

Mizrahi, T. (1986). *Getting rid of patients: Contradictions in the socialization of physicians*. New Brunswick, NJ: Rutgers University Press.

Moll, L. (Ed.). (1990). *Vygotsky and education*. Cambridge, UK: Cambridge University Press.

Montgomery, D. (1987). *The fall of the house of labor: The workplace, the state, and American labor activism, 1865–1925*. Cambridge, UK: Cambridge University Press.

Montague, J. (1984). *The dead kingdom*. Winston-Salem, NC: Wake Forest University Press.

Moraes, M. C. M. (1996). Os 'pós-ismos' e outras querelas ideológicas, *Perspectiva*, Florianópolis: NUP/CED/Editora da UFSC, 16(25), 45–69.

Moraes, M. C. M. (2001). *O recuo da teoria. Revista Portuguesa de Educação*. Braga, Pt.: Universidade do Minho, Centro de Educação e Psicologia, 14(1), 7–25.

Moraes, M. C. M. (2003). Ceticismo epistemológico, ironia complacente: considerações acerca do neopragmatismo de Richard Rorty. In M. C. M. Moraes (org.), *Iluminismo as avessas: produção de conhecimento e políticas de formação docente* (pp. 34–52). Rio de Janeiro, Brazil: DP&A.

Moraes, M. C. M., and Muller, R. G. (2003). História e experiência: contribuições de E. P. Thompson à pesquisa em educação. *Perspectiva*. Revista de Educação do CED/UFSC, 21(2), 329–349.

Moser, R. (1999). The new academic labor system and the new academic citizenship. *Radical Historian Newsletter*, 80, 1.

Mouffe, C. (2000). Rorty's Pragmatist Politics. *Economy & Society*, 29(3), 439–453.

Murray, P. (Ed.). (1988). *Genius: The history of an idea*. New York: Basil Blackwell.

National Education Association. (1986–1987). *Report and recommendations on part-time, temporary and nontenure track faculty appointments*. Standing Committee Report. NEA: Office of Higher Education, Washington, DC.

National Education Association. (1999). *The NEA 1999 almanac of higher education*. NEA: Office of Higher Education, 1201 16th Street NW, Washington, DC 20036.

National Education Association. (2001). *The NEA Almanac of higher education*. National Education Association: Washington, DC.

National Center for Education Statistics. (1998). *Fall staff in postsecondary institutions 1995*. US Department of Education Office of Educational Research and Improvement: Washington DC.

Naville, P. (1946). Psychologie, Marxisme, Matérialisme: Essai Critique. Paris: Marcel Rivière.

Negt, O., and Kluge, A. (1993). *Public sphere and experience: Toward an analysis of the bourgeois and proletarian public sphere*. Minneapolis: University of Minnesota Press.

Nelson, C. (Ed.). (1997). *Will teach for food: Academic labor in crisis*, Minneapolis: University of Minnesota Press.

Nelson, C., and Watt, S. (1999). *Academic keywords: A devil's dictionary for higher education*. New York: Routledge.

Nelson, D. (1980). *Frederick W. Taylor and the rise of scientific management*. Madison: University of Wisconsin Press.

Nelson, D. (Ed.). (1992). *A mental revolution: Scientific management since Taylor*. Columbus: Ohio State University Press.

Ngwenyam, O., and Nielson, P. A. (2003). Competing values in software process improvement: An assumption analysis of CMM from an organizational culture perspective. *IEEE Transactions on Engineering Management*, 50(1), 100–112.

Noble, D. (1986). *Forces of Production: A Social History of Industrial Automation*. New York: Oxford University Press.

Norris C. (1993) *The contest of faculties*. New York: Methuen.

Norris, C. (1995). Truth, science, and the growth of knowledge. *New Left Review*, 210, 105–123

Norris, C. (1996). *Reclaiming truth*, Durham, NC: Duke University Press.

Norris, C. (1997). *Against relativism*. Oxford, UK: Blackwell.

Norris, C. (2000). Treading water in neurath's ship: Quine, Davidson, Rorty. *Minding the gap*. Amherst: University of Massachusetts Press.

Nyland, C. (1998). Taylorism and the mutual gains strategy. *Industrial Relations*, 37(4), 519–542.

Ollman, B. (1976). *Alienation*. (2nd edition) New York: Cambridge University Press.

Ollman, B. (1993). *Dialectical investigations*. New York: Routledge.

Organization for Economic Cooperation and Development. (2004). Policy brief on lifelong learning, *OECD Observer*, (February) Paris: OECD.

Osborne, R. (1937). *Freud and Marx: A dialectical study*. New York: Equinox Co-operative Press.

Osborn, D. K. (1991). *Early childhood in historical perspective*. (3rd edition) Athens, GA: Day and Press Education Associates.

Packer, M. (2001). *Changing classes: School reform and the new economy*. Cambridge, UK: Cambridge University Press.

Panofsky, C. P. (2003). The relations of learning and student social class: Toward re-'socializing' sociocultural learning theory. In A. Kozulin and B. Gindis (Eds.), *Vygotsky's educational theory in cultural context. Learning in doing* (pp. 411–431). New York: Cambridge University Press.

Pearl, A. (1997). Democratic education as an alternative to deficit thinking. In R. Valencia (Ed.), *The evolution of deficit thinking* (pp. 160–210). London: Falmer Press.

Piore, M. J., and Sabel, C. J. (1984). *The second industrial divide: Possibilities for prosperity*. New York: Basic Books.

Politzer, G. (1928). *Critique of the foundations of psychology*. Paris: Editions Sociales.

Politzer, G. (1969). To which direction is concrete psychology oriented?. In *Ecrits II: Les fondements de la psychologie* (pp. 136–188). Paris: Editions Sociales.

Politzer, G. (1929/1969). Note on individual psychology. In *Ecrits II: Les fondements de la psychologie* (pp. 235–244). Paris: Editions Sociales.

Powell, W., and DiMaggio, P. (Eds.). (1991). *The new institutionalism in organizational analysis*. Chicago: University of Chicago Press.

Prasad, M. (1998). International capital on 'Silicon Plateau': Work and control in India's computer industry. *Social Forces*, 77(2), 429–452.

Putnam, R. (2000). *Bowling alone: The collapse and revival of American community*. New York: Simon & Schuster.

Ranciere, J. (1991). *The ignorant schoolmaster*. Stanford, CA: Stanford University Press.

Ratner, C. (1991). *Vygotsky's sociohistorical psychology and its contemporary applications*. New York: Plenum Press.

Ratner, C. (1996). Activity as a key concept for cultural psychology. *Culture & Psychology*, 2, 407–434.

Ratner, C. (1997). In defense of activity theory. *Culture & Psychology*, 3(2), 211–223.

Reich, B. (1996). The paradoxes of education in Rorty's liberal utopia. *Philosophy of Education*. (Available On-line at: www.ed.uiuc.edu/EPS/PES-Yearbook/96_docs/reich.html)

Reich, R. (1991). *The work of nations*. New York: Addison-Wesley.

Reich, W. (1929/1966). Dialectical materialism and psychoanalysis. *Studies on the Left*, 6(4), 5–46.

Reich, W. (1934/1972). What is class-consciousness? In W. Reich (Ed.), *Sex-pol: Essays 1920–1934* (pp. 277–357). New York: Random House.

Rey, F. G. (2002). L. S. Vygotsky and the question of personality in the cultural-historical approach. In D. Robbins and A. Stetsenko (Eds.), *Voices within Vygotsky's non-classical psychology: Past, present, future* (pp. 129–142). New York: Nova Science Publishers Inc.

Rhoades, G. (1998). *Managed professionals: Unionized faculty and restructuring academic labor.* Albany, NY: SUNY Press.

Ricardo, D. (1820/1911). *The principles of political economy and taxation.* New York: E. P. Dutton.

Rinehart, J., Huxley, C., and Robertson., D. (1997). *Just another car company? Lean production and its discontents.* Ithaca: ILR Press.

Riu, A. M., and Morato, J. C. (1996). *Dicionário de filosofía en CD rom.* Barcelona: Herder.

Robbins, D., and Stetsenko, A. (Eds.). (2002). *Voices within Vygotsky's non-classical psychology: Past, present, future.* New York: Nova Science Publishers.

Rodwin, M. A. (Ed.). (1993). *Medicine, money, and morals: Physicians' conflicts of interest.* New York: Oxford University Press.

Rojo, R. H. R. (2001). Family interactions as a source of being in society: Language-games and everyday family discourse genres in language construction. In S. Chaiklin (Ed.) *The theory and practice of cultural-historical psychology* (pp. 56–83). Aarhus: Aarhus University Press.

Rorty, R. (1979). *Philosophy and the mirror of nature.* Princeton, NJ: Princeton University Press.

Rorty, R. (1982). *Consequences of pragmatism.* Hempstead: University of Minnesota Press.

Rorty, R. (1987). Science as solidarity. In J. S. Nelson, A. Megill, and D. M. McCloskey (Eds.), *The rhetoric of the human sciences* (pp 38–52). Madison: University of Wisconsin Press.

Rorty, R. (1989a). *Contingency, irony and solidarity.* Cambridge: Cambridge University Press.

Rorty, R. (1989b). Education without dogma; Truth, freedom, and our universities, *Dissent,* 36, 198–204.

Rorty, R. (1989c). Two meanings of 'logocentrism'. In R. W. Dasenbrock (Ed.), *Redrawing the lines: Analytic philosophy, deconstruction, and literary theory* (pp. 204–216). Minneapolis, MN: Minnesota University Press.

Rorty, R. (1990). The danger of over-philosophication. Reply to Arcilla and Nicholson, *Educational Theory,* 40(1), 41–44.

Rorty, R. (1991a). *Objectivity, relativism, and truth: Philosophical papers, Volume. 1.* Cambridge, UK: Cambridge University Press.

Rorty, R. (1991b). *Essays on Heidegger and others; Philosophical papers, Volume 2.* Cambridge, UK: Cambridge University Press.

Rorty, R. (1994a). *A filosofia e o espelho da natureza.* Rio de Janeiro: Delume Dumará.

Rorty, R. (1994b). Relativismo: encontrar e fabricar. In A. Cicero and W. Salomao (Eds.), *Relativismo enquanto visão de mundo.* Rio de Janeiro: Francisco Alves.

Rorty, R. (1998a). *Achieving our country.* Cambridge, MA: Harvard University Press.

Rorty, R. (1998b). That old time philosophy. *The New Republic,* (April), 28–33.

Rorty, R. (2000). *Verdad y progreso, Escritos filosóficos, 3*, Buenos Aires, Barcelona, México: Paidós.

Rose, N. (1990). *Governing the soul: The shaping of the private self.* New York: Routledge.

Rosenow, E. (1998). Towards an aesthetic education? Rorty's conception of education. *The Journal of the Philosophy of Education of Great Britain*, 32(2), 253–265.

Rossi-Landi, F. (1968/1983). *Language as work and trade.* South Hadley, MA: Bergin and Garvey.

Rubenstein, S. (1934/1987). Problems of psychology in the works of Karl Marx, *Studies in Soviet Thought*, 33, 111–130.

Rubenstein, S. (1945). Consciousness in the light of dialectical materialism. *Science & Society*, 10, 252–261.

Rubenstein, S. (1987). Problems of psychology in the works of Karl Marx. *Studies in Soviet Thought*, 33, 111–130.

Rückriem, G. (2003). *Tool or medium? The meaning of information telecommunication technology to human practice: A quest for systemic understanding of activity theory.* Helsinki: Center for Activity Theory and Developmental Work Research.

Sacks, M. (1994). *On-the-job learning in the software industry.* Westport, CT: Quorum.

Sadovnik, A. (Ed.). (1995). *Knowledge and pedagogy: The sociology of Basil Bernstein.* Norwood, NJ: Ablex Publishing.

Said, E. (1993). *Culture and imperialism.* London: Chatto and Windus.

Sartre, J. P. (1960). *Critique de la raison dialectique* (Tome 1). Paris: Editions Gallimard.

Saviani, D. (1997). *Critical-Historical Pedagogy.* Campinas, Brazil: Autores Associados.

Sawchuk, P. H. (2003). *Adult learning and technology in working class life.* Cambridge, UK: Cambridge University Press.

Sayers, S. (1998). *Marxism and human nature.* London: Routledge.

Schachter, H. L. (1989). *Frederick Taylor and the public administration community.* Albany NY: SUNY Press.

Schell, E. E., and Stock, P. L. (Eds.). (2001). *Moving a mountain: Transforming the role of contingent faculty in composition studies and higher education.* Urbana, IL: National Council of Teachers of English.

Schneider, B. (1987). The people make the place. *Personnel psychology*, 40, 437–454.

Scott, W. R. (1995). *Institutions and organizations.* London: Sage.

Scott, W. R. (2003). *Organization: Rational, natural and open systems* (5th edition). New York: Prentice Hall.

Seccombe, W. and Livingstone, D. W. (1999). *Down-to-earth people: Beyond class reductionism and postmodernism.* Toronto: Garamond Press.

Selleck, R. J. W. (1968). *The new education.* London: Sir Issac Pitman & Soons Ltd.

Sève, L. (1966). Psychology and Marxism. *La nouvelle critique*, 180, 1–23.

Sève, L. (1975). *Marxism and the theory of human personality.* London: Lawrence & Wishart.

Sève. L. (1977). *Toward a Marxist critique of psychoanalysis.* Paris: Editions Sociales.

Sève. L. (1978). *Man in marxist theory and the psychology of personality.* Brighton, UK: Harvester Press.

Sève. L. (1984). *Structuralisme et dialectique* [Structuralism and dialectic]. Paris: Editions Sociales.

Sève, L. (1989). Vygotsky on dialectic and psychology. *Enfance,* 42(1/2), 11–16.

Shames, C. (1984). Dialectics and the theory of individuality. *Psychology & Social Theory,* 4, 51–65.

Shames, C. (1987). The dialectic of abstract and concrete activity. In M. Hildebrand-Nilson and G. Rückriem (Eds.), *Proceedings of the first international congress on activity theory* (pp. 43–51). Berlin: Hochschule der Kunste.

Shames, C. (1988). Toward a psychology of emancipation. *New Ideas in Psychology,* 6(1), 127–135.

Shames, C. (1990). Activity theory and the global community. *Activity Theory,* 5/6, 3–9.

Sharp R., Hartwig, M., and O'Leary, J. (1989). Independent working class education: A repressed historical alternative. *Discourse,* 10(2), 1–26.

Slaughter, S., and Lesley, L. (1997). *Academic capitalism: Politics, policies and the entrepreneurial university.* Baltimore: Johns Hopkins University Press.

Smith, A. (1776/1994). *An inquiry into the nature and causes of the wealth of nations.* New York: Random House.

Smith, C., and Thompson, P. (1999). Reevaluating the labor process debate. In M. Wardell, T. L. Steiger, P. Meiskins (Eds.), *Rethinking the labor process* (pp. 205–232). Albany, NY: SUNY Press.

Software Engineering Institute. (2003). *Process maturity profile: 2002 year end update.* (Available online at: http://www.sei.cmu.edu/sema/profile_SW-CMM.html)

Sohn-Rethel, A. (1976). *Intellectual and manual labor.* Atlantic Highlands, NJ: Humanities Press.

Sohn-Rethel, A. (1978). *Intellectual and manual labour: A critique of epistemology.* Atlantic Highlands, NJ: Humanities Press.

Soley, L. C. (1995). *Leasing the ivory tower: The corporate takeover of academia.* Boston: South End Press.

Sontag, S. (2001). *Illness as metaphor and AIDS and its metaphors.* New York: Picador.

Spender, D. (1980). *Man made language.* London: Pandora.

Spenner, K. I. (1988). Technological change, skill requirements, and education: The case for uncertainty. In R. M. Cyert and D. C. Mowery (Eds.), *The impact of technological change on employment and economic growth* (pp. 131–184). Cambridge MA: Ballinger.

Standish Group. (1994). *Chaos study report.* (Available online at: www.standishgroup.com)

Steiger, T. L. (1999). Forms of labor process and labor's share of value. In M. Wardell, T. L. Steiger, and P. Meiskins (Eds.), *Rethinking the labor process* (pp. 189–204). Albany: SUNY Press.

Stetsenko, A. (1999). Social interaction, cultural tools and the zone of proximal development: In search of a synthesis. In S. Chaiklin, M. Hedegaard and U. J. Jensen (Eds.), *Activity theory and social practice: Cultural-historical approaches* (pp. 235–252). Aarhus: Aarhus University Press.

Stetsenko, A., and Arievitch, I. M. (1996). The zone of proximal development: Resolving the contradiction between idea and method in post-Vygotskian psychology. In J. Lompscher (Ed.), *Development and learning from a cultural-historical point of view, Volume 1* (pp. 81–92). Marburg, Germany: BdWi-Verlag.

Struik, D. (1964). Introduction. In Karl Marx, *The economic and philosophical manuscripts of 1844* (pp. 9–56). New York: International.

Strzalka, D. (2001). Protests don't stop city colleges layoffs. (February 16), *Chicago Tribune*, 16.

Sunday Los Angles Times. (2001). "School Lockers Making a Comeback" (September 2) (Orange Country ed.)

Swanson, K., McComb, D., Smith, J., and McCubbrey, D. (1991). The application software factory: Applying total quality techniques to systems development. *MIS Quarterly*, (December), 567–579.

Swartz, D. (1997). *Culture and power: The sociology of Pierre Bourdieu.* Chicago: University of Chicago Press.

Thévenot, L. (2002). Justifying critical differences: Which concepts of value are sustainable in an expanded coordination. In K. S. Tong and C. Sin-wai (Eds.), *Culture and humanity in the new millennium: The future of human values* (pp. 45–65). Hong Kong: The Chinese University Press.

Thompson, M. (1979). *Rubbish theory: The creation and destruction of value.* Oxford, UK: Oxford University Press.

Thompson, P. (1989). *The nature of work* (2nd edition). London: Macmillan.

Thompson, P., and McHugh, D. (2002). *Work organizations: A critical introduction* (3rd edition). Houndmills: Palgrave.

Thompson, P., and Smith, C. (2001). Follow the redbrick road: Reflections on pathways in and out of the labor process debate. *International Studies of Management and Organization*, 30(4), 40–67.

Tinker T. (2002). Spectres of Marx and Braverman in the twilight of postmodernist labour process research. *Work, Employment & Society*, 16(2), 251–279.

Tobach, E. (1995). The uniqueness of human labor. In L. Martin, K. Nelson, and E. Tobach (Eds.), *Sociocultural psychology: Theory and practice of doing and knowing* (pp. 43–66). New York: Cambridge University Press.

Tobach, E. (1999). Activity theory and the concept of integrative levels. In Y. Engeström, R. Miettinen and R-L. Punamaki. (Eds.), *Perspectives on activity theory* (pp. 133–146). New York: Cambridge University Press.

Topper, K. (1995). Richard Rorty, liberalism and the politics of redescription. *The American Political Science Review*, 89(4), 954–965.

Torrance, J. (1977). *Estrangement, alienation, and exploitation.* New York: Columbia University Press.

Tough, A. (1978). Adults' major learning efforts: Recent research and future directions. *Adult Education*, 28, 250–63.

Touraine, A. (1969). *Post-industrial society.* Paris: Editions Minuit.

Triandis, H. C. and Gelfand, M. J. (1998). Converging measurement of horizontal and vertical individualism and collectivism, *Journal of Personality and Social Psychology*, 74(1), 118–128.

Tucker, R. (1978). *The Marx-Engels readers.* New York: Norton.

Tulviste, P. (1999). Activity as explanatory principle in cultural psychology. In S. Chaiklin, M. Hedegaard and U. J. Jensen (Eds.), *Activity and social practice* (pp. 66–78). Aarhus: Aarhus University Press.

United Kingdom Adult Education Committee. (1919). The 1919 Report of the Adult Education Committee to the United Kingdom Ministry of Reconstruction. Nottingham: University of Nottingham.

University of Maine. (1999). *Developments and trends in the academic workplace.* Orono, ME: Bureau of Labor Education, University of Maine.

U.S. Bureau of the Census. (1975). *Historical statistics of the United States.* Washington DC: U.S. Government Printing Office.

U.S. Bureau of the Census. (2000). *Statistical abstract of the United States.* Austin, Texas: Hoover's Business Press.

U.S. Government. (1935). *National Labor Relations Act.* Section 157 [sec. 7] U.S. Code, Title 29, Sections 141–187.

Van der Pijl, K. (1998). *Transnational Classes and International Relations.* London: Routledge.

Van Der Veer, R., and Valsiner, J. (Eds.). (1994). *The Vygotsky Reader.* London: Blackwell.

Van Iterson, A., Mastenbroek, W., Newton, T., and Smith, D. (Eds.). (2002). *The civilized organization: Norbert Elias and the future of organization studies.* Philadelphia: John Benjamins.

Van Maanen, J., and Barley, S. R. (1984). Occupational communities: Culture and control in organizations. *Research in Organizational Behavior,* 6, 287–365.

Varenne, H., and McDermott, R. (1998). *Successful failure: The school America builds.* Boulder, CO: Westview Press.

Verret, M. (1999). Dialogues avec La Vie. Paris: L'Harmattan.

Vojskunsky, A. J., Zhdan, A. N., and Tikhomirov, O. K. (Eds.). (1999). *Traditions and perspectives of the activity approach in psychology: A. N. Leontyev's school.* Moscow: Smysl.

Volosinov, V. N. (1929/1973). *Marxism and the philosophy of language.* New York: Seminar Press.

Vygodskaja, G. L., and Lifanova, T. M. (1996). *Lev Semjonovich Vygotsky; Life, activity, lines to a portrait.* Moscow: Smysl.

Vygotsky, L. S. (1921–1923/1997b). *Educational psychology.* Boca Raton, FL: Saint Lucie Press.

Vygotsky, L. S. (1924, 1925, 1930/2003). *Consciousness, the unconscious, emotions.* Paris: La Dispute.

Vygotsky, L. (1925/1994). Consciousness as a problem for the psychology of behavior. *Société française,* 50, 35–50.

Vygotsky, L. S. (1927/1997a). *The collected works of L. S. Vygotsky. Problems of the theory and history of psychology, vol. 3.* New York: Plenum Press.

Vygotsky, L. S. (1930/1994). The socialist alteration of man. In R. Van Der Veer and J. Valsiner (Eds.), *The Vygotsky reader* (pp. 175–184). Oxford, UK: Blackwell.

Vygotsky, L. S. (1928–1933/1993). *The collected works of L. S. Vygotsky: The fundamentals of defectology: Abnormal psychology and learning disabilities, Volume 2.* New York: Plenum Press.

Vygotsky, L. S. (1933–1934/1987). *The collected works of L. S. Vygotsky: Problems of general psychology, Volume 1.* New York: Plenum Press.

Vygotsky, L. S. (1987). Thinking and speech. *The collected works of L. S. Vygotsky: Problems of general psychology, Volume 1* (pp. 375–383). New York: Plenum Press.

Vygostky, L. S. (1962). *Thought and language.* Cambridge, MA: MIT Press.

Vygotsky, L. S. (1978). *Mind in society: The development of higher psychological processes.* Cambridge, MA: Harvard University Press.

Vygotsky, L. S. (1984). *A Formação Social da Mente.* São Paulo, Brazil: Martins Fontes.

Vygotsky, L. S. (1989). Concrete human psychology. *Soviet Psychology*, 27(2), 53–77.

Wallace, M. E. (Ed.). (1984). *Part-time academic employment in the humanities*. New York: Modern Language Association.

Wallon, H. (1925). Lèufant tur bulent [The Troublesome Child]. Paris: Alcan.

Wallon, H. (1936). Introduction. In H. Wallon (Ed.), *In the light of marxism* (pp. 9–16). Paris: Editions Sociales Internationales.

Wallon, H. (1937). Introduction. In H. Wallon (Ed.), *In the light of marxism* (pp. 7–15). Paris: Editions Sociales Internationales.

Wallon, H. (1946/1990). Dialectical materialism and psychology. In H. Wallon (Ed.), *Psychology and dialectic* (pp. 128–139). Paris: Messidor.

Wallon, H. (1951/1963). Psychology and dialectical materialism. *Enfance*, (1–2), 31–34.

Wardell, M. (1999). Labor processes: Moving beyond Braverman and the deskilling debate. In M. Wardell, T. L. Steiger, P. Meiskins (Eds.), *Rethinking the labor process* (pp. 1–16). Albany: SUNY Press.

Wardell, M, Steiger, T. L., and Meiskins, P. (Eds.). (1999). *Rethinking the labor process*. Albany: SUNY Press.

Waring, M. (1988). *If women counted: A new feminist economics*. San Francisco: Harper and Row.

Warren, B. (1980). *Imperialism: Pioneer of capitalism*. London: Verso.

Weber, H. (Ed.). (1997). *The software factory challenge*. Amsterdam: IOS Press.

Weber, M. (1904). *Protestant ethic and the spirit of capitalism*. New York: Scribner's.

Wertsch, J. V. (Ed.). (1979). *The concept of activity in Soviet psychology*. Armonk, NY: M.E. Sharp.

Wexler, P. (1983). *Critical social psychology*. Boston: Routledge and Kegan Paul.

Wexler, P. (1993). *Becoming somebody*. Philadelphia: Falmer Press.

Wheen, F. (1999). *Karl Marx: A life*. New York: Norton.

White, G. (Ed.). (2000). *Campus Inc.: Corporate power in the Ivory Tower*. Amherst, NY: Prometheus.

Wiener, C., Fagerhaugh, S., Strauss, A., and Suczek, B. (1983). What price chronic illness? *Society*, 19, 22–30.

Williams, R. (1977). *Marxism and literature*. New York: Oxford University Press.

Willis, P. (1977). *Learning to labour*. Westmead: Saxon House.

Wilson, R. (2001). Bennington president fired professor who criticized her fiercely and openly. *Chronicle of Higher Education*, (April 28), 20.

Worthen, H. (2001). The problem of the majority contingent faculty in the community colleges. In B. Alford and K. Kroll (Eds.), *The politics of writing in the two year college* (pp. 42–60). Portsmouth, NH: Heinemann.

Worthen, H., and Berry, J. (1999). *Contingent faculty in public higher education in Pennsylvania, spring 1999: Focus on the community colleges*. Harrisburg, PA: Keystone Research Center.

Wright, E. O., Levine, A., and Sober, E. (1992). *Reconstructing Marxism: Essays on explanation and the theory of history*. London and New York: Verso.

Yudin, E. G. (1978). *Systemic approach and the principle of activity*. Moscow: Nauka.

Zazzo, R. (1995). Psychology and marxism. *Bulletin de Psychologie*, 48(15–18) n.421: 592–611.

Zimbalist, A. (Ed.). (1979). *Case studies on the labor process*. New York: Monthly Review Press.

Zinn, H. (2003). Growing up class conscious. *Z Magazine*. (Available online at: http://zena.secureforum.com/Znet/zmag/zmag.cfm)

Zollo, M., and Winter, S. G. (2002). Deliberate learning and the evolution of dynamic capabilities. *Organization Science*, 13(3), 339–351.

# Index